PROGRAMMING IN C & C++

For Examination in Engineering Degree, Diploma and B.Sc., M.Sc., C-DAC and DOE

Dr. S.S. KHANDARE
M.E., P.G. Diploma in Computer Science, Ph.D,
Principal, B.D. College of Engineering, Sewagram,
Ex-Principal, LDRP Institute of Technology, Gandhinagar

S. CHAND PUBLISHING

S. Chand And Company Limited
(ISO 9001 Certified Company)

S. CHAND PUBLISHING

S. Chand And Company Limited

(ISO 9001 Certified Company)

Head Office: D-92, Sector–2, Noida – 201301, U.P. (India), Ph. 91-120-4682700

Registered Office: A-27, 2nd Floor, Mohan Co-operative Industrial Estate, New Delhi – 110 044
Phone: 011-49731800

www.**schandpublishing.com**; e-mail: **info@schandpublishing.com**

Marketing Offices:

Chennai	:	Ph: 23632120; chennai@schandpublishing.com
Guwahati	:	Ph: 2738811, 2735640; guwahati@schandpublishing.com
Hyderabad	:	Ph: 40186018; hyderabad@schandpublishing.com
Jalandhar	:	Ph: 4645630; jalandhar@schandpublishing.com
Kolkata	:	Ph: 23357458, 23353914; kolkata@schandpublishing.com
Lucknow	:	Ph: 4003633; lucknow@schandpublishing.com
Mumbai	:	Ph: 25000297; mumbai@schandpublishing.com
Patna	:	Ph: 2260011; patna@schandpublishing.com

First Edition 1998
Subsequent Editions and Reprints 1999, 2002, 2006, 2009, 2010, 2011, 2023
Sixth Revised Edition 2013

Reprint 2024

ISBN: 978-81-219-1691-2

Product Code: H7CPC50COMP10ENAF23R

PRINTED IN INDIA

By Vikas Publishing House Private Limited, Plot 20/4, Site-IV, Industrial Area Sahibabad, Ghaziabad – 201 010 and Published by S Chand And Company Limited, A-27, 2nd Floor, Mohan Co-operative Industrial Estate, New Delhi – 110 044

ACKNOWLEDGEMENT

I am grateful to the staff members and programmers of various Institutions for their suggestions during the development of the book.

I would like to thank to Mr. Navin Joshi, Executive Vice-President, S.Chand & Company Pvt. Ltd., New Delhi for their efforts in the published of this book.

I am thankful to Mr. Bhagirath Kaushik General Manager (Sales & Marketing) S.Chand & Company Pvt. Ltd., New Delhi for his dedicated efforts and co-operation during the publishing of the book.

I am very much thankful to Mr. C.L. Patel, Chairman, Charota Vidya Mandal for their encouragement. I am very much thankful to Prof. B.K. Raghunath, Principal, ADIT for providing suggestions for improvement of the book.

I am thankful to the programmers who have helped me in the preparation of the book.

Dr. S.S. Khandare

PREFACE TO SIXTH EDITION

I am thankful to the readers of the book for their overwhelming response for the Fifth edition. It is a great pleasure in presenting this improved edition of the book on C-programming. The book contains the topics of computer fundamentals, hardware and software, control and looping statements, arrays as simple C-language programming and the advance C-programming which contains string functions, pointers and structures. The extension of C-language to C++ is also included which helps the programmer to migrate from C to C++ programming. It include the object oriented programming in C++.

In this book, the basic programming methods and software technologies used in C & C++ programming are presented. In the Sixth and improved edition more number of trial programs and error programs in C++ are provided for practice.

The book is very useful for beginner and those who are appearing for competitive examination and private interview.

The author is thankful to the teachers and programmer who made valuable to contributions by providing suggestions for improvement.

Dr. S. S. KHANDARE
Ph. No. : 9732307842, 9732304151
e-mail : shashikhan_ngp@hotmail.com

CONTENTS

1
COMPUTER FUNDAMENTALS

OBJECTIVES

In this chapter you will be able to learn the

1. Functions of computer
2. Application of computer
3. Fundamentals of information technology
4. Basics of information system

1.1 COMPUTER

It is an electronic machine device which carries out calculations at high speed. It has a memory to store large amount of data and it does comparisons between two values and accordingly executes the decisions.

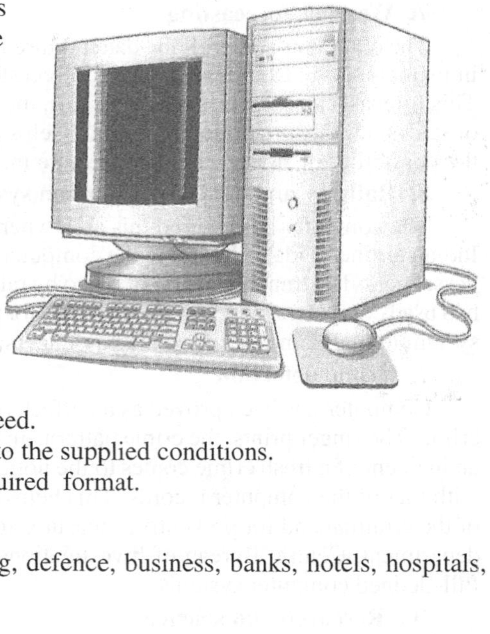

1.2 FUNCTIONS OF COMPUTER

The computer can perform large number of functions, but some important functions carried out by the computer are :

1. It is capable of carrying out calculations at very high speed.
2. It is makes calculation to a very high degree of accuracy.
3. It is capable of storing large amount of data and is able to retrieve the data at very fast speed.
4. It is capable of taking decisions according to the supplied conditions.
5. It is capable of providing output in the required format.

1.3 APPLICATIONS OF COMPUTER

It is used in the field of science and engineering, defence, business, banks, hotels, hospitals, office etc. for various purposes. Some of them are :

1. Inventory control

The computers are used in Inventory control to avoid the dead inventory. The information about the position of the stock of raw materials, finished goods and semi-finished goods is updated regularly. The daily receipt of stocks have to be added to the books. The issue of raw materials for processing is deducted from the stock and the stock at the end of the day can be known to plan the future procurement.

2. Production planning and control

Computers have been the best aids to planning of the production schedules. The clientwise demand of the goods, productwise manufacturing requirements, itemwise actual production, capacity wise manufacturing planning, various such combinations for planning the production control of an industry can be made possible by the use of computer.

3. Costing and budgetary Control

The product having passed through a series of manufacturing processes, the product costing would involve number of calculations and a range of decision-makings. Computers can take up this job and provide the necessary costing figures to control the manufacturing costs.

4. Sales analysis and market research

The efficient marketing management of an industry can be supported by the information on computer software.The analysis can be datewise, partywise, productwise, territorywise and salesmanwise sales figures. Computers can also prepare product invoices if required. This type of analysis can certainly become a strong base for marketing manager.

5. Financial accounting and pay roll

Computers has become the most efficient tool in financial accounting and auditing. The entire book–keeping is carried out through the computers. The preparation of trial balances, profit and loss statements can be obtained very easily. The computer gives excellent output formats, and exact figures.

6. Space technology

It is used in space technology. The assembling of space shuttles followed by an adequate quality control and testing is normally performed with the help of large computers. Even the path control of space shuttles is done entirely through computers. Also the counting of angles for target hitting in space is done by the computer. Apart from this, number of information regarding atmospheric pressure, temperature, movements of planets and all relevant information is stored in computer which helps in making the space program a success.

7. Weather forecasting

The computer stores all the data required about the pressure in air, temperature, hot currents etc. in its memory and supplies the daily forecast after proper calculations and certain logical decisions. This forecast can be – possibility of rains, the temperature in different parts of the country and trends of sea water. The prediction of rainfall helps the farmers for better crops, warns the fisherman about the possibility of storms and temperature information of the benefit of the public.

8. Railway and airline reservation system

The computer has entered this area where it schedules the running of every train in the country. Indian airlines and Air India use the computers to schedule their flights for domestic and international passengers. The transportations of cargo by rail and air both are managed by computer system. Airlines had used computers for reservation of seats for passengers much earlier. It is used for railway reservation system to maintain records of the passengers for next three months.

9. Crime detection

Computer has been proved as an effective tool in keeping track of perfect information regarding crime. The finger prints, the crime pattern, an all the relevant details are stored in the computer. When an incident of a fresh crime comes to the notice of the authorities, the execution of crime is compared with that of the computer records. This helps in the detection of a criminal, checking the past record of the criminal and for preventive measures to control the crime level in a particular area. The police department, Central Bureau of Investigations, the Regional Forensic Laboratory are equipped with full-fledged computer systems.

10. Research and science

The computers are used in science and research because of their basic characteristics of high speed in calculations and wide storage, in arriving at a required result.

11. Educational

Now–a–days computers have also entered the schools and colleges. Number of universities and the premier institutes of India have already introduced computer science as a full–fledged faculty at undergraduate and graduate levels. According to the new educational scheme, learning of computer is also introduced at school. Computers can also be helpful as an aid for learning of academic subjects like mathematics, physics, economics etc. They can be learned by computer with the help of a specialized software prepared for the relevant topics. The time will come in a very short future when most of the schools and colleges will have at least one computer in their premises.

12. Recreation

Computers have a variety of software for games and recreations. The games are designed for all the level of people, game for a small child for example to flight simulator for the professional air pilot. There are more than 1000 softwares available for such recreational purposes. This fact has made computer the most popular amongst all the age groups of people.

13. Applications in Engineering

In Engineering, they find wide applications in different fields like Mechanical, Production, Civil, Automobile, chemical, metallurgical engineering etc.

In Mechanical Engineering they are used for design of machine parts, analysis of complex system like thermal , crygenic, hydraulic, management etc. They are used for producing the drawings of components and parts. They are used in geometric modelling and creating operating machines on screen.

In production engineering they are used for manufacturing of components and parts on CNC system. They are used in industrial engineering, stores, assembly operation etc.

In civil engineering they are used for design of structures like bridges, dams etc.They are utilized for preparing drawings of the building. It is also used for architectural designing.

In automobile engineering they can be used for design of components, testing machines and measurement of vehicle parameters , drawing of components etc.

1.4 INFORMATION TECHNLOGY

The information can be defined as collection of data in the formatted form such that the storage of data, retrieval of data or processing on data becomes easy. The information stored on the paper is difficult to analyse and trace. The processing of data becomes tedious when the information is stored on the paper files.The deletion of data can be done by rubbing or erasing the information on paper. The analysis of information becomes difficult and tedious on the paper system.

The information is the processed data. Normally the data is in the raw form for producing the information. The information becomes the basis for executive decisions. Therefore the processing of data is carried out according to the requirements and suitable instructions. The data consists of the facts related to the people , places ,events or things ,items. It may consists of alphbets,numericals or both. The simple examples are name, age and address etc.

The computer system allows for storage of voluminous information in the storage devices. It allows for fast speed calculations even more than the speed of human brain. The use of computer system provides large number of advantages for processing of information. The advantages are

1. The data can be stored permanently.
2. Large number of calculations can be performed at very fast processing speed.
3. The degree of accuracy is very high.
4. The operations like deletion of data, modification of data can be done very easily.
5. The operation of retrieval of data can be performed and the data can be searched immediately from the stored data.
6. The operations such as indexing or arranging the data is possible.
7. The variety of functions can be utilized in the operations.
8. It allows for the decisions and logical comparisons.
9. It allows for creation of standard libraries.
10. It is possible to obtain the result in the formatted form.
11. It allows for production of graphics and aesthetics.

The ***information technology revolution*** has occurred because of the above advantages which are obtain in processing of the data. The difficult situation has a arised because of the complexities of the data and the amount of data to be handled in the business. The complex channels of distributions and the needs of the customer is rising every day. A simple example could be the railway reservation system which maintains huge data of the reservation of passengers travelling in the train at different destination. The data has become very complex because large number of trains have been introduced and variety of classes have been placed in every train. The passenger travelling in the train have varying destinations and the number of berth in every class are also varying. Because of these complexities it has become very difficult to maintain records on paper. A computer reservation system has eliminated all the problems arising in maintenance of the reservation system informations.

1.5 INFORMATION SYSTEM

It is an interaction of the man and the machine which is like the interaction between the human designer and the hardware of the system. The information system is used for operating the hardware therefore this is the set of devices, procedures and operating systems which is used to produce information and communicate this to the user for planning , control and performance.

1.6 COMPONENTS OF INFORMATION SYSTEM

The computer system consists of three main components

1. Hardware
   Hardware is a science of the electronic circuits and components of computer. These are electronic equipments.The hardware is controlled by the software.It processes the data and creates the information.
2. Software
   Software is an interface which performs the work of translation between human designer and the hardware. These are the sets of programs or instructions which converts the raw data into useful information.
3. Human designer
   Human resource is a man power and skilled personal available to perform the operation on computer system
4. Procedures
   These are the guidlines which the human operator follow while using the software. These are the manual provided by the manufacturers as operating instructions for data processing.
5. Data
   This is consisting of raw and unprocessed facts. After the data is processed through the computer information is generated.

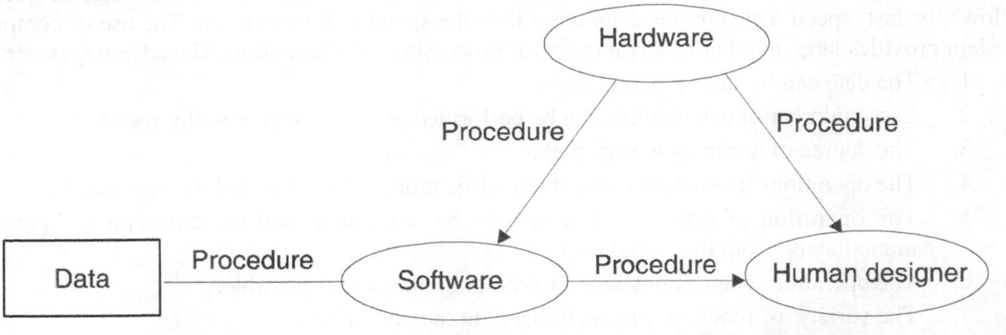

Fig.1.1 Shows the sketch of the 3 components of information system.

1.7 TYPES OF INFORMATION SYSTEM

The computer based information system are divided in two main categories

1. Office automation system
2. Transaction processing system

The office automation system are the systems are among the newest and rapidly expanding computer based information systems. These are used for increasing the efficiency of the system. The transaction processing systems are used for processing of the transactions such as banks,airlines,railways etc.

1.8 AREAS OF INFORMATION TECHNOLOGY

There are various areas of information technology. These areas could be broadly classified as

1. Hardware engineering
   It is science related to electronic circuits and components.

2. Networking
   It is science related to internent and interconnected network of computers.
3. MIS
   It is a tool used by management for improving the productivities.
4. Internet and softwares
   It is the area in which the sharing of resources and communication can be performed.
5. Enterprise Resource Planning
   It is the area in which the planning of available resources and forecast of the demand of the customer is performed by use of computer system.
6. GUI applications
   These are front end tools used for customisation of software.
7. DBA applications
   These are the data base related applications software.
8. Operating system
   This is a science of study of operational system of computer.
9. Computer aided design
   It is the design of the product by use of the computer softwares.
10. E-commerce
    It is the commercial activity performed by use of the electronic media.
11. Web page development
    This is a development of customise marketing documents placed on the internet site for the view of the customers.
12. Application developers
    This is a area of software development of the commercial applications, business and engineering application.
13. Multimedia systems
    These are the recreational systems used for entertainment, games, fun etc.

1.9 COMPUTER AND ITS HISTORY

The word computer is derived from the word 'compute' which means to calculate. The computer was initially a device known as Abacus which was developed by chinese during 3000 B.C. In 1617, John Napier who is a Scottish mathematician developed a device called Napier bones. With the help of the device multiplication and addition are possible. In 1942, blaise Pascal who is the French mathemetician invented the first mechanical calculator. In 1673 , Gottfried Wilhelm Leibniz who is the German invented the leibniz calculator which was used for addition, subtraction and multiplication.Then the French weavers son Joseph Marie Jacquard has developed a pleate with multiple holes to store the data which is known as punched cards.

1.10 COMPUTER SCIENCE

The computer science is a science related to the processing of information and data on the computer system. The computer science is a branch of information technology which the deals with the electronic data processing system. This consists of the studies of hardware and components of computer and the related software technology. The computer science uses tools and techniques for processing of data and information.

1.11 PROBLEM SOLVING TECHNIQUES

The various problems in engineering and science are of the complex nature and these problems use the complex mathematical system for analysis. The various tools in the mathematics are used such as matrix operations, co-ordinate geometry, surfaces and solids of revolutions. In order to solve these complex mathematical equations the help of computers and information technology makes it easier to obtain the solutions. The computer programming is the most important tool which allows conversion of mathematical equations into useful programming commands. These programming commands are executed by the computer system. The basic need of programming by the user was to avoid tedious procedure of calculations for any engineering problem in which large number of calculations are involved and the input data vary continuously. The accuracy expected in calculation is very high and the process of selection and decision making is to be performed by the program. The powerful techniques of solving problems is numerical methods.

1.12 ALGORITHM

These are the step of the programming used obtaining the results of the program for the given inputs. These are the sets of rules or instructions for performing the desired task to obtain the results. These may consists of steps of the program or part of the program or the logic of the program. The logic is a way of performing the given task by utilizing magic steps such that the results are very easily available. The Algorithms are very useful in development of the program.

1.13 APPLICATION OF COMPUTERS IN ENGINEERING

The computer programming is used in wide areas of application in engineering.

1. **CAD/CAM technology**

It is used in CAD/CAM technology in which the design of machine component, drawing of components and manufacturing components on the computerised system. The programmer prepares a program which can be utilized from computer processing and manufacturing. The use of computerised system allows the user to modify the existing design or to animate the design to a new variety of design. The manufacturing performed by used of computer result in high precision and accuracy in manufacturing.

2. **Civil engineering**

It is used in civil engineering to performed calculation of structural design and preparation of building plans and their structure. It is also used for costing and estimation of construction materials and site calculations.

3. **Electrical engineering**

It is used in electrical engineering for preparing the layouts of transmission system. The load estimation and calculations of electrical network. It is also used for design of transformers and electric motors.

4. **Chemical Engineering**

It is used in chemical engineering for calculation of reaction, heat generation and fuel combustion.The design of furnaces and heat exchangers can be performed by use of programming. It also allows for calculation of combustion systems and cooling systems.

5. **Automobile engineering**

The use of programming is more prominent in the vehicle design and development system.The design vehicle frames,car body and other transmission component can be made for strength and cost. The design of engine and fuels system can be done by using programs.

6. **Packaging technology**

The programming technique could be utilized for design of packages of different varieties. The costing and estimation of the packages can be performed by use of computer programs.

This book deals with the computer programming techniques and methods in C-language. It is language widely used for solving complex problem solving techniques.

EXERCISE

1. Explain the functions of computer.
2. Write the various applications of computers in engineering.
3. What is information technology ?
4. Explain various components of IT.
5. Explain various types of information systems.
6. Explain various areas of IT.
7. Explain the history of computers.
8. What are the applications of computer in Engineering ?
9. What is meant by problem solving technique ?
10. Explain what do you mean by algorithm.
11. Explain the history of computer.

2
HARDWARE

AN OVERVIEW

In the previous chapter , we have studied the application of computer in the various fields. The information technology is new science used for processing data or information. The important components of information technology have been discussed and the various area of computer science were presented.

In this chapter we will discuss about very important component of information technology as hardware which is physical component which performs the operation of computer system. The hardware works on the binary system and therefore the binary arithmetic is dicussed here.

OBJECTIVES

In this chapter you will study the hardware construction of computer.

The various objectives are

1. Study of binary arithmetic
2. Study various components of computer
3. Study memory devices
4. Study of binary language

2.1 BINARY ARITHMETIC

The digital circuit works on binary system and binary systems has arithmic which performs the calculations on binary system.

2.1.1 Digital Fundamentals

The digital circuits and systems involves two positional states. The two state system is called binary and its two digits are 0 and 1. A binary digit is called a bit. A digital circuit is a circuit which expresses voltage or current values as digits. There the digital circuits used in the computer are working on two digits 0 and 1. A numbering system which uses only two digits is called binary number system. Computer does not work with decimal numbers but operates on decimal numbers and processes the binary numbers.All of us are familiar with decimal number system which has ten digits as 0,1,2,3,4,5,6,7,8,9. Any number can be represented by 10 digits. Therefore, the base or radix of decimal system is ten.

2.1.2 Decimal Number System

A ***base*** or radix of a number system specifies the total number of different digits that are used for counting in each places.If a number larger than 9 is to be represented then additional columns of the digits are added. In this system the first place (least significant position) has a value of 1. The place to the left has value ten times that of the first place. As we go further to left, the value increases exponentially.

Example :

$$25 = 2 \times 10 + 5 \times 1$$

The value of the number is sum of the digits after each has been multiplied by its weight. In decimal number system , the weight of least significant position(LSP) is 1 or 10^0 . Then the power of 10 goes on increasing with increase in places.

Example :

$425 = 4 \times 10^2 + 2 \times 10^1 + 5 \times 10^0$

2.1.3 Binary Number System

A binary number system uses only two digits 0 & 1 to represent any number. For binary number base or radix is two because it uses only two digits. This system has become popular in the digital circuits.

In this system of numbering , the first digit (extreme right) has a value of 1 or 10^0 . The first digit is known as least significant bit(LSB).The place to the left of LSB has a value twice that of the first place i.e. 2^1 .A place 2 places to the left of LSB has a value of 4 or 2^2. The places further to the left are counted as 8 or 2^3 ,16 or 2^4 and 32 or 2^5. The last or extreme left digit is known as most significant bit(MSB).

Example :

The following binary numbers are expressed in the decimal form

$101 = 1 \times 2^2 + 0 \times 2^1 + 1 \times 2^0 = 4 + 0 + 1 = 5$

There binary equivalent of the decimal number 5 is 101.

Similarly

$1100 = 1 \times 2^3 + 1 \times 2^2 + 0 \times 2^1 + 0 \times 2^0 = 8 + 4 + 0 + 0 = 12$

2.2 BIT

In digital circuits only two values are permissible as 0 or 1. A 0 or 1 is the bit formation and string of bits with 0 or 1 becomes the word. A four bit word is known as a nibble and eight bit word is known as byte.

A bit can assume any two values 1 or 0. The communication of the electronic system occurs due to the electronic signals which are represented by the binary numbers called bit. These are the numbers representing the circuit 'break' and 'make' conditions.

2.3 BYTE

In binary system the power of 2 is considered as base for representation of bits. The combination of 8 bits is considered as a byte and a byte is a string of eight binary digits. Every character in the English language is represented by byte.The numbers are represented in the binary system by using the bits forming a byte.The construction of byte is explained as below,

Example : A byte is represented below by combination of 8 bits.

01100100

represents the power of 2 according to their locations.

Locations (n)	7	6	5	4	3	2	1	0
values	0	1	1	0	0	1	0	0

The values of bits are multiplied by 2^n and resulting summation which is an equivalent number.

$$0*2^7 + 1*2^6 + 1*2^5 + 0*2^4 + 0*2^3 + 1*2^2 + 0*2^1 + 0*2^0$$

$$= 0 + 64 + 32 + 0 + 0 + 4 + 0 + 0 = 100$$

∴ The equivalent number representation of binary number can be written in a general form as

$$x = \sum_{n=0}^{7} i\,2^n$$

where, n – location of binary number .

i – binary number

2.4 BINARY NUMBER EQUIVALENTS

The binary number equivalents of numbers upto 20 are as shown below

Binary No.	Number equivalent
0	0
1	1
10	2
11	3
100	4
101	5
110	6
111	7
1000	8
1001	9
1010	10
1011	11
1100	12
1101	13
1110	14
1111	15
10000	16
10001	17
10010	18
10011	19
10100	20

2.5 CONVERSION OF BINARY NUMBER TO NORMAL NUMBER

For converting a binary number to a decimal number,the procedure is adopted by considering the bits and location of binary number with power of 2. The following binary number is converted to decimal number by using the following procedure.

Binary Number 1 0 1 1 1 1

Decimal Number $1*2^5 + 0*2^4 + 1*2^3 + 1*2^2 + 1*2^1 + 1*2^0 = 47$

2.6 CONVERSION OF NORMAL NUMBER TO BINARY NUMBER

To convert a normal number into a binary number. The following procedure is adopted.

1. Divide number by 2, obtain remainder R1
   This is rightmost binary number.
2. Divide the quotient by 2, obtain remainder R2
   This is second right most binary numbers carry this process is succession upto 7 digits.

Example :

quotient	remainder
47/2 = 23	1
23/2 = 11	1
11/2 = 5	1
5/2 = 2	1
2/2 = 1	0
1/2 = 0	1

2.7 REPRESENTATION OF DECIMAL NUMBERS

The decimal number consists of integer part and decimal part. This decimal part of number is represented as

Decimal Number	Binary number
$0.5 = 1/2 = 2^{-1}$	0.1
$0.25 = 1/4 = 2^{-2}$	0.01
$0.125 = 1/8 = 2^{-3}$	0.001
$0.0625 = 1/16 = 2^{-4}$	0.0001
$0.03125 = 1/32 = 2^{-5}$	.00001
$0.015625 = 1/64 = 2^{-6}$	.00001

Example :

In binary form 3/4 is represented as

$$\begin{aligned} 3/4 &= 0.5 + 0.25 \\ &= 2^{-1} + 2^{-2} \\ &= 0.1 + 0.01 \text{ in binary form} \\ &= 0.11 \end{aligned}$$

2.8 REPRESENTATION OF NEGATIVE NUMBERS

The leftmost bit represents sign of a binary number. If this bit is 1, then number is negative otherwise the bit is zero, the number is positive. The remaining bits represent the value of number.

The remaining bits represent the value of number. The compliment action of reversing bit occurs due to leftmost bit being 1 if it is represented in binary system as

00000001

then –1 is represented as

11111111

This is done by adding 1 to –1, which gives 0 number represented by bits

00000000

and reverse bits of this will represent –1

11111111

2.9 BINARY CODING SYSTEM

The characters are represented in the electrical signal by 0 & 1. This is known as binary coding system. There are 3 types of coding systems used.

System Unit

1. ASCII system

In this system, the binary codes are generated by combination of eight bits . This American Standard Code for International Interchange (ASCII). Every character is assigned with eight bits code and combination of 8 bits of 0 or 1 results into 256 characters being represented on this system.

For example

A is represented by 0100 0001

B is represented by 0100 0010

2. EDCDIC system

This system has been developed by IBM and used for large computers. It is Extended Binary Coded Decimal Interchange Code. The EBCDIC is used for

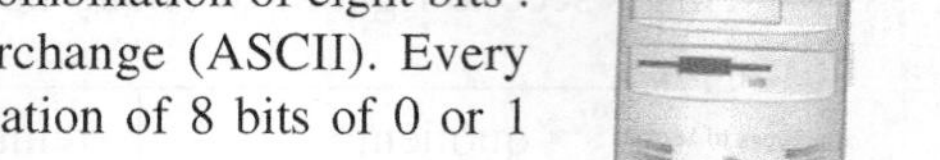

representing characters as similar to ASCII system.This uses eight bits to represent the characters.

For example

A is represented by 1100 0001

B is represented by 1100 0010

3. Unicode system

It is a 16 bit code designed to support international languages like Chinese and Japanese. These languages have large number of characters.

2.10 COMPONENTS OF A COMPUTER

Every computer system consists of three basic components:

1. Input device
2. Central Processing Unit
3. Output device

1. Input devices

This is a device used for supplying data or program to the computer in a particular language. There are different types of devices used :

(i) Magnetic tape/disk
(ii) Key board
(iii) Digitizer
(iv) Optical mark reader(OMR)
(v) Optical character reader(OCR)
(vi) Magnetic INK character reader (MICR)
(vii) Voice data entry terminal
(viii) Machine vision system
(ix) Cursor control devices
(x) Scanner

The keyboard is primary input device and any type of character or numeric data can be fed through the keyboard.The keyboard is the most important input device for the computer.It is a primary device used in the computer.

The magnetic tapes and disk are the memory devices which are capable of storing and retrieval of the data.

The OCR / OMR device uses the optical rays principle to read the available information. These devices can read only ready-made information. The bar code are codes through which items are recognised. These bar codes are recognised through the scanning device. This device decodes the information stored as bars and converts them into electrical pulses. The signals are compared with the patterns and OCR program recognises the matching pattern. Then the rates and sale record of the item is transfered to the computer.

Digitizer are the graphic instrument used on CAD workstations. It is a work surface which cantains hundreds of copper lines that form a grid.Each copper line receives electric pulses. A special pen or stylus is attached to the digitizer which is sensitive to the pulses and creates the drawing on screen.

MICR devices use magnetic field for reading of data or information. The banking industry uses a code to uniquely identify the bank and their cheque.The code and amount can be written on the cheque by using magnetic ink which consists of magnetic particles. These characters are read by using magnetic ink character readers.

The voice data entry terminal is used to enter the data through the voice.This method is very convenient for entry of the data.These devices converts the human spoken words to machine understandable form. A microphone or telephone is used to convert human speech into electric signals.

The signal pattern is then transmitted to a computer where it is compared to a dictionary of patterns which have been previously stored. When the match is found a word is recognised and then computer produces the output.

Machine vision system are the devices which converts visual images to computer understandable form. It consists of TV or camera to see the images and details. Some times the camera captures the images and then images are compared to view their differences. These systems are used in the factories and robots recognise the components..

There are various types of cursor devices used such as

1. Light pen
2. Track ball
3. Thumb wheel
4. Mouse
5. Joy stick

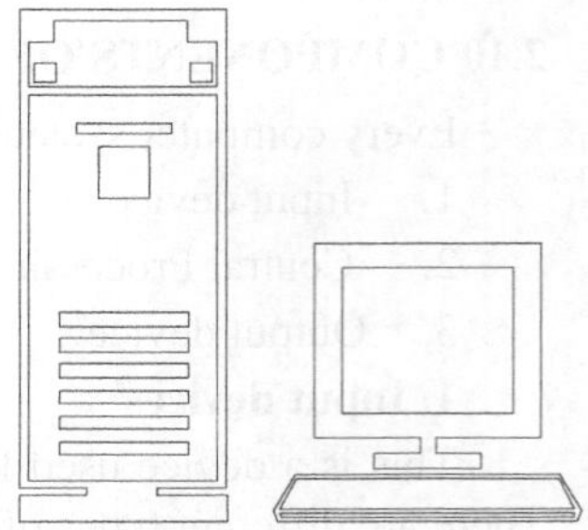

The mouse is commonly used cursor control device which can move the cursor of the computer to any desired position on the screen of the computer. It allows operations of various functions available on the computer screen.The scanner is a device used for the purpose of scanning of the required data or figure or picture.

2. Central Processing Unit

A computer receives instructions and data from the input unit and stores them in its memory. It has to execute the instructions given to it through a central processing unit.

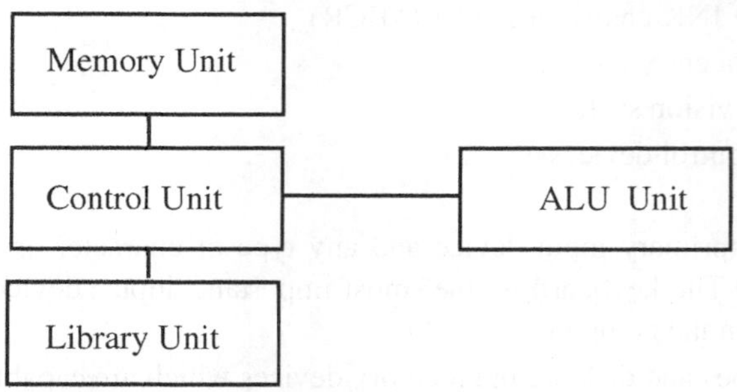

It consists of memory unit, control unit, library unit and arithmetic logic unit. The control unit controls operation of all units of the computer. It brings one instruction at a time from the memory, interprets it and obeys it by coordinating the working of all the other units. The control unit tells the input unit as to which information is to be read and the location in the memory where it is stored.

It instructs the memory to store the result in the specified address. It orders the arithmetic logic unit, as to which arithmetic operations are to be performed, where to find the required data and where to store the result. The standard functions are obtained from the library unit. The files are stored in library unit.

3. Output devices

The purpose of the output devices is to provide the results to the programmer after execution of the program.There are different types of output devices used :

(i) Magnetic tape/disk (ii) Visual display unit
(iii) Printers (iv) Plotter.
(v) COM

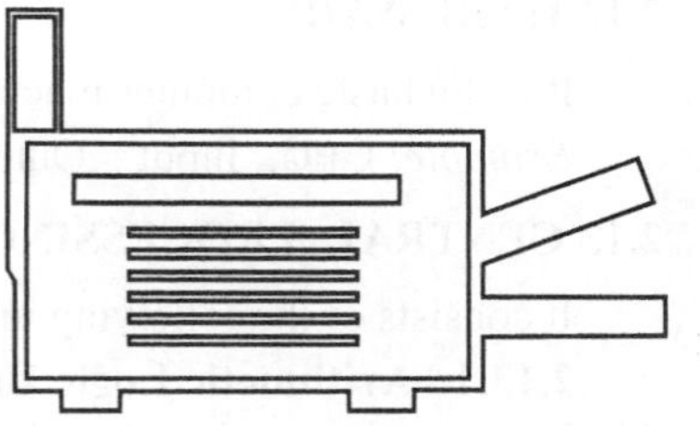

The most popular output device is the Visual Display Unit (VDU)in which a display of the figures and pictures is available. All the results are temporarily available on the screen of the display unit.These are referred to as monitors.The VDU uses cathod ray tubes(CRT) and recently the monitors uses Liquid Crystal Display(LCD). The VDU is 12" or 15" diagonal size screens. The visual display screen is divided into rows and column of tiny dots known as pixels. These pixel can switched on or off by any colour and collection of the pixels will be used to represent the characters. The screen is capable of displaying large number of pixels which is called a high resolution screen. The high resolution screen is capable of displaying sharp images.

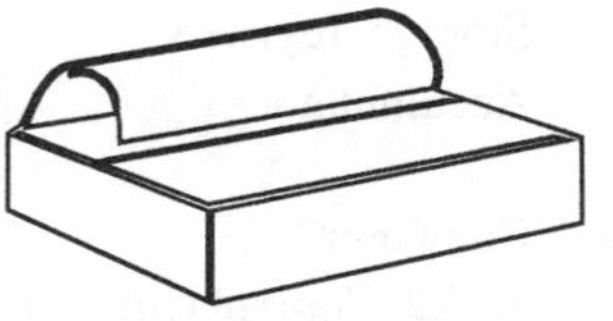

The permanent copy of the result is available on the printers. These devices provide a print of the result or picture or graphics. There are three types of printers

1. Dot matrix printers
2. Ink jet printers
3. Laser printers

The plotter are very useful tools for printing of the CAD drawings. If the drawing is to be obtained on large size sheet, then it is obtained on the plotter.

Computer output Microfilm is used to record computer output as microscopic film images. The information is printed on a page and then recorded on a sheet or roll of micro-film.

2.11 TYPES OF COMPUTERS

These computers; processes the digital data, which is supplied to them and perform numerical calculations. The results are available in the form of numbers or characters.

Computers are classified on the basis of their size and capacity:

1. Micro

These are Single user (Personal Computer) computer. These are ranging from calculator size to desktop size. The micro-computer CPU is microprocessor. These microprocessor are manufactured by Intel corporation company. The major brand of intel microprocessors is Intel 89586 known as Pentinum. These are also referred as PC , Desk top computers or lap-top or Home computers.

2. Mini

These are multiuser computers. These are small general purpose system. These are called multi-user system.

3. Supermini

These are multiuser having more computer power.

4. Mainframe

These are large memory computers and connected to large number of users at different locations.These offer faster processing speed. These are also multi-user system.

5. Supercomputers

These are high speed computers. These are designed to process scientific jobs like whether forecasting, AI , research etc. These are largest,fastest and expensive system in the world.

The personal computers (PC) are microcomputer, which are used by majority of persons. According to their memory, speed and capacity these are classified as :

(i) PC – XT (Extended technology).
(ii) PC – AT (Advanced technology).
(iii) PC – AT– 286 – Low speed computations.
(iv) PC – AT– 386 – Medium speed computation.
(v) PC – AT– 486 – Medium speed computation.
(vi) PC – AT– 586 – high speed computation.

2.12 HARDWARE

It is the basic computer machine which is made of electronic and mechanical parts.

Example: CPU, Input , Output devices are hardware units.

2.13 CENTRAL PROCESSING UNIT

It consists of the following units as shown earlier in the flow chart.

2.13.1 Arithmetic Logic Unit —This unit carries out arithmetic operations and comparisons. ALU receives instructions and data from the control unit.

ALU consists of :

Adder	–	This carries out arithmetic operations.
Storage registers	–	These are for keeping or storing data temporarily.
Accumulator	–	This is a special register which receives and stores the output from the adder.
Comparer	–	This compares two data items.

2.13.2 Control Unit —It is like the nervous system of human body. It supervises all the operations of the CPU. It co-ordinates the working of different parts of the computer. It is a link between input device, memory, ALU and output device.The control unit interprets and executes the instructions with the help of special purpose storage called Registers.

Functions

It accepts instructions in the proper sequence

– It interprets the instructions

– It sends the necessary data and operations to ALU

– It obtains data or results from ALU

– It transfers data to the appropriate unit

Registers

Registers are high speed memory locations used to store temporary results.

The various registers are

Instruction register	–	This keeps the instructions to be executed.
Address register	–	The address is stored for data on which operation is to be performed.
Instruction counter	–	This keeps the address of the next instruction.
Decoder	–	It interprets the operations and finds what is exactly to be done.

2.13.3 Memory Unit

The memory unit stores the data in registers in the form of bits.

Register

It is a hardware unit which can store the data or information either in numbers or characters. The collection of 8 bits is called a Byte. A character in a computer is represented by a Byte. The collection of 8 bits is one byte, therefore combination of such bits provides us 256 different characters to carry out our computations.These coding systems are known as ASCII system.

Purpose of Memory

The data instructions and intermediate results are stored in the memory of the computer. It consists of large number of bytes in sequence.

Unit of Memory

The memory capacity is specified by the number of bytes.

1 KB $= 2^{10} = 1024$ bytes

1 MB $= 2^{20} = 1024 \times 1024$ bytes.

2.13.4 Types of Memory

These are two types of memories used

(i) Semiconductor memory

(ii) Magnetic disc memory

(i) Semiconductor Memory

The memory devices come in the form of chips made of silicon, which are semiconductor devices. It is known as MOS (metal oxide semiconductor). It is a microprocessor unit used as memory.

There are different types of memories used in computers :

1. RAM (Random Access Memory)

It is a temporary memory storage where the information or program is fed and executed. When it is switched off any information stored in this memory is lost.The RAM is an essential memory for every computer, which is temporary memory for execution of the program or data.

2. ROM (Read Only Memory)

The information is stored in the memory at the time of manufacturing which cannot be altered and fresh information cannot be entered.

(a) PROM (Programmable Read Only Memory)

It can be programmed by a programmer to record the information.

(b) EPROM (Erasable Programmable Read only Memory)

The information can only be read and the information remains on the chip until it is erased.

(c) EEPROM(Electrically Erasable Programmable Read Only Memory)

The information can erased electrically.

3. Cache memory

It is used to store operating instructions and data that are likely to be needed for next instructions. This increases the speed of processing. It is a static memory chip Cache size varies from 64 K to 320 MB.

(ii) Magnetic Disc Memory

It is a circular plate with a number of circles called Tracks. The data is recorded on the disk by magnetising the spots on the tracks. The disc is placed on the drives. There is read/write head which moves on the surface of the disc to access a particular record on the track. The data is written on the disc along the concentric circles called Tracks. The read/write head of the drives moves back and forth from one track to another as the disk spins over it.

1. Floppy disc

The floppy can be used as an input media for computer as well as the output media. It is made of plastic material with magnetic coating on one or both sides. These plastic discs are permanently sealed in square plastic jacket to protect it from dust and scratches. A hole is cut in the jacket to enable read/write head of a computer to access the information from any area in the hole.These are permanent removable memories .

The floppies are available in two sizes

(i) Floppy with 5 1/4" diameter.

(ii) Floppy with 3.5" diameter.

The disc has different number of tracks depending upon the drive for which they are used. For a 5 1/4" floppy, number of tracks per inch are either 48 or 96. The floppy has sectors in which information is stored.

Usually a disc contains 40 tracks,(0–39), each track is divided into 32 sectors which are 512 bytes long.

2. Hard disc

The hard disc is a thin metal disc having diameter ranging from 8 to 10 cm. It is located on both sides with magnetic ferric oxide. The data is recorded in magnetised spots on circular tracks on the disk surface. A storage segment stores one or several records of a file. Since each storage segment is identified by an address consisting of track number, sector number etc. The hard disc contains 3 or more plates as one unit. The disc capacity varies from 2100 MB to 4600 MB. These discs use random access method to read or write data. The data transfer is at the rate of 5 MB per second. These are non-removable memories which store the data permanently.

3. Magnetic Tapes

These are used for sequential processing and accessing is required. It is the medium to store large files and for back up purposes.The data is stored in tiny spots on the magnetizable material that coats one side of a plastic tape. Since the tape is a continuous length medium to differentiate between different data records gaps or spaces are left in between records called inter record gaps(IRG).

4. Optical Disc

The data is recorded by burning a permanent pattern onto the surface of the disc by means of a high precision laser beam. The data is read by using the laser at a lower intensity. These are read only memories and the matter can be stored once cannot be erased. These are called compact disc read only memories(CD-ROM). There are memories used such as CD-RW which are rewritable memories.

5. Other memory devices

There other memory devices like

1. Zip drive
2. Pen drive

(iii) Formatting

This is a process of checking the condition of the disc and arranging the tracks and sectors in a proper sequence and locating the bad sectors.

(iv) Write – Protect

To protect the disc from transfer of any data, a notch is provided which is write-protect notch which must be covered by paper.

2.14 Bus

The microprocessor is connected to the memory and other peripheral devices through a collection of wires called Bus. There are 3 types of Buses

1. Data Bus

   A set of lines which are used to transmit and receive "Data". This set of lines is referred to as a Data Bus. They transmit and receive data. The current processors have 32 or 64 bit data buses.

2. Control Bus

   This is used to transmit and receive control signals between the processor and other devices.

3. Address Bus

   The addresses of devices and memory locations are transmitted on the address lines.

2.15 Wordlength

The number of bits that a micro-processor can process at one time is referred as the Wordlength. Any word consists of a fixed number of bits which are treated as a unit and can be used to represent an element of data or program instruction. The 32 or 64 bit processors can operate on 32 or 64 bits of data at a time.

EXERCISE

1. Explain the binary system and binary arithmetic.
2. Explain how decimal numbers are represented in the binary form.
3. Convert binary number 101 , 1100, 1101 and 10110 in the decimal form.
4. Determine decimal value of binary number 0.1101.
5. Convert decimal number 13, 21 & 29 to binary form.
6. Explain bit and byte.
7. Explain the components of a computer.
8. What are the various input devices used in computer ?
9. What do you mean by cursor control devices ?
10. What are the various output devices used in computer ?
11. Explain the components of the CPU.
12. What are the different types of computers used ?
13. What are the registers ?
14. Explain the different types of memories used.
15. Explain magnetic disc drives.
16. What is the use of RAM ?
17. What do you mean by Bus?
18. What is the word length? explain.
19. What do you mean by coding system ?
20. Explain the ASCII and EBCDIC code system to represent the characters.

3

SOFTWARE

AN OVERVIEW

In the previous chapter we have studied the Hardware as most important component of the system.The hardware work on the binary language known as language of bits. The numbers and characters can be represented in the binary form.The hardware consists of the input , CPU and output devices.

In this chapter, we will study the software components which is an interpreter to carry out the work of converting the instructions of the user to binary form suitable for operation on the CPU.

OBJECTIVES

The objective in this chapter are

1. study of software
2. study of various operating system
3. study of compilers
4. Efficient programming techniques

3.1 SOFTWARES IN INFORMATION TECHNOLOGY

It is a program which provides instruction to the computer for execution.The software can translate instructions of the user into machine language commands or vice versa to obtain the communication between the user and CPU .The software controls and directs the hardware operation of the computer.

The software broadly divided into four parts

1. application software
2. Operating system software
3. Languages
4. Packages

These are described as below :

1. Application software:

The application software are the softwares used for specific area of application.

2. Operating system software:

Operating system software are the software used for satisfactory operation of system

3. Languages :

Languages are used for development of the application software

4. Packages:

Packages are useful for performing customer oriented job work.

These are explained as below :

a) Application software

It is a software developed by the programmer to solve the user's specific problems. These softwares are menu-driven softwares used for specific purposes by the user. They can carry out the work in the specific area of application.

Ex : Softwares on payroll, inventory control, medical diagnosis, accounting, education.

b) Operating system

It is a set of programs which forms vital links between the user and the computer hardware to control. It activates, monitors and executes the instructions on the computer. These softwares initially check the hardware components and load the related translator of files and provide some basic functions for instructions to the machine. It is a program developed by a company to control operation of a computer. This program activates the component of computer and prepares them for operation.

There are various types of operating system used:

1. DOS (Disc operating system)
2. Unix
3. LAN Novell
4. Zenix.
5. Window–95

DOS is the most widely used system. The DOS compiler if loaded activates and prepares the computer for operations.

The UNIX system is a multi-user system used to run the software by sharing between the different uses. This system works on waiting-line method where the different users feed their jobs and get them processed.

The LAN system is also a multiuser system which utilizes the sharing of files and softwares but without any waiting time.

The window–95 system uses fast speed processing of data and results. It also provides number of functions on the screen for satisfactory operation of the system.

c) Compilers

The compilers are assemblers or the programming language translators. These translate user programs into executable instructions on the computer.

These are of two varieties :

1. Languages
2. Packages

They are described as below :

1. Programming languages

A computer hardware understands only machine language which is in a binary form. This is known as low level language.

Also it is called as assembly language which is language near to machine language. The high level languages are the languages written by the programmer in English Language. A compiler/Interpreter program is used in the computer to convert the language instructions into machine language.

There is a variety of high level languages :

(i) BASIC
(ii) FORTRAN
(iii) COBOL
(iv) PASCAL
(v) C–language
(vi) C^{++}–language
(vii) Java programming

2. Packages

There is a variety of semi–high level languages or software packages :

(i) word star
(ii) D-Base / Fox-base
(iii) LOTUS

(iv) Ventura
(v) PageMaker
(vi) Corel draw
(vii) Fontacy
(viii) Auto–cad

3.2 CODING

The writing of instructions in a definite language which a computer can understand is called "coding ", and the language is known as "Computer language".

3.3 COMPUTER PROGRAMMING

It is a sequence of steps to be performed and must be translated into detailed instructions which the computer is capable of understanding. These instructions are arranged in the proper order causing the computer to perform a desired task. They are called statements and this set of instructions is called a "Program". The preparation of this program is called programming. The execution of the program consists of the following parts.

3.3.1 Source program

It is a program to provide instructions for the ultimate operations to be performed by the computer to solve a problem. This is prepared by a programmer in a programming language.

3.3.2 Processor/Compiler

It is a program developed by the firm in the required programming language. Its purpose is to inform the computer as to how to translate the source program into appropriate sequence of machine language instruction. There is a separate compiler for every language.

3.3.3 Object program

This is an input program to be executed by the hardware of the computer. This follows the instructions from the processor to convert the source program into a machine language called the "Object Program" to obtain desired results.

3.4 STEPS OF PROGRAMMING

The programming of any problem in any area has to be done by using certain steps. These steps are needed for preparation of program.

1. Defining the problem
2. Planning and analyzing solution of problem
3. Programming into computer language
4. Testing of the program
5. Running of the program
6. Documentation of the program

Any problem in engineering or commercial field has to be solved by using above step. The problem must be defined and analyzed using the basic theory behind the problem. A language is selected and a program is prepared, which can be tested by operation of the program. Then the final document of the program operation is prepared.

3.5 PROGRAM PLANNING

The method of solving problem using programming technique is called Planning of program before preparing a program planning must be carried out by finding sequence of step to be perform. The details about the input data and output results are prepared. The choice of programming language or tools can be made from variety of software languages and packages. The flowchart are the useful tolls which could be prepared to indicate sequence of operation of the program. The flowcharts also help in creation of logic of solution to a problem.

3.6 PROCEDURE OF PROGRAMMING

The efficient programming can be done by programmer if the procedure of programming is followed by programmer. It involves following phases for programming.

1. Objective of programming :

The programmer must decide about the objective of programming.

2. Identification of probable inputs / outputs :

The input variables and output variables must be decided by the programmer in the initial stage.

3. Formula or analysis :

It is necessary for the programmer to collect the required equations of analysis to be performed by the program.

4. Logics or decisions involved in programming :

The programmer should think and develop the required logic involved in the program.

5. Cyclic operations :

The programmer has to decide about the cyclic operations in the program.

6. Format of presentation of outputs :

The format of presentation of output should be constructed by the programmer.

7. Preparation and development of flow charts :

The flowcharts are very useful for indicating the flow of program and thecontent of the program.

8. Preparation of a program :

The flow charts should be converted into a software program using programming language.

9. Identification of errors :

The errors in the program must be removed and the program is executed on the CPU.

10. Testing of program :

The software program must be tested for different inputs and results of the program must be checked.

3.7 PROGRAMMING METHODS

The method followed in the programming is such that it involves these steps

1. Title of the program
2. Finding inputs of the program
3. Finding outputs of the program
4. The mathematical model involved
5. The decisions taken in the program
6. Logic used in the program
7. Presentation of outputs.
8. Use of standard functions.

The flowchart can be used as a guide line and the flowchart can be developed to understand the complexities of the program.

3.8 PROGRAM TESTING

Every program developed by the programer must be tested for error free operation there are 2 types of testing.

1. Syntax Testing
2. Logical Testing

In Syntax testing is a testing of program for grammatical error which are normally indicated by the compiler. In the Logical testing the logical errors during the execution of program are tested.

3.9 PROGRAM DOCUMENTATION

This involves preparation of the manual. There are 2 types of the manuals.

1. System manual

It contains the program descriptions, algorithms and flowcharts.

2.User manual

It return for the user for actual day to day operations of each and every menu used in the program.

3.10 EFFICIENT PROGRAMMING

The programming is regarded to be effecient when the program requires less memory and runs at very fast speed. The program must require very less space for storage. The program should have clarity about the problem and should provide step by step solution. The effecient programming can be done by skilled programer by using following techniques :

1.The memory space for symbols operations and functions should be reduced by reuse of symbol to a large extent.

2. The repetition of sets of calculations may be placed in the function program.
3. The use of readymade functions
4. Integer variable require less space and time for calculations.
5. Over dimensioning of array variable is undesirable.
6. Simple logic should be check by hand on calculations
7. Insertion of securities and checking of input data are to be installed

3.11 BENEFITS OF C & C++

The C-language has been regarded as one of the best language of programming because of the its ability to handle complex analysis situations. It is capable of performing operation on strings and characters. It can perform operation on the file to store the data. It has capability to produce graphics.The use of pointers in C-language helps in processing of data at fast speed .The use of structure in programming allows the programmer to store the data in a formatted form. The c-language has been further extended to C++ by use of modified command. The C++ contains object oriented programming which allows for creation of classes and objects which uses the function program and allows structured programming. The new techniques of inheritance and polymorphism allows for creation of new classes from the existing classes which helps us in reusability of software.

3.12 C– LANGUAGE

The C–language is a high level language which has many advantages over other languages. The variables which are used in C-language can have large number of variety of declaration for variable names and it can have wide accuracy in calculations. The nature of variables can be changed temporarily. The statements do not require a statement number and iterations can be carried out easily. It accepts long statements and writing procedure of statements is easy. The use of readymade functions can be done by inclusion of library files.

The advanced features of C allows graphic operations. Programming with pointers, arrays and functions makes calculations and execution easier. The corruption of data can be prevented by use of structures.File operation allows creation of files to store data or results.

3.13 EXECUTION OF PROGRAM IN C–LANGUAGE

The C–language program is written in a file with ".C" extension name. This file is typed on the editor screen. The program is compiled with the help of compiler of C–language. This is known as compilation. The grammar of C–language program is checked and if there are no errors, then the compilation is successful and object file '.obj' will be created to convert C–program to machine language program. This object file contains the object program, which can be linked with libraries to generate '.exe' file, which can be executed by the computer. This execution of 'exe' file is known as running of program.

If there are any logical or calculation errors in the execution of the program, the program will be terminated and error will be indicated.

3.15 DEVELOPMENT OF C–LANGUAGE

Turbo–C is a version of C–language with features which provides menues for faster operation through windows. The development of C-language resulted into extension of C-language to C^{++}-language. The C–language has been modified to include some readymade functions and some of the difficulties in operation of C-language have been resolved. The C^{++} – language provides new system of input /output statement and the string operation has been simplified. It also provides new system of file operation and other statements. The object oriented programming technique has been utilized for preparation of program in C^{++} – language. The OOP provides a better way of dealing with problems of complex nature by use of classes and objects which allows for storage of data in a formatted form. The C++ – language has been further extended by visual C^{++} package. In this case the frontend GUI components could be inserted in the software and can be customised according to the requirements.

3.16 MANAGEMENT SYSTEMS FOR CPU

There are differnet types of management system for CPU. These are

1. Multi-tasking
2. Multi-programming
3. Multi-processing

1. Multi-tasking

In this system, the computer is capble to perform the multiple tasks at the same time such as editing a file , printing a file. This is known as multiple tasking. In this system the operating system and the buffer make it possible to use the CPU time effectively.

2. Multi-programming

In this case the computer can run multiple programs running at the same time. The multi-programming is necessary for multi-user system. The multi-user system has many users to share the same CPU and therefore the operating system has to manage the CPU usage. In this case , same CPU is shared by various programs on time sharing basis.

3. Multi-processing

In this system, multiple CPU helps in processing multiple instructions simultaneously.

3.17 FILE SYSTEMS

These are the system used for storage of the files on the memory device. All computer applications needs to store and retrieve information. Any computer system can have number of files and there is a need to organise the files and keep track of the files. This is done by the file systems. It consists of two parts as collection of files storing their related data and a directory structure to organise and provide information about files.

There are various systems used

1. FAT

This is File Allocation Table. In this system 8.3 file name conventions are used i.e. file name can be 8 characters long and 3 character extension names to indicate the file type. The files are stored into the clustors whose size is determined by the size of the partition size. A file can be stored in the sigle or multiple cluster. When a file is created an entry is created in the directory which contains the file name , file attributes and the starting cluster number which indexes into the FAT.This entry in the fat table indicates that this is the last cluster of the file. In order to protect the data two copies of FAT are maintained in case one is damaged.

2. VFAT

This is extension of FAT. It contains upto 255 characters , spaces and multiple periods. This system is not case sensitive. The maximum size of VFAT is 4 GB.

3. FAT32

It is extension of FAT and VFAT. It is 32 bit addressing system. This result into smaller cluster size than FAT. These system are supported by Win 95/98/2000 system but not by window NT.

4. NTFS

This New Technology File System. File and directory names can be upto 255 characters long.File names preserve case but are not case sensitive. The maximum size of an NTFS partition is 264 bytes. The NTFS system provides reliability ,fault tolerance and secutrity. It supports multiple data stream.These additional stream contains data that describe the file attributes. The NTFS supports last access ,last write , file creation date /time stamp and security access restrictions. The user can add own user defined attribute to a file. This is because each attribute of a file is an independent byte stream that can be created , deleted , read and written. The NTFS system allows the operating system to recover without having to use disk checking utilities like chkdsk which is required under the FAT and FAT32 systems.

5. Ext2fs

This file system is mostly used in Linux system. The directory structure used in this system is simple with each entry containing just file name and its i-node number. The i-node is a structure which describes the file. All information about the file type ,size ,time stamp,ownership, access right ,file type pointer to data block is contained in the i-node. When the file is accessed ,the directory is checked for the file name to find the i-node number. The i-node is located and the disk locations of the files block are read. Then using these block addresses the file is read from the disk. File blocks are similar to the clusters used in the FAT to store files.

6. Ext3fs

This is similar to the Ext2fs file system with a transaction log similar to the NTFS file system. it is known as journaling- file system which has the transaction log known as journal.

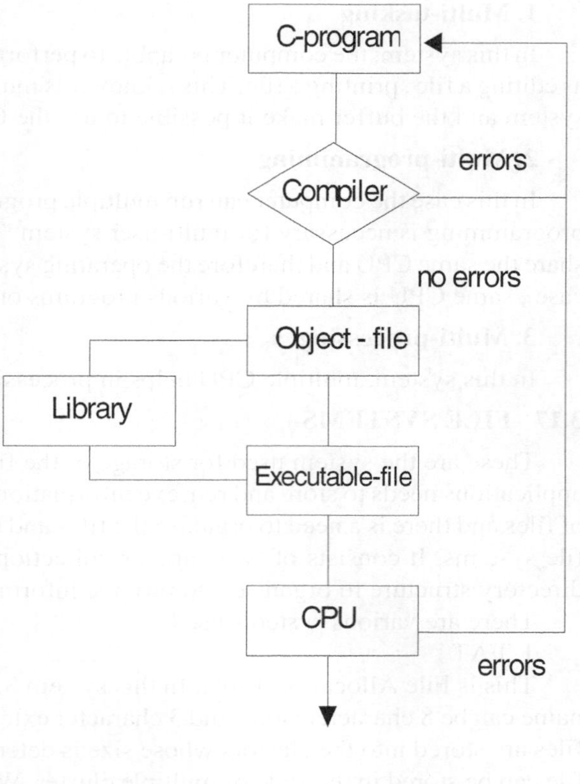

In case if there is power loss and system reboots the integrity of the file system is preserved.

7. Reiser file system

This is new system used under Linux operating system. It is similar to journaling file system like Ext3fs and provides crash recovery , speeds up booting process and helps to prevent data loss due to mechanical or serious errors.

3.18 GRAPHIC USER INTERFACES

This are the various interfaces provided to the user for smooth operation of the system. The interfaces are graphics in nature and they provide access to the system. the operation of the software modules can be done by operating or clicking these interfaces. The messages can be given by use of the interfaces and acceptance of the alternative operations can be doen by clicking these interfaces. The mouse or cursor control device allows to access the interfaces and click the interfaces which further performs the operation. The advantage of these interfaces is that it is able to provide large number functions and operations on the monitor.

The various types of interfaces used are

1. Menu - drop down , pull down
2. Buttons - radio, click, check boxes
3. Scroll bar
4. Text field
5. Text area
6. dialog boxes
7. Pop up menu
8. Boxes - list box , combo box
9. label

These are very useful elements required for any type customised software.

EXERCISE – 3

1. Explain types of softwares used.
2. Explain the classifications of the software
3. Explain the purpose of operating system software
4. Explain various types of operating system softwares
5. Explain what do you mean by compilers
6. Explain the various languages used for programming
7. What are the different type of packges used in IT
8. Explain the method of execution of the program
9. Explain what do you mean by programming
10. Explain the efficient programming
11. What is source and object program
12. What are the programming methods used for programming
13. Why program testing is necessary
14. What do you mean by flow chart
15. Why C–language has been a popular software development language.
16. What the different type of file systems used
17. Explain what do you mean by GUI

4
NETWORKING & E-COMMERCE

AN OVERVIEW

In the previous chapter we have it studied the software and programming techniques. The software are very improtant elements of any system. The software provide facility of interacting with the computer hardware and provides large number of readymade function and operations for convenience of the user.

In this chapter we will study the networking of computer and the world of the internet which connects large number of users all over the world.

OBJECTIVES

The major objective are

1. Study networking system
2. To understand the internet
3. To obtained the knowledge of E-commerce
4. Understand online business systems

4.1 NETWORKING

A group of computers and other devices connected together is called a network. The inter connected computers can share resources which called networking.It is linking of two or more different entities together to form a group or network to perform some specific task. The networking enhances the capacity of computer to share, exchange, preserve and protect information. When the computers are connected over a network it is possible to exchange the information easily and faster. A group of computer connected together is a network.

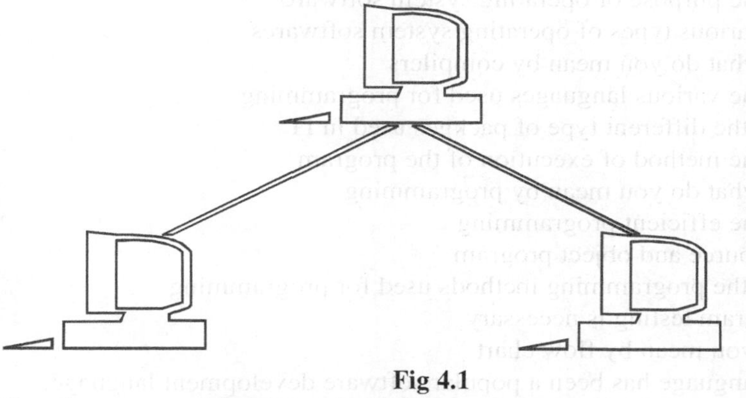

Fig 4.1

The client server relationship exists in networking in which client requests that some action to be performed and server performs the action returning the results to the client. The client first has to established the connection to server and then the data can be transmitted. The server may deny or accept the connection. If the connection is accepted then the client and server communicate through sockets as similar to the operations being performed on the input/output file. When the connection is not required the client server can terminate their connection and the networking is stops.

4.2 TYPES OF NETWORK

There are two types of networks :

1. Local area network (LAN)
2. Wide area network (WAN)

4.3 LOCAL AREA NETWORK

It is a network of number of computers connected to each other by a cable in a single location or building or area.

4.4 WIDE AREA NETWORK

It is network of number of computers connected to each other at separate distance.

4.5 USES OF NETWORK

It can be used for sharing of resources such as

1. Sharing information
2. Sharing hardware resources
3. Sharing software resources
4. Preserving information
5. Protecting information
6. E-mail

4.6 SYSTEMS OF LAN

There are three system of LAN. They are described below

1. Client-servers

These System do not provide network resources. These are client server models. In these model the server is connected to various clients. They provide data to the client and clients use their own resources.

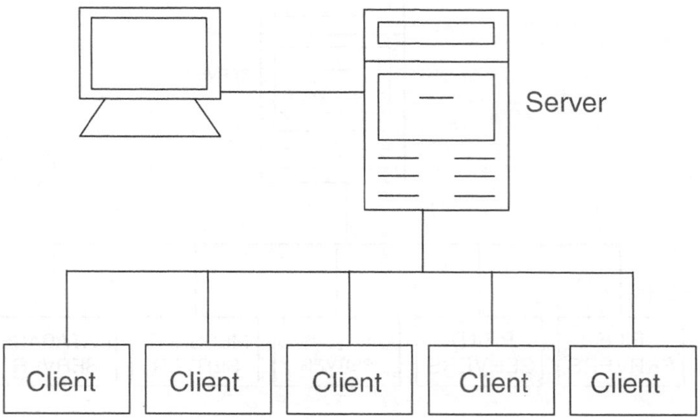

Client Server

Fig. 4.2

2. Peer to peer (P2P)

These are the system which do not use but provide resources. These are peer to peer models. All the computer are connected together by network card and cables. The sharing of resources occurs because of the connection between the different computer terminal and printers, memory devices can be accessed very easily.

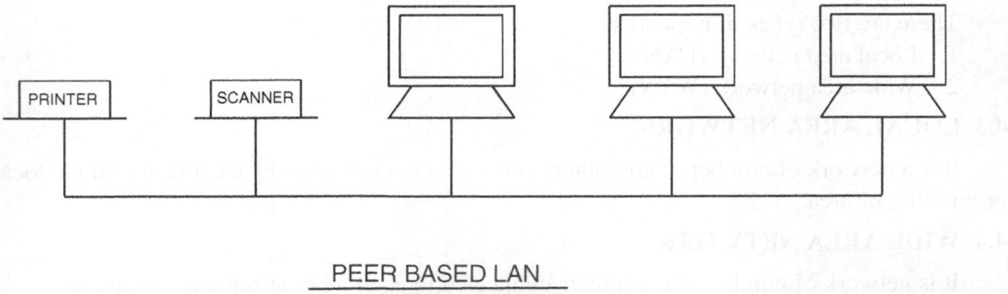

Fig. 4.3

3. hybrid

These system provide resources. These are hybrid network. In these model server provide all resources and client can access the resources.

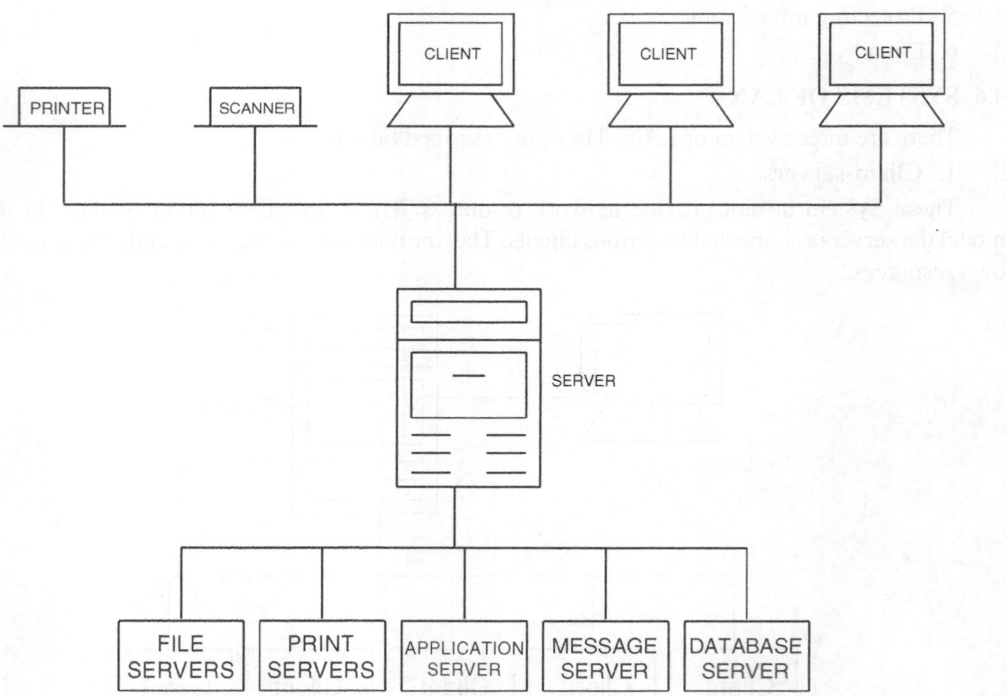

Fig. 4.4

4.7 NETWORK PROTOCOLS

These are the bases on which the information can be exchanged.There are different types of protocols used.

1. NetBEUI
2. NWLINK
3. TCP/IP

1. NetBEUI

   It is a netBIOS extended user interface which implements the NETBIOS frame.

2. NWLINK

   It is a networking component that provides the protocol. It is easy to connect & supports routing between networks.

3. TCP/IP

   It is Transmission control protocol/internet protocols. This is used in the internet.

4.8 INTERNET SERVICE PROVIDER

These are the companies which provide access to user on a pay and use basis. The ISP provide service through dial up telephone or ISDN lines.

4.9 ISDN

It is an Integrated Services Digital Network. These are two or three times faster than ordinary telephone lines.

4.10 LEASED LINE

It is phone line connection that is rented for exclusive use from one computer to another for constant access.

4.11 DSL

These are Asymmetric Digital Subscriber line model technology which transform ordinary telephone line into high speed digital lines for instant internet access.

4.12 WEB SITE

It is location or memory space where the user can store his data and the data can be accessed by large number of users.

4.13 SEARCH ENGINE

This is a software which actually searches the entire world wide web. It utilizes indexing software agents like robots or spiders.

4.14 WEB DIRECTORIES

These are the editors to compile, index and categorised the information.

4.15 COMMON GATEWAY INTERFACE

This is used for server side solution used to develop web applications. The application processes the data it receives and sends it back to the server. This is used for dynamic web development.

4.16 ACTIVE SERVER PAGES

These are the pages which allows development of dynamic web content. This allows connection to a particular web server.

4.17 INTERNET TECHNOLOGY

The Java technology or net technology is an internet friendly science which allows the operation to be performed on the internet. The internet is a world wide network of computer through the telephone links which allows various user to share the data, communicate to each other, perform the transactions etc.

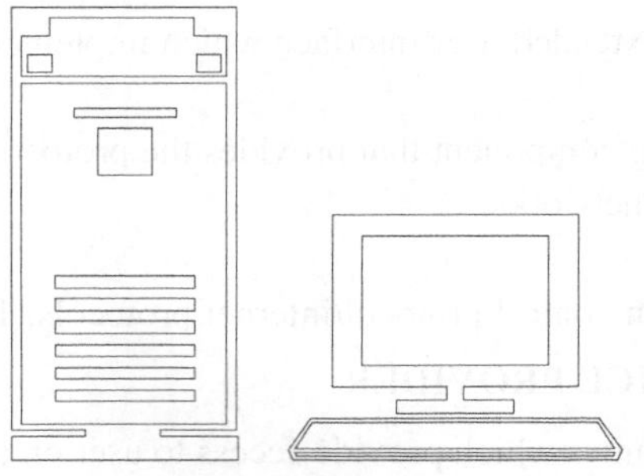

Fig 4.5

4.18 HYPER TEXT

This is a text which works like a reference book. In this text the file or page is tagged to every text and on clicking the text the file or page is open. This allows each page of book to be linked to other pages and these hyper links can be obtained by clicking mouse pointer on them. The hyper links of text are underlined and marked with blue colour.

Example.

<u>**Contents**</u>

4.19 HTML

This is a hyper text makeup language. This language allows variety of data different types to be integrated seamlessly and permits links between data situated anywhere on the internet.

All the files of internet are written in HTML language which contents tags to indicate the customization of the page.

4.20 HTML FILE

This is the main file of the internet in which HTML tags are written and the file has an extension".html".

Example.

main.html

The internet based languages allows these files because of which it utilizes the hyper text. The hyper text is a text which is connected to a another page or it has a link to another page. This makes it easier to access and create the chain of the pages. The facility of preparing hyper text is available in the HTML language. The language allows creation of web pages and HTML file.

4.21 WEB BROWSERS

The screen which allows us obtain the world wide web is call a browser.

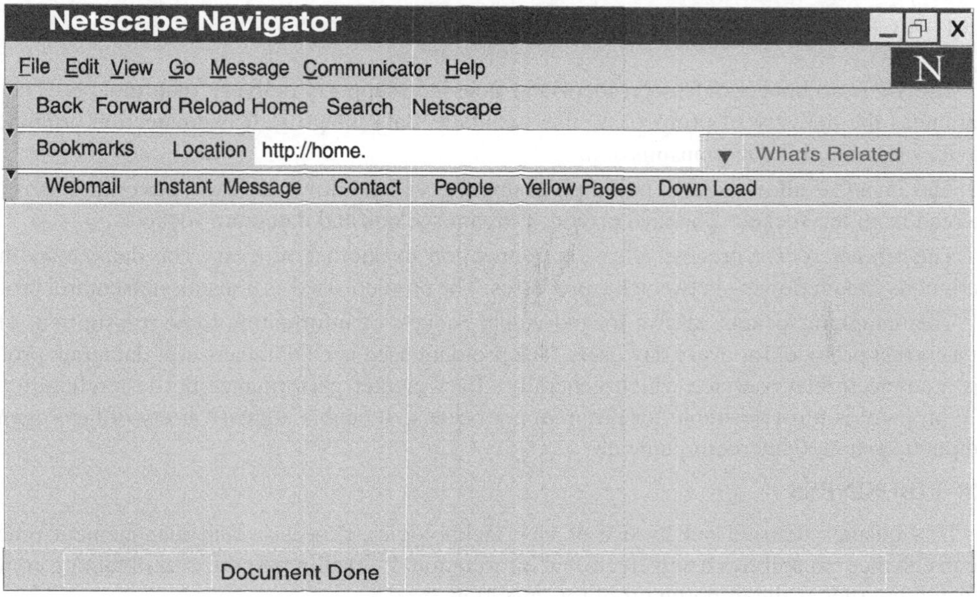

Fig. 4.6

4.22 UNIFORM RESOURCE LOCATOR

The site of an internet connection can be specified by the uniform resource locator (URL). The internet browser is a screen connected to internet having an text field to write the address of the site. It is used for accessing the data at any location or site to obtain the informations.

It is specified by

xxx:\\www.yyy.zzz\pq.html

Where,

xxx	–	It is a service descriptor
www	–	It is a world wide web
yyy	–	It is a name of the company
zzz	–	It is a extension name
pq.html	–	name of HTML file

Example :

http:\\www.rise.com\rais.html

The URL indicates the name of service descriptor , site name and the name file on the site.

4.23 HTTP

This is a *Hyper Text Transfer Protocol*. This is used in the internet technology for accessing the address of the site. This protocol is used by world wide web servers. It allows for access of web pages in the HTML format.

4.24 HTML LANGUAGE

In this language , the English characters are used and tags are written for preparing the web page. The tags are used for variety of properties like background colour,heading,text colour , text size, justification, images etc.

4.25 TCP/IP

This is Transmission Control Protocol/Internet Protocol. It is most widely used protocol & it is internet protocol. It consists of main protocols

1. TCP
2. IP

The IP is a connectionless protocol and does not supports delivery of protocols. The TCP guarantees the delivery of protocol & also maintains data integrity. It is connection oriented and provides reliable full data transmission.

The Java/C # allows socket based programming which allows to view networking as if like a file read from the socket. The java provides stream sockets and datagram sockets.

The *stream socket* process allows a connection to another process. The data flows due to continuous stream flowing between the processes. The protocol used is transmission control protocol.

The datagram sockets, allows for individual packets of information to be transmitted. This is not a correct protocol for every day users. The protocol used is UDP means user datagram protocol. It is a connectionless service which generally offers greater performance but less reliability. The TCP protocol is most desirable for programmer because it enable a great variety of heterogeneous computer system to intercommunicate.

4.26 E-BUSINESS

It is business carried out by use of new technologies, processes and management practices which enhance capabilities using electronic information. It is selling products or obtaining contracts by using internet as the important tool for operation.

4.27 E-COMMERCE

The virtual world of business is e-commerce. The internet has interconnected number of users creating a new world markets and new business opportunities.

It is the selling product on internet. It is commercial activity performed by using electronic media by executing business transaction such as contract ordering, invoicing payment on interactive electronic media. This refers to all types of transactions relating to commercial activities based on processing and transmission of digitised data, text, sound and images.

It is defined as any transfer involving some exchange of value over an iternet. The E–commerce involves a user with a computer linked to the internet who employs an internet browser to contact websites in order to exchange the value for goods or services or transfer of funds between accounts. The goods exchanged may be electronic documents, images and sound files. The electronic services may include A. T. M. , Financial planning, online games etc.

The commerce is considered as business or trading done by transaction money or goods. The commerce involve exchange of products and in return value of money.

The e-commerce is commercial operation performed by using electronic media.It is business carried out by use of new technologies, processes and management practices which enhance capabilities using electronic information. It is selling products or obtaining contracts by using internet as the important tool for operation.

E-commerce involves display of product on the internet and allowing customer to choose the product from the range. He can place order online and receive invoice indicating the payment. The payment can be made on line using credit card, paypal or on line account transfer system.

The customer can receive the date of dispatch of product through the courier agency. The E-commerce can be used with shopping cast where the products can be purchased and placed in the shopping cast.

4.28 BENEFITS OF E-COMMERCE

There are large number of benefits of e-commerce

1. The transactions can be easily performed. Because every user can be contacted or informed about the nature of transaction occured.
2. It allows displays of products for marketing. The product could be placed on display and the user can access the product details and perform analysis.
3. The customer gets competitive market easily. It is possible access large number of supplier and idea about their product and prices can be obtained.
4. The searching products and supplier is easier. The product can be traced or the suppliers can be searched and contacted without any difficulty.
5. Paperless and fast communication can be done.This system has paperless work and all the communication could be made electronic medium.
6. The transaction can be done easily by on line payment system. The payment can be done on line system for transfer money from one account to another account.
7. The quotation, bills etc can be send easily. The bills could be prepared very easily and calculation can be performed by software programs.

4.29 E-COMMERCE OPERATIONS

In the e-commerce operations, the customer accesses the web site and submit enquiry on the web site which contains various options. The web site has programs and data libraries which provides the desired data to the customer.

The customer accesses the web site. The web site must be constructed with customised format using GUI components to select various options. The customer require to perform various operations like

1. Searching of data on site.
2. Select the required product or item on site.
3. Obtain the display of the product and its features.
4. Ask for the bill of the productz.
5. On line payment of the product.

The e-commerce operation is performed by the customer when the web site displays the contents of the site and the various products available on site. The user has a option to select the desired product or he makes an enquiry. The programs on the web site approaches to the data library and the data is brought from the library and displayed in a customized form to the user. If the user selects the products then the bill is calculated and is provided with facility of payment on line or by cheque or draft.

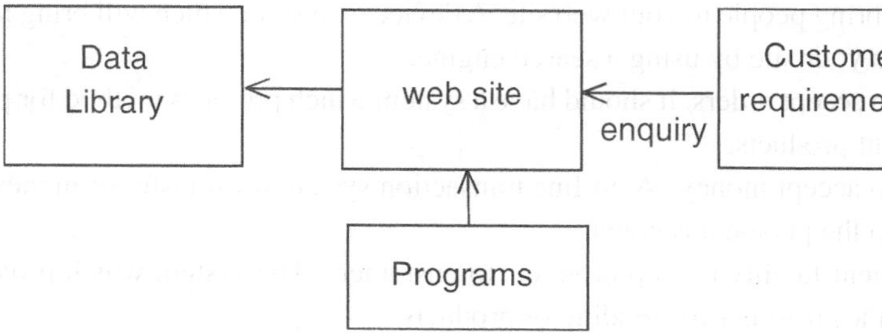

Fig. 4.7

4.30 VARIETIES OF E-COMMERCE SITE

There are different variety of e-commerce sites

1. Sites used for marketing of product
   In these sites the products are displayed on the sites and user can obtained information about the products supplied by the company. Such site allows access of the user during surfing operation for appropriate categary of product.
2. Sites used for placing of orders
   On these sites the information about the product is acquired by the user and site allows user to make selection or place the orders for the product.
3. Sites used for commercial operations
   These are the site on which the user select his products or services and the orders are placed with the company. The payments are translated using on line payment system.
4. Sites allows for meetings and negotiation. These are the sites on which meeting and negotiation are performed through discussion.
5. Site meant for finding other sites and establishing connection using e-mail or e-connection facility.

4.31 ELEMENT OF E-COMMERCE

The e-commerce activity normally contains following operation

1. Selling of products to customers as a producer or distributor. The customer can be display the product/services available for consumer.
2. This is a place from which the products are sold. The product can be sold on the web site by placing the order for the products.
3. The way of finding the people who can purchase the products by marketing technique. It means locating the shop, sending information order or quotations.
4. Accept the order by e-mail or e-process.
5. Accept the money by e-payments by billing and collection.
6. Deliver the product or service by e-fulfillment.

4.32 CONDUCT OF E-COMMERCE

The e-commerce should contains the following systems for smooth conduct

1. A product . The details about the product its main features are maintained on the site
2. The memory device permanently connected to the world wide web and any user can be able to access the site. Place to sell the product.
3. A way to bring people to your web site. A device or system which will bring large number of persons to your site by using a search engine.
4. Method to accept orders. It should have a system which provides method for placing of order of different products.
5. Method to accept money. A on-line transaction system for transfer of money from the user account to the personal account.
6. A fulfillment facility to ship products to customers. The system which provides a bill and instructs the customer for sending of products.
7. Way to accept returns. The receipt of product is to be obtained.
8. Way to provide customer service. Any services to the customer regarding products should be provided.

4.33 APPLICATIONS OF E-COMMERCE

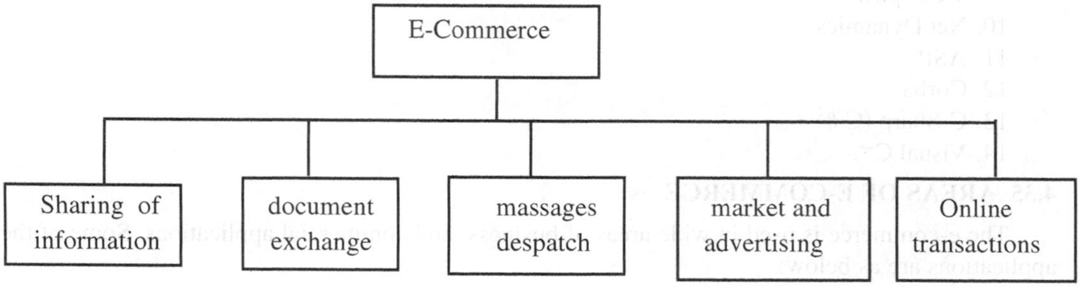

Fig. 4.8

The e-commerce is used in major of fields such as

1. **Sharing of information**
   The sharing information can be performed by a system of video conferencing system where the user can perform discussion and meet the persons at remote location. The information can be transferred by face to face discussion with different persons.
2. **Document exchange**
   The document could be transfered by creating files either in form of web pages or by creating file in other packages and can be transferred to the user using FTP protocols.
3. **Despatch of messages**
   The messages can be send by using e-mail facility from one site to another site using e-mail address of the user.
4. **Marketing and advertising**
   This can be done by creating websites on a connected server having ID on world wide web on which complete information about product is stored. The user can be allowed to access the information using search engines which brings the customer to the sites.
5. **On Line transaction**
   This system allows for the user to access a known site at which their account is maintained for money or any other product. They can supply information for transfer of money or products on the site, which allows the transactions to occur.

The electronic commerce can be fully automated transaction or partially automated transactions using human and physical interfaces.

4.34 SOFTWARES USED IN E-COMMERCE

There are various types of softwares used in E-commerce technology. These are as below :

1. HTML
   This allows created of web pages which loaded on the web sites.
2. Java language
   This is object oriented programming language which allows the user to create softwares for e-commerce operation.
3. Java servlet
   The static web pages can be created by HTML programming and servlet allow dynamic web pages using Java programs.
4. Java server pages
5. Enterprise Java beans
6. Remote method invocation
7. XML
   This is extended Markup language allows for dynamic web page development.

8. Weblogic
9 Web sphere
10. Net Dynamics
11. ASP
12. Corba
13. C-Sharp (C #)
14. Visual C^{++}.

4.35 AREAS OF E-COMMERCE

The e-commerce is used in wide areas of business and commercial applications. Some of the applications are as below:

1. Web site development

The website can be created for any business organization which contains the information of the organization, the products manufactured and the location, capacity etc. of the company. The web site contains number of files having photograph and picture of the company products. It also provides information about the communications to be done with different departments.

2. On line training

It is possible to provide training to the students by using the internet and video conferencing system. The training can be given in various areas of engineering, science, medical etc.

3. Shopping

It is used for purpose of shopping where the products could be displayed and the information regarding the product can be provided. The orders could be accepted .

4. Real estate

The e-commerce for real estate business for display and choice of various properties and their locations.

5. Customer services

It can be used for providing various services to the customers like the information about trains, buses, hotels etc. The e-mail service can also be provided.

6. Medical consultation

It can be used for consultation of the expert doctor regarding the diagnosis.

7. On line library

It can be used for the library in which on line books could be provided and e-books could be obtained on the internet.

8. On line banking

It can be used for on line banking services where the transactions of payment could be made on the internet through the credit cards system.

4.36 E-COMMERCE PROCEDURE

The e-business depends upon the user aspect of the site for marketing purposes. The e-commerce site need good appearance, content and product organization. The aesthetics of site are main factors to determine customer attraction towards the site. The site should also have a automatic back office which provides link between the user and actual delivery of goods. The e-commerce site must contain product information, pricing, inventory, invoicing and final order placing.

The figure shows e-business procedure. The customer approaches the site and obtains the display of the product. The product is selected and the order will be placed by the customer. The order placed will checked and varified by a programs. The order will be captured by a program and it is transmitted to the order executor, which will process the order and the products are then transferred to the customer.

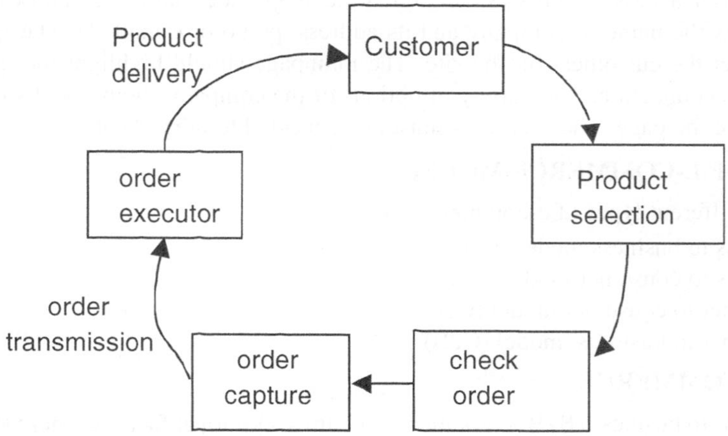

Fig.4.9

There are series of processes which will be performed between a customer browsing an e-commerce site and actually purchasing and receiving an ordered product.

The site must communicate to the customer which products are available for sale. The facilities of browsing and selecting the product. The order can be placed for the product. The facility of e-payment and preparation of bills is essential and finally the order must be placed in the order executor.

4.37 DESIGN OF E-COMMERCE SITES

The E-commerce sites should be designed according to the area and the type of site. It is necessary to know about following system

1. Information about type of product/services.
2. Mechanism of bringing the customers.
3. The number of alternative or selection available.
4. Mechanism for placing and checking of orders.
5. Method/mode of making payments.

It may be possible that all the systems may not be listed or available required on the site.

4.38 SYSTEM OF DESIGNING OF THE SITE

The web site should contain a front page which will display the name and address of the company very clearly as main heading

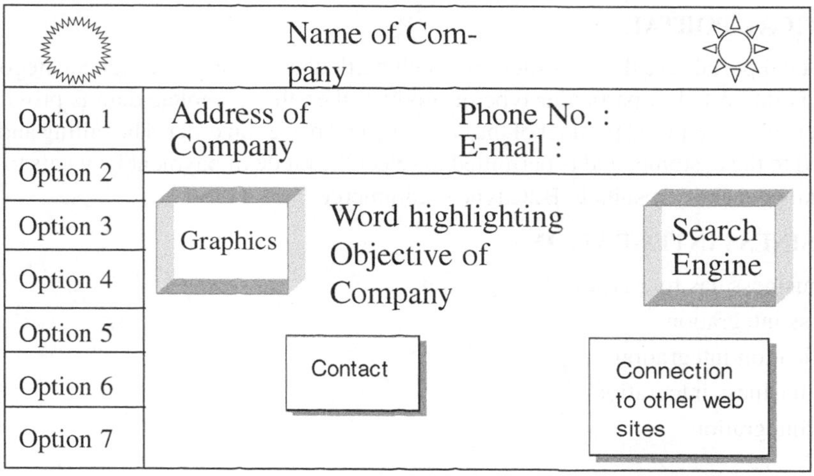

Fig.4.10

When the user access a web site the web site contains the main page known as index.html should highlights the name of company and its address, ph.no or e-mail ID. The graphics can be utilized to attract the customers on the site. The mainpage should highlight the objective of the company and its connection. The variety of options of the company should be displayed either on top or left side of the page. These options must be connected to other databases.

4.39 TYPES OF E-COMMERCE MODEL

These are different types of e-commerce model

1. Business to business model (B2B)
2. Business to consumer model (B2C)
3. Consumer to consumer model (C2C)
4. Consumer to business model (C2B)

4.39.1 B2B E-COMMERCE

The business to business (B2B) e-commerce requires additional facilities more than online web stores. It requires numerous processes for even the simplest transactions. Most of the organizations use the internet or a virtual private network (VPN) as the primary mechanism for conducting business on-line. This implies internet enabling applications such as supply chain management system, procurement applications, electronic storefronts, customer relationship management, software and enterprise resource planning systems.

4.39.2 B2C E-COMMERCE

These sites display large number of advertisement on the site to attract the customers. These customers provide various requirements and then the transactions are performed. The primary aim of such sites is to obtain customer for business or selling of products.

4.39.3 C2C E-COMMERCE

In this case, the seller get listed on the web site for the product they want to sell and the buyer accesses the site. The suitable seller is selected. These site are services site which acts like exchanges or broker for transaction of data from one customer to another.

4.39.4 C2B E-COMMERCE

In this case, the consumer places an estimate of the amount of money he is willing to spend for a particular service. Then the supplier provides the product. These are consumer oriented sites on which the consumer requirement are placed and the supplier provide products according to the needs of consumers.

4.40 VERTICAL PORTAL

The vertical portals are the web sites on which particular industry or product category is listed. If customer is interested in particular type of product, then the complete data is provided on site. The customer selects required product of the company and places an order. The billing and quotations are submitted to the customer and is permitted to select the mode of payment he wants to make. The vertical portals generally results in B2C type e-commerce.

4.41 E-BUSINESS INTEGRATION

The e-business has four types of integration

1. Access integration
2. Application integration
3. Inter business integration
4. Data integration

1. Access integration

The user must have access to the relevant and upto date information without having surfed through different web sites.

2. Application integration

The business processes involving multiple application require integration of application logic and functions. The selling of products must be integrated with payments at the site.

3. Inter business integration

It is imperative for business to participate in a market place of B2B exchange environment. These environment brings the buyer and supplier to same platform.

4. Data integration

The data integration is important for B2B environments because the data comes from different sources. It allows applications to work with data from different computing platforms, databases and operating systems.

4.42 PAYMENT GATEWAY

The payment gateway is third party network which acquires transactions from an e-commerce portal and processes it through the banking or credit card system. It links the banking network with the internet. It is a link into banking network and internet user. It uses enhanced security features such as digital envelopes and content key.

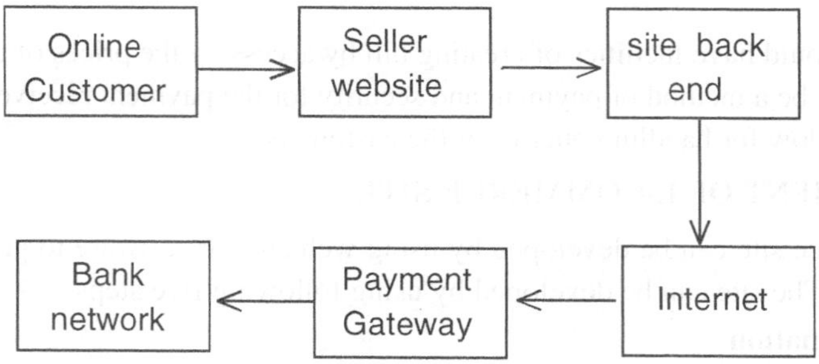

Fig.4.11

The customer click his buy order on the website and make payment. He selects the gateway services by using credit card, digital cash or bank account to make payment to website.

The gateway provides on interface between the merchant and bank's payment processing system. The payment gateway translates messages into other message format which are used for authorization and settlement of merchant transactions. The payment gateway takes a transaction, then certifies it and routes with encryption. They use secure electronic transaction (SET) technology to ensure the security of financial transaction on net.

4.43 ADVANTAGES OF E-COMMERCE

The e-commerce technology provides large number of advantages to the customers.

1. It has low transaction cost because the customer services could be provided with less expenditure. The cost of printing and mailing of catalogs is very less. The distribution cost is almost negligible and the processing can be done at low cost.
2. It allows for larger purchases for every transactions made in the e-commerce stores because the customer get access to the large number of products hence the purchases are increased.
3. It allows for more information to be stored for the product and display of information can be very easily done.

4. The person can shaft the product according to their liking and their requirement.
5. It has ability to configure product and display prices according to the configuration.
6. It has to ability to compare to prices between multiple vendor easily.
7. It is possible to search large number of catalogs easily.
8. The company can mention data in huge catalog and automatic searching can be very easily performed.
9. The complicated orders can be placed very easily.
10. The billing and forwarding can be done by the e-commerce site.

4.44 E-COMMERCE SITES

The E-commerce site are developed and must contain large number of features on the sites.

1. Easy navigation and good site architecture. The site must have capabilities for easy navigation and the content of the site must be displayed on the first page and customer should be in a position to select according to his requirement.
2. It should have search engine facilities to search the required data.
3. There must be a procedure of registration. A registration form should be made available on the site.
4. It must have help and facilities of e-mail for correspondence on the site.
5. The site should allow customer to make changes in the selection or deletion of selected items on the site.
6. The site should have facilities of creating bill by accessing the prices of the product.
7. There must be a method of payment and security for the payment received online.
8. It should allow for handling queries of the customers.

4.45 DEVELOPMENT OF E-COMMERCE SITE

The e-commerce site can be developed by using web creator software to generate HTML file and Java program. The site can be developed by using following five steps.

1. Basic information

It must contain basic information about company name, address, logo, phone number etc. It provides help and should contain the ways of placing order by e-mail, form, order with list or order form with entry fields.

2. Creation of libraries

The library can be created by entering the data into the database and libraries can be linked together.

3. Order placing and confirmation

It should contain procedure for placing order and confirmation of the order can be made by customer.

4. Mode of payment

The mode of payment by credit card or money transfer is indicated. The payment can be done by cheque or draft.

5. Customization of site

The site can be customized by adding the GUI component like buttons, menu lists etc.

EXERCISE

1. Explain the networking.
2. Explain different types of networking system.
3. What is internet explain ?
4. What meant by hypertext?
5. Explain the web browser.
6. Explain what is HTTP.
7. Explain what is of E-commerce.
8. What are the different field of E-commerce?
9. Explain the applications of E-commerce.
10. What are the benefits of e-commerce technology?
11. Explain different areas of E-commerce.
12. Explain the different software used in e-commerce.
13. Explain procedure of E-commerce.
14. Explain various types of E-commerce.
15. Explain various features of E-commerce.
16. Explain the payment gateway.

5

ALGORITHMS & FLOW CHARTS

An Overview

In the previous chapter, we have studied the internet and networking process in which various aspects of internet operation and networking between the different computers has been studies.

In this chapter, we will study the tools which can be used before programming is carried out such as algorithm and flow charts. These are used for development of software in C & C++. These provide convenience in development of program .

OBJECTIVES

The objective in this chapter are

1. study of algorithm
2. study of flow chart
3. study of pseudocode
4. Efficient programming techniques

5.1 INTRODUCTION

The programming of any problem in any area has to be done by using certain steps.The problem solving technique is used for solving of the problem. The computer can not solve problem on their own. But they assist in solving problems. Therefore to solve the problem the following factors are considered very important:

1. Define the problem
2. Identify the input and output values
3. Identify the conditions to be fulfilled
4. identify contrainst and limitations
5. Identify alternative theories and solutions
6. Choose best alternative
7. Compute result
8. Varify correctness of result

Therefore it is necessary to develop a algorithm of any program in the beginning of any complex problem solving process. The algorithm describes the method of doing a task.

5.2 ALGORITHM

It is a set of precise rules that specify the way doing the task or method of solving problem.These are the sequence of logical steps required to perform a specific task of solving problem.The development of algorithm is carried out for solving problem. The algorithm helps us to define and refine out programming problems.

5.3 TYPES OF ALGORITHM

There are two types of algorithms

1. Definitive

2. Subjective

5.3.1 Definitive algorithm

This algorithm performs the tasks which have a definite answer and a best method of processing. The example is searching a word in a dictionery or searching a telephone number in directory are definitive algorithms.

5.3.2 Subjective algorithm

This algorithm processes information based on an assumption in which the correct answer is matter of opinion.These are used in business, commerce etc.

5.4 PROPERTIES OF GOOD ALGORITHM

The algorithm consists of finite steps which shows detailed sequence of actions to be performed to solve problem and complete the task. A good algorithm less time for execution. The properties of good algorithm are

1. Finiteness

This means the algorithm must terminate after a finite number of steps

2. Definiteness

Each step in the algorithm must be precisely defined

3. Effectiveness

All operations can be carried out exactly in finite time

4. Input

An algorithm has zero or more input

5. Output

An algorithm has one or more outputs

The algorithm is displayed by pseudocode.

5.5 PSEUDOCODE

It uses an informal language and some notations. It is an ouline of the program. It is written in form that it can be easily converted to a computer program. It allows the programmer to write logic of the algorithm. It the algorithm is expressed using pseudocode then it is easier to convert it into computer program. There are different methods or styles of wrting pseudocode. It do not follow rigorous notations and there is no universal standard for the pseudocode. Pseudocode is an English-like code to represent the outline or logic of a program.

It is not a particular type of programming code, but it can be used as an intermediate step for developing program code.

The various methods of expressing the pseudocode are discussed here.

Variable

It indicates the location in the memory of the computer in which the value is placed. The values may be supplied by using keyboard. The are indicated as

N ← 5

This means value of variable N is 5

The arithemetic operations are shown as

N ← A +B

The means N is addition of A & B

N ← N+5

This means value of N is increamented by 5

Read(A,B,C) or Input A,B,C

This means read value of A,B,C

Write(B,C) or display B,C

This means write value of variable B and C.

A loop indicates some operation to be repeated as long as the condition is true. The loop denotes repetition of algorithm till some condition holds true. The while loop can be used in algorithm by

While condition

End while

Endwhile

This is sequence of actions to be performed one over the other. This is loop or cyclic operation over certain statements till the condition is true.

To form the condition we can use relational operators like >, <, ≤ , ≥ , =, ¹

Example

```
   N ¬ 5
While N <  10
         N ¬  N+2
Endwhile
write(N)
```

This is case where N is initially 5 and while condition check it. The N is increamented by 2 to 7 and the cycle terminates when the vlaue of N becomes more than or equal to 10.

The algorithm can be used to construct the IF statement in the decision making process. This allows the decision to be taken by the algorithm when a condition has been satisfied. It is written as

```
If condition
then
        Decision1
Else
        Decision2
Endif
```

In this case if the condition is satisfied then the decision1 is executed or else the decision2 is executed.

Example

```
if N< 40
Then
        C= A+B
Else
        C=A-B
Endif
```

Example 5-1: Algorithm for arranging two numbers in order

```
1  INPUT Num1, Num2
   2 IF Num1 < Num2 THEN
3  Num1=Num2
4  Num2=Num1
5  ENDIF
6  DISPLAY Num1, Num2
7  ENDIF
```

Example 5-2 : Algorithm to display of grades

```
IF Score >= 80 AND Score < 90 THEN
DISPLAY "B"
ENDIF
```

Example 5-3 : Algorithm to display of comment and count

```
INPUT count
WHILE count <> "5"
IF a < b THEN
DISPLAY "hi"
IF a = 10 THEN
IF b <= -99 THEN
        DISPLAY "bye"
ENDIF
DISPLAY "what"
IF a + b = 0 THEN
        DISPLAY "good"
ENDIF
DISPLAY "yuh"
ENDIF
ENDIF
INPUT count
ENDWILE
END
```

Example 5-5 : Algorithm to perform calculations

```
INPUT x, y
IF x < y THEN
        INPUT y
        z = x ^ 2
        total = x + y
        w = x + total + z
        z = z + 1
        DISPLAY x, y, z, w, total
ELSE
        INPUT y
        z = x ^ 2
        total = x + y
        w = x - total + z
        z = z + 1
        DISPLAY x, y, z, w, total
ENDIF
DISPLAY "bye"
END
```

Example 5-6 : Algorithm to count even or odd numbers

```
Max = 6
Evens = 0
Count = 1
WHILE Count <= Max
        INPUT Number
IF Number % 2 = 0 THEN
        Evens = Evens + 1
ENDIF
        Count = Count + 1
ENDWHILE
DISPLAY Evens
END
```

Example 5-7 : Find largest number

```
1.  [Read the first number]
    Read(LARGEST)
2.  [Read the second  number]
    Read(CURRENT)
3.  [Update largest number so far]
    If  LARGEST > CURRENT
    Then LARGEST — CURRENT
    End if
4.  [Read third number]
    Read(CURRENT)
5.  [Update largest number so far]
    if(CURRENT>LARGEST
    Then LARGEST — CURRENT
    End if
6.  [Display largest value]
    Write(LARGEST)
7.  [Finished]
    Halt
```

5.6 FLOWCHART

A flow chart is a diagrammatic representation of the sequence of operations to be performed to obtain solution of the problem. The flow chart are prepared in the early stage of program development. They provide solutions to the problem by diagrammatic methods. They ar useful in understanding the logic of complicated and lengthy problems. If the flow chart is drawn then it is easy to write programs. The flowcharts are used in programming for purpose of indicating the sequence of operation of the program. The flowchart also indicate the transfer of control and the cyclic operation performed in the program. These are the graphical tools which could be used for development of complete program. The flowchart uses symbol or blocks of different shape for representing statements of the program. The various symbol used are

1. Computation box - rectangular shape
2. Decision box - diamond shape
3. Input box - circular box or parallogram
4. Output box - Cut box
5. oval - Start and end of program

The flow lines denotes the direction of logic flow in a program.

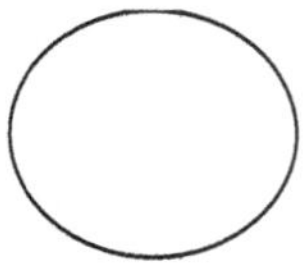

This is used for start and end of flowchart

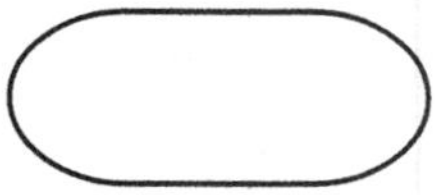

This block is use for representing supplier data to the program.

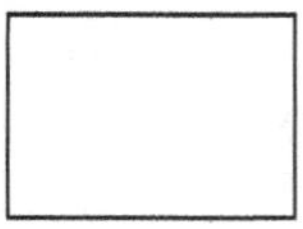

This block is used writing of arithmetic statements

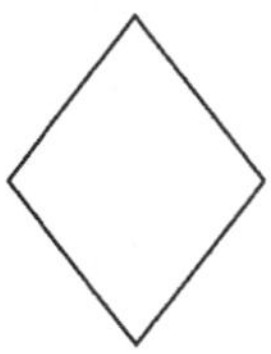

This block is used for decision making statement

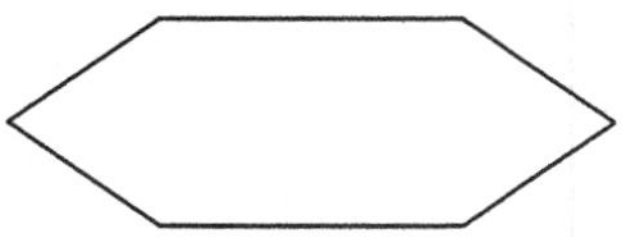

This block is used for iteration or looping statement

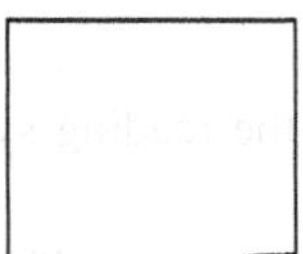

This block is used for writing of output statements.

5.7 EXAMPLES OF FLOW CHARTS

Following are the flow charts prepared by using the above symbols for given examples.

5.7.1 Flow chart to find root of an equation

$ax^2 + bx + c = 0.$

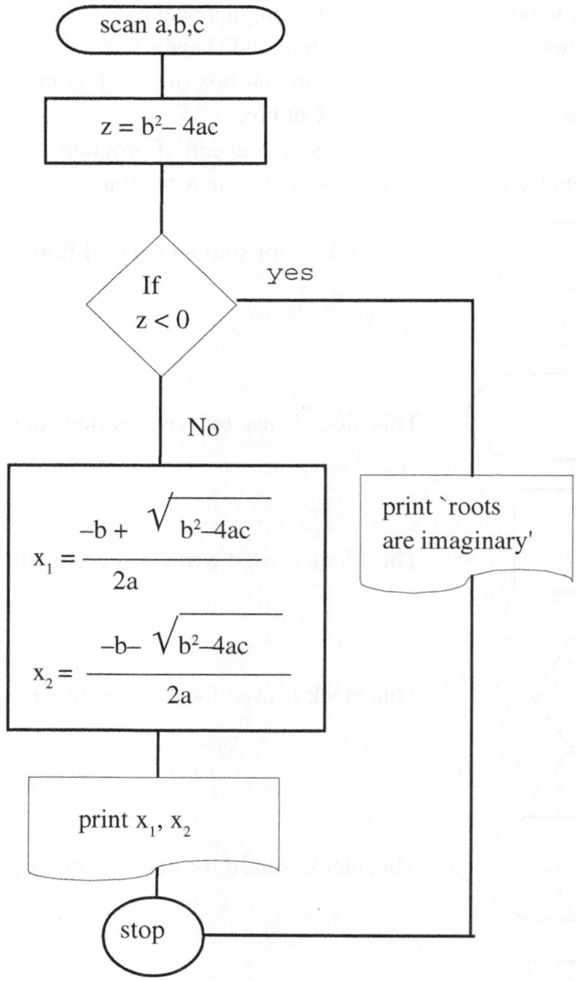

In this flowchart, a, b & c are scanned which is indicated by the reading symbol. Then arithmetic statement is used to find value z, indicated by box symbol.

The decision making box is used, to check whether it is less than 0 or not. If it is less than zero, then printing is made as roots are imaginarry. But if z is greater than zero, then x1 and x2 are calculated using arithmetic statement and are printed by the program.

5.7.2 Flow chart to calculate sum of series

$$S = \sum_{r=1}^{n} x^r$$

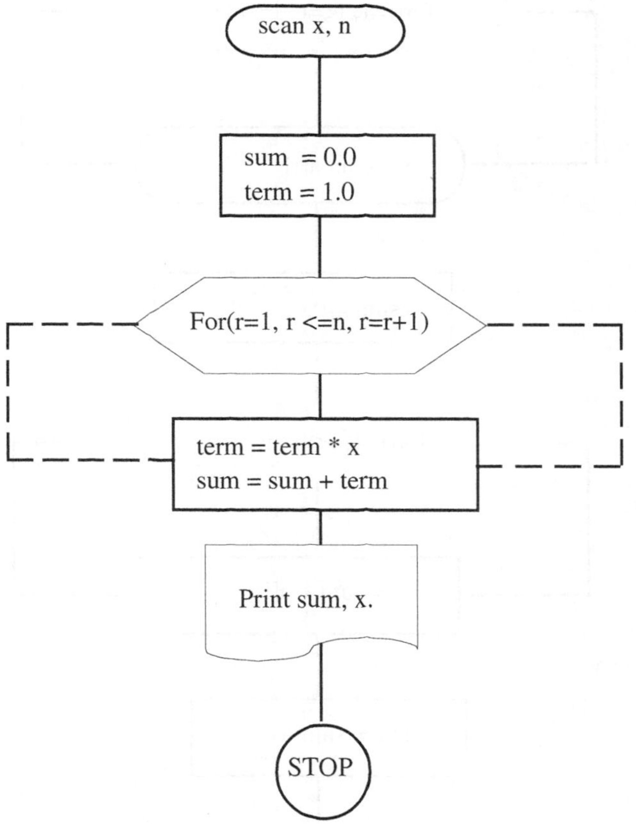

In this flow chart, sum of series is made by supplying input values as x and n. The `sum' and `term' are initialized. Then by using `for' statement `r' index varies from 1 to n in steps of 1, the `term' is multiplied and added to `sum' shown by the rectangular box. The cycles are continued, which is shown bydotted line. The printing of sum and x is shown by the `printing box'.

5.7.3 Flow chart to calculated average of `n' given numbers

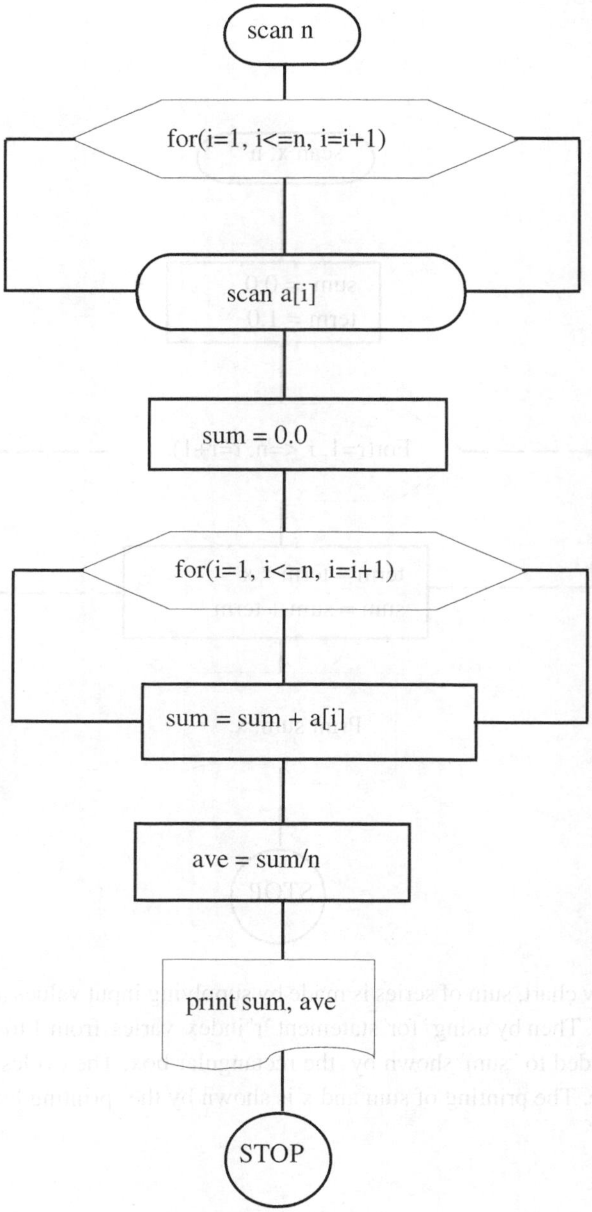

5.7.4 Flow chart to calculate sum of diagonal elements of matrix

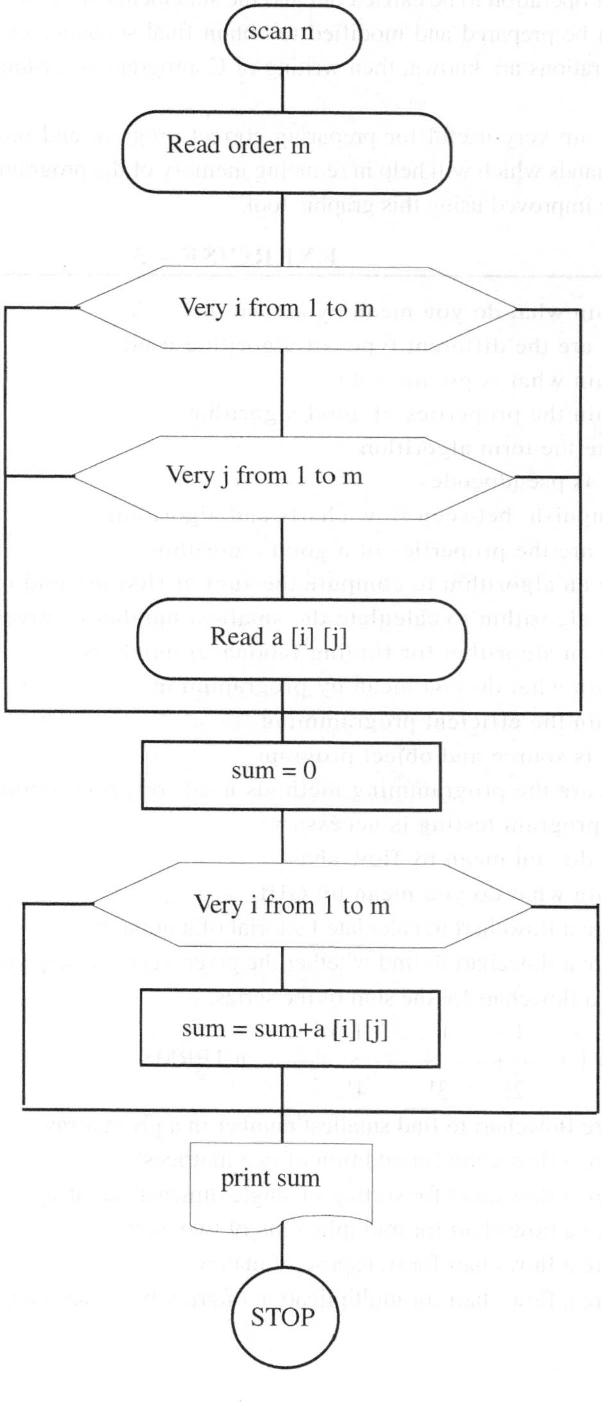

5.8 USE OF FLOW CHARTS

Flow charts are prepared before writing any program. These charts indicate the flow of program and sequence of operation to be carried out and the statements or variables used in the program. The flow charts can be prepared and modified to obtain final sequence of operations to be perfomed. Once these operations are known, then writing of C–program according to flowchart is very easily possible.

The charts are very useful for preparing correct program and proper way of writing the C–language commands which will help in reducing memory of the program. The speed and accuracy of program can be improved using this graphic tool.

EXERCISE – 5

1. Explain what do you mean by algorithm
2. What are the different types of algorithm used
3. Explain what is pseudocode
4. Explain the properties of good algorithm
5. Define the term algorithm
6. What is pseudocode
7. Distinguish between flow charts and algorithm
8. What are the properties of a good algorithm
9. Write an algorithm to compute the sum of first ten odd numbers
10. Write algorithm to calculate the smallest number of given number
11. Write an algorithm for finding fabonacci numbers
12. Explain what do you mean by programming
13. Explain the efficient programming
14. What is source and object program
15. What are the programming methods used for programming
16. Why program testing is necessary
17. What do you mean by flow chart
18. Explain what do you mean by GUI
19. Prepare a flowchart to calculate factorial of a number.
20. Prepare a flowchart to find whether the given year is a leap year or not.
21. Draw a flowchart for the sum of the series.

$$S = 1 + \frac{1}{2!} + \frac{1}{3!} + \frac{1}{4!} + \text{———} \text{ n TERMS}$$

21. Prepare flowchart to find smallest number in a given array.
22. Prepare a flow chart for addition of two matrices.
23. Prepare a flow chart for sorting of single dimensional array.
24. prepare a flow chart for multiplication of two matrices.
25. Prepare a flow chart for transpose of matrix.
26. Prepare a flow chart for multiplication of array by scaler using function program.

6
C-FUNDAMENTALS

AN OVERVIEW

In the previous chapter we have studied the networking of computers and networking through the telephonic link all over the world is internetworking. The internet has allowed to connect the persons all over the world and the web sites have been able provide them large amounts of data. The field of E-commerce made it possible to perform the online operations. The C-language plays important role in the e-commerce operations.In this chapter, we will study the basics C-language.

OBJECTIVES

After completing this unit you will be able to :

* Explain the constants
* Define variables
* Discuss types of variables
* Describe arithmetic operators
* Develop arithmetic expressions
* Write arithmetic statement

6.1 INTRODUCTION

In C–language, the English characters are used to write any type of program. It consist of:

6.1.1 Alphabets

It uses small case alphabets of English language.

a,b,c ....z.

These are used to write an executable statement of the program. The non–executable statement may also be written in upper case English alphabets.

6.1.2 Numbers

It uses basic numbers from mathematics

0,1,2,3....................9

Any number can be generated by using these basic numbers.

6.1.3 Characters

It uses different types of characters such as :

–	minus	=	equal to
+	plus	!	exclamation
/	slash	&	and
*	star	,	comma
%	percent	;	semicolon
[,{,],}	brackets	#	not equal to
:	colon	_	underscore
.	dot	"	inverted comma

6.2 CONSTANT

It is a single or multiple digit number formed by using basic numbers whose value is constant throughout the program.

Ex. 128, 58.0, 20, 0, -- 22.5

The negative number is assigned with a –ve sign.

There are three types of constants used in C–Language, They are :

6.2.1 Float Constant

It is a string of numbers containing decimal values.

Ex : 20.4, 58.6.

6.2.2 Integer Constant

This constant is a string of numbers without any decimal values.

Ex : 20,58.

6.2.3 Exponent Constant

The floating point constant can be written in the exponent form if the value is too large or small.

Ex : 1.7e4 means 1.7×10^4

where, e indicates the exponent 10.

6.2.4 Character Constant

It is a constant whose value is a character which may be alphabet, number or special character.

Ex : "SA"

6.3 VARIABLES

A value which varies continuously during the execution of program is a variable of the program. A variable can be written by a variable name formed by string of alphabets, underscore and digits. But the variable name must start with alphabet or underscore, it should not start with digit. The digit can be inserted in the variable name any where.

Ex : Sum, piece_flat,i, j5xl,number_of_moves, _sysflag are valid variable names.

Invalid variable name

sum$value	–	This is not valid variable name due to $.
piece flag	–	This is not valid due to blank space.
5spencer	–	Check because it starts with a digit.

There are different types of variables used in the program :

6.3.1 Integer variable

It is a variable whose value during the execution of the program remains as an integer value. This variable name can be declared at the starting of the program by the word "int".

Ex : int a,b,c;

The a,b,c are the integer variable names, which are declared as integer variables by a word "int". These variables accept the value between – 32000 to + 32000.

6.3.2 float variable

It is a variable name whose value remains real or decimal during the execution of the program. This variable name can be declared at the starting of the program by a word "float" These variables have upto 6 decimal accuracy.

Ex : float extra, cost;

The 'extra' and 'cost' are the floating variable names. These are declared as real value variable by the word "float". These variables have upto 6 decimal accuracy.

6.3.3 double variables

This is similar to float variables. It is used when the accuracy provided by a float variable is not sufficient and more accuracy is expected. These are declared by the word "double".

Ex : double second, time;

These variables have upto 12 decimal accuracy.

6.3.4 char variables

These variables contain a string of alphabets or characters or numbers as characters. These can be declared by using the word "char".

Ex : char call, make;

The call and make are character variables. These variables accept one character.

6.3.5 long variables

If the word "long" is placed before any declaration of variable, then the declared variable will be of extended accuracy on many computer systems for double and integer variables.

If 'long ' is used for the 'int' variable then the variable accepts the value upto -1×10^{21} to $+ 1\times 10^{21}$.

Ex : long int factorial;

If 'long ' is used for the 'double ' variable, then the variable accepts the value upto 24 decimal accuracy.

Ex. : long double fact;

6.3.6 short variables

If the word "short" is placed before any declaration, then the declared variable will be used to store fairly small accurate values.

Ex : short int factorial;

6.3.7 unsigned variables

If the word "unsigned" is placed before any declaration, then the declared variable will be used to store positive numbers.

Ex : unsigned int counter;

All the variables which are likely to be used in the program must be declared before the starting of the "C" program.

6.4 DATA TYPES AND RANGES

The following are the ranges of the various data types for the variables defined earlier.

Data Type	Range or precision
Char	Characters
Unsigned char	0–225 characters
Signed	–128 to 127
int	–32768 to 32767
Unsigned int	0 to 65535
Signed int	same as int
Unsigned short int	0 to 255
Signed short int	same as short int
Long int	–2147483648 to 2147483649
Unsigned long int	0 to 4294967296
Singed long int	same as long int
float	apr. 6 digits of precision
double	12 digits of precision
long double	24 digits of precision

6.5 ARITHMETIC OPERATORS

When the arithmetic operations are to be carried out in C-language, then the following mathematical operators are used.These operators allows mathematical operations to be performed on the numbers.

language symbol	operation
+	addition
–	subtraction
*	multiplication
/	division

Two types of special operators are used to perform the specific operation.

(i) Unary minus operator

If the value of any variable is –ve, then it is assigned with a negative sign by the use of Unary minus operator. A unary operator is the one that operates on single value as opposed to a binary operator which operates on two values.

Ex : –a; where –ve is a unary minus operator.

(ii) Modulus operator

The modulus operator is indicated by % sign. This operator provides us a remainder of any value between division of the two integer variables. It is used for integer variable expressions only.

Ex : a%b

This means that a is divided by b and remainder is the result.

In "C" programming, no operator is used for raising a number to a power. C-compiler provides a function in the program library for performing exponentiation or integer power which can be obtained by multiplying with original value.

6.6 ARITHMETIC EXPRESSIONS

If the variables and constants are joined by a mathematical operators to carry out calculations of algebraic equation, then it is an arithmetic expression.

Ex :

(i) a + b — where a and b are variables and + is an operation carrying addition of values a and b.

(ii) a – b — it is subtraction between a and b.

(iii) a * b — it is multiplication between values a and b.

(iv) a /b — it is division between values a and b.

(v) a % b — it is calculation remainder between a when divided by b.

(vi) (a+b)*c — In this operation brackets are used to indicate the operation to be performed first and next.
Here because of brackets "a" is added to "b" and then it is multiplied by "c".

(vii) (a+b)/(c+d) — In this case (a+b) and (c+d) are executed, then the division between the two occurs.

6.6.1 Hierarchy of operation of the expression

The modulus operator has equal precedence to the multiplication and division operators. These three operations are performed first and then subtraction and addition are performed. The operations are performed from left to right. The brackets receive first preference for calculations.

6.7 ARITHMETIC STATEMENT

In this statement, right hand side can contain arithmetic expression, constant or variable or function call and left hand side contains a variable name only. The numerical or character value on right hand side which is calculated and assigned to the variable name on the left hand side.

Ex : a = b + c/d

where (b+c/d) is executed and a variable will be assigned with the value of expression.

6.7.1 Rules for writing arithmetic statement

(1) If the floating point value is assigned to an integer variable, then the decimal portion of the number gets truncated.

(2) For writing the expressions the circular brackets are used and brackets can be placed any number of times, but opening brackets must be equal to closing brackets.

(3) The arithmetic expression on the right hand side of the statement must be all variables or constants of either integer or floating\double type, but mixed mode variables are not permitted.

(4) If the nature of variable is changed in the expression from integer to float\double or vice versa, then the variable can be modified by using a declaration of int or float\double in bracket near to the variable.

(5) No subscript or superscripts are permitted.

6.7.2 Examples of arithmetic statement

The following are the examples of arithmetic statement :

(i) $$\frac{2\pi a^2}{(a^2+x^2)^2} = y$$

This algebric equation is written as arithmetic statement.

y = 2.0*pi*i*a*a/((a*a+x*x)*(a*a+x*x))

(ii) $2.6 \times 10^{-5}\,(1.0+ 0.7854/V_o)\ LD^2\ R = I_o$

io=2.6e–5*(1.0+0.7854/vo)*l*d*d*r

(iii) $(x/y)^5 + C^3 + X^2 = z$

z=((x/y)*(x/y)*(x/y)*(x/y)*(x/y)+c*c*c+x*x

(iv) Remainder of $(x+y+z)/(q^2+ c^2) = a$

a=(x+y+z)%(q*q+c*c)

(v) $-a^2 + by + cz = d$

d=(–a)*a+b*y+c*z

(vi) $b_o = -x^2/y^3 + z^2 + .01x$

bo =(((–x)*x)/(y*y*y))+z*z+0.01*x

(vii) $i_c = 2.2\ v + 4.4\alpha^2 + \beta^2$

ic=2.2*nu+4.4*alp*alp+bet*bet

(viii) $tc = 1000.672/(-1.6\ b^2+Y^2/Z^3)$

tc=1000.672/((–1.6)*b*b+y*y/(z*z*z)

(ix) $ax^3+ bx^2+ cx + d = k$

k= a*x*x+b*x*x+c*x+d

6.8 METHODS OF WRITING "C" PROGRAM

Every column of screen accepts one character on one line. Each character of the statement should be written on one line in the program. At the end of every statement semicolon ";" must be provided, which indicates that the statement is complete. If the space for statement is not sufficient, it can be written on the next line. The statement instruction should be written in continuation of the sequence of the statement. If the program is a main program, then it is to be written by the first statement as "main()".

```
main ( )      ────────►  main program
{             ────────►  start of program
  ───;  ┐
  ───;  ├     ────────►  program statement
  ───;  ┘
}             ────────►  end of program
```

The opening "{" brace is used to start the program on one line and written below 'main()' statement. The statements are inserted after opening brace and at the end of program, it is closed by "}" closing brace on one single line.

6.9 COMMENT STATEMENT

The comment statement is enclosed in the two slashes "/" with "*" on both sides of the statements. This statement is useful for the reading of the program by the operator.

It can be used for giving a title to the program. The comment statement can be inserted anywhere in the program. It is non–executable statement of the program. It can be used for supplying information or describing variables or their nature in the program.

EX : /* India is my country */

/* I like my country */

EXERCISE

1. Explain the difference between float and double variable.
2. Explain whether following variable names are valid / invalid.

   (i) x > y_8 (ii) sum + g_6 (iii) 5_next_

   (iv) n_3_5 (v) x_y_4 (vi) _3_a_b
3. Write the arithmetic statements for the following

   (i) $\frac{x^2 + y^2}{a^2 + b} = Z$ (ii) $\frac{a \,.\, b}{c + z} = p$ (iii) $\frac{(a+b)^2}{(c + d)} + F^2 = q$

   (iv) $(x^2 + y^2 + z^2)^3 = n$ (v) $\frac{d}{k + z} + 5\,j^2 = m.$
4. Explain the comment statement of C.
5. Explain how a statement of C–language is closed.
6. Correct the following statements in C–language.

   (i) float c,d

   (ii) int a, b float c;

(iii) float char a, b, c;

(iv) long a, b, c;

(v) /* This is a C–Program

(vi) a + b = c + d;

(vii) c = (((a + b) * c) / d;

(viii) c = [(x + a) / (c + d)];

(ix)
```
main ( );
{
        int a,b,c;
        a=2,b=3;
        c=a+b;
        printf("c=%d\n",c);
}
```

7. Explain the results of the following statements in C–program.

(a)
```
int a, b, c;
a = 15;
b = 4;
```
If (i) c = a%b; (ii) c = a/b; (iii) c = (b*3)/a;

(b)
```
float a, b; int c; float x; double y;
a = 22.0;
b = 7.0;
c = a/b;
x = a/b;
y = a/b;
```

(c)
```
float x, y, z; int a, b, c;
x = 6.784;
y = 3.269;
z = x * y;
a = z/3.0;
b = a * z/3;
c = a + b;
x = c;
y = b;
z = x * y;
```

8. Explain whether the following are valid variable names and if not, why ?

(i) w.h.o.

(ii) x++

(iii) a$b

(iv) 1 alp

(v) al1p

(vi) y*x

(vii) raman

(viii) in-charge

(ix) Vishwas

(x) –beg.

9. Write arithmetic statements for the following :

(i) $t = (\alpha + \beta^3 + \alpha\beta)^2 / (\alpha + \beta - 1)$.

(ii) $\beta = \frac{L}{\pi ab}\left[1 - \frac{u^2}{\alpha^2} - \frac{V^2}{\beta^2}\right]$

(iii) $L = 4C^2 - (D-d)^2 + \pi\left[\frac{D+d}{2}\right]$

(iv) $x = \frac{a + b + \pi}{2x + 5y}$

(v) $6 = \frac{6_x + 6_y}{2}$

(vi) $q = \frac{\sigma A_1 (T_1^4 - T_2^4)}{\frac{1}{\varepsilon_1} + \frac{A_1}{A_2}\left[\frac{1}{\varepsilon_2} - 1\right]}$

(vii) $\frac{1}{U} = \frac{1}{h_1} + F_1 + \frac{b}{k} + F_2 + \frac{1}{h_2}$

10. Explain the following :
    (i) Hierarchy of arithmetic operation
    (ii) Use of braces `{ }' in C–language.
    (iii) 'main()' name of program.
    (iv) Executable and non executable statement
    (v) Purpose comment statement
    (vi) Integer division

11. Explain the output of following arithmetic statements
    (i) 1 = 4.3;
    d = 3.6
    x = 1 * 1 * 1 + d * d / 2.0;
    y = 1 * 1 * (l + d) * d/2.0;
    z = 1 * 1 * ((l + d) * d)/2.0;
    (ii) a = 6.4;
    b = 5.6;
    a = a * a + b * b;
    c = (a * b)/3.0;
    b = c;
    d = a * b + c * a
    (iii) a = 7.9
    b = 5.2
    c = a/b * a
    d = (a/b) * a
    e = a/(b*a) * d

12 . Explain whether the following statements are correct, if wrong indicate the errors.
    (i) int a b c;
    (ii) int a, float b;

(iii) x + a = y + b;
(iv) Z = ((x+y) / (c+d) * e;
(v) y = x ** 2 * 3;
(vi) p = 9 $ 5
(vii) /* This is a base program /

13. Find the incorrect floating point constants and give reasons.
    (i) 40.123.67
    (ii) 345.65
    (iii) 34E2
    (iv) 34
    (v) 345
14. Write which of these constant are integer, float and exponent.
    10,–15, 6.25, –10.26, 5.0e5, 22.6982, 1.2e–5
15. Explain which of these variables are valid variables
    aa, _ia5, ia_5, number very, 5abs, aa5$, %aaxx, _&xy
16. Explain the capacities and types of these variables.
    int a, bx, cz;
    float aa, by, xz;
    double xx, yy, zz;
    char x,y, z;
    long int a, bb,cc;
    long double aa, cc,dd;
17. Explain various types of arithmetic operator.
18. Can modulus operates on the float value ?

7

INPUT AND OUTPUT STATEMENT

AN OVERVIEW

In the previous chapter we have seen that constant and variable are the two main element responsible for creating arithmetic statement.The variables are of different types which must be declared in the begining of the program.The arithmetic statement consists of variable on LHS and arithmetic expression on RHS.

In this unit we will study the statements which are used for reading of data and writing of results. The input statement is optional whereas the output statement is compulsory. Every program must have output statement which will print the result of the program. The input statement generalizes the program and the results to be calculated for the given input.The input and output statements are used in the computer program for supplying the data and printing the results.

OBJECTIVES

After completing this unit you will be able to :

* Explain statement used for reading of data
* Compose statement used for writing of result
* Understand the formats
* Explain the character operation
* Define interation statement
* Consider post-script and pre-script increments

7.1 INPUT STATEMENT

This statement is used for the supplying of data to the program .This statement is optional and can be used whenever the program is to be made as a general computer program.

The input statement of the "C" program is indicated by a "scanf" statement.

The general form of the statement is scanf ("%xa" ,&y)

where

a is a format conversion character.

y is a variable to be read by the computer.

x is the format conversion modifier.

In this statement, the value of 'y' variable is read through 'xa' format from the data screen.

7.1.1 Format conversion character (a)

The following format conversion characters are used in the program.

Character	*Use*
d	This is used for reading of integer variable values.
f	The value to be read is expressed in floating values of variables or Double values.
e	This format character is identical to the f format but used for exponent values.
c	This format is used for reading of character, numbers, alphabets, special characters etc.
s	Sequence of character or string.

7.1.2 Format conversion modifiers (x)

Character	Description
*	This specifies that the value is to be skipped and not assigned to a variable.
field width number(n)	This indicates the maximum number of positions the field occupied is n.
h	This is used before d format specifying that the corresponding argument is a pointer to the short.
l	This is used for integer values indicating that the pointer is long. When used for float indicates that the pointer is double.

The format along with the modifier if required is used for every variable present in the 'scanf' statement. The variables use formats in their sequence.

Ex:

The following examples show the data input for the given variables.

(1) scanf ("%d%d%d ",&hour,&minutes,&seconds);
data : 10 20 30

(2) scanf("%5d%5d%5d",&a,&b,&c);
data : 10 20 30

(3) scanf("%d%f %e",&a,&b,&c);
data: 10 2.654 2.1e–5

Some Examples:

In the following example you will see the method of reading the data by scanf statement.

1. **scanf("%d%d%d",&a,&b,&c);**

In this scanf statement a,b,c are integer variables whose value is to be read by using %d format which is to be used for integer variables.The number of format should match with number of variables. The data values are supplied from the data screen using the following pattern

10 20 30

The data values are supplied as a = 10, b = 20, c = 30 which are separated by a blank space.

2. **scanf ("%d %f %e",&a,&b,&c);**

In this case we see that a is integer variable , b is float variable, c is float variable but the format used for b is f and for c is e. It means that value of a will be read by d format , value of b will be read by f format and value of c is read by e format.

10 2.36 2.0e5

This indicates that value of a = 10, value of b = 2.36 and value of c $= 2.0 \times 10^5$

3. **scanf ("%5d%5d%5d", &a,&b,&c);**

In this case a ,b,c are integer variables and the format used is d with modifier 5 which means that 5 spaces are to be reserved for reading of values of a,b,c.

```
   10    20   30
| a |  b | c |
```

Here we see that the variables a , b,c are provided with five spaces and the values of variables are to be supplied in these five spaces. The values of variables are written at the end of the field . It becomes necessary in these cases that the values must be supplied in the given field.

4. **scanf ("%-5d%-5d%-5d", &a,&b,&c);**

In this case a ,b,c are integer variables and the format used is d with modifier 5 which means that 5 spaces are to be reserved for reading of values of a,b,c.

```
10    20    30
| a |  b | c |
```

The modifier used in these cases is a negative modifier which means that the values of variables are to be supplied at the begining of the field . In the earlier case the modifier was positive but negative modifiers changes the printing from the start of field.

7.2 OUTPUT STATEMENT

This statement is used for printing of variables and arithmetic expressions etc.It can be used for printing of some comments along with the results.The general form of the statement is

printf("%xauv ",y);

where, x – format conversion modifier.

a – format conversion character.

u – comment

y – variable or arithmetic expression

v – white space character

In this statement,the value of 'y' variable is printed through 'xa' format along with the comment 'u' and by executing white space character 'v'. The comment and white space character can be written anywhere in double inverted comma, " ".

The following format conversion modifier and characters are used in output statement.

7.2.1 Format conversion modifier

The format conversion modifiers are used for modification of the results to be printed in the program. These are optional and can be used if required. The format may contain modifier if essential.

Character	Description
–	This is used when the printing is to be done from the start of the field
blank space	indicates that non–negative numbers are to be preceded by a blank space.
n–field width number	This indicates the minimum number(n) of positions that are to be used to display the values.
l	To indicate that the value to be displayed is a long integer.
. m	It indicates number of decimal values to which number precision printing should be done. Where m is integer number t\o indicate decimal precision.

7.2.2 Format conversion characters

These are the format conversion characters used for printing of results.The values of variable and arithmetic expression could be printed by using this character.

Character	Use/purpose
d	The value is displayed as an integer variable or expression.
u	The value of variable is displayed as an unsigned decimal number.
f	The value is displayed in floating point form either(float or double).
e	The value is displayed in exponential form.
g	This use is for float or double value in e or f format whichever takes less space.
c	The value is displayed as a single character.
s	The value is displayed as a character string and used for char array.

7.2.3 White space characters

The white space characters are used alongwith printing of variables to shift control to the desired place. These are as below :

(i) blank space : This leaves a blank space at the time of printing.

(ii) \t – tab : This leaves five blank spaces at the time of printing.

(iii) \n – new line character : This shifts the control to a new line.

(iv) \f – form feed character : This shifts the control to a new page.

7.2.4 Examples on 'printf' statement

In the following examples the results printed or likely to be displayed by different formats are as shown:

1. printf ("Programming in \tC is very intersting \n\n");
   Output : Programming in C is very nice.
   This statement prints a comment on the result screen.

2. If a = 10 ,b = 20 , c = 30 ,then the result will be printed by following :
   printf(" %d %d %d",a,b,c);
   Output : 10 20 30

3. printf("% 5d %5d %5d",a,b,c);
   Output: 10 20 30

4. printf("% –5d% –5d% –5d",a,b,c);
   Output: 10 20 30

5. printf("a = %d, b = %d, c = %d\n",a,b,c);
   Output : a = 10,b = 20, c = 30

6. printf("d = %d\n", b + c);
   Output : d = 50

7. If the value of f = 12.978 it will be displayed as :
   printf (" %f %e %g\n", f,f,f):
   Output : 12.978000 1.297800e1 12.978

8. printf (" % 0.2f %0.2e\n", f,f);
   Output : 12.98 1.30e1

9. printf ("% 0.0f % .0e\n", f,f);
   Output : 13 1.0e1

10. printf (" %07.2f %07.2e\n",f,f);
    Output : 0012.98 1.30e1

7.3 CHARACTER OPERATION

Any character of keyboard can be a character value of C-language. The char variable is capable of accepting one character of C–language.The character variable can be supplied with a character value by the following statement :

7.3.1 By assignment

x = 'A';

The character variable x is supplied with value of the character by providing inverted comma of right side (' ') on both sides of character.

7.3.2 Using 'scanf' statement

The characters can be supplied to a char variable on the user screen through 'c' format in the 'scanf' statement.

Ex:

```
scanf("%c%c",&a,&b);
```

Input : XY

In this case, X & Y are the values and a and b are char variables supplied from the user screen.

The following programs in C–language use declaration of variable, arithmetic statement and Input/Output statement of C–language.

Program 7–1

Program on printing of a comment.

```
/*PRINTING OF A COMMENT*/
main()
{
    printf("Programming in C is highly exciting \n");
}
```

Output : Programming in C is highly exciting.

This program prints a comment written in " " in printf statement as output.

Program 7–2

Program on arithmetic calculation.

```
/*Program on addition of two variables*/
main()
{
    int a,b,c;
    a=2;
    b=3;
    c=a+b;
    printf("c=%d+%d=%d\n",a,b,c);
}
```

Output : c=2+3 = 5

This program adds value a to b and c value is printed.

Program 7–3

Program on scanning and printing of variable.

```
/*Program on scanning and printing of variable */
main()
{
    float a,b,c,d;
    printf("enter the value of a & b\n");
    scanf("%f%f",&a,&b);
    c=a;
    d=b;
    printf("c=%g  d=%g\n",c,d);
}
```

Input	:	enter the value of a & b 10 20
Output	:	c = 10 d = 20

In this program 'a & b' are supplied through data screen and these are substituted in 'c & d', then 'c & d' are printed.

Program 7–4

Program to calculate volume of a box.

```
/*CALCULATION OF VOLUME OF A BOX*/
main()
{
    float l,b,h,v;
    printf("enter the value of length,breadth & height\n");
    scanf("%f%f%f",&l,&b,&h);
    v=l*b*h;
    printf("volume of the box is %g\n",v);
}
```

Input	:	enter the value of length, breadth & height 10 20 30
Output	:	volume of the box is 6000.

In this program length , breadth and height of box are scanned and volume is calculated and printed.

Program 7–5

```
/* program on char variable */
main()
{
    char c;
    c='A';
    printf(" ascii value c=%d, c=%c\n",c,c);
}
```

Output	:	ascii value c=65, c=A

In this program the char variable is declared and a character value is supplied to the variable using arithmetic statement . Then using printf statement the character value is printed which gives ascii value of the character using %d format and the character using %c format.

Program 7–6

```
/* program on scanning and printing of the char variable */
main()
{
    char a,b;
    printf("enter two characters \n");
    scanf("%c%c",&a,&b);
    printf("a=%c,b=%c\n",a,b);
}
```

In this program, the two characters are scanned from the user screen and printed by using '%c' format.

Input	:	enter two characters
		sg
Output	:	a = s,b = g

7.4 POSTSCRIPT AND PRESCRIPT INCREMENTS STATEMENT

(i) If the value of 'i' has to be incremented by 1, then we write an arithmetic statement as :

i = i+1;

This can be written by an equivalent statement

++i;

or

i++;

The difference between the above two statements is that the first is pre-script increment and second is post-cript increment.The pre-script increment is increment before the operation is performed whereas the postscript increment is a increment after the operation is performed.

(ii) If the value is to be reduced by 1, then we write an arithmetic statement as

i = i–1;

This can be written by an equivalent statement

– –i;

or

i– –;

This case is similar to the previous case where pre-script or post-script decrement is given.This can be seen in the following program :

The difference in the two statement is in case of pre-script the value is incremented in the operation and then the calculations are done whereas in the post-script increment the operation is performed and increment is done afterwards.

This concept will be more clear to you in the following arithmetic statement.

c = (a + 1) – b;

This statement is just similar to the next statement means (a + 1) is replaced by ++a.

c = (++a) – b;

In this case a is incremented by 1 and b is subtracted from a.

c = (a++) – b;

In this case b is subtracted from a and then a is incremented.

Example:

If value of a = 20 and value of b = 10, then the results would be given as

c = (++a) – b;

c = 21 – 10 = 11

a = 21

b = 10

If the statement is

c = (a++) – b;

In this case b is subtracted from a and then a is incremented.

c = 20 – 10 = 10

a = 21

b = 10

The value of a is 21 in both the cases whereas the value of c is 11 in the first case and it is 10 in the second.

Program 7–7

```
/*program on post-script and pre-script increment*/
main()
{
    int a,b,c,d;
    a=4,b=3;
    c=(++a)*b;
    printf("a=%d,b=%d,c=%d\n",a,b,c);
    a=4;
    d=(a++)*b;
    printf("a=%d,b=%d,c=%d\n",a,b,c);
}
```

Output	:	a = 5,b = 3,c = 15 a = 5,b = 3,c = 15

In this program , the value of c and d is calculated by using pre-script and post-script increment operator,whereas both values are found to be different because of the difference that, in the first case 'a' is incremented before multiplication with 'b' whereas in the second case 'a' is incremented after multiplication with 'b'.

Program 7–8

```
/*program on post–script and pre–script decrement*/
main()
{
    int a,b,c,d;
    a=4,b=3;
    c=(--a)-b;
    printf("a=%d,b=%d,c=%d\n",a,b,c);
    a=4;
    d=(a--)-b;
    printf("a=%d,b=%d,c=%d\n",a,b,c);
}
```

Output	:	a = 3, b = 3, c = 0 a = 3,b = 3, c = 0

In this program , the value of c and d is calculated by using pre-script and post- script decrement operator,whereas both values are found to be different because of the difference that in the first case 'a' is decremented before subtraction with 'b' whereas in the second case 'a' is decremented after subtraction with 'b'.

EXERCISE

1. Explain whether the following statements are correct or not.
   (i) scanf("%d%d ", a,b);
   (ii) scanf("%d%d", &a, &b, &c);
   (iii) scanf("%d%d\n", &a, &b);
   (iv) scanf("a = %d, b = %d", &a, &b);
   (v) printf("%d%f%d", a,b);
   (vi) printf("a = %d b = %f\n", a,b,c);
   (vii) printf("a=%d%b = %d\n", a,b);
   (viii) printf("a=%3.5f,b=%0.5e", a,b);
   (ix) printf("%fg, %5c\n", a,b);
   (x) printf("%0.02f, %0.–1e\n", a,b);

2. Explain how the values will be supplied in the following cases.
   a = 2.2 b = 3.2 x = +
   (i) scanf("%f%f", &a, &b);
   (ii) scanf("%7f%5f", &a, &b);
   (iii) scanf("% -7f%-7f", &a, &b);
   (iv) scanf("%f%e", &a, &b);
   (v) scanf("%f%c%f", &a, &x, &b);
   (vi) scanf("%f %c %f", &a, &x, &b);

3. Explain the output of the following values.
   x = 4.396 y = 50.727 z = 97.56
   (i) printf("%f%f%f", x,y,z);
   (ii) printf("%e%e%e", x,y,z);
   (iii) printf("%f%e%g", x,y,z);
   (iv) printf("%5f%g%5e", x,y,z);
   (v) printf("%10f%g%5e", x,y,z);
   (vi) printf("%10.2f%g%10.2e", x,y,z);
   (vii) printf("%0.2f%g%0.2e", x,y,z);
   (viii) printf("%0.5f%g%0.5c", x,y,z);

4. Explain the result of following execution.
   (i)
   ```
   x = 5.69;
   z = x;
   y = x * x / 2.0;
   y = y/2.3;
   z = (x * y)/z
   printf("%5.2f, %5.1f, %5.3f", x,y,z);
   ```
   (ii)
   ```
   p = 10.269999;
   q = 22.0/7.0;
   r = p * q /(p * q/10)
   printf("%5.8f, %5.9f, %g", p,q,r);
   ```

5. Explain how the data is supplied in case of following scanf statements.
   (i) scanf("%d%d%d",&a,&b,&c);
   (ii) scanf("%5d%5d%5d",&a,&b,&c);
   (iii) scanf("%10d%10d%10d",&a,&b,&c);

(iv) scanf("%d%f%e",&a,&b,&c);

(v) scanf("%5d%10f%e",&a,&b,&c);

6. Write the output produced by using following printf statement.

 (i) If a = 10, b = 20, c = 30.

  (a) printf("%d%d%d",a,b,c);
  (b) printf("a=%d b=%d c = %d",a,b,c);
  (c) printf("%10d%10d%10d",a,b,c);
  (d) printf("%d   %d   %d",a,b,c);
  (e) printf("%d,%d,%d",a,b,c);
  (f) printf("%d\t%d\t%d\t%d",a+b,a-b,a*b,c);
  (g) printf("%d\n%d\n%d\n%d",a+b,a-b,a*b,c);
  (h) printf("\fthe programming is essential \tfor software engineer\n");
  (i) printf("%-10d\t%-10d\t%-10d\t",a,b,c);

 (ii) If f= 48.6785 then what is the print ?

  (a) printf("%f%g%e",f,f,f);
  (b) printf("%10f%5g%10e",f,f,f);
  (c) printf("%-10f%-5g%-10e",f,f,f);
  (d) printf("%10.2f%5.4g%10.2e",f,f,f);
  (e) printf("%5.2f%5.2g%5.2e",f,f,f);
  (f) printf("%0.2f%0.2g%0.2e",f,f,f);
  (g) printf("%0.1f%5.2g%0.2e",f,f,f);
  (h) printf("%-5.2f%-5.2g%-5.2e",f,f,f);

7. Write a program to evaluate the expression.

 (i) A+B (ii) A–B (iii) A´B (iv) A/B (v) Remainder of A/B
 use integer, float or double, exponent formats and variables for printing with different types of modifiers.

8. Write a program to calculate total amount, total interest on a fixed deposit of amount (P) kept in bank for (N) year at the rate of (R) simple interest (I) P.A.

9. Write a program to calculate power (P) developed by a machine rotating at the speed of (N) RPM with force (F) at radius (R).

 $P = 2\pi\ N T / 60$ & $T = F \times R$

10. Write a program to calculate the average of five given numbers.

11. Write a program to calculate oF temperature to oC temperature and kelvin temperature.

 $C/5 = (F-32)/9$

 $K = C + 273$

12. If X,Y are the two co-ordinates of a point which lie on the circumference of a circle whose centre is origin, calculate area of such a circle.

 $Z = X^2 + Y^2$

 $A = \pi \times Z$

13. Write a program to find equation to a straight line, passing through points (X_1,Y_1), (X_2,Y_2).

 $Y = m X + C$

 $m = (Y_2-Y_1) / (X_2-X_1)$

 $C = Y_1 - m X_1$

14. Write a program to print a character "X".

15. Write a program to scan any two characters `P', `Q' and print the characters.

16. Write a program to scan and print a name which has maximum eight characters.
17. Write a program to calculate square of area of a triangle using following equation :

$$Area^2 = S(S-A)(S-B)(S-C)$$

$$S = \frac{A+B+C}{2}$$

Where A,B,C are lengths of three sides of the triangle.
18. The quantity of heat Q across the two surfaces of a solid block of thickness `b' in time `t' is given by

$$Q = \frac{K A (T_1 - T_2)t}{b}$$

A	–	Cross sectional area
T_1, T_2	–	Temperature of two surface
K	–	Thermal conductivity
b	–	Thickness of block

Write a program to calculate heat flow rate through a solid slab.
19. Write a program to calculate focal length of a lense.

$$\frac{1}{f} = (\mu-1)\left(\frac{1}{R_1} - \frac{1}{R_2}\right)$$

where,

R_1, R_2 – Radius of curvature of two sides

μ – refractivity index
20. Write a program to calculate rise of a liquid `h' in a tube of radius ` r ' which is given by

$$h = \frac{2\tau z}{\rho g}$$

Where ,

τ – Surface tension.

z – cosine of angle of contact of liquid with walls of tube.

ρ – density of liquid.

g – acceleration due to gravity.
21. When power is transmitted by belt, the ratio of tight to slack side tension (k) is given by

$$\frac{T_1}{T_2} = k$$

The belt velocity is given as

$$V = \frac{\pi DN}{60}$$

H.P. transmitted is given by

$$H.P. = \frac{(T_1 - T_2)V}{75}$$

Write a program to calculate the power required if T_1,T_2,N , D are the values supplied as input parameter.

8

CONTROL STATEMENT

AN OVERVIEW

In the previous, unit we have seen that the operation on characters can be performed and any string can be read and printed through program.The iteration statements are used in programming to save the memory required for storage of characters.

In this unit we are interested in studying the statements which allows the central processing unit to make decisions. These are the statements used for the purpose of decision making process. The central processing unit is capable of taking decisions on the basis of the supplied conditions. If the conditions and decisions are known then the CPU takes the decision correctly.

OBJECTIVES

After completing this unit you will be able to:

1. Discuss statements used for decision making
2. Develop logical expression
3. Write decision statement
4. Demonstrate decisions according to supplied conditions

8.1 INTRODUCTION

Control statements are used for taking the decisions and then transferring the control to the given statement.These statements check logical conditions and if the condition is found to be true, then the decisions are executed.

There are different types of statements used , which are known as "if" statements.

1. simple "if" statement
2. "if–else" statement
3. compound "if" statement
4. nested "if" statement
5. "else–if construct" statement

8.2 Simple "if" Statement

This statement is used when the given condition is true, then the decision is executed. The general form of this statement is :

```
if(x1)
        y1;
```

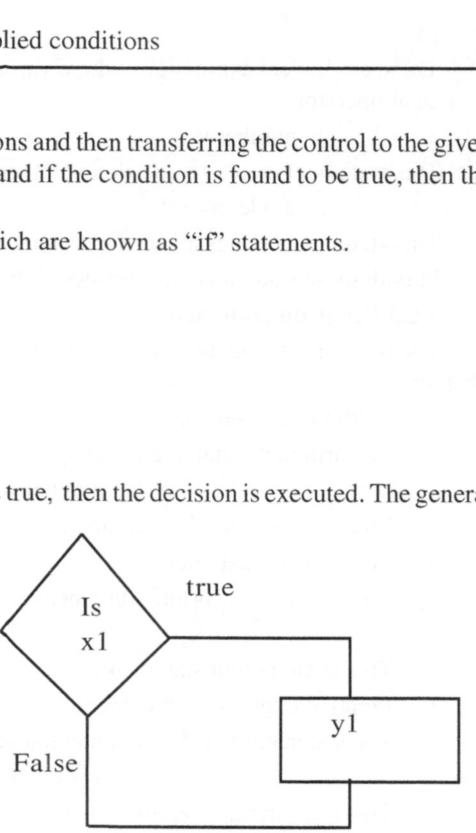

where, x1 – relational expression which creates a condition.

y1 – program statement.

This statement is executed as if 'x1' condition is true, then 'y1' decision is executed.

The x condition is created by a relational expression which is a question being asked to the compiler which may be true or false.

The decision may be a statement or bunch of statements enclosed in braces.

The relational expression and program statements are explained as below :

8.2.1 Relational expression (x1)

If the variable is joined to a constant or variable by a logical operator, then it is a relational expression.This expression uses a logical operator which creates a question in the statement .

8.2.2 Types of relational operators

There is a variety of relational operators used in C–language. These relational operators create a condition which could be checked by the compiler.

Relational operators	*Meaning*
<	less than
<=	less than or equal to
>	greater than
>=	greater than or equal to
==	equal to
!=	not equal to

Ex :

These are logical expressions where variables "number" and " grade" are joined to constant by a logical operator.

number < 0

This statement creates a question whether the number is less than 0.

grade >= 60

This statement creates a question whether the grade is greater than or equal to 60.

In both these statements,it is observed that the result will be either true or false.

8.2.3 Program statement (y1)

The program statements can be of three varieties which are already explained in the previous chapters.

1. Arithmetic statement :

   The arithmetic statement can be used as program statement.

   number = y+x ;

   This is an arithmetic statement.

2. Input/output statement :

   The 'scanf' and 'printf' statement can be used as program statement.

   printf ("%d %d", x,y);

   This is an output statement.

3. Iterative expression statement:

   The statement which gives increment of 1 to a variable.

   + + count ;

   This is an iterative expression statement.

Example :

The following are the examples of simple 'if' statement.

```
1 . if(a>b )
        c=a+b;
2.  if(a>b)
        printf("c= %d \n",c);
3.  if(a>b)
        ++i;
```

In all the above statements if the result of logical expression (a>b) is true,then the program statement is executed.

8.3 "IF–ELSE" STATEMENT

This statement is used for taking two decisions in the program. If the condition is found to be true, then the first decision is executed and if the condition is found to be false, then the second decision is executed. This executes any one decision depending upon the logical condition found to be true.

The general form is

```
if (x1)
        y1 ;
else
        y2 ;
```

where, x1 – logical expression

y1,y2 – program statement.

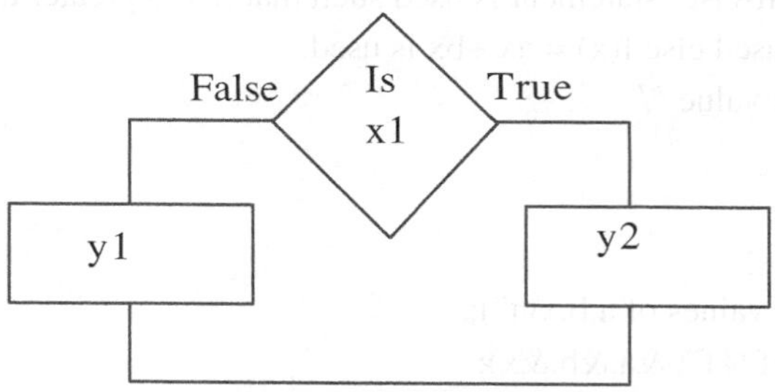

In this statement, if the result of the evaluation of logical expression 'x1' is true, then 'y1' is executed and if false, 'y2' is executed.

Ex :

```
if (y = 0)
        x = a;
else
        x = b;
```

In this case , if y is equal to 0 , then x=a and if x is not equal to 0, then x = b.

Program 8–1

This program finds absolute value of a number. The absolute value of a number is a positive value of any number means if a number is negative then it is converted to a positive number but if a number is positive then it is retained same.The following program calculates the absolute value.

```
/* program to calculate the absolute value */
main ( )
{
    float number ;
    printf ("write your number\n");
    scanf  ( "%f", &number );
    if (number < 0.0)
            number = –number;
    printf (" the absolute value is %g\n ", number);
}
```

Input	:	write your number –7
Output	:	the absolute value is 7

This program scans a number from the user screen and converts negative number to positive providing absolute value of the number.

Program 8–2

This program evaluates the function

$$f(x) = ax^2 + b \quad \text{if} \quad b >= 2$$
$$= ax + bx \quad \text{if} \quad b < 2$$

In this program ,'if-else' statement is used such that if x is greater than or equal to 2, then $f(x) = ax^2 + b$ is used else $f(x) = ax + bx$ is used.

```
/* Evaluation of y value */
main ( )
{
    float a,b,x,y;
    printf ("enter values of a,b,x\n");
    scanf(" %f %f %f", &a,&b,&x);
    if (x >= 2.0)
            y = a*x*x+b ;
    else
            y = a * x +b *x ;
    printf ( "the value of y = % g\n", y);
}
```

Input	:	enter values of a,b,x 2 3 4
Output	:	the value of y = 35

This program evaluates the value of y according to the given expression if a particular condition is satisfied.

Program 8–3

This program determines whether the given number is even or odd.The criteria used in this program is that the number is divided by 2 and remainder is calculated.If the remainder is found to be equal to 0, then the number is even otherwise it is odd.

```
/* to determine odd or even number */
main ( )
{
    int   number, rem;
    printf (" enter your number\n");
    scanf (" %d", & number );
    rem = number %2 ;
    if (rem = = 0)
    printf ("the number is even\n");
    else
    printf("the number is odd\n");
}
```

Input	:	enter your number 3
Output	:	the number is odd

8.4 COMPOUND "IF" STATEMENT

In compound "if" statement if two conditions are to be checked simultaneously and the execution of decisions depends on these two conditions,then it is used for decision making . This statement takes the decision on checking of two or more conditions simultaneously.

This statement utilizes the logical operators for joining of two conditions

Operator	Meaning
&&	and
||	OR
!	Negation

It uses three logical operators , One is '&&' operator which means both must be satisfied and another is '||' operator which means either of the two must be satisfied. The third is '!' operator which reverses logical condition.

Examples :

```
1 . if((a>b)&&(b>c))
            d=a+b;
      else
            d=a–b;
```

In this case if both the logical expressions are true, then 'd=a+b' otherwise if both are false or either of them is false then 'd=a–b'.

```
2.  if((a>b) || (b>c))
            d=a+b;
      else
            d=a–b;
```

In this case if both or any one of the logical expression is true, then 'd=a+b' otherwise if both of them are false, then 'd=a–b'.

Program 8–4

```
/* compound if–statement */
main()
{
    int age;
    clrscr();
    printf("Enter the age of the student\n");
    scanf("%d",&age);
    if(age >5 && age <15)
    {
            printf("Student can appear for contest\n");
    }
    else
    {
            printf("Student  cannot appear for  contest\n");
    }
}
```

This program uses the compound 'if' statement which compares the age of the student, whether it lies between 5 and 15 .If the age is between this range ,then it is printed as being permitted to appear for the contest otherwise it is not permitted to appear for the contest.

Input	:	Enter the age of the student 12
Output	:	Student can appear for contest

Program 8–5

```
/* PROGRAM  ON  NEGATION  OPERATOR */
main()
{
    int x,y;
    clrscr();
    printf("Enter the value of x\n");
    scanf("%d",&x);
    if(!(x>5))
            y=6;
    else
            y=5;
    printf("The value of y=%d\n",y);
}
```

Input	:	Enter the value of x 3
Output	:	The value of y = 6

In this program the negation operator "!" is used to reverse the logical expression. The value of x is scanned in the above program and if x is less than 5, then y is 6 or else y is 5. The negation operator changes the logical expression from true to false or false to true.

8.5 Nested "if" Statement

These statements are used when there are two or more conditions to be satisfied but the checking of one condition is dependent on another condition and if both conditions are found to be true, then the decision is to be executed. In this statement, the 'if' statements are nested together and the decisions are executed after checking of various conditions.

The general forms of these statements are :

(1)
```
if (x1)
if (x2)
y1;
```
x1 , x2 — relational expressions,
y1, y2 — program statements.

This is similar to the form if x1 is true and x2 is true, then y1 is executed.

(2)
```
if (x1)
if (x2)
y2;
else
 y1;
```

This is similar to the form namely that if x1 is true and x2 is true, then y2 is executed, but if x2 is false y1 is executed.

(3)
```
if (x1)
{
if(x2)
        y2;
}
else
        y1;
```

This is similar to the form namely that if 'x1' and 'x2' are true, then 'y2' is executed otherwise 'y1' is executed.

Ex :

1.
```
if (a>0)
if (b>0)
c = d + e;
```

In this case ,if both a>0 and b>0 are true, then 'c=d+e'.

2.
```
if (a>0)
if (b>0)
c = d + f;
else
c = d + e;
```

In this case, if both 'a>0' and 'b>0' are true, then 'c=d+f ' but if b <= 0, then 'c=d+e'. But value of 'a' must be greater than 0.

3 .
```
if (a>0)
{
if (b>0)
c = d +f;
```

```
    }
else
c = d + e ;
```

In this case,if a>0 and b>0, then 'c=d+f ',but if a<=0 then 'c=d+e'.

Program 8–6

```
/* program on nested if statement*/
main()
{
    float a,b,discount;
    clrscr();
    printf("enter the price  and number  of product\n");
    scanf("%f%f",&a,&b);
    if(a>5000)
        {
        if(b>5)
            {
                discount=a*b*0.05;
            }
            else
                discount=0;
            }
        else
            {
                discount=0;
            }
        printf("The discount on the product is %g  ",discount);
}
```

Input	:	enter the price and number of product 5000 5
Output	:	The discount on the product is 0

This is a program on 'nested if' statement. In this program ,the price and number of product purchased by the customer is supplied. If the price is more than 5000 and number of products purchased are more than 5, then the discount is paid as 5% otherwise if price of product is less than 5000, then the discount given on product is zero.

8.6 "if–else" Construct Statement

This statement is used , when there are multiple conditions on which various decisions are dependent.This statement checks the multiple conditions in sequence and accordingly the required decisions are executed. But only one decision is executed when any one of the condition is satisfied.

The general form of the statement is

```
if (x1)
    y1 ;
else                                x1 , x2 , x3     — logical expression.
    if (x2)                         y1,y2,y3 ,y4     — program statements.
```

```
            y2;
            if(x3)
                y3;
            else
                y4;
```

This statement is similar to the form namely that if x1 is true, then y1 is executed else if x2 is true, then y2 is executed, otherwise y3 is executed.

```
Ex : if (a>0)
        c = d + e;
        else
            if (b>0)
                c = d + f;
                else
                    c = a + b;
```

In this statement, if a>0, then c=d+e. If a<=0, then the condition b>0 is checked.If b>0 is true, then 'c=d+f', but if b<=0,then 'c=a+b'. Therefore, only one value 'c' is evaluated.

Program 8–7

```
/* program on  if–else construct statement*/
main()
{
    int num, y;
    printf("enter the number \n");
    scanf("%d",&num);
    if(num > 5)
        y = 2*num;
        else
            if(num < 5)
                y = num + 2;
        else
        y = num – 2;
    printf(" The value of y is %d ",y);
}
```

Input	:	enter the number 3
Output	:	The value of y is 1

In this program , 'if-else' construct statement is used for comparing three conditions of 'num'.

if num > 5 , then

y = 2 * num

otherwise if num < 5

y = num + 2

otherwise if num = 5

y = num – 2

If one condition of 'num' is not satisfied then second condition is checked and if second is not satisfied then third condition is checked.

8.7 "switch " Statement

This statement is used, when we have to use the chain of if-else statement, where value of one variable is compared with different cases and then program statements are executed.This statement is useful when 'if-else' construct statement uses '= =' logical operator and has a central variable which checks various cases of variable and if any one is satisfied then the decision is executed.

The general form of the statement is

```
switch (x1)
{
    case z1:
            y1;
            y2;
            break;
    case  z2:
            p1;
            p2;
            break;
    default :
            a1;
            a2;
            break;
}
```

where x1 is a variable to be compared and z1, z2 are the values of variables with which x1 to be compared.

y1,y2 ....
p1,p2 ....   Program statement
a1,a2 ....

The above statements indicate that if value of x1 variable is z1, then y1,y2 statements are executed. If x1 is z2, then p1,p2...,, statements are executed, or in default a1,a2 are executed. The 'break' statement is used to break the control when one decision is executed.

Program 8–8

This program evaluates the expression according to the given operator:

```
/* program to evaluate operators*/
main ()
{
    char oper;
    float a,b,x,c;
    printf("enter the value of a, oper & b\n");
    scanf(" %f%c%f", &a,&oper,&b);
    switch (oper)
    {
        case '+' :
                x = a + b;
                break;
        case '–' :
```

```
                x = a – b;
                break;
        case '*' :
                x = a* b;
                break;
        case '/' :
                x = a/b;
        break;
        default :
        printf ("Please excuse me\n");
                c = 0;
                break;
    }
printf ("x = %g %c%g = %g\n",a, opr,b,x);
}
```

Input	:	enter the value of a, oper & b 2 + 3
Output	:	x = 2 + 3 = 5

In this program an arithmetic expression with two variables separated by a mathematical operator is supplied as data. The operator is accepted by character variable 'oper'. Then according to the type of operator, the arithmetic expression is evaluated. The switch statement compares the 'oper' variable with different cases and executes the statements. The 'break' is a statement available in C–language to terminate further operation of 'switch' statement.This statement is explained in the next chapter.

EXERCISE

1. Write a program to compute sum of the first ten numbers using iterative expression statement.
2. Write a program to find whether a quadratic equation has real or imaginary roots.

   $$ax^2 + bx + c = 0$$

3. Write a program to find whether the year is a leap year.
4. Write a program to find whether the given character is an alphabet, digit or special character using 'if-else' construct statement.
5. Evaluate the expression according to the supplied operator for any two values of a and b using 'if else' statement.
6. If a, b and c are three points whose co-ordinates are (x_1, y_1), (x_2,y_2) and (x_3,y_3) find out whether the points are colinear and if they are colinear find the equation of the line.
7. Evaluate a function f(x)

   $$f(x = Ax^2 + Bx + C \quad \text{if } x < D$$
   $$= 0 \quad \text{if } x = D$$
   $$= Ax^2 + Bx^2 - C \quad \text{if } x > D$$

   for each value of x, print x and f(x).
8. Write a program to compute f(x)

   $$f(x) = 1 + \frac{x}{1 + x^2} \quad \text{for } x < 0$$
   $$= 0 \quad \text{for } x = 0$$
   $$= 1 - \frac{x}{1 + x^2} \quad \text{for } x > 0$$

9. Radius of circle and (x,y) co-ordinates of a point are entered through keyboard. Write a program to find whether the point lies inside the circle, on the circle or outside the circle.

10. (x,y) co-ordinates of three points are entered through the keyboard. Write a program to find whether they form equilateral, isosceles or scalene triangle.
11. Write a program to find whether the given number is a prime number or not. A prime number is a number not divisible by any other number.
12. Write a program to find the value of Y for a particular value of K

    IF K = 1 $Y = ax + b$
    IF K = 2 $Y = ax^2 + b^2$
    IF K = 3 $Y = -ax$
    IF K = 4 $Y = a + x$

    The a, x, b, k are supplied through keyboard
13. Write the above program using `switch' statement.
14. Write a program to calculate the area of triangle, circle or rectangle depending upon the user option.
15. The formula for calculating z are given below :

    $Z = 3x^2 - 7x + 2$ for $x < 4.7$
    $Z = 3x^2 + 21.2x - 0.8$ for $x = 4.7$
    $Z = 3x^2 + 21.3x - 1.6$ for $x > 4.7$

    Write a program for evaluating value of Z.
16. When a cylinder of internal radius `a' and outer radius `b' is subjected to the internal pressure P, the maximum stress `σ' is given by

    $$\sigma = P\left[\frac{b^2 + a^2}{b^2 - a^2}\right] \quad \text{if} \quad b/a > 1.1$$

    $$\sigma = \frac{pd}{2t} \quad \text{if} \quad \frac{b}{a} <= 1.1$$

    $d = 2a$
    $t = b - a.$

    Prepare a program to calculate maximum stress in the material according to the diameter and thickness.
17. The rate of interest offered by a bank on fixed deposits is

(i)	Period < 6 Months	5%
(ii)	Period 6 < 12 Month	6%
(iii)	Between 1 Year to 3 Year	8%
(iv)	Between 3 Year to 5 Year	9%
(v)	Above 5 Year or more	10%

    Write a program to calculate monthly interest of customers.
18. The polar moment of inertia (J) of tube having inner diameter d and outer diameter D is given by the following two formulas.

    $$J = \frac{\pi}{32}(D^4 - d^4) \qquad \frac{D}{d} \geq 1.1$$

    $$J = \frac{\pi D^3 T}{4} \qquad \frac{D}{d} < 1.1$$

    $$\text{Where } t = \frac{D - d}{2}$$

    Write a program to calculate moment of inertia of the tube if D and t are supplied to the program as input.
19. The formula for calculating income tax is as under :

    Income Tax = 0   If Income $\leq$ 40000
    Income Tax = 0.15 (Income– 40000)   If Income > 40000

    Write a program to calculate income tax of a person having given income according to the above formula.

9
LOOPING STATEMENTS

AN OVERVIEW

In the previous unit, we have seen that the central processing unit can be made capable of taking decisions on the basis of supplied conditions.It is necessary for the programmer to write conditions and decisions in the program. Then the compiler can execute the program and the decision will be taken according to the supplied conditions.The switch statement allows multiple decisions for multiple conditions.

In this unit, the looping statements are discussed .These are used for the cyclic operation which are performed by using the statement. The statement allows repeated execution of various statements in a cyclic fashion such that the statements are executed repeatedly and the value of certain variable is modified in every cycle and such cycles continue till a particular condition is reached. The cycles are terminated when we reach a value.

OBJECTIVES

After completing this unit you will be able to:

* Understand cyclic operations
* Explain statements for cyclic operation
* Demonstrate 'for' statement
* Describe 'while' and 'do while' statement

9.1 INTRODUCTION

These statements are used, when repeated operations are to be performed by iterative calculations. In these statement, loops are to be used for computing large number of values of certain variables. These statements allow the user to perform the calculations of same variables with same statement having modifications of the variables in the cycle till a condition is not reached to terminate the cyclic operation.

There are different types of such statements used :

1. "for" statement
2. "while" statement
3. "do-while" statement
4. `Nested' for statement
5. `Parallel' for statement
6. `goto' statement
7. 'continue' statement
8. "break" statement

9.2 "for" STATEMENT

In this case, repetitive calculations of a set of statements are performed by changing the values of variables between the initial value and the final value of the variable with a particular stepsize. This statement is used when iterations are to be carried out between initial and final value with a stepsize.

The general form of the statement is

```
for (z1; z2;z3)
{
        y1;
        y2;
        –
}
```

where,

z1 – arithmetic statement indicating initial value of the index variable.

z2 – logical expression indicating maximum possible value of the index variable.

z3 – arithmetic or iterative expression statement indicating increment or decrement of the index variable.

y1,y2 – program statement.

Ex:

```
for (x=1; x<= 10; x = x+2)
{
    a = b + x;
    d= x + a;
}
```

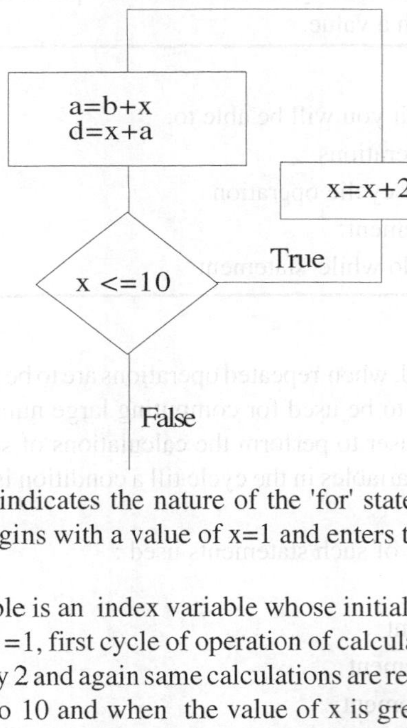

The flow chart shown above indicates the nature of the 'for' statement .In this flow chart it is observed that the 'for' statement begins with a value of x=1 and enters the cycle to evaluate the value of 'a' and 'd' .

In the above example, x variable is an index variable whose initial is 1 and final value is 10 and stepsize is 2. With initial value of x =1, first cycle of operation of calculation a and d is performed and then the x variable is incremented by 2 and again same calculations are repeated.This process continues till the value of x becomes equal to 10 and when the value of x is greater than 10 then the logical expression becomes false and the cyclic operations are terminated. The iterations are carried out with value of variables varying from x =0, 2, 4, 6, 8, 10 for total 6 values of x and the values of a & d are computed.

This same operation can be performed by using a reverse cycle as

```
for(x=10;x>=1;x=x–2)
    {
        a=b+x;
        d=x+a;
    }
```

In this case the initial value of 'x ' is 10 and the terminating value of x is 0. Every cycle of calculation is carried out by using value of x and it is decremented by 2 in every cycle .

Program 9–1

A triangular number is sum of all numbers upto that number. In this program the summation of all the numbers upto the given number is calculated.

Ex : Triangular number of 6 is

= 1+2+3+4+5+6 =21

```
/* Program to calculate triangular number */
main ( )
{
    int n, sum, m;
    printf(" enter the value for triangular number\n");
    scanf (" %d", &m);
    sum = 0;
    for (n=1; n<=m; ++n)
    {
        sum = sum + n;
    }
    printf ( "n= %d sum=%d",n,sum);
}
```

Input	:	enter the value for triangular number 3
Output	:	n=4 sum=6

Program 9–2

This program calculates factorial of a number. The factorial of the number means it is a multiplication of all the numbers upto that number.

Ex : 6! = 1.2.3.4.5.6

```
/* factorial of a number */
main()
{
    int n, fac,m;
    printf("enter the value of number\n");
    scanf ("%d", &m);
    fac = 1;
    for (n = 1; n<= m; ++n)
    {
        fac = fac * n;
    }
    printf (" the factorial of a number %d is %d",m,fac);
}
```

Input	:	enter the value of number 4
Output	:	the factorial of a number 4 is 24

In this program factorial of number is calculated by using multiplication.

Program 9–3

This program calculates the sum of even numbers upto 100

S = 2 + 4 + 6 + ...100

```
/* sum of the even numbers */
main ()
{
    int n,sum;
    sum = 0;
    for( n =2; n<= 100; n = n+2)
    {
            sum = sum +n;
    }
    printf ("n = %d sum=%d", n,sum);
}
```

Output	:	n=102 sum=2550

Program 9–4

This program evaluates the sum of a series

s = 1 + 1/2! + 1/3! + ... n terms.

```
/* program to calculate the sum of the series */
main ( )
{
    int n, m,x,y; long int fac;
    float sum;
    printf (enter the number of terms\n");
    scanf ("%d" , &y);
    sum = 1.0; fac = 1;
    for (x =1; x=<y; ++x)
    {
            fac = fac * x;
            sum = sum+ ( 1.0/(float) fac );
    }
    printf ( "number of terms = %d sum of series %g" , y,sum);
}
```

Input	:	enter the number of terms 2
Output	:	number of terms = 2 sum of series 1.5

In this program the sum of series is calculated by generating every term of a series as reciprocal of factorial and adding the term in every cycle.

Program 9–5

This programs evaluates the sum of a series.

sum = 1 + x + x^2 + x^3 ....x^{49}

```
/* to calculate sum of series */
main ( )
{
    float n,x, sum,term,i;
    printf(" enter the value of maxm term and x\n");
    scanf (" %f%f ", &n,&x );
    sum = 1; term = 1;
    for (i = 2; i<= 50; ++i)
    {
        term = term + x;
        sum  = sum +  term;
    }
    printf ("The sum of series for %g upto %g is %g\n",n,x,sum);
}
```

Input	:	enter the value of maxm. term and x 2 3
Output	:	The sum of series for 2 upto 3 is 3725

In this program every term of series is multiplied in every cycle by 'x' and added to sum of previous cycle.

Program 9–6

This program calculates Fabonacii series in which every number is generated by sum of two previous terms. The first two terms are generating terms.

Ex :

The fabonacii series can be shown as below

1 1 2 3 5 8 13 21 .... n terms

```
/* program for fabonacii series */
main ()
{
    int fa, fb,n,fc;
    printf (" enter the initial value of fa & fb\n");
    scanf ("%d%d", &fa &fb);
    for ( n= 3; n<=10; ++n)
    {
        fc = fa + fb;
        printf("%d fabonacii number is %d\n", n,fc);
        fa = fb;
        fb =  fc;
    }
}
```

Input	:	enter the initial value of fa & fb 4 6
Output	:	3 fabonacii number is 10 4 fabonacii number is 16 5 fabonacii number is 26 6 fabonacii number is 42 7 fabonacii number is 68 8 fabonacii number is 110 9 fabonacii number is 178 10 fabonacii number is 288

In this program, the term of fabonacia series is calculated in every cycle using addition of two previous terms. 'fa' and 'fb' variable stores two previous terms and fc is calculated which is the current term.

Program 9–7

This program calculates safe loading in the columns by using two formulas. The safe loading S is given by

S = (18000 – 0.485 r^2) if r ≤ 120
= (18000/1+ r^2/18000) if r < 120

The values of safe loading 's' are calculated for various values of r between 125 to 'rm' with a step size of 'rs'.

```
/* Calculation of same loading */
main ()
{
    float r, rm,rs,s;
    printf (" enter the value of maximum number and step size\n");
    scanf(%f%f", &rm, &rs);
    for (r = 125; r >= rm; r= r+rs)
    {
        if (r <= 120)
        {
            s = (18000.0 – 485.0 *r*r);
        }
        else
            s = (18000.0/(1.0+r*r/18000.0));
        printf (" r = %d s= %g\n, r,s);
    }
}
```

Input	:	enter the value of maximum number and step size 300 25
Output	:	r=125 s=9635.69 r=150 s=8000 r=175 s=6663.24 r=200 s=5586.21 r=225 s=4721.31 r=250 s=4024.84 r=275 s=3460.61 r=300 s=3000

In this program, the safe loading is calculated for various values of r and 'if-else' statement is used to find the type of equation applicable for safe load 's'

9.2.1 Limitations of 'for' Statement

In 'for' statement the index variable cannot be modified or calculated in 'for' loop. If stepsize or increment is not fixed, then 'for' statement cannot be used.

Example :

```
for(i=0;i<=5;++i)
{
        i=i+3;
}
```

Here the index is modified again in the 'for' statement,which is wrong.

9.3 "while" STATEMENT

This statement is used, when the iterative calculations are to be done till a particular condition is true and when the condition is false, the iterations or cycles of operation are to be terminated.

The general form is

```
while (x1)
{
        y1;
        y2;
}
```

where , x1 — logical expression

y1,y2 — program statement

In this statement, if the condition 'x1' is true, then 'y1' and 'y2' statements are executed for the first cycle and again 'x1' is checked.If the condition is found to be true ,then y1 & y2 are executed for the second time .The calculations of y1 & y2 continues ,till 'x1' condition is false and the cycles of execution are discontinued.

This statement may be used ,when the index variable is calculated in every cycle and the increment of index is unknown. This can be used if increments are not fixed, but calculated in the loop.

Ex :

```
count=1;
    while ( count <=15 )
    {
            printf (" %d\n",count );
            count=count * 2;
    }
```

In this case 'count' will be printed five times till the count value exceeds fifteen.

9.4 "do–while" STATEMENT

This statement is used when the statements are to be executed initially and the result of the statement is compared. In case, if the condition is satisfied or true, iterations are continued otherwise iterations are terminated.

The general form is

```
do
{
        y1 ;
        y2 ;
        y3;
```

```
}while (x1);
```

where, y1,y2,y3 – statements of the program
x1 – logical expression indicating the condition.

In this statement, the first cycle of y1,y2,y3 statements is executed and at the end of the execution, the condition x1 is checked by logical expression. If x1 condition is true, then control shifts to 'do' statement and again the second cycle of operation of y1, y2, y3 is executed and the cycles continue till x1 is false.

Ex:

```
do
    {
        a = b + c;
        d = e + f;
        num = d/10.0;
    } while (num ! = 0.0);
```

If the value of num is not equal to zero then iterations are terminated.

This statement becomes necessary when the initial value of index is unknown or is computed in the first cycle or reinitialization of index to initial is necessary in every cycle.

Program 9–8

In this program sum of series is obtained till the value of the term is above 0.02.

sum = 1+ 1/2 + 1/3 + 1/4 .... upto accuracy of 0.02

```
/* sum of the series*/
main()
{
    float i,n,x,sig=1;
    i = 1;
    do
    {
        x = ++i;
        term = 1.0/x;
        sig = sig + term;
    }while (term >= 0.02);
    printf("number of terms = %g the sum of the series=%g\n", i,sig);
}
```

Output : number of terms=50 the sum of the series=4.49921

In this program, the 'do–while' statement is used because the final value of index variable at which the termination occurs is unknown and is calculated in the cycle itself. The term is calculated in every cycle and the value of the term is checked in every cycle. In case if the term is below 0.02 then the cycle is terminated.

9.5 NESTED 'for' STATEMENT

The 'for' statement are 'nested' means one 'for' statement is executed inside the other 'for' statement. This statement provides more number of cycles of execution because for every value of index of outer 'for' statement the index of inner 'for' statement is varied.

Example:

```
for (i = 1; i < = 3; + + i)
{
for (j = 1; j < = 3; + + j)
{
printf("i=%d,j=%d\n",i,j);
}
}
```

In this case i varies from 1 to 3 with stepsize of 1 and j varies from 1 to 3 in steps of 1.For every value of i the j is varied from 1 to 3. Therefore, total 3×3 = 9 cycle will be performed.

9.6 PARALLEL 'for' STATEMENT

The 'for' statement can be written as parallel where we have two indexes varying simultaneously upto maximum value. This statement allows the variation of two indexes simultaneously .

```
for (i = 1, j = 1; i < = 5; + + i,j=j+0.2)
{
    x = x + i + j;
    y = y – i – j;
    printf("x=%d,y=%d\n",x,y);
}
```

In this case, the 'for' statement for i and j are varying simultaneously. The i and j will be varied upto 5 in step 1 and j will be varied upto 5 in step of 1 and total 5 cycles are executed.

9.7 "Goto" STATEMENT

In C-language 'goto' statement is used to shift the control to any other statement which is not in sequence. This is written as

goto p ;

Where ,

p – Label name

Then the control is shifted to the statement where label name is written.

Ex :

```
top :
        x = x + 1 ;
        y = x + 2 ;
        goto top;
```

In this statement, the 'goto' statement indicates that the control should be shifted to the 'top' label which is written in the starting.

Program 9–9

```
/* Program on goto */
main()
{
    int sum,i,j;
    clrscr();
    for(i=1;i<=5;++i)
    {
```

```
        printf("Enter value of j\n");
        scanf("%d",&j);
        if(j<5)
        {
                printf("Sum will be done only if value of j is greater than 5\n")
                goto bot;
        }
        sum=i+j;
        printf("i=%d,j=%d,Sum=I+J=%d\n",i,j,sum);
    }
    bot:
    printf("The cycle is terminated\n");
}
```

Input	:	Enter value of j 5
Output	:	i=1,j=5,Sum=I+J=6
Input	:	Enter value of j 4
Output	:	Sum will be done only if value of j is greater than 5 The cycle is terminated

In this program, if the value of 'j' supplied is less than 5, then the control is shifted above 'for' statement by 'goto' statement and 'for' statement is again repeated.

9.8 'Continue' STATEMENT

This statement is used when the execution of further statements of the cycle is to be skipped. This statement bypasses the execution of further statements and transfers control to start of the cycle for execution of next cycle.

It is written as

```
continue;
```

Ex : The following part of program shows the example of 'continue' statement.

```
sum=0;
for (i=0; i< = 5; ++i)
{
        sum=sum+i;
        if(i==2)
                continue;
}
```

In this statement the sum of the numbers upto 5 is obtained but if i is equal to 2, then 'continue' is executed and execution of that cycle or all further statements is discontinued and control is shifted for execution of the next cycle of 'for' statement. Therefore, the value of 2 is excluded from summation.

Program 9–10

Program to calculate sum of all numbers upto 10 excluding 5.

sum = 1+ 2 + 3 +4 + 6 + 7 + 8 + 9 + 10

```
/* sum of the numbers upto 10*/
main()
{
```

```
    int i,sum=0;
    for(i=1;i<=10;++i)
    {
        if(i==5)
            continue;
        sum=sum+i;
    }
    printf("sum=%d\n",sum);
}
```

Output : sum=50

In this program sum of the first 10 numbers excluding 5 is calculated by using continues statement. Every number in generated and added to sum in cycle of 'for' statement. If number is equal to 5 then the addition is skipped by continued statement and the next cycle is started.

9.9 'break' STATEMENT

This statement is used when we want to break the cycle of execution after satisfying the condition. This statement breaks the further operation of loop or cycle and iterations are stopped. The control comes out of the statement.

It is written as

```
break;
```

Ex :

```
for(i = 1; i < = 5; ++i)
{
    scanf("%d", &s[i]);
    if(s[i] > = 20)
        break;
}
```

In this case, the program scans 5 values and if value supplied is greater than 20 for any value of i cycle is terminated.

Program 9–11

```
/*Program on break */
main()
{
    int sum,i,j;
    for(i=1;i<=10;++i)
    {
        printf("Enter value of j\n");
        scanf("%d",&j);
        if(j<5)
        {
            printf("j's value entered is less than 5\n");
            break;
        }
        sum=sum+i+j;
        printf("i=%d,j=%d,sum = %d\n",i,j,sum);
    }
}
```

Input	:	Enter value of j 3
Output	:	j's value entered is less than 5

In this program, if the value of 'j' is less than 5, then the 'for' statement breaks the cycle of operation, otherwise every number 'j' supplied in the cycle is added to 'sum' along with value of 'i'.

EXERCISE

1. Write a program to find sum of a series :

   $S = 1 - 2/3^2 + 2^2 / 5^2 - 2^3/7^2$..... 50 terms
2. Write a program to print 50 fabonacii numbes r whose first two numbers are given. The fabonacii numbers are the numbers generated by the sum of the two previous number of the series.
3. Write a program to find the sum of a series

   S = 1 + 1/2! + 1/3! + 1/4! +..........N terms

5. Write a program to calculate value of `g' at different altitudes 'h'

   $g = 32.17\ [4390/(4390+h)]^2$ IF $h > 0$

   $g = 32.17\ [1 + h/4390]$ IF $h <= 0$

   If 'h' varies from 10 to 200 in steps of 5.
6. Write a program to evaluate :

   $X = \sum_{K=0}^{500} C\,Y^K$ Where , $C = K^2$ FOR K= 0 − 250

   $C = 4\,K^3$ FOR K= 251–500
7. Write a program to find sum of the series :

   $S = 1+1/(x^2 +1) + 1/(x^3 +2)+ 1/(x^4 +3)+$.....N terms
8. Write a program to find a 3 digit number below 1000 such that the sum of cubes of digits of the number is equal to the number.
9. The displacement of particle is given by

   $s= ut + 1/2\ at^2$

   write a program to prepare a table of displacement versus time for given values of initial velocity u and acceleration at uniform increments of 1 second from 0 to 50 seconds.
10. Prepare a program to read a 10 digit number and rewrite in reverse order of digits.
11. Out of the 100 given +ve integers it is desired to find out those which are exact multiples of four and total no. of such numbers.
12. Write a program to find sum of following series correct upto 5th decimal place.

    $$S = 1 - \frac{X^2}{2!} + \frac{X^4}{4!} - \frac{X^6}{6!} + \ldots\ldots$$
13. Write a program to find a prime number upto 100. A prime number is a number not divisible by any other number.
14. Prepare a program to find the sum of

    S=1 + 2 + 3 + 4 + 6 .... + 15 in which 5 is excluded.

15. Write a program to find the sum of series

$$\text{Log}_e\, x = \left[\frac{x-1}{1}\right] + 1/2\left[\frac{x-1}{2}\right]^2 + 1/3\left[\frac{x-1}{3}\right]^3 + \ldots..$$

and $\log_e x$ should be correct upto fifth decimal accuracy.

16. Write a program to compute value of π

$$\frac{\pi^6}{6} = 1 + \frac{1}{2^2} + \frac{1}{3^2} + \frac{1}{4^2} + \ldots\ldots\ldots.$$

17. Write a program to evaluate

$$S = \frac{1.0}{5^3} + \frac{1.1}{5^4} + \frac{1.2}{5^5} + \ldots...$$

correct upto six decimal places.

18. Write a program to evaluate for different values of x

$$P = x.\frac{x^2}{3}.\frac{x^3}{5}.\frac{x^4}{7}\ldots.\frac{x^{10}}{19}$$

where x value varies as

$x = 0.9, 0.95, 1.0, \ldots\ldots\ldots., 1.4$

10

NUMERIC ARRAY

AN OVERVIEW

In the last chapter you have studied the statements related to the programming which allow you to prepare program which involve simple calculation. The statement which allows the decision being taken using computer program are studied there has been repetative calculation which could be performed by looping statement which allows for cyclic operations. Find the answer of following program which involves decisions and cyclic operations.

Like

$$S = \sum_{n=1}^{500} C X^n \qquad \text{Where} \quad C = k^2 \quad \text{if } n < 250; \qquad = 4k \quad \text{if } n \geq 250$$

Here it involves a series summation and every term to be generated and value 'C' has two equations in which either of two is selected. This may be possible by ' for ' and ' if - else' statement.

OBJECTIVES

After completing this unit you will be able to:

* Write declaration of numeric array variable
* Identify various types of methods for supply of values to array variable.
* Discuss methods of printing of array variable
* Define two dimensional numeric array variable
* Demonstrate storage in 2-D array variable

10.1 INTRODUCTION

If multiple values are to be stored under the same variable name, then arrays are used. In an array a single variable can be assigned with a number which acts as an index number or subscript. The values are stored in the array in different memory locations indicated by the indexes. These variables allow storage of number of values under the same variable name.

If there are many values for a particular variable, then in mathematics they are indicated by subscript number.

For example five given number are :

2   –5   6   9   22

If these numbers are stored under same variable name, then we write in mathematics as

$x_1 = 2$

$x_2 = -5$

$x_3 = 6$

$x_4 = 9$

$x_5 = 22$

This procedure is also used in C– programming in the form of array variables.

There are two types of array variables :

1. Single dimensional array variable
2. Two dimensional array variable

10.2 SINGLE DIMENSIONAL ARRAY

The single dimensional array variable is a variable in which the values are stored in one dimension. All the values of the array are stored in memory available in columns. Every element of the array can be retrieved by indicating location number or index of the memory.

10.2.1 Declaration of array

Before using an array it must be declared in the initial stage by a variable type and the maximum memory required for the array.

The general form in which they are declared is

x y [z];

where,

x	–	indicates type of variable int or float or char.
y	–	indicates the name of variable as usual to normal variable.
z	–	maximum no. of memories required for the variable.

Ex :

```
float a[10];
```

The above declaration creates memory spaces of floating type for storing the 10 values, of "a" variable.

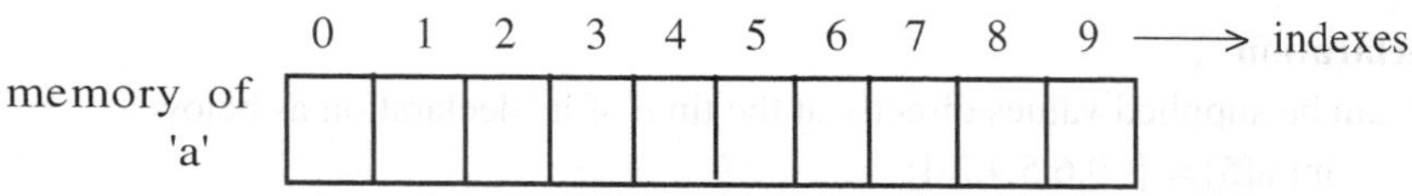

The memory of 'a' consist of 10 spaces and are indexed by a number for different memory location from 0 to 9.

10.2.2 Supply of values to array variable

After declaration of array, the values of the array variables are supplied in the memory by following three methods :

(a) Arithmetic statement.

(b) 'scanf' statement.

(c) By declaration

(a) Arithmetic Statement

The values of the array variable can be supplied in the memory by use of the arithmetic statement.

Ex :

```
a [0] = 10.2;
a [1] = 13.6;
a [2] = 19.6
```

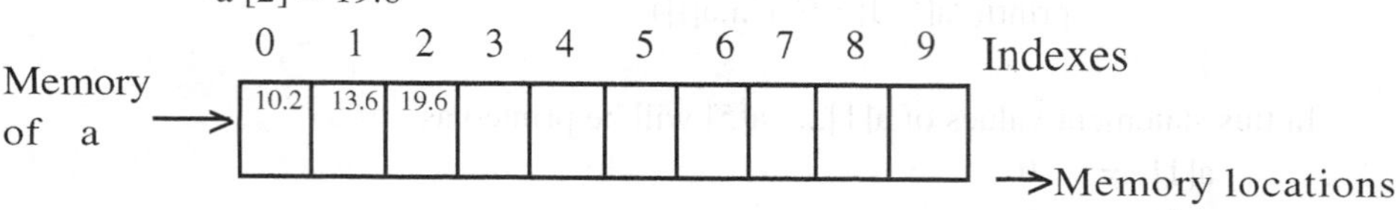

In this case, the memories are filled by using arithmetic statement.

The above statements are the arithmetic statements where value of 'a' variable is stored under different memory locations indicated by the index number in the rectangular bracket to represent the memory location.

(b) "scanf" statement

The values of the array variable can be supplied by a 'scanf' statement. In this case, any general value of array can be supplied in the program through the data screen. The array is entered by using "scanf" statement in the ' for' loop.

Ex :

```
for (i=1;  i<=5; ++i)
{
        scanf ("%f", &a[i ]);
}
```

In the above statement ' i' value starts from 1 and ends at 5. It reads 5 values of 'a' variable. These five data values can be supplied on the data screen as :

10.2 13.6 19.2 5.67 8.31

These are filled in the memory as

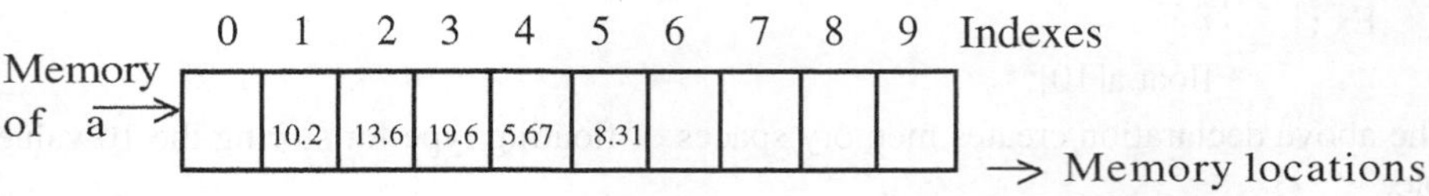

(c) By declaration

The array can be supplied values directly at the time of its declaration as below :

```
int a[5] = {–9,6,5,4,3 };
```

In this case, the value of array is supplied at the point of declaration and the 5 values are supplied as

a[0] = –9, a[1] = 6, a[2] = 5, a[3] = 4, a[4] = 3

These are filled in the memory as :

0	1	2	3	4
–9	6	5	4	3

10.2.3 Printing of array variable

The values of array variable can be printed by using "printf" statement in the 'for' loop.

Ex:

There are two methods of producing values of variables :

```
(i) for (i=1; i<=5; ++i)
    {
            printf("a[%d]= %d",i,a[i])
    }
```

In this statement values of a[1],.....a[5] will be printed as

a[1] = –9
a[2] = 6
a[3] = 5
a[4] = 4
a[5] = 3

```
(ii) for (i=1; i<=5; ++i)
     {
```

```
            printf("%d- ",a[i])
        }
```

In this statement values of a[1],.....a[5] will be printed in one row with two blank spaces.

−9 6 5 4 3

Program 10–1

This Program calculates the fabonacii series using arrays. Every term of fabonacci series is sum of two previous terms of series and first two terms are generating terms.

```
/* To calculate the fabonacii number */
main()
{
    int m,i,f[1000];
    printf( "enter the value for maximum number\n");
    scanf("%d", &m);
    printf("enter first two fabonacii number \n");
    scanf ("%d%d", &f[0],&f[1]);
    for (i=2;i< m; ++i)
    {
            f[i] = f[i–1]+ f[i–2];
    }
    for (i=0; i<m;++i)
    printf ("the %5d fabonacii  number %5d\n,i+1,f[i]);
}
```

Input	:	enter the value for maximum number	3
		enter first two fabonacii number	2 3
Output	:	the 1 fabonacii number	2
		the 2 fabonacii number	3
		the 3 fabonacii number	5

Program 10–2

This Program scans and prints the array of numbers .

```
/*Scanning and printing of array */
main()
{
    int x[30],i,m;
    printf("Enter your number\n");
    scanf("%d",&m);
    printf("Enter %d elements of array\n",m);
    for (i=1; i<=m; ++i)
    {
            scanf(" %d",&x[j]);
    }
    for (i=1; i<=m; ++i)
    {
            printf ("%d  ",x[i]);
    }
}
```

Input	:	Enter your number 4 Enter 4 elements of array 2 3 4 5
Output	:	2 3 4 5

In this program the memory is opened by using declaration of memory and a maximum number is scanned. The scanf statement is executed in 'for' statement to scan given numbers and the printf statement is executed to print the array.

Program 10–3

This Program calculates sum of given numbers.

```
/* to calculate the sum of the number */
main ()
{
    int i, sum, m;
    int s[100];
    printf ("enter maximum value of number\n");
    scanf ("%d",&m);
    printf (" enter the  numbers\n");
    for (i=1; i<=m; ++i)
    {
        scanf (" %d", &s[i] );
    }
    sum = 0;
    for (i=1; i<=m; ++i)
    {
        sum = sum+s[i];
    }
    for(i=1;i<=m;++i)
    {
        printf (" the sum of number is %d \n",sum);
    }
}
```

Input	:	enter maximum value of number 4 enter the numbers 3 2 9 6
Output	:	the sum of number is 20 the sum of number is 20 the sum of number is 20 the sum of number is 20

In this program sum of the given numbers is calculated. The program is supplied with the maximum number and the elements of array are scanned and then the sum of all the elements is calculated by using a 'for' statement.

10.3 TWO–DIMENSIONAL ARRAY

The matrix in mathematics is a two-dimensional array written in columns and rows. The element of the matrix is indicated by the row and column number in which it is located.

The element of matrix is detected by writing a_{ij}

where, i stands for row and j stands for column, 'a' stands for name of the matrix.

Ex :

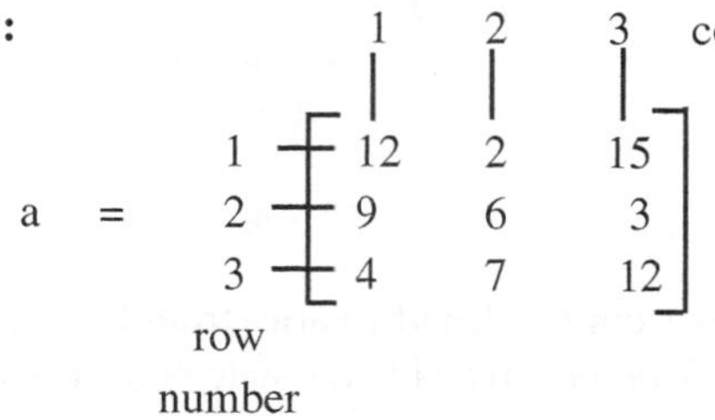

The element a_{12} is traced by supplying the values of the subscript 12

$a_{12} = 2$

where, 12 is indicating 1 row and 2 columns of the matrix whose value is 2.

The two dimension array variable is capable of storing the matrix of mathematics because it contains elements arranged in rows and columns.

10.3.1 Declaration of 2–D array

The two dimensional array can be declared as :

```
int a[5][5];
```

This creates a memory in two dimesion as :

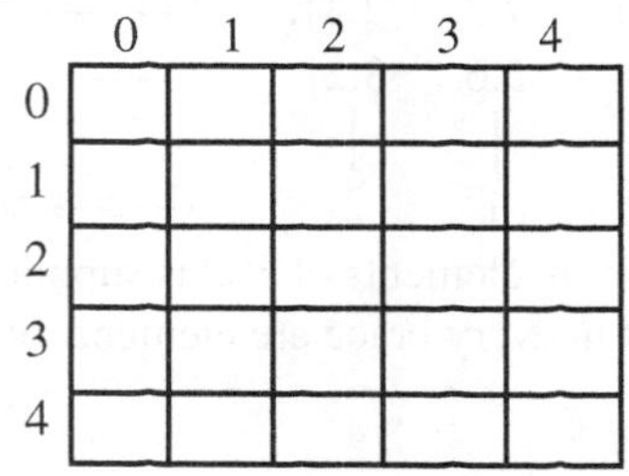

This is a two dimensional matrix of the order 5×5 having integer type memory. This array is capable of storing 25 values of the elements of array in 5 rows and 5 columns.

10.3.2 Supply of values to array

The value can be assigned to 2–D array by 'arithmetic statement' or 'scanf' statement or by way of declaration.

(a) Arithmetic Statement

The elements of the array can be supplied by using arithmetic statement by supplying the row number and the column number as below :

```
a[1][1]=10;
```

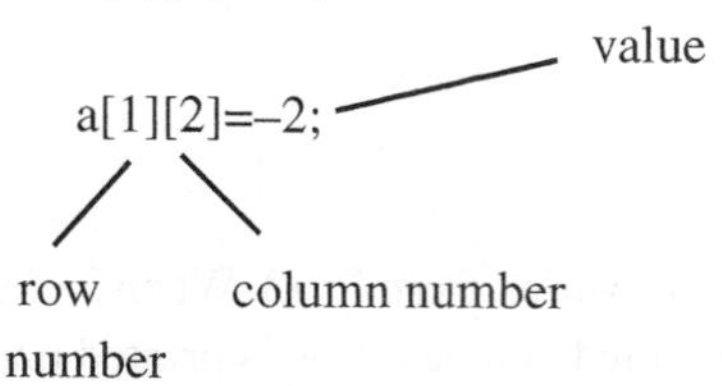

(b) 'scanf' Statement

The values can be supplied to a two-dimensional array using 'scanf' statement in 'nested for' statement as below :

```
for (i = 1; i<=3; ++i)
{
for (j = 1; j<=3; ++j)
{
    scanf("%d", & a[i][j])
}
}
```

where, a is two-dimensional integer array, i varies from 1 to 3, and j varies from 1 to 3. For every value of 'i', j varies from 1 to 3. Hence a matrix of 3×3 order is read by this statement. The elements are supplied in the format

```
–2    5    6
 7    9    2
22    6   19
```

All these elements are arranged in the form of rows and columns.

(c) By declaration

The array can be supplied at the time of declaration in the program as :

```
float  a[3][3] = {                          row number
            { 1.2,   6.4,   1.3},  ———— 0
            {2.1,    7.3,   2.4},  ———— 1
            {1.1,    5.6,   3.2}   ———— 2
        };   |        |      |
             0        1      2      ————> col. number
```

In this case, a matrix consisting of floating elements of 3×3 is supplied with row number from 0 to 2 and columns from 0 to 2. The element in every brace are elements of a row and are in sequence of column.

10.3.3 Printing of array

The two dimensional array can be printed by using nested ' for' statement.

```
for(i=1; i<3; ++i)
{
for(j=i; j<=3;++j)
{
        printf("%d    ", a[i][j]);
}
printf("\n");
}
```

```
–2    5    6
 7    9    2
22    6   19
```

A 3×3 matrix is printed using nested 'for' statement. 'i' varies from 1 to 3. When 3 elements are of first row of printed by 'j', a new line control '\n' is executed and next row is printed on a new line.Hence the printing is obtained in the form of a matrix on screen.

Program 10–4

The following program prints the elements of 2×2 matrix.

```
/* printing of matrix */
main()
{
    int a[20] [20],i,j;
    a[1][1]= 2; a[1][2]=3; a[2][1]= 4; a[2][2] =6;
    for (i=1; i<=2; ++i)
    {
        for( j=1; j<=2; ++j)
        printf (“%d”, a[i][j]);
        printf (“ \n”);
    }
}
```

Output	:	2	3
		4	6

In this program a matrix of order 2×2 is supplied by using arithmetic statement and it is printed by using 'printf' statement executed in 'for' statement.

Program 10–5

This program calculates the sum of all elements of the matrix.

```
/* sum of all elements of matrix */
main()
{
    int a[20][20], sum;
    int i,j,m,n;
    printf(“ enter the order m x n of the matrix\n”);
    scanf(“%d%d”, &m,&n);
    printf(“enter the %d x %d elements of the matrix\n”,m,n);
    for (i = 1; i<= m; ++i)
    {
        for (j = 1; j<=n; ++j)
        scanf ( “%d”,&a[i][j]);
    }
    sum = 0;
    for (i=1; i<=m; ++i)
    {
        for (j=1; j<=n; ++j)
        sum =sum + a[i][j];
    }
    printf(“ sum of all elements is  %d “,sum);
}
```

Input	:	enter the order m x n of the matrix 3 3 enter the 3 × 3 elements of the matrix 1 2 3 4 5 6 7 8 9
Output	:	sum of all elements is 45

In this program sum of all elements of the matrix is calculated by addition of all elements of the matrix. The matrix supplied is a matrix of any order m x n. The values of ' m ' & 'n' are scanned in the program and then the matrix is scanned using 'nested for' statement. All the elements of the matrix are added by extracting them from the memory.

Program 10–6

This program does addition of two matrices [a] & [b].In this case the elements of the matrices at corresponding locations of [a] & [b] are added to form a new matix [c]. The order of both the matrices [a] & [b] is same and the third matrix [c] is of the same order.

Ex :

[c] = [a] + [b]

$$\begin{bmatrix} 2 & 23 & 19 \\ 22 & 15 & 26 \\ 17 & 19 & 18 \end{bmatrix} = \begin{bmatrix} 5 & 13 & 17 \\ 9 & 12 & 19 \\ 12 & 17 & 13 \end{bmatrix} + \begin{bmatrix} -3 & 10 & 2 \\ 13 & 3 & 7 \\ 5 & 2 & 5 \end{bmatrix}$$

```
/* addition of matrices */
main()
{
    int a[20][20],b[20][20],c[20][20],,j,m,n;
    printf(" enter the order m x n\n");
    scanf ("%d %d", &m &n);
    printf (" enter the elements of matrix A\n");
    for (i=1; <=m; ++i)
    {
        for (j=1; j<=n; ++j);
        scanf ( "%d", &a [i][j]);
    }
    printf (" enter the elements of B matrix\n");
    for (i= 1; i<=m; ++i)
    {
        for(j=1; j<=n; ++j)
        scanf ( "%d", &b[i][j]);
    }
    for (i=1; i<=m; ++i)
    {
        for(j=1;J<=n; ++j)
```

```
            {
                c[i][j] = a[i][j]+b[i][j];
            }
    }
    printf("the elements of c matrix are  \n");
    for (i=1; i<=m; ++i)
    {
            for (j=1; j<=n; ++j)
            printf ( " %d     ", c[i][j] );
            printf ("\n");
    }
}
```

Input	:	enter the order m x n 2 2 enter the elements of matrix A 1 1 1 1 enter the elements of B matrix 2 2 2 2
Output	:	the elements of c matrix are 3 3 3 3

Program 10–7

The transpose of matrix means if [a] matrix is of the order of 2× 3, then [b] matrix is of the order 3 ×2 which is transpose of [a]. The transpose of [a] is created by converting the rows into columns and columns into rows.

Ex :

$$\underset{m\times n}{[a]} \xrightarrow{\text{transpose}} \underset{n\times m}{[b]}$$

$$\begin{bmatrix} 3 & 2 \\ 5 & 6 \\ 2 & 9 \end{bmatrix}_{3\times 2} \xrightarrow{\text{transpose}} \begin{bmatrix} 3 & 5 & 2 \\ 2 & 6 & 9 \end{bmatrix}_{2\times 3}$$

```
/* Transpose of matrix */
main()
{
    int a[20][20], b[20][20], i,j,m,n;
    printf (" enter the order m & n\n");
    scanf ("%d%d ",&m,&n);
```

```
        printf (" enter the elements of matrix A \n");
        for (i=1; i<=m; ++i)
        {
                for (j=1; j<=n; ++j)
                scanf("%d",&a[i][j]);
        }
        for(i=1;i<=m;++i)
        {
                for(j=1;j<=n;++j)
                b[j][i]=a[i][j];
        }
        printf("the elements of matrix B are\n");
        for (j=1 ; j<=n; ++j)
        {
                for (i=1; i<=m; ++i)
                printf ("%d   ", b [j][i];)
                printf ("\n");
        }
}
```

Input	:	enter the order m & n 3 3 enter the elements of matrix A 1 2 3 4 5 6 7 8 9
Output	:	the elements of matrix B are 1 4 7 2 5 8 3 6 9

Program 10–8

```
/* MULTIPLICATION OF THE COLUMN AND ROW*/
main()
{
        int i,j,m,n;
        int a[10][10];
        clrscr();
        printf("Enter the max value m and n\n");
        scanf("%d%d", &m,&n);
        for(i=1;i<=m;++i)
        for(j=1;j<=n;++j)
        {
                a[i][j] = i * j;
```

```
        }
        printf("The matrix is\n");
        for (j=1 ; j<=m; ++j)
        {
                for (i=1; i<=n; ++i)
                printf ("%d  ", a [i][j];)
                printf ("\n");
        }
}
```

In this program a matrix of specific order has been developed as below :

$$a = \begin{matrix} 1 & 2 & 3 & 4 \\ 2 & 4 & 6 & 8 \\ 3 & 6 & 9 & 12 \\ 4 & 8 & 12 & 16 \end{matrix}$$

Every element of the matrix consists of multiplication of row and coloumn number.

EXERCISE

1. Write a program to find largest or smallest number in given array.
2. Write a program to calculate average of given numbers using arrays and to calculate variance.
3. Write a program to obtain sum of the diagonal elements of a matrix.
4. Write a program to multiply single dimensional array by a scalar.

$$\begin{bmatrix} a_{11} & a_{12} & a_{13} \\ a_{21} & a_{22} & a_{23} \\ a_{31} & a_{32} & a_{33} \end{bmatrix}$$

The diagonal elements are the elements of matrix where column number is equal to row number such as a_{11}, a_{22}, a_{23}.

5. Write a program to obtain multiplication of two matrices.
6. Write a program to compute the value of 'c' array generated by using 'a' and 'b' arrays of order 'n'.

$$C = \sum_{i=1}^{n} (A_i - B_i)^2$$

7. Write a program to obtain determinant of 2×2 matrix.

$$|A| = \begin{bmatrix} a_{11} & a_{12} \\ a_{21} & a_{22} \end{bmatrix}$$

8. Write a program to find all prime numbers upto 100. A prime number is a number not divisible by any other number.
9. Write a program to separate all the digits of a five digit number.
10. Write a program to find sum of all individual rows and coloumns of 5×5 matrix.
11. Write a program to indicate whether the given matrix is symmetrical or not.

12. Write a program to print a given 5 digit number in the reverse order.
13. Write a program to find the values of 'b' matrix such that after addition to 'a' matrix all diagonal elements of 'a' matrix becomes zero.
14. Write a program to reverse the array of given numbers.
15. Write a program to calculate norm of a matrix which is sum of squares of all elements of matrix.
16. Write a program to multiply a 2–D matrix by a scalar number.
17. Write a program to find a negative number in a matrix and print its location.
18. Write a program to find the largest number in a 2–D array with its row and column number.
19. Write a program to calculate sum of individual digits of 3 digit number consider 312 number whose sum of individual digit number is sum = 3+1+2 = 6
20. Write a program to interchange the rows of 2–D matrix of 3×3 order. The exchange of rows occurs between 1 to 2, 2 to 3 and 3 to 1.
21. Create a two dimensional array (size 10 × 10). Fill this two dimensional array with the values from the first single dimensional array. Determine the maximum of each column. Display the two-dimensional array and the maximum of each column.
22. Repeat number 21, but this time instead of a 10 × 10 array, prompt the user for the size of the rows and columns.

11
CHARACTER ARRAY

AN OVERVIEW

In the previous unit you have studied the numeric array which is capable of storing the numeric values. The numeric array can store integer, float, double values depending on the declaration of the variable. The values are stored by using indexes and called by using indexes. The 2-D numeric arrays are very useful in storing the values in the matrix form and provides better storage of values.

UNIT OBJECTIVES

After completing this unit you will be able to:

* Write declaration of char array variable
* Identify various types of methods for supply of values to char array.
* Discuss methods of printing of char array variable
* Define two dimensional char array variable
* Demonstrate storage in 2-D char array variable
* Explain character arrays.

11.1 SINGLE DIMENSIONAL ARRAY

The single dimensional array variable is a variable in which the characters are stored in one dimension. All the characters of the array are stored in memory available in columns. Every element of the array can be retrieved by indicating location number or index of the memory.

11.1.1 Declaration of array

Before using an array it must be declared in the initial stage by a char variable type and the maximum memory required for the array.

The general form in which they are declared is

```
char y [z];
```

where,

y – indicates the name of variable as usual to normal variable.
z – maximum no. of memories required for the variable.

Ex :

```
char a[10];
```

The above declaration creates memory spaces of char type for storing the 10 values, of "a" variable.

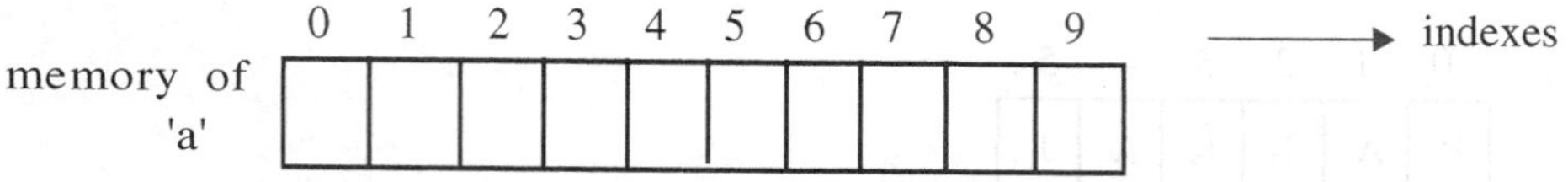

The memory of 'a' consist of 10 spaces and are indexed by a number for different memory location from 0 to 9.

11.1.2 Supply of values to array variable

After declaration of array, the values of the array variables are supplied in the memory by following three methods :

(a) Arithmetic statement. (b) 'scanf' statement. (c) By declaration

(a) Arithmetic Statement

The values of the array variable can be supplied in the memory by use of the arithmetic statement.

Ex :

```
a [0] = 'A';
a [1] = 'B';
a [2] = 'C';
```

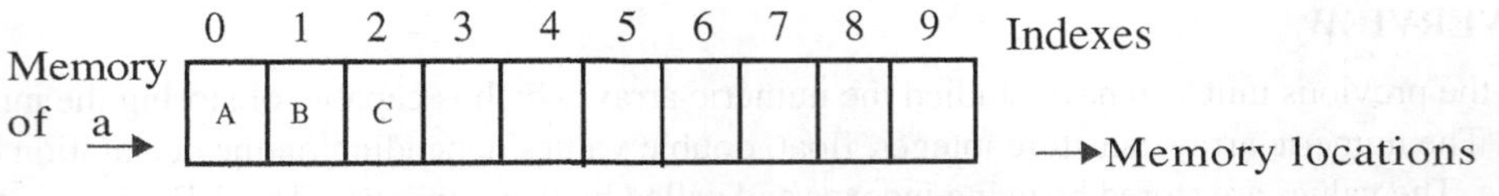

In this case, the memories are filled by using arithmetic statement.

The above statements are the arithmetic statement where value of 'a' variable is stored under different memory locations indicated by the index number in the rectangular bracket to represent the memory location.

(b) "scanf" statement

The values of the array variable can be supplied by a 'scanf' statement. In this case, any general value of array can be supplied in the program through the data screen. The array is entered by using "scanf" statement in the ' for' loop.

Ex :

```
for (i=0; i<6; ++i)
{
        scanf ("%c", &a[i ]);
}
```

In the above statement ' i' value starts from 0 and ends at 5. It reads 6 values 'a' variable. These five data values can be supplied on the data screen as

PANKAJ

They are filled in the memory as

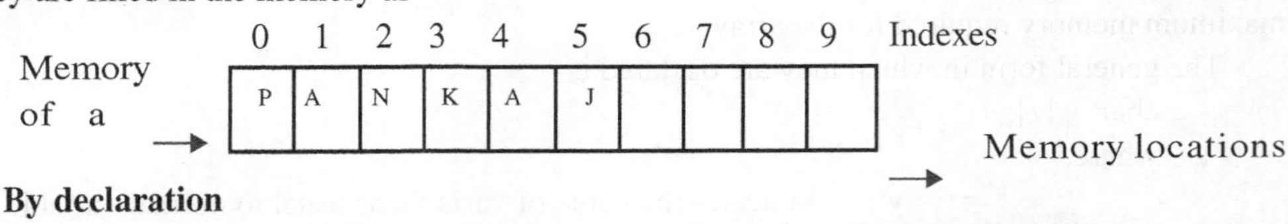

(c) By declaration

The array can be supplied values directly at the time of its declaration as below :

```
int a[5] = {'P','A','N','K','A','J'};
```

In this case, the characters of array is supplied at the point of declaration and the 6 characters are supplied as

a[0] = P, a[1] = A, a[2] = N, a[3] = K, a[4] = A, a[5] = J

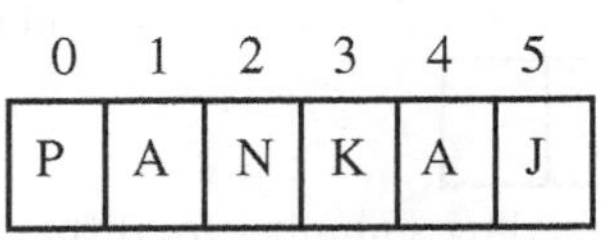

11.1.3 Printing of array variable

The values of array variable can be printed by using "printf" statement and '%c' format in the `for' loop.

Ex:

```
(i)  for (i=0; i<6; ++i)
        {
                printf(" %c",a[i])
        }
     PANKAJ
```

Program 11–1

The single dimensional char array is similar to a numeric array. This array is capable of storing the characters like name of person which consist of characters. This Programs prints a name which has been scanned by the computer.

```
/* to print a name using char array */
main()
{
    char w [100];
    int i,m;
    printf (" enter the value of maximum characters\n");
    scanf ("%d", &m);
    printf( "enter a word\n");
    for (i =0; i<=m; ++i)
    {
            scanf(" %c",&w[i]);
    }
    for (i =0; i<= m; ++i)
    {
            printf( "%c", w[i]);
    }
}
```

Input	:	enter the value of maximum characters 5 enter a word smita
Output	:	smita

11.2 CHARACTER MATRIX

A 2–D char array is a character matrix which stores a string of characters in every row. It means a line of page can be one row of character matrix and every column of line accepts one character. Therefore, a page can be generated in memory using a char matrix by a program.

It is declared as :

```
char a[10][10];
```

0	0	1	2	3	4	5	6	7	8	9
1	S	A	N	J	A	Y				
2	V	I	J	A	Y					
3	S	U	R	E	S	H				
4	R	A	M	E	S	H				
5										
6										
7										
8										
9										

A 2–D array created by a name 'a' with 10 rows × 10 columns counted from 0 to 10. In every row, 10 characters can be stored in columns.

It can be 'scanned' or supplied by using the following method:

```
for (i=0; i<10; ++ i)
{
for (j = 0; j<10; ++ j)
{
        scanf("%c",&a[i][j]);
}
}
```

The char matrix can be printed by using the following method

```
for(i=0; i<10; ++i)
{
for(j=0; j<10; ++j)
{
printf("%c", a[i][j];
}
}
```

The characters are stored in the char matrix by using 'scanf' operation in the 'nested for' statement. The names of persons can be supplied as character from data screen. These are printed by using `nested for' statement to print characters through `%c' format.

Program 11–2

```
/* character matrix */
main()
{
    char a[120][30];
    int i,j,m;
    printf ("enter the order\n");
    scanf ("d", &m);
    for (i=1; i<=m; ++i)
```

```
    {
        printf (" enter name for roll number %d\n ,i);
        {
            for (j=0; j<=15; ++j)
            scanf ("%c", &a[i][j];
        }
    }
    printf("the roll no. & names of the students are\n");
    for ( i=1; i<=m; ++i)
    {
        printf(" the roll number is %d\n", i);
        {
            for (j=0; j<=15; ++j)
            printf ("%c", a[i][j]);
        }
    }
}
```

Input	:	enter the order 2 enter the name for roll number 1 shital enter the name for roll number 2 anita
Output	:	the roll no. & name of the students are the roll number is 1 shital the roll number is 2 anita

In this program, a roll list of students is prepared by using char matrix. The names of students are scanned and placed in rows of matrix. These row numbers are used for giving roll numbers to the students name. Then the roll list is printed alongwith roll number.

11.3 INITIALIZATION OF THE CHAR ARRAY

The character array can be initialized by declaration of array and by supplying all characters of array at the time of declaration. The maximum number of elements can be supplied or may be allowed to be calculated by the compiler.

Example :

In case of char arrays, the string 'Hello !' can be supplied by using 'static' statements or by automatic statement at the time of its declaration.

```
char word [] = {'H', 'e', 'l', 'l','o', '!'};
                or
char  word[6]  =  {'H',  'e',  'l',  'l', 'o',  '!'};
```

These types of the statements are used when the char array receives a word or a string is fixed in the program and does not become input to the program.

The char variable is used in the program for very useful work of supplying name, address, department, area no., consumer no., etc. These data values are processed and stored in the memory. They can be retrived from the memory or can be utilized for decision making process.

11.4 NULL CHARACTERS

In the 'C' language, the special character that is used to signal the end of a string is known as the 'null character', and is written as '\0'.

The null character is a terminating blank space of string which means it is an end of the string. A word of English language terminates when blank space occurs whereas a string of C–language can contain a blank character and the blank character which terminates the string is a null character. In other words it is a terminating blank of the string.

Ex : The word 'Hello!' can be supplied with null character.

```
char word [] = {'H','e','l','l','o','!','\0'};
```

In this case the 'Hello!' string is terminated by null character means the string ends by a blank space.

11.5 ALTERNATE METHOD OF SUPPLYING THE STRING

The initialization of string 'Hello !' was made earlier using

```
char word[]={'H','e','l','l','o','!','\0'};
```

This initialization can also be made by

```
char word [] = {"Hello!"};
```

Both statements are equivalent and null is automatically available in second statement.

Therefore, any string inserted in " " is treated to be a string of C–Language terminated by a null character.

11.6 INPUT/OUTPUT FORMATS FOR STRINGS

The scanning and printing of characters done by using %c format is tedious and difficult for data entry. The counting of characters is necessary if a string is to be supplied to an array. To avoid the problem of data entry "%s" format is used.

The string can be read or printed by using %s format character.

It can be written as :

```
scanf ("%s", sa);
```

sa is a char array which receives characters from the user screen or data screen. The string is supplied on screen and when the blank space appears the string is terminated. This format is used for scaning of one word of English language from the user screen.

```
printf("%s", sa);
```

Where, sa is the char array containing string which can be directly printed on result screen through '%s' format.

Program 11-3

```
/* program for scanning and printing of string */
main ()
{
    char s1[81], s2[81], s3[81];
    printf ("enter three string text : \n");
    scanf ("%s %s %s", s1, s2, s3);
    printf ("s1 = %s\ns2 = %s\nS3 = %s\n," s1,s2,s3);
}
```

Input	:	enter three string text :
		Anita Vanita Sunita
Output	:	s1=Anita
		s2=Vanita
		s3=Sunita

In this program three strings s1, s2, s3 can be read and printed on the output screen.

11.7 DECLARATION OF 2-D CHAR ARRAY

The 2-D char array can be declared and supplied with number of strings using declaration and supply of strings at the same time. It can be declared as :

```
char c[3] [6] = {"Suresh", "ramesh", "smita"};
```

This indicates that c is a 2-D char array having memory of 6 characters each and 3 strings are supplied where;

c[0] string is Suresh
c[1] string is ramesh
c[2] string is smita

Every string is stored in a single row or line and receives the row number.

11.8 SCANNING OF 2-D CHAR ARRAY

The 2-D char array is capable of storing number of strings and the strings could be supplied to the char array using scanf statement. The scanning of 2-D char array allows supply of any string to the program. The scanf statement utilizes %s format for scanning of char array and the rows are varied using a 'for' statement.

```
for(i=0; i<3; ++i)
        scanf("%s", c[i]);
```

where

c is a 2-D char array

In this case , the rows are varied from 0 to 2 and three strings are read by using 'scanf' statement with %s format.

11.9 CHARACTER & ASCII VALUES

The operation on the character is important in all variety of the software because the data is supplied to all the software and is stored or retrieved by using the character operation.

Any character of the keyboard can be made character of the C–language by placing the character in a right sided single quotes.The value of a char variable is supplied through an assignment statement by placing the character in single quote.

```
c = 'x';
```

Every character of the keyboard has an ASCII value which may be represented by its number. The char variable which receives a value can be printed by using "%c" format.But if the value of char variable is printed by using "%d" format then the ASCII number would be printed by the variable.

Program 11–4

In this program the values of character which represent the ASCII number and the given characters are printed using "%c %d" format.

```
/* PROGRAM ON ASCII CODES AND NUMBERS*/
main()
{
    char c;int i;
    c='A';
    printf (" %d  %c \n",c,c);
    for(i=1;i<=255;++i)
```

```
{
        printf(" %d  %c \n",i,i);
        getch();
    }
}
```

Program 11–5

This program prints the value of various ASCII numbers and their characters.

```
/* PROGRAM ON ASCII CODES AND NUMBERS*/
main()
{
    int a;
    for(a=0;a<=255;a++)
    printf("%c   %d  ",a,a);
}
```

Program 11–6

This program produces a smiling face on the screen by printing of the character at code 1.

```
/* smiling face on the screen*/
main()
{
    char c;int i;
    c=1;
    for(i=1;i<=50;++i)
    {
        printf("  %c ",c);
        getch();
    }
}
```

EXERCISE

1. Write a program to arrange five given characters in alphabetical order.
2. Write a program to scan names of different persons and arrange these names in alphabetical order.
3. Write a program to arrange characters in a word in alphabetical order.
4. Write a program for reversing of a string.
5. Write a program to seperate alphabets of string.
6. Write a program to accept a sentence consisting of 'n' words.
7. Write a program to arrange the alphabets in a string in alphabetical order.
8. Write a program to locate an alphabet in a string and its location number.
9. Write a program to count number of words in a sentence.
10. Write a program to print characters A, B, C

    A B C

    C B A

    B A C
11. Write a program to obtain a sub-string from a large string
    (*i*) 'Me' from 'Meet'
    (*ii*) 'Gain' from 'Against'
    (*iii*) 'Vices' from 'Services'

12
FUNCTION PROGRAM

AN OVERVIEW

In the previous unit we have seen the treatment of character array of single and two dimensional type.The character arrays are utilized for storage of strings and a string in c-language consists of bunch of characters or bunch of words of English language. The character arrays are utilized for storage of name, roll no, address,code etc.The two dimensional char array are capable of storing number of strings in the different rows.The two dimensional char array are very useful in enumeration of strings.

In this unit you will be studying the concept of functions programs and their applications to the programming. There are different types of function used in the programming. The function programs are the sub programs which perform certain type of function to assist the main program. The use of the function program is necessary because repetitive type of function is performed by the functions programs when they are called by the main program.

OBJECTIVES

After completing this unit you will be able to

* Explain functions programs.
* Demonstrate the use function program.
* Develop the call of a function program.
* Describe function program.
* Study various types of function programs.

12.1 INTRODUCTION

The function program is a small program used as sub-program. If there are repetitive calculations or set of calculations to be computed in the main program, then the function programs are used. These are sub-programs used for the main program. As we indicate the main program by name " main ()", similarly the function program can be named by any desired name.

The function programs perform a variety of functions which are required in the main program. These function programs are written outside the main program and they are named by the desired name. The function program also uses similar statements which are used in the main program.These function programs are called in the main program by giving a call to a function program.

Every file contains one main program and it can use any number of function programs for a set of calculations by different names. But two function programs with the same name cannot appear in the file.The function programs are supplied with the input values using the arguments of fuction program and the calculated result may be supplied to the main program or printed by the function program. Sometimes, they may be displaying the graphic output or image in the program.

12.2 CONCEPT OF FUNCTION PROGRAM

The function programs are the sub programs assisting the main program. The function programs are the programs written out of main program placed either below or above main program.The function program perform the described function and to perform the function they are called in the main program or may be called by other function programs.The function program can be written by any name as similar to a variable name.Every file contains one main program and large number of functions programs.The main program is executed initially by compiler and incase if the call is made to the function programs they will be executed in sequence.

The concept of a function program is just similar to a situation of a company in which the general manager acts as a main person to organize the working of the company.The general manager utilizes functional managers as production manager, account officer, personal manager and stores officers to perform the given work.The work of a production manager is to manage the production, the account officers maintains the account , personal manager maintains the records of employees where as the stores officers maintain the inventory in store.In order to operate the company smoothly the general manager gets the work done through these officers to perform the given work by calling these officers and co-ordinating them to perform the given work.

12.3 USE OF FUNCTION PROGRAM

The function program can be written below or above main program and can be named similar to a variable name. The function program name can be written and preceded by () as similar to the main program. The body of function program containing number of statement can be enclosed in a { }. The function program can be called in the main program any number of times and any place in the main program.

```
f()
{
        -----;
        -----;
}
main()
{
        f();
        f();
        ------;
        f();
        ------;
}
```

In this case f is a function program which is declared by f() and this function program contains number of statements.The function program is called in the main program three times to perform the given function.

The following program shows the utilization of function program.

12.4 PROCEDURE OF WRITING FUNCTION PROGRAM

The function programs are normally written in the initial stages of file and main program is written at the end. When the function is called for the output values to be calculated by function program, then the input values can be supplied in the main program through arguments.

The following program shows the function program which prints a comment.

Program 12–1

```
/* this is a sub-program for printing a sentence */
print_c()
{
    printf (" programing in "C" is very interesting \n");
}
main ()
{
    print_c();
    print_c();
}
```

Output	:	programming in 'C' is very interesting programming in 'C' is very interesting

In this program 'print_c' function program prints a 'comment' and is called in the main program twice to print the comment two times.

12.5 TYPES OF FUNCTION PROGRAMS

There are three ways of writing function programs :

1. Non-returnable function program.
2. Returnable function program.
3. Input/Output argument function program.
4. 'void' function.
5. Recursive function.

In a function program normally input values are supplied through arguments. These input values or variables are supplied in the main program when a call is given to function program. The function program can be written in three ways as given below:

12.5.1 NON-RETURNABLE FUNCTION PROGRAM

In this function program, the input values to the program are supplied through argument and output variables are printed immediately in the following program.

This program computes values of c using function program which is multiplication of a & b.

Initially p and q are input to the program, which are supplied in the main program and a call is given to function program. The function program is executed and value of 'c' is calculated and printed in function program. Then the value of r and s are calculated and again a call is given to function program using r and s as arguments which are substituted in a and b variables of function.

The a and b are variables as argument of function program, hence they must be declared immediately after writing the name of function program because they are the external variables as their values are obtained from outside the function program.

Program 12–2

```
/* to calculate value of C */
compute (a,b)
float a, b;
{
    float c;
    c = a * b;
    printf (" a= %g b= %g\n", a,b);
    printf (" c= %g", c);
}
main()
{
    float p,q,r,s;
    printf (" enter the values of a & b\n");
    scanf ( "%f %f", &p &q);
    printf ( " p=%f q=%f\n, p,q);
    compute (p, q);
    r = p + 2,0   s = q + 3,0;
    compute(r,s);
}
```

Input	:	enter the values of a & b 2 3
Output	:	p=2.000000 q=3.000000 a=2 b=3 c=6 a=4 b=6 c=24

12.5.2 Returnable function program

This function program returns a value output variable to the main program.This function program is capable of returning a single value to the main program.

Program 12–3

```
float compute (a,b)
float a,b;
{
    float c;
    c = a*b;
    return(c);
}
main ()
{
    float p,q,r,s,z;
    printf("Enter the values of a & b\n");
    scanf("%f %f", &p, &q);
    z = compute (p,q);
    printf("c = %g\n", z);
    r = p + 2.0; s = q + 3.0;
    z = compute (r,s);
    printf("c = %g\n", z);
}
```

Input	:	Enter the values of a & b 2 3
Output	:	c=6 c=24

In this function program, a and b are supplied from outside as argument and the program calculates value of c, which is returned to the main program by a 'return (c)' statement. This function program calculates a single value and returns to main program, since this value is a floating value. The program is declared as 'float' 'compute (a,b)'.

In the main program, p & q are supplied and a call is given to function program by its name 'compute (p,q)'. The p,q are the arguments of a function program in the call of function program by main program. The values of p,q are substituted in a & b variable of function program. This function call returns a value of 'c' to the main program, which is obtained by 'z' variable. Then value of r & s are calculated and a call is given to function program using r, s as argument, which returns value of c substituted again in 'z' variable and this value is printed.

12.5.3 Input/Output argument function program

This program uses input variables and output variables as an argument of function program. The input variables are supplied as an argument and the output variables are calculated in the function program and they are returned to the main program through the output arguments.

Program 12–4

```
compute(a,b,c)
float a[10],b[10],c[10];
{
     c[1] = a[1]*b[1];
}
main ()
{
     float p[10],q[10],r[10],s[10],z[10];
     printf("Enter the values of p & q\n");
     scanf("%f%f",&p[1], &q[1]);
     compute(p,q,z);
     printf("c = %g\n", z[1]);
     r[1] = p[1] + 2.0 ;
     s[1] = q[1] + 3.0;
     compute(r,s,z);
     printf("c = %g\n", z[1]);
}
```

Input	:	Enter the values of p & q 3 3
Output	:	c=9 c=30

In this case, the function program has three arguments a,b,c. Where a & b are input arguments which receive the value from the main program and c is output argument which receives values calculated by function program and returns this value to the main program.

In the main program, the p and q are supplied. A call is given to function program with input values p, q and output variable z which is substituted in a and b. The c value calculated in function program is substituted in z in main program. Again r and s are calculated and function call is given, then 'r' and 's' are substituted in a and b. The value of c is calculated by function program and placed in z variable of main program. But in this case all the variables must be array variables.

Program 12–5

This program calculates the value of the factorial of any given number.

```
/* to calculate factorial */
long int fact (n)
int n;
{
     int i;long int fac;
     fac=1;
     for (i=1; i<=n; ++i)
     fac = fac * i;
     return (fac);
}
```

```
main()
{
    int n;
    long int z;
    printf ("enter the value\n");
    scanf ( "%d", &n);
    z = fact(n);
    printf ( " the factorial %d is %ld\n", n,z);
}
```

Input	:	enter the value 3
Output	:	the factorial 3 is 6

This is a returnable function program which returns a value to the main program.This program is utilized to calculate the value of factorial of the given number. In this program the value of the factorial is returned by function program to the main program.

Program 12–6

This program calculates sum of series

$$s = 1 + \frac{1}{2!} + \frac{1}{3!} + \frac{1}{4!} \ldots\ldots \text{ n terms.}$$

```
/* to calculate sum of series */
long int fact (n)
int n;
{
    int i;long int fac;
    for (i=1; i<=n; ++i)
    fac = fac * i;
    return (fac);
}
main()
{
    int m,j,n;
    float sum;
    printf (" enter the number of terms \n");
    scanf ("%d", &m);
    sum=1.0;
    for ( j=1; j<=m; ++j)
    {
        sum=(float) (sum + (1.0/fact(j)));
    }
    printf ("sum of the series is %g", sum);
}
```

Input	:	enter the number of terms 2
Output	:	sum of the series is 0.999999

In this program, the value of sum of the series is calculated. The series involves addition of reciprocal of factorial of the number of that term. For this purpose a call is given to the function program which calculates the factorial and then by supplying input everytime the ouput is calculated by calling the function program.This program uses 'fact(n)' function program to evaluate sum of series.

Program 12–7

This program finds the minimum value in an array of given numbers.

```
/* to find minimum value in an  array */
mini_value (array, n)
int array [],n;
{
    int  min , i, l;
    min = array [0];
    for ( i=1, i<=n; ++i)
    {
            if (array [i] < min)
            {
                    min = array [i];
                    l = i;
            }
    }
    printf ("minimum value is %d at %d location\n, min, l);
}
main ()
{
    int array [100], n, j,minimum ,1;
    printf (" enter the number of variables \n");
    scanf ("%d" &n);
    printf (" enter the values of variables \n");
    for ( j=0; j<=n; ++j)
    {
            scanf ("%d", array [j]);
    }
    mini_value (array, n);
}
```

Input	:	enter the number of variables 4 enter the values of variables 3 5 2 7
Output	:	minimum value is 2 at 3 location

In this program, an array is scanned and entered in the program. Then a call is given to the function program to calculate minimum value in the array and it is printed in function program.

Program 12–8

This program calculates whether a given number is divisible by 3 or not.

```
/* program on number divisible by 3*/
divisible(x)
int x;
{
    int rem;
    rem = x%3;
    if (rem==0)
        printf("The number is divisible by 3\n");
    else
        printf("The number is not divisible by 3\n");
}
main()
{
    int y,x;
    printf("Enter your number\n");
    scanf("%d",&y);
    divisible(x);
}
```

Input	:	Enter your number 12
Output	:	The number is divisible by 3

In this program, the main program accepts a variable value 'y' and gives a call to a function program 'divisible' which finds whether the given number is divisible by 3 or not and the printing is done by the function program.

Program 12–9

In function program of Input/Output argument type the input argument can be utilized as an output argument. The input values are passed to the function program by use of the array and the array is modified. This array will be returned to the main program by use of the same argument.

```
/* function program on Input/output argument */
main()
{
    int i;
    int a[5]={2,9,3,7,4};
    multiply(a);
    for(i=0;i<5;++i)
    {
        printf("%d\t",a[i]);
    }
}
```

```
multiply(a)
int a[5];
{
      int i;
      for(i=0;i<5;++i)
      a[i]=a[i]*2;
}
```

Output :	4	18	6	14	8

In the above program a function program 'multiply ' is used by the main program to multiply all elements of the array.In the main program the array 'a' is supplied and the function program 'multiply' is called in the main program. This function program receives 'a' as input argument and all the elements of array are multiplied by 2. This array is returned to the main program and printed by the main program.

Program 12–10

In this program, the main program plays a role like a Manager of a Company. In a company the manager calls different persons to perform a particular type of activity or function and gets the work done from them.Similarly, the main program becomes a manager of the file and plays a role of calling different function programs for performing a particular type of the function.

```
/*Main as function operating program */
/*program on operation of main program as function operating program */
re(x)
int x[20];
{
      int i;
      for(i=1;i<=5;++i)
      scanf("%d",&x[i]);
}
add(x,y,z)
int x[20],y[20],z[20];
{
      int i;
      for(i=1;i<=5;++i)
      z[i]=x[i]+y[i];
}
subtract(x,y,z)
int x[20],y[20],z[20];
{
      int i;
      for(i=1;i<=5;++i)
      z[i]=x[i]-y[i];
}
pr(x)
int x[20];
{
```

```
    int i;
    printf("\n");
    for(i=1;i<=5;++i)
    printf(" %d\t",x[i]);
}
main()
{
    int a[20],b[20],c[20],d[20];
    clrscr();
    printf("\n enter five elements of a array\n");
    re(a);
    printf("\n enter five elements of b array\n");
    re(b);
    add(a,b,c);
    subtract(a,b,d);
    printf("\nThe five elements of a array are\n");
    pr(a);
    printf("\nThe five elements of b array are\n");
    pr(b);
    printf("\nThe five elements of c array are\n");
    pr(c);
    printf("\nThe five elements of d array are\n");
    pr(d);
}
```

Input	:	enter five elements of 'a' array 1 2 3 4 5 enter five elements of ,b, array 5 4 3 2 1
Output	:	The five elements of 'a' array are 1 2 3 4 5 The five elements of 'b' array are 5 4 3 2 1 The five elements of 'c' array are 6 6 6 6 6 The five elements of 'd' array are –4 –2 0 2 4

In this program, the main program simply gives call to different function programs and they perform the required function and call can be given to them as many times as it is required in the main program. The main program gives a call to a function program 're' to read the array 'a'. The 're' function program is assigned with a work of reading only an array. Then it is again called to read 'b'. Then a call is given to a function program 'add' which does the work of addition of elements of array 'a' and 'b' to obtain 'c'. Then a call is given to a 'subtract' function which does subtraction between elements 'a' and 'b' to obtain 'd'. Then a 'pr' function is called four times to print value 'a','b','c' & 'd' arrays.

Therfore the main program only calls function program as many times as it is required and obtains the work from these function programs.

12.5.4 'void' function

A function declaration is made by a word 'void'. A function declaration that is preceded by the keyword 'void' explicitly informs the compiler that the function does not return a value.

The general form is

void x (y1,y2,y3);

where,

x	–	function name
y1,y2,y3	–	argument of the function.

Ex :

void cal (int a,int b,int c);

The void functions are non-returnable functions, which can be declared in the main program if the function program is written below main program.

Program 12–11

```
/* void declaration of function */
main()
{
      void compute(int ,int);
       int a=2,b=3;
     compute(a,b);
}
void compute(int x , int y)
{
     int c;
     c= x*y;
     printf("C=%d\n",c);
}
```

Output : C = 6

This is a non-returnable function program 'compute' of void type. This function program is declared as void function program in the main program having two varieties of integer argument.

12.5.5 Recursive function

In this function, the function itself can be called in that function i.e. the function uses its own function to make repetitive calculations. The recursive function gives call to itself in its own area by modification of its own argument. This is seen in the following example of factorial of a number .

6! = 6. 5!

6! = 6.5.4!

6! = 6.5.4.3.2.1 0!

In this case of the factorial of a number 6, the factorial is calulated by multiplying the same function with the reduction in the argument value.As factorial 6 is 6 multiplied with factorial of 5, this process of creating recursion of the argument by reducing its value is continued till the factorial of 0 is calculated. Then the recursive process of factorial stops because the factorial of negative quantity is 0 and this becomes a termination point.

Then the recursive function can be written as:

factorial(n) = n × factorial(n–1)

The following program explains the recursive function.

Program 12–12

```
/* Recursive function to calculate the factorial of a positive integer */
long int factorial(n)
int n;
{
    long int result;
    if (n = = 0)
            result = 1;
    else
            result = n * factorial ( n – 1);
    return(result);
}
main ()
{
    int j;
    printf("enter your number \n");
    scanf("%d",&j);
    printf ("% d! = %ld\n", j, factorial(j));
}
```

Input	:	enter your number 4
Output	:	4!=24

In this function program, the recursive function is used to find the factorial of a number. The main program gives a call to a function program 'factorial' and supplies an input through the argument. The recursive function checks the value of 'n' and if it is not equal to n, then the 'result' is calculated by multiplying 'n' with the call of 'factorial' function having new argument as 'n–1'. Therefore, a call of the function program is made by reducing the value of argument by 1. This process continues in recursion and in every cycle the call is given to a function program by reducing its argument till the value of argument reaches to 0.If the value of n becomes 0, then the recursion stops and the complete 'answer' of all such cycles is a factorial of the number.

Program 12–13

```
/* Recursive function to calculate power of any number*/
int mypower(int x, int n) {
  if (n == 0) {
    return 1;
  }
  else {
    return x * mypower(x, n–1);
  }
}
main(){
  printf("recursive power is %d", mypower(2, 10));
}
```

12.6 FUNCTION DECLARATION

In case if the function program is written below 'main' program then it is necessary to declare the function program in the 'main' program according to the nature of function program means if the function program is returnable then it is declared by type of 'return' value otherwise it should be a 'void' function program. The declarations of functions are the advanced intimations for the nature of function and the number of arguments as well as the name of function written below the 'main' program.

Program 12–14

```
/* to calculate value of C */
main()
{
    float p, q, r, s;
    void compute(int,int);
    printf (" enter the values of a & b\n");
    scanf ( "%f %f", &p &q);
    printf ( " p=%f q=%f\n, p,q);
    compute (p, q);
    r = p + 2,0   s = q + 3,0;
    compute(r,s);
}
void compute (a,b)
float a, b;
{
    float c;
    c = a *  b;
    printf (" a= %g b= %g\n", a,b);
    printf (" c= %g", c);
}
```

Input	:	enter the values of a & b 23
Output	:	p=2.000000 q=3.000000 a=2 b=3 c=6 a=4 b=6 c=24

In this function program the 'compute' function program is a 'void' function program and the function program is declared in the 'main' program. This function program is written below the 'main' program. Therefore, it becomes necessary to declare the function program in the 'main' program as advanced intimation of function program.

Program 12–14

```
main ()
{
    float p,q,r,s,z;
    float compute(float,float);
    printf("Enter the values of a & b\n");
    scanf("%f %f", &p, &q);
```

```
        z = compute (p,q);
        printf("c = %g\n", z);
        r = p + 2.0; s = q + 3.0;
        z = compute (r,s);
        printf("c = %g\n", z);
}
float compute (a,b)
float a,b;
{
        float c;
        c = a*b;
        return(c);
}
```

Input	:	Enter the values of a & b 2 3
Output	:	c=6 c=24

In this program the returnable function program is used to return a value to 'main' program. But the function program is written below 'main' program. Therefore, it must be declared in the 'main' program as an advance intimation to the 'main' program. The function program is declared by a 'float' word because it is a returnable function program.

12.7 ARRAY AS AN ARGUMENT OF FUNCTION PROGRAM

If an array variable becomes argument of a function program then the whole array is passed to a function program. This means if the array contains 10 elements then all the elements are passed to function program by making array to be argument of function program. This process of passing an array to a function program when a call is given is called 'call by reference'. The advantage of this process is to pass the multiple values to the function program.

It is possible to send a single element of the array to a function program. This results in sending a single value to a function program. The modification on this value is possible. This process is known as 'call by value'.

If a array is made to be an argument of a function program as an input argument and output argument. In such a case the array is passed on to the function program and the array is modified and returned to the function program. This function program has already been explained as input/output argument function program.

Program 12–15

```
/* Array as an argument of function program passed by reference */
sum_array(a,n)
int a[5],n;
{
        int i;
        int sum=0;
        for(i=0;i<5;++i)
        {
```

```
        sum = sum + a[i];
        }
        clrscr();
        printf("Sum = %d",sum);
}
main()
{
        int i;
        int a[5] = {1,2,3,4,5};
        sum_array(a,5);
}
```

Output :	Sum = 15

In this function program, the 'call by reference' system is used in which the complete array 'a' has been made as an argument of function program. The function program receives the array and the sum of the all elements of the array is calculated by function program. This situation provides number of elements of array to be transferred to the function program.

Program 12–16

```
/* Array as an argument of function program call by value */
int sum=0;
sum_array(b)
int b;
{
        sum = sum + b;
}
main()
{
        int a[5] = {1,2,3,4,5};
        int i;
        for(i=0;i<5;++i)
        {
                sum_array(a[i]);
        }
        printf("Sum = %d\n",sum);
}
```

Output	:	Sum = 15

In this program the array is declared in the main program and single element of array is passed to the function program and the element of array is captured by a normal variable of the function program. Therefore, the sum of all elements is calculated by passing the individual elements to the function program which is called 5 times. This situation is 'call by value'. The sum of all elements is calculated by using global variable 'sum' which is explained in the next chapter.

Program 12–17

```
/* Array as an input / output argument of function program */
```

```
sum_array(a,n)
int a[5],n;
{
      int i;
      for(i=0;i<n;++i)
      {
              a[i] = a[i] * 3;
      }
}
main()
{
      int a[5] = {1,2,3,4,5};
    . int i,n=5;
      sum_array(a,n);
      clrscr();
      for(i=0;i<n;++i)
      {
              printf("%d\t",a[i]);
      }
}
```

Output : 3 6 9 12 15

In this program, the array becomes the argument of a function program and it is passed from 'main' program to function program. Every element of the array is multiplied by factor of 3 and is returned to the 'main' program as an output argument. In this situation all the elements of array are modified and automatically returned to the 'main' program.

12.8 NESTING OF FUNCTIONS

In the nesting of functions the functions are called to each other and also main program calls the functions. The call to the function programs can be in the following two structures :

1. Hierarchical call
2. Intermixed call

1. Hierarchical call

In this structure the 'main' program calls the function program and the function program calls another function program. Therefore, the hierarchical calls are made to different function programs in a sequential manner. The call of 'main' program goes to a function program and in turn it goes to another function program. The program 8–18 highlights the hierarchical calls to different function programs. The 'main' program calls 'min_max' program and the 'min_max' program calls the 'absolute' program to calculate absolute value of a number.

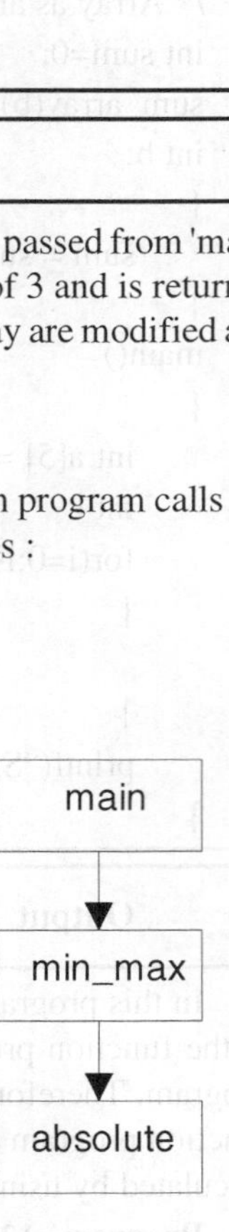

The fig. shows the Hierarchical call in which the main program calls min_max function program and that function program calls absolute function program.

Program 12–18

```
/* Program on Nesting of functions (hierarchical) */
main()
{
    int a,b,c;
    clrscr();
    printf("Enter the values of a and b \n");
    scanf("%d%d",&a,&b);
    c = min_max(a,b);
    printf("C = %d\n",c);
}
min_max(a,b)
int a,b;
{
    int z;
    z = a – b;
    z = absolute(z);
    return(z);
}
absolute(z)
int z;
{
    if(z<0)
            z = –z;
    return(z);
}
```

Input	:	Enter the values of a and b 2 3
Output	:	C = 1

2. Intermixed call :

In this case, any function program can call to each other according to the requirements. The function programs can call each other when ever it is required and the main program can also call any function program.

12.9 CHAR ARRAY AS AN ARGUMENT OF FUNCTION PROGRAM

As similar to a numeric array the char array can become argument of a function program. The character array is capable of storing a string and the string is passed to a function program through an array. This string can be received by a char array in the function program as an argument of function program.

In the following program, the char array is made to be an argument of function program and it is scanned by a function program. The argument of a function program is an output argument. The 'scan_char' function program scans an array and it is passed through a function program to the main program. This array is further passed to a function program 'print_char' as an input argument and it is printd by the 'print_char' function program.

Program 12–19

```
/* Program on char array as an argument of function program */
main()
{
    char c[10];
    scan_char(c);
    print_char(c);
}
scan_char(c)
char c[10];
{
    int i;
    clrscr();
    printf("Enter the string\n");
    for(i=0;i<10;++i)
    {
            scanf("%c",&c[i]);
    }
}
print_char(c)
char c[10];
{
    int i;
    printf("The string is\n");
    for(i=0;i<10;++i)
    {
            printf("%c",c[i]);
    }
}
```

Input	:	Enter the string Flower _
Output	:	The string is Flower _

12.10 FUNCTION PROGRAM NUMERICAL MATHEMATICAL TECHNIQUE

The function program in C–language can be utilized to create usermade functions by using numerical mathematical technique. This method indicates how a user can create his own function program for evaluating the regularly and frequently required usermade functions.

This calculates square root of the value by Newton Raphson method using function programs. This method utilizes the technique of trial and errors in a scientific manner to evaluate a square root of the function. The cycle is started by using a value of 'guess' variable as 1considering to be a square root of the number and then the value of 'guess' is improved in every cycle using the given procedure. The cycle is terminated if square of the 'guess' reaches to an accuracy of 1×10^{-5} for the given number.

This method is performed in the following manner:

step 1 : set the value of 'guess' to 1

step 2 : If $|guess^2 - x| < \varepsilon$,then proceed to step 4.

step 3 : set the value of 'guess' to (x/guess + guess)/2 and return to step 2

step4 : 'guess' is the approximation of the square root.

Where,

guess	–	guess value as a root of the x .
ε	–	accuracy of the true root desired as 1×10^{-5}
x	–	number whose root is to be calculated.

This process can be indicated by a flow chart as below :

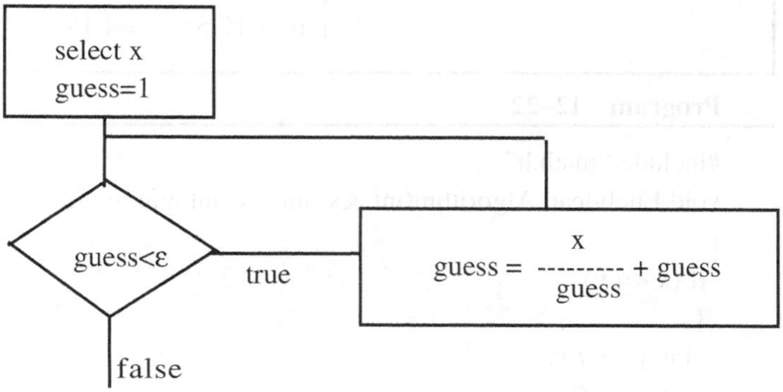

In this program, some value is initially guessed and if absolute value of difference of number and square of guess is below a desired accuracy then guess is root of the number. But if this condition is not satisfied in the beginning, then a new guess is calculated by given formula and again checking of 'guess' is done. This cycle should continue, so long as guess is not correct.

The program is as below :

Program 12–21

```
/*  function to calculate the square root of  a number */
float abs _value (x)
float x ;
{
    if (x<0)
            x = –x;
    return (x);
}
/* Function to compute square root of a number /*
float sq_root (X)
float x;
{
    float epsilon = 0.00001;
    float guess   = 1.0;
    while(abs_ value (guess * guess–x) >= epsilon)
                    guess=(x/guess + guess )/2.0;
```

```
    return(guess);
}
main ()
{
    printf ("sq_root (2.0)        = %g\n", sq_root (2.0));
    printf (" sq_root (144.0)     = %g\n", sq_root (144.0));
    printf (" sq_root (17.5)      = %g\n", sq_root (17.5));
}
```

Output : sq_root(2.0) =1.414216
sq_root(144.0) =12.000000
sq_root(17.5) =4.183300

Program 12–22

```
#include "math.h"
void Euclidean Algorithm(int &x, int &y, int &a, int &b, int &g)
{
 if (x <= y)
 {
  int q = y / x;
  int r = y % x;
  if (r == 0)
  {
   a = 1;
   b = 0;
   g = x;
  }
  else
  {
   int ap;
   Euclidean Algorithm(x, r, ap, b, g);
   // a = ap + b * q;
   a = b;
   a *= q;
   a += ap;
  }
 }
 else
 {
  int ap, bp;
  Euclidean Algorithm(y, x, bp, ap, g);
  // a = y - ap;
  a = y;
  a – = ap;
```

```
    // b = x - bp;
    b = x;
    b -= bp;
  }
}
/*
This function will fail in undefined ways if either x or y is zero.
*/
void Greatest Common Divisor (int &x, int &y, int &g)
{
 if (x <= y)
 {
   int r = y;
   r %= x;
   if (r == 0)
     g = x;
   else
     Greatest Common Divisor (x, r, g);
 }
 else
   Greatest Common Divisor (y, x, g);
}
int main(){
   int x1 = 180;
   int x2 = 420;
   int h, i;
   int r;
   Greatest Common Divisor (x1, x2, r);
   printf("GCD=%d\n", r);
   Euclidean Algorithm(x1, x2, h, i, r);
   printf("EA=%d\n", r);
}
```

EXERCISE

1. Prepare a program to print roll number and names of students using a character matrix.
2. Prepare a function program to calculate sum of series

$$\text{Sum} = 1 + \frac{1}{2!} + \frac{1}{3!} + \frac{1}{4!} + \ldots\ldots\ldots\ldots\ldots\ldots \text{n terms.}$$

3. Prepare a function program to print the minimum or maximum values in an array.
4. Prepare a function program to sort an array of integers into ascending order.
5. Prepare a function program to calculate value of x in a quadratic equation.
6. Write a function program to find smallest number in a matrix allocation of rows and columns in which element is available.
7. A function is defined as :

Cube (p,q,r) = $p^3 + q^3 + r^3$
use this function to evaluate

$$C = (u + 2.2)^3 + (v + 2.7)^3 + (\frac{1}{c} + (d - 3.9))^3$$

$$L = [s^3 + t^3] / [8.0 + [g^3 + h^3 + w^3]]$$

using a program.

8. Evaluate a funciton f(x) using function program :

$$f(x) = 7x^2 + 2x - 3 \quad \text{for} \quad x < 2.5$$
$$= 13.5x + 3 \quad \text{for} \quad x = 2.5$$
$$= -2x^2 + 6x - 2 \quad \text{for} \quad x > 2.5$$

9. For a set of 15 data points (x,y) write a program to compute the co-relation coefficient 'r' given by

$$r = \frac{n\,\Sigma xy - \Sigma x \,.\, \Sigma y}{(n\,\Sigma x^2 - \Sigma x^2)\,(n\Sigma y^2 - \Sigma y^2)}$$

where n is number of data points

10. Write a function program for addition of two matrices.

$$[c] = [a] + [b]$$

$$= \begin{bmatrix} a_{11} & a_{12} \\ a_{21} & a_{22} \end{bmatrix} + \begin{bmatrix} b_{11} & b_{12} \\ b_{21} & b_{22} \end{bmatrix}$$

$$= \begin{bmatrix} a_{11} + b_{11} \\ a_{21} + b_{21} \end{bmatrix} \quad \begin{bmatrix} a_{12} + b_{12} \\ a_{22} + b_{22} \end{bmatrix}$$

11. Write a function program to obtain multiplication of two matrices.

$$[c]_{mxl} = [a]_{mxn} \times [b]_{nxl}$$

$$= \begin{bmatrix} a_{11} & a_{12} \\ a_{21} & a_{22} \\ a_{31} & a_{32} \end{bmatrix} \times \begin{bmatrix} b_{11} & b_{12} & b_{13} \\ b_{21} & b_{22} & b_{23} \end{bmatrix}$$

12. Write a function program to scan and print a square matrix and find sum of diagonal elements of matrix.
13. Write a function program to calculate cube root of a number using numerical method.
14. Write a function program to multiply an array by a scalar .
15. Write a function program to find maximum and minimum value of two given numbers.
16. Write a function program to calculate surface area and volume of a sphere .
    The surface area of sphere is given by $4\pi\ r^2$
    The volume of sphere is given by $4/3\ \pi\ r^3$
    where r is radius of sphere
17. Write a program to search a number from a given array using 'search' function program.
18. Write a function program to accept a two digit number and separate the digits of the number.
19. Write a function program to accept two digits of a number and join the two digits to form a complete number.
20. Write a function program to calculate the surface area and volume of cylinder.
    The surface area of cylinder is given by $2\pi\ L\ r$

The volume of cylinder is given by $\pi r^3 L$

where r is a radius of cylinder and L is a length of cylinder.

21. Consider the following program written in C syntax:

```
void main() {
int value = 2, list[5] = {1,3,5,7,9};
swap (value, list[0];
swap (list[0], list[1]);
swap (value, list[value]);
}
void swap (int a, int b) {
int temp;
temp = a;
a = b;
b = temp;
}
```

For each of the following parameter-passing methods, what are all of the values of the variables value and list after each of the three calls to swap?

a. passed by value
b. passed by reference
c. passed by name
d. passed by value-result

22. Given an array of 100 random numbers in the range from 1 to 999, write a program with functions that will do the following:

Print an array ten values to a line.

Make sure that the values are aligned in rows.

Return a count of the number of even values.

Return the sum of all values in the array.

When building the array, if 3 or 7 evenly divide the random number, store it as a negative number.

23. Implement a function calculate to take in two integer parameters num1, num2 and a third parameter operator of character type and return the resulting operation. The function should use the 'switch ' keyword to determine the operation depending on the given operator. For example, if num1 = 2, num2 = 3 and operator = "+" then the returned result should be 5. The function should display an error message for invalid operator other than *,/,- and +.

24. Implement a function deviation that take in an array call numarray containing floating numbers and its size. The function should calculate print out its average and deviation of each number in the array.

For example if numarray = {1.0, 2.0, 3.0} then average = 2 and deviations of first, second and third number are –1.0, 0 and 1.0 respectively.

25. Implement a function called FindFactorsN that take in a numarray of size 5 and a second integer parameter N. Assuming numarray contains the values 2,3,5,7,11, the function FindFactorsN should check whether N can be divisible by the values in numarray.

For example if N=20, FindFactorsN display on the screen 25 (as 2 and 5 are factors of 20)

26. Implement a function called IntChange that take in an array intarr of 3 integers and 3 integer parameters i0,i1,i2. The 3 integer parameters specify that new positions of intarr to be returned after calling IntChange whereby i0 contain the position of the integer in intarr to be copied to position 0 and so on.

For example, if the IntChange is called with intarr = {1,2,3} and i0=2, i1=1 and i2=0 then it returns an array with {3,2,1}

27. Implement a function called TotalMultiple that take in an array called floatarray of 3 float numbers and a reference parameter called TM. For each floating values in the floatarray, the function multiplies it by TM and total up these values and store it into TM.
    For example, if floatarray has {2.0,4.0,2.0} and TM = 2.0,
    TotalMultiple store 16.0 (2.0 * 2 + 4.0 * 2 + 2.0 * 2 = 16.0) to TM.
28. Implement a function called BackOrForward that take in a string parameter str, an integer parameter position and a character parameter direction. If direction is 'F' the function returns a string from position to end of str. If direction is 'B' the function returns a string start to position of str.
    For example, if the function is called with BackOrForward ('hello', 2, 'F'), it returns the string 'llo'. If it is called with BackOrForward ('hello', 2, 'B'), it returns the string 'he'.
29. Implement a function called ShiftLOrR that take in a string parameter and a character parameter LOrR. If LOrR is 'L', then all characters in str are shifted by 1 ASCII value to the left.If LOrR is 'R', then all characters in str are shifted by 1 ASCII value to the right.
    For example, ShiftLOrR ('bcd, 'L') returns 'abc'.
30. Implement a function InsertInt that take in 2 integer arrays IntArr1, IntArr2, 2 integer parameters IA1, IA2 and a character parameter FOrB. If FOrB is 'F', then array IA2 is inserted in front of IA1. If FOrB is 'B', then array IA2 is inserted after IA1. IA1 and IA2 indicate the number of integers in IntArr1 and IntArr2 respectively.
    For example, If IntArr1 = {1,2,3}, IntArr2 = {4,5,6}, IA = 3, IA = 3 and FOrB = 'F' then IntArr1 would have {4,5,6,1,2,3} after the function call.
31. Implement a function called xypower that take in 2 reference parameters x and y.
    Upon exit the function xypower stores the value of x to the power of y back to x and stores the value of y to x back y.
    For example, if x = 2 and y = 3, upon exit of xypower, x will have the value 8 (2 to power of 3) and y the value 9 (3 to the power of 2).
32. Implement a recursive function called recurstr that take a string parameter str and an integer parameter n. The function should display the n number times string str is printed on the screen. For e.g. recurstr('C is Fun!', 10) will print hello on the screen 10 times. The function header is given as void recurstr(char str[], int n)
33. Implement a recursive function PrintInt that take in an array of integers intarr and an integer parameter num. The recursive function should print out the values in intarr in reverse order.
34. Implement a recursive function Half_Of that take in an integer num and display half of its integer value in each recursive call as long as the values are greater than 0.The function returns the number of times it has half num. For example, Half_Of (21) displays 10 5 2 1 on the screen and returns 4.
35. Implement a recursive function called DisplayProduct that take in an float parameter num and a second float parameter factor. DisplayProduct displays the product of num and factor on the screen (on every recursive call) up to and including 300.
    For example Display(20.0, 2.0) displays 40.0, 60.0, 160.0 on the screen(the next value 320.0 is not displayed because it is greater than 300).
36. Write a function that dynamically allocates an array of integers. The function should accept an integer argument indicating the # of elements to allocate. The function should return a pointer to the array.

37. Write a program that dynamically allocates an array large enough to hold any # of test scores the user wishes to enter (use the function from question #1). Once all the scores are entered, the array should be passed to a function that sorts them in ascending order. Another function should then be called that calculates the average score. The program should display the sorted list of scores and average, with appropriate headings.Drop the lowest score. The score should not be included in the calculation of the average.
38. A function to convert a decimal to a fraction and result (returned as a string) should be calculated with LCM (least common multiple) in mind, example.
    0.75 = 3/4 and not 75/100
    1.3 = 1 1/3
    and that the function returns, fractions by:
    #/2, #/3, #/4, #/5, etc... that is the most common fractions possible which a user can easily interpret!!!

13
AUXILIARY STATEMENTS AND OPERATIONS

AN OVERVIEW

In the previous unit we have seen the function program as the sub program used in the main program. The sub program are used in the main program to perform certain function and these programs are called in the main program as many number of times. In a file there can be any number of function program with different names. These function program are called by the main program or by other function programs. The function programs can be supplied with arguments and the number of arguments must match in the name and call of function. The function program may return a value or they may be non-returnable function programs.

In this unit we are going to study some of the auxiliary statements which are used in the programming to provide convenience and benefit during the execution of program.These are the statement used as auxiliary statement to improve the facilities in the programming. There are number of statements used in programming to reduce the memory for storage, speed of execution etc.

OBJECTIVES

After completing this unit you will be able to

*Define equivalent statement
*Explain user specified data
*Describe c-pre processor
*Define new variables
*Explain static and automatic variable
*Analyze register variable

13.1 EQUIVALENT STATEMENT

This is an equivalent statement which is used in programming. If a value of a variable is modified in the program by a simple statement, then equivalent statement can be used. This statement reduces the memory for storage of file by one byte.

This is represented by a general form :

x opr = z;

which is equivalent to

x = x opr z;

where,

opr – mathematical operator
x – variables
z – variable or constant.

Example :

(1) a[i] = a[i] * 2 ;
can be represented as
a[i] * = 2;

(2) counter = counter + 5;
is equivalent to
counter += 5;

(3) a = a/(b+c)
is equivalent to
a /= b + c;

(4) a = a – 5;
is equivalent to
a – = 5;

13.2 TYPES OF VARIABLES

There are different types of additional variables used in C–language. Their use arises in the function programs.

13.2.1 Automatic and Static Variables

Automatic Variable :

The variables declared without any storage are assumed to be "automatic variables". These work inside the block in which they are declared after the execution of the block or function where all such variables are disposed off. These are declared by using a word 'auto'.

Ex . auto int i= 9;

is equivalent to declaring

int i=9;

This means every time this statement is executed 'i' is equal to 9.

Static variable

These are permanent within the function or file in which it is declared. They work in the similar manner as the auto variables, but they retain the latest value so that, when the block or function in which they are declared is reinvoked, it holds its latest value. These are declared by a word 'static'.

Ex : static float a=9;

'a' is floating static variable, which receives a value of 9 for the first time and static statement is not executed for the second time.

13.2.2 global variables

The variables are declared before the function program or the main() program and are globally existing for all the functions inside the program. These are known as global variables.

Ex : float x, y;

If these variables are declared outside the main program and function program and in the beginning of file, then x & y are global variables.

13.2.3 Register variables

If access to some variables is required to be faster, then variables can be declared as of register type. If some variables are frequently called in program many times, then such variables can be declared as 'register' variables.

Ex. : register int i;

Rules for using register variables :

1. Only a few variables can be declared as register variables.
2. Type of register variables must be int, char or pointer.
3. Address of register variable can not be retrieved.

Program 13–1

This is a program on global variables.

```
/* Global variables */
float span, load, moment;          ———————▶ global variable declaration
main()
{
    printf ("Beam span = \n");
    scanf ("%f", & span);
    printf ("UDL on beam = \n");
    scanf ("%f", & load);
    mfunc();
    printf ("The bending moment = %g\n", moment);
}
mfunc()
{
    moment = load * span * span/2.0;
}
```

Input	:	Beam span=20 UDL on beam=20
Output	:	The bending moment = 4000

In this program, all the variables are declared as global variables. They are declared in the begining of the file and out of main program and function program. The function program calculates the 'moment' by using 'load' and 'span' variables. The values of input/output variables passes through the global variable from main and function program.

Program 13–2

This is a program on automatic and static variables.

```
/* Program to illustrate auto and static variables */
auto_static()
{
    int a = 0;    static int s = 0;
    printf ("automatic 'a' = %d, static 's' = %d\n",a,s);
    ++a;
    ++s;
}
main()
{
    int i;
    for ( i=0; i<4; ++i)
    auto_static();
}
```

Output : automatic 'a'=0, static 's'=3

In this program 'a' maintains a value of zero in every cycle whereas 's' variable is static whose value is incremented in every cycle because static statement is executed for the first and not for the second time.

Program 13–3

```
/* expression statement */
expression(a,n)
float a[10];
int n
{
    int i;
    for(i=0;i<n;++i)
    a[i] *= 2;
}

main()
{
    float value[4] = {1.2,--3.7, 6.2, 8.55};
    float i;
    expression(value,4);
    for(i=0;i<4;++i)
    {
            printf ("%0.2f\t",value[i]);
    }
}
```

In this program a 'value' array having four numbers is supplied at the time of declaration and every element of the array is multiplied by 4 using 'expression' function. The function program is a non-returnable function program, which is supplied with the array and scalar. This function uses equivalent expression to multiply every element of array by scalar.

Program 13–4

This function program performs multiplication of the elements matrix by scalar.

```
/* Multiply scalar to a matrix */
scalar (a,s)
int a [3] [5];
int s;
{
    int  i, j;
    for (i=0; i<3; ++i)
    for (j=0; j<5; ++j)
    a[i][j] * = s;
}
display (a)
int a[3][5];
{
    int i, j;
    for (i=0; i<3; ++i)
```

```
{
for (j=0; j<5; ++j)
{
        printf("%5d", a[i][j]);
}
}
main()
{
    int b [3][5] =
                {
                        {7,10,52,0,7},
                        {12,10,52,0,7},
                        {-2,1,2,4,9},
                };
    printf("original matrix :/n");
    display (b);
    scalar (b,2);
    printf("matrix multiplied by 2\n");
    display (b);
}
```

Output	:	original matrix: 7 10 52 0 7 12 10 52 0 7 –2 1 2 4 9 matrix multiplied by 2 14 20 104 0 14 24 20 104 0 14 –4 2 4 8 18

This program multiplies all elements of matrix by a scalar 2 and displays the matrix using function program.In this function program the matrix is supplied at the time of declaration. Then a function program is called as 'display' which performs the work of printing of the matrix. The main program gives a call to another function program 'scalar' which supplies the matrix and the scalar value of 2 and the matrix is multiplied by the scalar using the above function. Then again a 'display' function is called which displays the new matrix.

Program 13–5

```
/* Program to multiply and add individual elements of matrix */
float a[100], b[100], c[100],n;
main ()
{
    float i;
    printf ("Enter the max element of array\n");
    scanf("%f",&n);
    printf ("Enter the %g element of [a] array\n",n);
    for (i=1; i<=n; ++i)
    {
        scanf("%f",&a[i]);
    }
```

```
        printf ("Enter the %g element of[b] array\n",n);
        for (i=1; i<=n; ++i)
        {
                scanf("%f",&b[i]);
        }
        mult();
        printf ("The multiplied array axb is \n");
        prn();
        printf("\n");
        add();
        printf ("The added array axb is \n");
        prn();
    }
    add()
    {
         float i;
         for (i=i;<n;++i)
        {
                c[i] = a[i] + b[i];
        }
    }
    mult()
    {
        float i;
        for(i=1; i<=n;++i)
        {
                c[i]= a[i] * b[i];
        }
    }
    prn()
    {
        float i;
        for (i=1; i<=n; ++i)
        {
                printf ("%g\t", c[i]);
        }

    }
```

Input	:	Enter the max element of array
		3
		Enter the 3 element of [a] array
		1 2 3
		Enter the 3 element of [b] array
		4 5 6

Output :	The multiplied array a x b is 4 10 18 The added array a x b is 5 7 9

In this program, 'a' and 'b' are two arrays declared as global array variables in the beginning of the file. The 'a' and 'b' arrays are read in the main program and a function ‘mult’ is called which carries out multiplication between elements of two arrays and 'c' array is calculated in the 'mult' program. The ‘prn’ function program is called to print elements of 'c' array, which is possible because 'c' array is a global variable.

Again in the second phase ‘add’ function program is called which does addition of elements of array 'a' and 'b' and then again the 'c' array is printed by calling ‘prn()’ function.

In the above program, a call of function is made without using any argument because all input output variables of function program are global variables and they are accessible in the function program.

13.3 USER SPECIFIED DATA

The statement allows the developer to create new data types. The data can be supplied by the user according to his requirements, whereas the compiler will accept the data in its own format.

13.3.1 Enumerated Data Type

It is user created data type in which the values appropriate to the data type are specified in the user defined list. It is identified as “enum”, followed by the user selected name of the data type and listing of acceptable values of the data type.

Ex :

```
enum time {am ,pm};
```

In this case value of time ‘am’ is 0 and‘pm’ is 1

```
enum colour {red, green, yellow};
```

The value of colour red is 0, green is 1 and yellow is 2.

The ‘colour’ is integer variable, which enumerates the different colours as given in the bracket. Then,

```
colour = red;
```

means colour value equal to 0

13.3.2 typedef statement

The programmer is allowed to create new names for the existing data types. This statement clearly specifies the equivalent string likely to be used for the regular string.

Ex : `typedef float REAL;`

This allows the name REAL to be used in place of ‘float’ any where in the program.

13.3.3 Unions

If one single variable is to be used to store different types of values like char, float and int, then unions are used. But union is capable of storing one single value at a time.

It is written as

```
union xx
{
        char ch;
        float fl;
        int in;
};
```

This means that xx is a union of ‘ch’, ‘fl’ and ‘in’. If 'xx' is used with 'ch' , then a character value can be stored, if used with 'fl', then a float value can be stored or if used with 'in', then integer value can be stored.

This xx union can be used for any other variable by declaring,

Union xx y;

Then y accepts the union of xx.

Any of these three values can be given to the union.

(1) y.ch = ‘+’;

(2) y.fl = 9.824;

(3) y.in = 9;

But 'y' can be used for either of three variables in the program.

Program 13–6

```
/* Program on union */
main ()
{
    union  xx
    {
            int x;
            float y;
            char c;
    };
    union  xx  z;
    clrscr();
    z.x = 10;
    printf ("z = %d\n", z.x);
    z.y = 10.2;
    printf ("z = %g\n", z.y);
    z.c = 'H';
    printf ("z = %c\n", z.c);
}
```

Output : z = 10
z = 10.2
z = H

In this program union of ‘xx’ is used which has three variables which stores int, float, char values. This allows 'z' to store any type of three values provided it stores one value of any nature at a time.

Program 13–7

This is program on the enumerated data type.In this program, the supports are enumerated as ‘hinge’,‘roller’,‘fixed’. The support variable is referred to another variable ‘boundary’ whose value is supplied as 'hinge'. The number of 'hinge' is 0, hence the ‘boundary’ receives a value of 0 and is printed in the program. Then the value of ‘boundary’ is supplied in the program and the value is numeric which is compared with the string whose value is specified by 'enum' statement.

```
/*Program on Enumerated data type*/
main()
```

```
{
    enum support {hinge, roller, fixed};
    enum support boundary = hinge;
    printf ("\n The support is %d", boundary);
    printf("\n Enter a value:");
    scanf(" %d", & boundary);
    if (boundary == hinge)
            printf ("\n The support is hinge");
    else
    if (boundary == roller)
            printf ("\n The support is roller");
    else
    if (boundary == fixed)
            printf ("\n The support is fixed");
    else
            printf ("\n The support condition is not defined");
}
```

Output	:	The support is 0
Input	:	Enter a value : 1
Output	:	The support is roller

13.4 C–PREPROCESSOR

The string replacement and inclusion of files through a pre-processor is easier. It is a program that processes the source code before it passes through the compiler.There are three types of C–preprocessors

(i) Simple string replacement
(ii) Macro expansion
(iii) File inclusion.

The C–preprocessor is represented by a sign # and it is written in the beginning of the file before writing of any other statement of the program.

13.4.1 Simple string replacement

It is the replacement of another string which is done by # define statement. This statement allows declaration of the constants in the program.

The general form is

```
#define x c ;
```

where,

x – String whose value is c, which can be written in capital alphabets.

Ex : `#define PI 3.141593`

and here 'PI' is a string whose value is 3.141593. 'PI' can be used any where in program. Then in its place the value of 3.141593 can be substituted.

13.4.2 Macro expansion

When the equivalent text consists of more than a single value, operator or variable, the symbolic name is referred to as micro and substitution of the text in place of the symbolic name is called a macro expansion.

Ex : # define cube (x) (x * x * x)

Here 'cube' is a function program name, which calculates cube of x. This is a one line function, which can be defined.

13.4.3 File Inclusion

If a function program in another file is required in the current program, then that file can be included in current program by 'include' statement. Then all function programs written in included file can be used in the current file. This saves rewriting of ready functions in current file.

The file can be included for execution of the program in the main program. It is defined as

include < file name >

or

it can be written by alternate method

include "file name"

The name of file consists of any name of seven characters and an extension name seperated by a dot. Because of this statement the function programs which are written in the given file are included in the current file eventhough they are not written in the current file.

It is written as first executable statement of the program even before writing any program in the file.

Ex :

```
# include <math.h>
        or
# include "ramesh1.xx"
```

Program 13–8

This program finds whether the given value is even or odd.In this program the main program calls a function program 'even'to check whether the given value is even or odd.If the value is divisible by 2, then the answer is TRUE or 1. If the value is not divisible by 2, then the answer is FALSE or 0 because of the define statement which allows writing of string in place of number and substitutes it automatically.

```
/*Program On Define Statement */
# define TRUE 1
# define FALSE 0
/* function to determine if an integer is even */
even (number)
int number;
{
    int answer;
    if (number %2 == 0)
            answer = TRUE;
    else
            answer = FALSE;
    return (answer);
}
```

```
main()
{
    if (even (17) == TRUE)
            printf ("yes\n");
    else
            printf ("no\n");
    if (even(20) == TRUE)
            printf ("yes\n");
    else
            printf ("no\n");
}
```

Output	:	no
		yes

Program 13–9

This is a program on C–preprocessor,in which simple string replacement is used to substitute the value of 'PI' as 22.0/7.0.The 'square' function is used to supply the square value of x and 'cube' function is used to supply cube value of x.

These C–preprocessors can be called in the function program by their direct substitution like wherever 'PI' is written value of 22.0/7.0 is substituted.

/* Function to calculate area, circumference of a circle, and the volume of a sphere of a given radius */

```
# define PI   22.0/7.0
# define square(x) (x*x)
# define cube(x) (x*x*x*)
double area (r)
double r;
{
    float ar;
    ar= PI*square(r);
    return(ar);
}
double circumference (r);
double r;
{
    float ci;
    ci = 2.0 * PI * r;
    return(ci);
}
double volume (r)
double r;
{
    float vo;
    vo= 4.0/3.0 * PI * cube(r);
```

```
        return(vo);
    }
    main ( )
    {
        float r;
        printf("enter the radius \n");
        scanf("%f",&r);
        printf("\nradius = %g,area = %0.4f \n", r,area (r));
        printf("radius = %g, circumference= %0. \n",r,circumference (r));
        printf("radius = %g, volume = %0.4f \n", r,volume (r));
    }
```

Input	:	enter the radius 4
Output	:	radius=4,area=50.2857 radius=4,circumference=25.1429 radius=4,volume=268.1905

In this program, the radius is supplied in the main program and the call is given in a printf statement to function program area which is returnable function program to print the area of circle.

Then in the next statement call of circumference function program is given and the circumference of the circle is printed.

Then in the next statement the call is given to volume function program to print volume of the sphere.

All these function programs are returnable function programs which utilize the C–preprocessor as constant definition as 'PI' and micro–functions square and cube of x.

13.5 LIBRARY OF MATHEMATICAL FUNCTIONS IN 'C' LANGUAGE

A library is available for execution of the mathematical or trigonometrical function as 'math.h'.Whenever mathematical functions are required a library is available in C–language which can be utilized to access readymade mathematical functions.The function in this library can be accessed by inclusion of 'math.h' header file in the program.

This library defines variety of mathematical functions which are listed as below :

The different functions available in this library are as below :

Functions	Names
c	sqrt(c);
a^x	pow(a,x)
sin (t)	sin(t)
cos (t)	cos(t)
tan (t)	tan(t)
$\sin^{-1}$ (t)	asin(t)
$\cos^{-1}$ (t)	acos(t)
$\tan^{-1}$ (t)	atan(t)
sin (t)	dsin(t) t –> degrees
cos (t)	dcos(t)

tan (t)	dtan(t)
$sin^{-1}(t)$	dasin(t)
$cos^{-1}(t)$	dacos(t)
$tan^{-1}(t)$	datan(t)
$\|x\|$	abs(x)
Cosh(x)	Cosh(x)
Sinh(x)	sinh(x)
e^x	exp(x)
$Log_e x$	log(x)
$Log_{10} x$	log10(x)

For using the above functions in the program "math.h" library should be included in the program by using the statement

include <math.h>

Program 13–10

```
/* Program on mathematical library functions */
#include "math.h"
main()
{
    float x,x1,x2,x3,x4,x5;
    printf ("Enter the value of x\n");
    scanf ("%f",&x);
    /* square root of x*/
    x1=sqrt(x);
    /* cube root of x*/
    x2=pow(x,0.333);
    /* exponent of x*/
    x3=exp(x);
    /* naturallogarithm of x*/
    x4=log(x);
    /* sine of 30 degree*/
    x=30.0/180.0 * 3.142;
    x5=sin(x);
    printf ("x1=%g, x2=%g, x3=%g, x4=%g, x5=%g,x=%g\n",x1,x2,x3,x4,x5,x);
}
```

Input	:	Enter the value of x 3
Output	:	x1=1.73205,x2=0,x3=20.0855,x4=1.09861,x5=0.500059,x=0.523667

In this program the x1,x2,x3,x4,x5 calculates square root, cube root, exponent, logrithm and sine of x using readymade library functions available in the "math.h" library.

13.6 CONDITIONAL EXPRESSION OPERATOR

If it is desired that the choice of value should depend on a condition , then we can write it using 'if-else' statement as

```
if(x1)
        z = y1;
else
        z = y1;
```

This can be written in another form by conditional expression operator as below :

z = x1 ? y1 : y2;

Where,

z	–	Value to be calculated
x1	–	Logical expression
y1,y2	–	Arithmetic expression, variables or constants

This will be evaluated as if x1 is true, then z = y1 and if false then z = y2

Ex : z = (a>b) ? p1 : p2;
if a > b , then z = p1
if a < b , then z = p2

Program 13–11

In this statement a conditional operator is used to solve the equation. If the value of x supplied to the program is more than five then the conditional operator directly provides the value as 3 and if x is less than 5 then the value will be taken as 4. This operator reduces the number of lines required for the decision making process. This is also seen by if-else statement which is given in the program which does similar work of conditional operator.

```
/* CONDITIONAL OPERATOR */
main()
{
    int x,y;
    clrscr();
    printf("Enter the value of x\n");
    scanf("%d",&x);
    y=(x>5?3:4);
    printf("the value of y=%d\n",y);
    if(x>5)
            y=3;
    else
            y=4;
    printf("the value of y=%d\n",y);
    return;
}
```

Input	:	Enter the value of x 4
Output	:	the value of y=4

Program 13–12

The norm of a matrix is under root of sum of the squares of all elements of matrix. In this program a matrix is supplied and the sum of squares of all elements of matrix is calculated using normal procedure of summation by use of the 'nested for' statement.

```
/* PROGRAM TO CALCULATE THE NORM OF MATRIX */
#include<math.h>
main()
{
     float a[10][10],b[10][10],i,j,n,m,norm;
     float sum=0;
     printf("ENTER THE VALUES OF MATRIX m & n\n");
     scanf("%f %f",& m,&n);
     printf("ENTER THE VALUES OF ELEMENTS OF MATRIX %gx%g \n",m,n);
     for(i=1;i<=m;++i)
     {
     for(j=1;j<=n;++j)
          scanf("%f",&a[i][j]);
     }
     for(i=1;i<=m;++i)
     {
     for(j=1;j<=n;++j)
     {
          sum += (a[i][j] * a[i][j]);
     }
     }
     norm=sqrt(sum);
     printf("norm=%g\n",norm);
}
```

Input	:	ENTER THE VALUES OF MATRIX m & n 2 2 ENTER THE VALUES OF ELEMENTS OF MATRIX 2×2 1 2 3 4
Output	:	norm = 2.23607

13.7 AUXILIARY FUNCTIONS AND OPERATOR

13.7.1 'sizeof ' operator

This is used to obtain required storage of memory according to the size of the variable.

It is written as :

sizeof(y);

Where,

y – array variable, data type to indicate type of memory

This statement allows required memory storage for 'y' array variable.

13.7.2 'malloc' function

In analysis of complex system, if memory requirement of array is unknown and can vary depending upon the type of problem. But the programmer wants to run the program with minimum memory location. Therefore, in the beginning small memory is allocated and any extra memory can be further provided by this statement.

float *a;

a = malloc(50);

This statement allocates a first memory of 100 bytes.

13.7.3 'calloc' function

This function is similar to malloc but uses two arguments that specifies the number of elements to be reserved and size of each element.

calloc(n, sizeof(y))

Where,

n – number of elements

y – array variable or pointer

13.7.4 'free' function

When the work with memory which has been dynamically allocated is over, then the memory is freed by 'free' function.

free(y);

EXERCISE

1. Write a program to provide values of displacement, velocity and acceleration of particle in SHM

$$X = a \text{ Sin } (\omega t + \phi)$$

$$V = a\ \omega \text{ Cos}(\omega t + \phi)$$

$$a_c = -a\omega^2 \text{ Sin } (\omega t + \phi)$$

where, ω a, t, ϕ are angular velocity, maximum amplitude, time and phase angle as input variables.

2. Write a program to calculate the diameter of a dead shaft(D) subjected to bending moment (bm) and safe stress in material is (fs)

$$bm = \frac{\pi}{32} \times D^3 \times f_s$$

3. Write expression for the following using library functions :

(i) $S = \left[\frac{5}{2\pi}\right]^{1/2} \text{ Sin } \frac{\pi}{b} e^a$

(ii) $\omega = 1 - \frac{1}{(R)^{r-1}}\left[\frac{P^r - 1}{p-1} \cdot \frac{1}{r}\right]$

(iii) $Q = \frac{UA(T_i - T_e)}{Log_e(T_i/T_e)}$

(iv) $Z = \text{ Sin } (x + 2y) + e^{xy} - x^2 - y^2$

(v) $R = \frac{2V^2 \text{ Sin}\theta \text{ Cos}\theta}{g(1+m)}$

(vi) $P = \text{Sin } (x\sqrt{1-x^2}) + \text{loge } (1x^2 + my + n)$

(vii) $T = |a| (x \sqrt{e^{-(w/z)} x})$

(viii) $C = I \,.\, (e^{35v} - 1)$

(ix) $6 = \frac{6_x + 6_y}{2} + \sqrt{\frac{(6_y - 6_x)^2}{2} + £_{xy}{}^2}$

4 . Explain the following :

(i) sum = 1; a[1] = 3;
sum * = a[1];
What is value of sum ?

(ii) static int a[5] = {5, –6, 2, 9, 7};
What is value of a[3] ?

(iii) global variables and register variables.

(iv) enum colour {red, blue, green, yellow};
colour = green;
What is the numerical value of colour ?

(v) # define f(x) (x * x * 2)
What is the value f(3 + 2) ?

(vi) Explain the purpose of 'static' statement in program .

5. Evaluate

$$y = e^{2x} \log_e \left(1+\frac{|x|}{\sqrt{1+x^2+x^5}}\right)$$

for x = 1.5, 1.55, 1.6, ... 10

Write a program for evaluation of y for these values.

6. Evaluate the value of w using computer program.

$W = 1 + \text{Sin } x + | A_x + B_y | e^{|x-A|}$

Write a program to evaluate W

For x varying in range of 0.1 to 0.9 in steps of 0.1
y varying in range of 10 to 50 in steps of 10

7. Write a program to obtain mean, median and standard deviation of given `n' numbers using static statement and function program.

8. Write a program to calculate triangular number of a number using recursive function where triangular number is sum of numbers upto that number.

$\Delta\, 6 = 1+2+3+5+6$

9. Write a program to calculate sum of all numbers in array using static and equivalent expression statement and also calculate average of numbers.

10. Write a program to add two matrices using `static' statement and global variables.

11. Write a program to calculate surface area, cross sectional area and volume of cylinder of radius r and height h using `define' statement for `π' and square and cube of radius with function program for calculation of the following.

Surface area of cylinder	=	$2 \pi r h$
Cross-sectional area	=	πr^2
Volume of cylinder	=	$\pi r^2 h$.

12. Write a program to arrange an array in ascending order using global variable, function program and static statement.

13. A projectile fired at an angle θ with an initial velocity V_o will travel distance r according to the formula :

$$r = \frac{V_o^2 \text{ Sin } 2\theta}{g}$$

The projectile will be in motion for a time

$$t = \frac{V_o^2 \, Sin\theta}{g}$$

It will reach a maximum height `h' given by,

$$h = \frac{V_o^2 \, Sin\theta}{g}$$

Write a program to print value of r,t and h for different angles varying from 10 to 360 in steps 5.

14. Write a program to find the greatest common divisor (gcd) of five given numbers.
15. Write a program to calculate heat flow rate through a heat exchanger

$$Q = UA \, \Delta T_m$$

$$\frac{1}{U} = \frac{1}{h_1} + \frac{b_1}{k_1} + \frac{1}{h_2}$$

$$\Delta T_m = \frac{\Delta T_o - \Delta T_i}{\log_e \Delta T_o / \Delta T_i}$$

Where,

h_1, h_2, b_1, k_1 are input variables,

ΔT_o , ΔT_i are the temperature differences at input and output,

A is the area of heat exchanger.

16. Write a program to find prime number using function program and global variables.
17. This program has to ask the user for 3 values and display what type of triangle is (isoceles,equilateral or scalene) it should display also if is not a triangle. It should use enum, switch and functions. Finally it has to ask the user if he want to try again.

14

STRING OPERATION

AN OVERVIEW

In the previous you have studied the concept of an array. The array is variable having multiple memories and allows to store the data in single and two dimension format. The 2 -D array was found to be suitable for storage of matrix. The single and two dimensional character arrays are suitable for storage of string and sentences of English language.

There are different types of strings operations being performed.In the previous chapters you have seen the concept of string and the methods of declaration of string.A **string** is bunch of characters or words of English language joined to represent name of person, number, designation and address of the person.

OBJECTIVES

After completing this unit you will be able to:

* Present char array variable
* Specify types of string functions
* Explain string operations

14.1 INTRODUCTION

In the earlier chapters, the concept of single dimensional and 2-D char array was discussed. The char array is useful for storage of string and 2-D char array stores number of strings. The operation of strings are the operations which allow modifications of strings or determine parameters related to string. The string operations are necessary because strings are used for storage of name, address, city, location, pincode number, roll number etc. The strings are used for storage of numeric character values.

14.2 TYPES OF OPERATIONS

There are various types of string operations being performed on string such as

1. Joining of two strings
2. Length of strings
3. Comparing two strings
4. Determining a character in a string
5. Copying of string

14.3 CONCATENATE TWO STRINGS

This means that the two strings are joined together by simple addition process. The second string is joined at the end of the first string. In this program the two strings are supplied in the program by automatic statement and 'join' function is called to join the characters of the second string with the first string.

Program 14-1

```
/* Program to join strings */
join (string1, n1, string2, n2, result)
char string1 [], string2[], result[];
int n1, n2
```

```
{
    int i, j;
    for (i=0; i<n1; ++i)
    result [i] = string1 [i];
    for (j=0; j<n2; ++j)
    result [n1+j] = string2[j]
}
main()
{
    char s1[5] = {'T','e','s','t',' '};
    char s2[6] = { 'w','o','r','k','s',' ' };
    char result[11];
    int i;
    join (s1,5,s2,6 ,result);
    for (i=0, i<11; ++i)
            printf ("%c", result[i]);
            printf ("\n");
}
```

Output : Test works

This program joins two strings s1 and s2 to form s3 by calling the function 'join'.

14.4 LENGTH OF A STRING

The length of string is number of characters in a string. The length of string is an integer value which can be known if the characters in the string are counted.

Program 14-2

```
/* function to count the number of characters in a string */
int string_length (string)
char string [];
{
    int count = 0;
    while (String [count] ! = '\0')
            ++ count;
    return (count);
}
main ()
{
    char word1 [] = {'a','s','t','e','r','\0'};
    printf ("length of string is %d \n",string_length(word1));
}
```

Output : length of string is 5

In this program the length of the string is calculated by use of null character. The function program string_length is used to find the length of string. In this function program a count variable counts the number of characters of string upto null character. This provides the length of string.

14.5 COMPARING TWO STRING

The two strings could be compared whether they are equal or not. This can be done by comparing length of the string initially. If the length of string is equal then every character in a string can be compared and if all the characters are same and string terminates with null character then the strings are regarded to be equal.

Program 14-3

This program is used to find whether the given strings are equal or not. The two strings are supplied to a function program 'equal' which initially determines whether the first character matches for both the strings and is not equal to null. Then all subsequent characters of both the strings are compared and if they do not match then a flag is provided as 0, but if both characters of the string reaches to null character then the strings are regarded to be equal and a flag 1 is received by the function program.

```
/* program for determining whether strings are equal */
int equal (s1,s2)
char s1[], s[2];
{
    int i = 0, answer = 0;
    while(s1[i] == s2[i] && s1[i]! ='\0' && s2[i]! ='\0');
    {
        ++i;
        if (s1[i] == '\0' && s2[i] == '\0')
                answer = 1;
        else
                answer = 0;
    }
    return (answer);
}
main()
{
    int z;
    char stra[] = {"string"};
     char strb[] = {"string"};
    z = equal (stra, strb);
    if (z==1)
        printf("The strings are equal\n");
    else
        printf("The strings are unequal\n");
}
```

Output : The strings are equal

This program determines whether two strings 'stra', 'strb' are equal or not using a function program that if all characters are equal in string and terminate at same points, then the strings are equal.

14.6 STRING FUNCTIONS

In C–language readymade functions for operation on string are available. In 'stdio.h' library file following readymade functions on strings are available. These can be used by inclusion of the file in program.

#include < stdio.h>

The readymade functions on string are as below :

14.6.1 'gets' FUNCTION

This function is used for supplying a bunch of characters

or strings from the data screen to a given char array. This statement scans a line of English language from data screen which consists of a bunch of words. It works like a 'scanf' statement.

Ex : gets (s);

It scans the string from screen and substitutes in char array 's'

14.6.2 'puts' FUNCTION

This function is used to provide output of the string from variable on user screen.

Ex : puts (s);

This prints the string from char array 's' to the output screen.

Program 14-4

This program utilizes readymade function 'gets' and 'puts'. The statement is scanned from the data screen using 'gets' function and is printed on result screen using puts function.

```
/* string functions */
main ()
{
    char string [20];
    printf("enter the string\n");
    gets (string);
    printf("the string entered was\n");
    puts(string);
}
```

Input	:	enter the string Anita
Output	:	the string entered was Anita

This program uses 'gets' and 'puts' function to enter and print the given string.

14.6.3 'sscanf' FUNCTION

This function reads the character array from another char array instead of from keyboard.

Ex : sscanf (buffer,"%s", num);

In this function the char array is read from another char array. The 'buffer' is a programmer selected variable name that must be declared as either an array of characters sufficiently large to hold the resulting string.

14.6.4 'sprintf' FUNCTION

This function writes a character array from one char array another char array instead of to the screen.

Ex : sprintf (buffer, "%s", num);

14.6.5 'getchar' FUNCTION

This function reads a character from standard input keyboard. The repeated calls to the getchar() function will return successive single characters from the input.

Ex : c = getchar();

where c is a char variable. One call of getchar results in reading of one character from data screen and storing it in c char variable.

14.6.6 'putchar' FUNCTION

This function prints the character 'c' to the user screen.

Ex : putchar (c);

14.6.7 'strcat' FUNCTION

This function concatenates two strings. The second string is joined to the first string by using this function.

Ex : strcat (s1,s2);

In this case string s2 is joined to s1 to form new string s1. Where s1 is a combination of s1 and s2.

14.6.8 'strchr' FUNCTION

This function locates the position of a character within a string. This returns the address of the character.

Ex : p = strchr ('x',s);

where ,	s	is a char array
	x	is a character which is to be traced in s1
	p	is a pointer variable.

14.6.9 'strcmp' FUNCTION

This function compares two strings to find whether they are equal or not. It returns the address of the first non-matching character.

Ex : c = strcmp (s1, s2);

This statement compares two strings s1, s2 and the address of non-matching character is returned to c pointer variable.

14.6.10 'strcpy' FUNCTION

This function copies one string to another string and replaces content of 1st string by 2nd strings.

Ex : strcpy (s1, s2);

In this case string s2 is copied to string s1. If s1 exists then it will be overwritter by s2.

14.6.11 'strlen' FUNCTION

This function returns the length of string which is an integer value.

Ex : i = strlen (s1);

where, i is integer variable.

The length of the string s1 is calculated by this function and stored in i integer variable.

14.6.12 'getch' FUNCTION

This function scans a character directly from a keyboard or a console device by bypassing the user screen.

c = getch ();

In this case , a call of 'getch' results in scanning of one character directly from keyboard and substitute in 'c' char variable.

Program 14-5

Program on 'getch' function.

```
# include <stdio.h>
main()
{
      int c, i;
      for (i=1; i<=5; ++i)
      {
            c = getch();
            printf ("%c   ", c);
      }
}
```

Output	:	anita

This program reads five characters directly from keyboard without displaying on screen and prints them on the screen.

Program 14-6

Program on 'strcpy' function.

```
# include <stdio.h>
/* strcpy function */
main()
{
      char string1[20], string2 [20];
      printf("Enter your first string\n");
      gets (string1);
      printf("Enter your second string\n");
      gets (string2);
      strcpy (String1, string2);
      puts(string1);
      puts(string2);
}
```

Input	:	Enter your first string
		Anita
		Enter your second string
		Vanita
Output	:	Vanita
		Vanita

This program copies string2 to string1 and replaces string1 by string2.

Program 14-7

Program on 'strcat' function.

```
/* strcat function */
# include <Stdio.h>
main()
{
    char string1 [20], string2 [20];
    printf ("enter the first string\n");
    gets (string1);
    printf ("enter the second string\n");
    gets (string2):
    strcat (string1, string2);
    printf ("the string is\n");
    put (string1);
}
```

Input	:	Enter the first string Anita Enter the second string Vanita
Output	:	the string is AnitaVanita

This program concatenates or joins 'string2' to 'string1' and forms a new joined 'string1'.

EXERCISE

1. Write a program for reversing the string using `strlen' function.
2. Prepare a program to separate alphabets of a string.
3. Write a program to arrange these alphabets in alphabetical order.
4. Write a program to locate an alphabet in a string and its location number.
5. Write a function program to accept a sentence consisting of `n' word.
6. Write a program to count number of words in a sentence.
7. Write a program to obtain a sub-string form a large string
   (i) 'Me' from 'Meet'
   (ii) 'Gain' from 'Against'
   (iii) 'Vices' from 'Services'
8. Write a program using function program to delete a string from a sentence.
9. Write a program using function program to find a string from a sentence.
10. Write a program using function program to insert a string at particular location in a statement.
11. Prepare a program to scan names of students and print roll list of students.
12. Write a program using function program to search a name of student, remove a name of student, replace the name by a new name.
13. Write a program to convert upper case characters of string to lower case characters.
14. Program to find length of string and print half string.
15. Write a program that accepts a sentence of words and then displays each word of the sentence on

different lines.

16. Write a program to calculate number of words in a sentence and print last two words.
17. Write a program to reverse the words of sentence.
18. Write a program to find whether a word is present in a sentence and if present find the length of the string.
19. Input a two digit number and convert it to an equivalent in words.
20. Write a program to accept a string and replace the beginning letter of every word with capital letter.
21. Write a program to convert a string from lower case to upper case.
22. Write a C– program to input a line of text and invoke a function search _line to count the number of vowels, number of consonants, number of digits, number of space character and other special characters in line of text.
23. Write a function to convert a character number into an integer number. Develop a program that allows the user to enter a string and performing the following operations on it:
    1 – Count Number of Characters In String
    2 - Count Number of Words In String
    3 - Remove Spaces In String
    4 – Add 1 ASCII value to every characters in String
    5 – Sum up each ASCII value in string
    6 – Reverse String
    7 – Reverse Words In String

The following screen suggests a possible user interface:

```
Enter String: C is Fun!

1 – Count Number of Characters In String
2 - Count Number of Words In String
3 - Remove Spaces In String
4 – Add 1 ASCII value to every characters in String
5 – Sum up each ASCII value in string
6 – Reverse String
7 – Reverse Words In String
```

whereby:

If option 1 is chosen, 7 (including any special characters but excluding spaces) is shown on the screen.

If option 2 is chosen, 3 is shown on the screen.

If option 3 is chosen, 'CisFun!' is shown on the screen.

If option 4 is chosen, add 1 ASCII value to every character in the string.

If option 5 is chosen, sum up and display total ASCII values in string.

If option 6 is chosen, '!nuF si C' is shown on the screen.

If option 7 is chosen, 'C si !nunF' is shown on the screen.

15
POINTERS

AN OVERVIEW

In the previous unit we have studied the concept of a string and the storage of a string in a single and two dimensional character arrays. The string is a bunch of characters or words or sentences of English language which can be stored in single or two dimensional array. There are readymade functions which can be utilized for operation on string.

In this unit the concept of a pointer has been discussed. The pointer is similar to a broker in human life. The broker operates between the seller and buyer and transacts the value between the two. The broker accepts a value from seller and transfer the value to a buyer. The pointer of c language performs the work in the similar fashion.

OBJECTIVES

After completing this unit you will be able to

* Define a pointer
* Demonstrate the operation of pointer
* Explain the use of pointer
* Evaluate functioning of pointer

15.1 INTRODUCTION

The pointers enable us to effectively represent complex data structure and to change values which are passed as arguments to functions, to work with memory that has been allocated dynamically. The concept of the pointer is just similar to the broker. The pointers accept a value from a variable store it and give it to another variable. Every variable receives an address in the memory and the address of variable in the memory is indicated by an integer number. The pointer variable is capable of accessing address of any other normal variable.

15.2 DECLARATION OF POINTER

It is defined as x *y;

where, x – declaration of pointer variable

y – variable name of pointer.

Ex : int *point;

where 'point' is a variable which is pointer of integer type.

The pointer variable is capable of receiving the value from the normal variable.If the pointer variable is represented by

*point ⟶ represents a value

point ⟶ represents an address at that value.

15.3 SUPPLY OF VALUE TO POINTER

The value can be stored in the pointer by attaching '&' character to the value of variable to be supplied.

Ex : point = &x;

In this case value of 'x' variable whose value is to be supplied to the pointer, can be given by equalizing address or location of x to 'point' pointer. To obtain address of variable '&' is attached to it. The address is a location number in memory of computer. If '*' is removed from pointer variable, then it represents an address of pointer variable and if '*' is attached, then it represents a value of pointer variable. Like,

point – represents address of pointer

*point – represents a value of variable.

Hence,

point = &x;

means address 'x' normal variable is given to pointer variable 'point'. This automatically means 'point' acquires address of x and can represent for value of x.

but if it is written as

*point = x;

Then 'x' normal variable supplies value to the 'point' pointer variable and address of pointer variable and x will be different, only value of x is substituted in 'point' pointer variable.

15.4 PRINTING OF VALUE OF POINTER

The pointer can be printed by using a 'printf' statement as

printf("the value of pointer is %d\n",*point);

The address of the pointer can be printed by removing its '*'

printf("the address of the pointer is %d\n",point);

Program 15–1

```
/* program on pointers */
main()
{
    int *ptr, a = 9,b;
    *ptr = a;
    b=*ptr;
    printf("a=%d,*ptr= %d, b=%d\n," a, *ptr, b);
    printf("address of a=%d,address of ptr=%d,address of b=%d\n", &a,ptr,&b);
}
```

In this program 'a' variable supplies value to pointer variable 'ptr' and 'ptr' supplies value to 'b' variable.The value of all three variables are printed by using 'printf' statement and the addresses are printed by another 'printf' statement.

Program 15–2

```
/* Program on pointers */
main ()
{
    int *ptr, a = 9; b;
    ptr = &a;
    b = *ptr;
    printf("a = %d, *ptr = %d, b =%d\n", a, *ptr, b);
    printf("address of a=%,address of ptr=%d,address of b=%d\n",&a,ptr,&b);
}
```

In this program, the address or location number of a variable is given to 'ptr'. Hence 'ptr' acquires address of 'a' and naturally 'ptr' receives any value stored in 'a'. This 'ptr' gives value to 'b' variable.

15.5 CONCEPT OF POINTER

The pointer works like a broker who accepts value from one variable and transfers to another variable. The pointer can be asked to accept the value of variable or address of variable. If it accepts the address of any variable, then changes in value of variable are automatically available to pointer or the values of variable can be changed by changing the value of the pointer.

Program 15–3

```
/* Pointer Program */
main()
{
    int a, *ptr, b;
    a = 9;
    ptr = &a;
    b = *ptr;
    ++a;
    printf("a = %d, *ptr = %d, b = %d\n", a, *ptr,b);
}
```

Output : a = 10, *ptr = 10, b = 9

In this program, 'ptr' receives address of 'a' variable and obviously value of 'a' variable. Then 'ptr' transfers value to 'b' variable. Then 'a' variable is incremented, because value of 'a' is 10 and pointer is located in the same address, hence receives value of 10.

15.6 TYPES OF POINTERS

There are different types of pointers, like integer, float and char pointers. These can be declared according to the declaration of type as int, float or char or double. Then the pointer will be able to store the value of declared type.

Program 15–4

```
/* types of pointers*/
main()
{
    int *ptr,a=9;float *ptr1,a1=9.23;char *ptr2,a2='+';
    int b;float b1;char b2;
    ptr=&a;
    b=*ptr;
    ptr1=&a1;
    b1=*ptr1;
    ptr2=&a2;
    b2=*ptr2;
    printf("b=%d, b1=%g , b2=%c\n",b,b1,b2);
}
```

Output : b=9, b1=9.23, b2=+

This program indicates the variety of pointers being used . The 'ptr' is an integer pointer, 'ptr1' is float pointer and 'ptr2' is character pointer.

Program 15–5

This is a program on the character pointer in which a value of character is given to a character pointer and it is printed by the pointer.

```
/*Character pointer */
main()
{
     char c = '+';
     char *cpoint = &c;
     printf ("%c %c \n", c,*cpoint);
     c = '/';
     printf ("%c %c\n", c, *cpoint);
}
```

Output	:	+ + / /

In this program the character pointer is receiving a character and it is printed by normal variable and pointer.

15.7 EXCHANGE OF VALUE BETWEEN TWO POINTERS

The values can be exchanged between two pointers by assigning their addresses or their values.The values of pointer can be assigned to each other by equalizing their addresses or their values .Ex:

If *ptr1 and *ptr2 are two pointers, then their values can be exchanged by equalizing their addresses or their values.

ptr2=ptr1

or

*ptr2=*ptr1

This can be seen in the following program :

Program 15–6

```
/* Exchange of value between two pointers */
main ()
{
     int a,b;
     int *ptr1, *ptr2;
     a = 5;
     ptr1 = &a;
     b = (*ptr1) * 2;
     ptr2 = ptr1;
     printf ("a = %d, b = %d, *ptr1 = %d, *ptr2 = %d\n", a,b,
     *ptr1, *ptr2);
}
```

Output	:	a=5,b=10,*ptr1=5,*ptr2=5

In this program 'ptr1' pointer receives address of 'a' and 'b' is obtained by multiplying 'ptr1' with 2. Then the address of 'ptr2' pointer is given to ptr1, which automatically transfers 'ptr1' value to 'ptr2' pointer.

15.8 POINTER AS ARGUMENT OF FUNCTION PROGRAM

The pointer variable can be used as argument of function program. This can be done by using the pointer variable as an argument in the call and is also an argument in the function program.

Program 15–7

The use of pointer with function.

```
/* pointer and function */
test (point)
int *point;
{
     *point = *point*2;
}
main()
{
     int i = 50, *p = &i;
     printf ("i original = %d\n", i);
     test(p);
     printf ("i new = %d\n", i);
}
```

Output	:	i original = 50 i new = 100

In this program , the pointer 'p' receives a value of 'i' and is supplied as an argument of the function program "test". Another pointer is used as argument of function "test" which modifies value of pointer and multiplies it with a value of 2.

Program 15–8

Program on the exchange of Pointers.

```
/* exchange of pointer */
exchange (point1, point2)
int *point1, *point2;
{
     int temp;
     temp = *point1;
     *point1 = *point2;
     *point2 = temp;
}
main()
{
     int a = –5, b = 66, *p1 = &a, *p2 = &b;
     printf ("a = %d, b =%d\n", b,b);
     exchange (p1, p2);
     printf ("a=%d, b=%d\n", *p1, *p2);
}
```

Output : a = 66, b = 66
a = 66, b = – 5

In this program, the values are exchanged between two pointers by use of function 'exchange'. This function program accepts the values of two pointers and supplies it to a function program which exchanges the value between two pointers.

15.9 USE OF POINTER IN AN ARRAY

The pointers are used in an array. If the pointer variable is used without '*' for representing an array it indicates the address of beginning value of array at 'o' index location and when used with the '*' it indicates the corresponding value of the zero index attached to the pointer variable.

The array has values in the memory as:

	0	1	2	3	4	5	6	7	8	9
array	3	7	–9	3	6	–1	7	9	1	–5

* array = array [0] = 3

The array becomes pointer of its own in a function program and acquires base address of array

* (array +1) = 7

* (array +2) = –9

* (array +3) =3

By incrementing the base address of array any element of array can be acquired.

This can be seen in the following programs.

Program 15–9

```
/* function to sum the elements of an integer array */
int add (array,n)
int *array[ ];
int n;
{
    int sum = 0, *point;
    int *as = array;
    int *aend = array + n;
    for (point = as; point<aend; ++point)
    sum + = *point;
    printf("sum=%d\n",sum);
}
main()
{
    int values[10] = {3,7,–9,3,6,–1,7,9,1,–5};
    add (values,10);
}
```

Output : sum=21

In this program sum of all elements of array 'value' are made by using a pointer. The array is supplied in the main program and 'add' function is called. The 'array' where 'value' is substituted is made pointer of its own in function program, hence it obtains start value of array as array [o], and address of this is given 'as' pointer and 'aend' pointer receives addresses and when a '*' is attached to the point, it represents a value of every element of array and adds all elements of array.

The same 'add' function program can be written by alternate method;

```
int add(array, n)
int *array [ ], n;
{
    int sum = 0, i;
    for(i=0; i<–n; ++i)
    sum + = *(array+i);
    printf("sum=%d\n",sum);
}
```

In this function program, the array is made pointer of its own. It receives begin value of array and address of that value.

Therefore, 'array' represents base address of array variable and '*array' represent the value at base address as array[0]. The (array+1) represents next address of 'array' variable means address of array[1], then *(array+1) represents value at array [1] locations. In this way all values can be added.

15.10 CHARACTER OPERATION USING POINTER

In similar fashion of using pointer to represent an integer array, the pointer can be used to obtain character array. A character pointer can be used to represent character value in an array.

Program 15–10

```
main ()
{
    char string1 [] = "string to be copied";
    char string2 [50] ;
    copy (string1, string2);
    printf (%s\n", string2);
    copy ("so is this", string2);
    printf("%s\n", string2);
}
copy (from,to)
char *from, *to;
{
    while (*from)
    {
        * to = *from;
        to++; from++;
    }
    *to = '\0';
}
```

Output	:	string to be copied so is this

This program copies string1 to string2, using two pointers 'from' and 'to'. If array is passed to these pointers in function program, they acquire begin address of strings and copies character value in address in the array. In while loop the characters are transferred 'from' to 'to' and addresses are incremented in every cycle. The 'while' terminates, when character do not exits in 'from' pointer.

Program 15–11

```
/* program to sort n numbers in ascending order */
main()
{
    int i,j,n,num [30];
    printf ("enter the maximum number\n");
    scanf ("%d", &n);
    printf("enter the numbers\n");
    get_array (num,n);
    printf("the elements of the array are\n");
    print_array (num,n);
    sort_array (num,n);
    printf("\nthe sorted elements of array are\n");
    print_array (num,n);
}
/* function to get the array elements */
get_array(num,n)
int n,num[30];
{
    int i;
    for(i=0;i<n;++i
    scanf("%d",&num[i];
}
/* This function sorts an array in the ascending order*/
sort_array (num,n)
int n, * num [ ];
{
    int i,j;
    for(j=0; j<n–1; i++)
    for (j=0; j<n–1;j++)
    if (*(num+j)>*(num+j+1)
    swap (num+j, num+j+1);
}
/*This function exchanges the value between two pointers*/
swap (int*a, int*b)
{
    int  temp;
    temp = *a;
    *a = *b;
    *b = temp;
}
```

```
print_array (m,n)
int n, *m[];
{
    int i, *ptr
    ptr = m;
    for (i=0; i<n; i++)
    printf ("%d", *(ptr + i));
}
```

Input	:	enter the maximum number 5 enter the numbers 3 1 2 5 4
Output	:	the elements of the array are 3 1 2 5 4 the sorted elements of array are 1 2 3 4 5

In this program on sorting of an array using pointer in ascending order, the main program uses function 'get_array for scanning of array, then 'sort_array' for sorting the elements of array in ascending order. Then 'print_array' for printing of sorted array.

15.11 FUNCTION POINTERS

The pointers can be used for the function as function pointers , where they can be used for calling a function. This can be seen in the following program.

Program 15–12

```
/*Pointer function*/
main()
{
    int n;
    void (*nptr)();                  ————→ declaration of function pointer
    printf("enter the values of nodes:");
    scanf("%d",&n);
    code(n);                   ————→ normal call of function program
    nptr=code;         ————→ function pointer receives the address of function name

    (*nptr)(n);                ————→ second call of function using function pointer
}
code(n)
int n;
{
    printf("the value of codes is %d\n",8*n);
}
```

Input	:	enter the values of nodes:4
Output	:	the value of codes is 4 the value of codes is 4

15.12 USE OF POINTER IN TWO DIMENSIONAL ARRAY

The pointers can be used in two dimensional arrays as similar to single dimensional array. These are especially required in the matrices. In this case also, the pointer variable without '*'takes a value of address at that index of the array and the pointer variable with '*' provides the corresponding value of the array at that address.

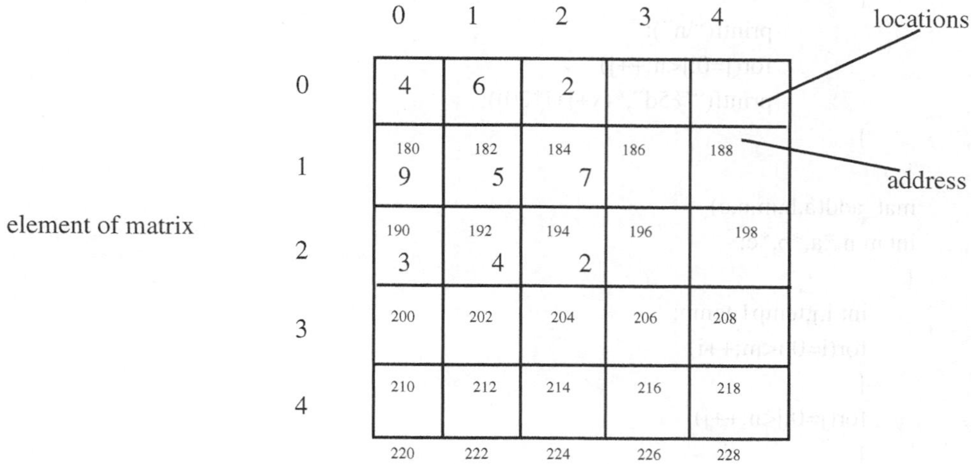

If 'a' matrix of order 3×3 is stored in a matrix of 5×5 as given above.Then elements of matrix can be obtained by accessing the base address of array as a pointer.

```
* a = a [0][0] = 4
a =  address of a [0][0]  = 180
Since     (a+1)=  182
*(a+1)          = a[0] [1]  = 6
*(a+2)          = a[0][2]  = 2
* (a+5+0)       = a [1][0] = 9
* (a+5+1)       = a [1] [1]=5
```

The following program is on addition of two matrices using pointers as below.

Program 15–13

```
/*Addition of the two matrices */
main()
{
    int i,j;int a[20][20],b[20][20],c[20][20],m,n;
    printf("\nEnter the order of matrices\n");
    scanf("%d%d",&m,&n);
    printf("\nEnter the elements of matrix A\n");
    get_array(a,m,n);
    printf("\nEnter the elements of matrix B\n");
    get_array(b,m,n);
    mat_add(a,b,m,n,c);
    printf("\n The addition of matrices A+B is \n");
    print_array(c,m,n);
}
print_array(x,m,n)
```

```
int *x,m,n;
{
    int i,j;
    for(i=0;i<m;++i)
    {
            printf("\n");
            for(j=0;j<n;++j)
            printf("%5d",*(x+j+i*20));
    }
}
mat_add(a,b,m,n,c)
int m,n,*a,*b,*c;
{
    int i,j,temp1,temp;
    for(i=0;i<m;++i)
    {
    for(j=0;j<n;++j)
    {
            temp1=*(a+j+i*20);
            temp2=*(b+j+i*20);
            *(c+j+i*20)= temp1+temp2;
    }
    }
}
get_array(x,m,n)
int x[20][20],m,n;
{
    int i,j;
    for(i=0;i<m;++i)
    {
    for(j=0;j<n;++j)
    {
            scanf("%d",&x[i][j]);
    }
    }
}
```

Input : Enter the order of matrices
3 3
Enter the elements of matrix A
1 2 3
4 5 6
7 8 9

		Enter the elements of matrix B 9 8 7 6 5 4 3 2 1
Output	:	The addition matrices A+B is 10 10 10 10 10 10 10 10 10

In this program, addition of two matrices is done by using pointers. The 'get_array' function 'scans' matrix. The 'mat_add' function adds two matrices 'a' and 'b' using pointers. The 'print_array' function prints the elements of matrix.

15.13 POINTER OF POINTER

In C–language a double pointer can be declared as a pointer of a pointer. This pointer can be declared by using ** operator.

int **ptr;

This means that the ptr pointer is a double pointer indicated by **. This pointer accepts the value from another pointer.

int a=9;

int *ptr1;

ptr1 = &a;

ptr = &ptr1;

In this case the double pointer receives the value from the normal pointer. So the double pointer acts as a pointer of a pointer.

Program 15–14

```
/* Double Pointer */
main()
{
int a = 100,*b,**c;
 clrscr();
  b = &a; /* b contains the address of int a, */
  /* hence b is an int pointer */
  c = &b; /* c contains the address of int pointer */
  /* hence c is a pointer to an int pointer*/
printf("%d %d %d",a,*b,**c);
return;
}
```

Output	:	100 100 100

EXERCISE

1. Write a program for multiplication of two matrices using pointers.
2. Explain what will be the output of the following program :

(i)
```
int a,b, *ptr;
ptr = &a;
a = 9;
b = *ptr;
a++;
```
What is the value of a,b,*ptr ?

(ii)
```
int a,b,*ptr; a = 9;
ptr = &a;
b = *ptr;
a++;
```
What is the value of a, b, *ptr ?

(iii)
```
int a, b, *ptr; a = 9;
ptr = &a;
b = *ptr;
*ptr + = 2;
```
What is the value of a, b, *ptr ?

(iv)
```
int a, b, *ptr; a = 9;
ptr = &a
&b = ptr;
++b;
```
What is the value of a, b, *ptr ?

3. Write a program to calculate sum of first ten numbers using pointer.
4. Write a program to calculate sum of odd numbers upto 50 using pointer.
5. Write a program to calculate average of given `n' number using pointer.
6. Write a program to calculate sum of all numbers in given matrix using pointer.
7. Write a program to calculate sum of diagonal elements of matrix using pointer.
8. Write a program to obtain transpose of matrix using pointers.
9. Write a program to find minimum and maximum values in a matrix using pointers.
10. Write a program to find factorial of number using pointer.
11. Write a program to reverse the characters of a string using pointers.
12. Write a program to exchange a string from one variable to another using pointers.

16

STRUCTURE

AN OVERVIEW

In the previous unit we have seen the application of pointers in c-programming. The pointers are not essential in programming but they are used in programming for improving the speed of execution of program by fast retrival of data. The pointers are capable of accessing the address of a any variable which makes it convenient for modification of data. The pointers can access the array and the movement on the array becomes easier by increasing the addresses. The pointer are capable of working on character arrays and they are also used for accessing the address of function programs.

In this unit we are going to discuss about the topic of structure which is an association of number of variables. The structures are use for representing bunch of variables. The structure provides convenience in the programming because of the combination of variables used to represent the data.

OBJECTIVES

After completing this unit you will be able to

* Define a structure.
* Distinguish variable and sub variable.
* Explain the application of structure in function program.
* Develop global structure.

16.1 INTRODUCTION

A *structure* is a bunch of variables representing a single quantity. It can be regarded as an association of variables representing certain quantity. In case if a quantity is defined by number of variables, then the use of structures in programming is desirable from the point of view of the structured programming. This prevents the corruption in the data and keeps the records in a formatted form through which data can be easily retrieved. The structures are capable of creating data cards for maintaining the information related to a particular quantity. The information can be retrieved very easily and stored in the correct format. The use of the structures is very useful for passing the values of numbers of the variables to the function programs by simply passing structures.

A simple example of the structure is a structure of the "day". A *structure* called "day" can be defined by three components which represents the day are date, month and year.

The *structure* of "day" can be declared as below:

```
struct day
{
     int date;
     int month;
     int year;
};
```

In this case the structure day consists of three sub-variables date, month and year. Every value of 'day' is represented by three quantities such as date, month and year.

The value of variables can only be supplied by reference of structure to another variable 'today' like

```
struct day today;
```

This indicates that structure 'day' is given to a new variable `today'. Then the value can be assigned to 'today', which is the main variable represented by three sub-variables date, month and year.

The value to variables can be supplied by using a variable in the form of ,

x.y = z;

where,

x	–	main variable
y	–	sub-variable
z	–	value of variable
x.y	–	structure variable which is used like a normal variable.

Ex : today.date = 10;

The 'today.date' is structured variable which can acquire a value similar to normal variable.

Program 16–1

```
/* program to illustrate a structure */
main()
{
    struct day
    {
        int month;
        int date;
        int year;
    };
    struct day today;
    today.month = 9;
    today.date = 25;
    today.year = 1996;
    clrscr();
    printf("today's day is %d/%d/%d \n", today. date,today.month,today.year);
}
```

Output : today's day is 25/9/1996

16.2 SCANNING OF STRUCTURE

The structure variables are scanned by the specification of sub variables and main variable.

The Scanning of a structure is made by attaching structured variable with the individual subvariable of structure by a dot and reading is made similar to normal variable.

It is written as:

scanf ("%d", & x.y);

Where,

x	–	structured variable name
y	–	sub-variable of structure to be read.

Ex : scanf("%d",&today.date);

The structure variable 'today.date' is scanned from the data screen.

Program 16–2

```
/* scanning and printing of structure variable */
main()
{
    struct day
    {
        int month;
        int date;
        int year;
    } ;
    struct day today ;
    scanf("%d%d%d", & today.date, & today.month, & today.year);
    printf("today's day is %d%d%d\n", today.date, today.month,today.year);
}
```

Input	:	27/6/2000
Output	:	today's day is 27/6/2000

In this program, a structure of 'day' is declared and referenced to 'today', the structure is scanned by using 'scanf' statement and printed.

Program 16–3

This program finds the next day from the current day in any month. This program uses 'if' statement to calculate the value of the next day.

```
/* Program to determine tomorrow's date */
main ()
{
    struct day
    {
        int month;
        int date;
        int year;
    };
    struct day today, tomorrow;
    static int dpm[12] ={31,28,31,30,31,30,31,31,30,31,30,31};
    print ("Enter todays day\n");
    Scanf("%d%d%d", & today.date,& today.month,& today.year);
    if(today.date<=dpm[today.month–1])
    {
        if(today.date!=dpm[today.month–1])
        {
            tomorrow. day = today. date + 1;
            tomorrow. month = today. month;
            tomorrow. year = today. year;
        }
        else
```

```
        if (today. month == 12)         / * year end */
        {
                tomorrow. date = 1;
                tomorrow. month = 1;
                tomorrow. year = today. year + 1;
        }
        else                            / * month end */
        {
                tomorrow. date = 1;
                tomorrow. month = today. month + 1;
                tomorrow. year = today. year;
        }
        printf ("Tomorrow's date is %d/%d/%d\n," tomorrow. date, tomorrow. month,
                        tomorrow. year);
        }
    else
    printf("Don't play with me, enter correct date\n");
}
```

Input	:	Enter todays day 27 6 2000
Output	:	Tomorrow's date is 28 / 6 / 2000

In this program, all the maximum number of days in the calander month are supplied to the array 'max_no_day' array. Then checking of whether the 'date' supplied is more than no. of days in month or no. of days in month or 'month' is more than 12 is carried out, then the day is correct.

Then it is checked where the given day is at the end of the year, then year is incremented, whereas date and month are 1. If it is not at the end of year, then checking will be carried out to find end of month by equalizing 'date' with maximum no. of days in month, if found to be true, then the month is incremented by 1 and date is considered as 1, then year for next day remains same. If both conditions fail, it means that the day is in the middle of the month, hence only date is incremented for next day, the 'month' and 'year' remains same.

16.3 STRUCTURE VARIABLE AS ARGUMENT OF FUNCTION PROGRAM

The structure can be used as argument of the function program by using a global structure which is just similar global variable. If a structure is declared in the beginning of file outside any program, then it becomes a global structure. In such a case global structure can be used as argument of function program.

If a structure is made argument of the function program then the transfer of a value is easily possible for large number of variables. When a structure is passed to a function program all the sub-variables maintaining the values of structure will be passed on to function program. The structure can be returned to the main program along with the content of all the values.

Similarly, a structured variable can also become an argument of function program.

Program 16–4

In this program, a structure of day is declared as a global structure by declaring it in the beginning of the file. The value of structure 'today' is supplied in the main program and the values are passed on to function program for further processing to find the next day.

```
/* program to determine tomorrow's date */
struct day
{
     int date;
     int month;
     int year;
};
main()
{
     int z;
     struct day today, tomorrow;
     clrscr();
     printf("Enter today's day :\n");
     scanf("%d/%d/%d",&today.month,&today.date,&today.year);
     z=number_of_days(today);
     if((today.date>z)||(today.month>12))
     {
               printf("you are a fool\n");
     }
     else
     if((today.date==31)&&(today.month==12))
     {
               tomorrow.date=1;
               tomorrow.month=1;
               tomorrow.year=today.year+1;
     }
     else
     if(today.month==z)
     {
               tomorrow.date=1;
               tomorrow.month=today.month+1;
               tomorrow.year=today.year;
     }
     else
     {
               tomorrow.date=today.date+1;
               tomorrow.month=today.month;
               tomorrow.year=today.year;
     }
     printf("Tomorrow'sdate is %d/%d/ %d\n", tomorrow.date, tomorrow.month,
               tomorrow.year);
}
int number_of_days(d)
struct day d;
```

```
{
    int answer;
    int dpm[12]={31,28,31,30,31,30,31,31,30,31,30,31};
    if(d.month==2)
    {
            answer=leap_year(d.year);
    }
    else
            answer=dpm[d.month–1];
    return(answer);
}
int leap_year(y)
int y;
{
    int zz;
    if(y%4==0)
            zz=29;
    else
            zz=28;
    return(zz);
}
```

Input	:	Enter today's day : 6 / 28 / 2000
Output	:	Tomorrow's date is 29 / 6 / 2000

In this program a global structure is declared and the 'today' is supplied to the structure. The maximum number of days are found by using 'number_of_days' function program. This function program supplied with 'today' is used as argument of function program to pass the values of structure. The main program uses function of 'number_of_days' to find maximum no. of days in month. Since 'February' has maximum days depending on leap year, therefore, a leap year function is called in 'number_of_days' function program to find whether the given year is leap year or not. The value of maximum 'number_of_days' for the given month is calculated by the function program and returned to the main program which further processes to find the next day using 'if–else' construct statement as it is done in the last program.

16.4 INITIALIZATION OF STRUCTURE

The structure can be initialized by using a static or automatic statement providing the values of the main variable along with the sub-variables. The structure can be pointed towards a specific variable.

Ex : Static struct day today = {7,2,1996};

or

struct day today = {7,2,1996};

In this case, the structure is referred and the values of subvariables are supplied using static or non-static statement. The date is 7, month is 2 and year 1996 for today.

16.5 ARRAY OF STRUCTURE

The structure can be used as an array and is stored by two or more independent sub-variables of the structure. This is done by assigning a structured variable to a structured array variable and the array variable will store the value in different indexes for different values of structures. The values to the structured array can be supplied by static or non-static statement or otherwise the values can be scanned by using 'scanf' statement.

Ex: static struct day holiday[5]={ {1,8,95},{10,8,95}, {15,8,95},{18,8,95},{29,8,95}};

The structure of day is given to a structure of array variable 'holiday'. In this case the days of holidays in a month are supplied using initialization statement.

Program 16–5

This program uses structure of 'time' which consists of hours, minutes and seconds. The current time is stored in an array and newtime after 1 second is determined by using a function program.

```
/* program to illustrate arrays of structures */
struct time
{
     int hour;
     int minutes;
     int seconds;
}
main ()
{
     struct time  time_update (); struct time u_time;
     static struct time c_times[5]=
     {
               {11,59,59}, {12,0,0}, {1,29,59},
               {23,59,59}, {19,12,17}
     };
     int i;
     for (i = 0;  i < 5 ; + + i)
     {
               printf (''Time is % 2d:%2d:%2d", c_times[i].hour,
               c_times[i].minutes, c_times[i].second);
               u_times [i] = time_update(c_times[i]);
               printf ("\tone second later it's % 2d:%2d:%2d\n",u_time[i].hour,
                                         u_time[i].minutes,u_times[i].seconds);
     }
}
/* Function to update the time by one second */
struct time  time_update(now)
struct time now ;
{
     struct time new_time ;
     new_time = now ;
     ++new_time. seconds ;
```

```
    if(new_time. seconds == 60 )
    {
        new_time.seconds = 0 ;
        ++new_time.minutes ;
        if(new_time.minutes == 60 )
        {
            new_time.minutes = 0 ;
            ++new_time.hour ;
            if (new_time. hour == 24)
                new_time. hour = 0 ;
        }
    }
    return (new_time);
}
```

Output	:	Time is 11 : 59 : 59	one second later it's 12 : 0 : 0
		Time is 12: 0 : 0	one second later it's 12 : 0 : 1
		Time is 1 : 29 : 59	one second later it's 1 : 30 : 0
		Time is 23 : 59 : 59	one second later it's 0 : 0 : 0
		Time is 19 : 12 : 17	one second later it's 19 : 12 : 18

In this program a global structure of time is declared and an array of 'c_time' is supplied to the structure. Then a call is given to function program to update the time by one second and 'new_time' is obtained in function program. This is accepted by 'u_time' in the main program.

16.6 ARRAY AS A SUB-VARIABLE OF STRUCTURE

The array variable can become a member of a structure i.e. the array becomes a sub variable of a structure. Then it is declared as an array while defining the structure.

Ex:

```
struct p
{
    int a[20];
    float b[20];
    char c[20]
};
```

In this case a structure p is declared which has three members all being array variables. This means that the main variable p has multiple memories for every sub-variable. Then in such a case all variables maintain number of values in structures.

Program 16–6

```
/* Character array as a member of structures */
main()
{
struct emp
{
char name[10];
int age;
```

```
int bsal;
};
struct emp e[30];
int i,m,n;
clrscr();
printf("Enter the no. of record\n");
scanf("%d",&n);
for(i=1;i<=n;i++)
{
printf("Enter the name, age and salary \n");
scanf("%s %d %d",&e[i].name,&e[i].age,&e[i].bsal);
}
printf("Information of Employees \n");
for(i=1;i<=n;i++)
{
printf("No.          : %d\nName          : %s\nAge     : %d\nBasic salary
: %d\n",i,e[i].name,e[i].age,e[i].bsal);
}
return;
}
```

```
Input   :   Enter the no. of record
            2
            Enter the name, age and salary
            Anita  20  2000
            Enter the name, age and salary
            Vanita  24  2300
Output  :   Information of Employees
            No.            : 1
            Name           : Anita
            Age            : 20
            Basic salary   : 2000
            No.            : 2
            Name           : Vanita
            Age            : 24
            Basic salary   : 2300
```

In this program the structure of employees is created to maintain the records of employees. The structure consists of name, age & salary of employees. The name of employee is a character array as a member of structure. This structure is referred to array variable and then the data of employees is scanned and then it is printed in a formatted form.

16.7 POINTERS AS A MAIN VARIABLE OF STRUCTURE

The pointer can be used to define a structured variable.

The main variable of structure can become a pointer variable.

Ex : struct day *day_pointer;

In this statement, structure of day is referred to '*day_pointer' pointer variable.

The main pointer variable can be given value by using a statement where the main variable is a pointer as attached to a sub-variable which is not a pointer.

(*day_pointer).date=21;

The main variable of structure can be a pointer and can receive a value when they are attached to normal variable. The general form of the pointer as a main variable of structure is:

(*x).y;

Where,

x – name of main variable as pointer

y – structured sub-variable

Which can be represented by an equivalent statement using

x –> y

Ex : '*day_pointer' main variable and 'month' is sub-variable.

if((*day_pointer).month==12)

Equivalent to

if(day_pointer –> month==12)

∴ '(*day_pointer).month' is same as 'day_pointer –> month'

Program 16–7

```
/* program to use pointer with structure */
main ()
{
    struct day
    {
        int date;
        int month;
        int year;
    };
    struct day today, *day_pointer;
    day_pointer = & today;
    day_pointer —> month = 30;
    day_pointer —> date = 27
    day_pointer —> year = 1995
    clrscr();
    printf (" Today's date is %d/%d/%d\n",day_pointer —> date_pointer —> month,
            day_pointer —> year);
}
```

Output : Today's date is 27/12/1995

16.8 STRUCTURE OF THE POINTERS

It is possible to create a structure of a pointer. This concept is just similar to an association of brokers attached to a main broker who controls and groups the brokers. In this case the sub-variables of a structure becomes pointer and this allows the transaction of values between the pointers.

The pointers can be structured to a particular variable by their declaration. In this case all the sub-variables of structure are pointer and the main variable is a normal variable.

Ex :

```
struct point
{
        int * p1 ;
        int * p2 ;
};
```

In this case, the structure of 'point' is two pointers '*p1' and '*p2'.

When a value is to be given to a structured pointer variable it is written as similar to the normal pointers by way of giving address of normal variable to the pointer of structure variable.

```
point.p1=&x1;
```

where,

x1 – normal variable

In this case, pointer p1 receives address of x1.

The value to a pointer structure variable can be given by normal variable using a statement

```
*point.p1 = x1;
```

When a structured pointer variable gives a value to a normal variable, then it is written as

```
y1 = *point.p1;
```

where,

y1 – normal variable

Program 16–8

```
/* structures containing pointers */
main ()
{
    struct point
    {
        int * p1 ;
        int * p2 ;
    };
    struct point  poin;
    int x1 = 100, x2 = 20;
    poin.p1 = &x1;
    *poin.p2 = x2;
    *poin.p1 = x2;
    clrscr();
    printf ("x1 = %d, *poin.p1 = %d\n," x1, *poin.p1);
    printf ("x2 = %d, *poin.p2 = %d\n," x2, *poin.p2);
}
```

Output :	x1 = 20, *poin.p1 = 20 x2 = 20, *poin.p2 = 20

16.9 STRUCTURE OF NORMAL VARIABLES AND POINTERS

This is an association of normal variable and pointer variable. It is also called as link list. In the linked list, a structure of the normal variables and pointer variables is created. Then the pointer variable becomes a sub-variable of structure alongwith the normal variable.

Ex:

If a structure is defined as:

```
struct e
{
        int x;
        int *z;
};
struct e y;
```

Where,

e – main variable

x – normal sub-variable

z – pointer sub-variable

In this case, 'y' is a main variable whose structure consists of a normal variable 'x' and pointer variable 'z'. The normal sub-variable can be utilised by using it along with the main variable.

```
y.x = 10;
```

The structured variable 'y.x' receives values of 10.

The pointer sub-variable can be utilised by using it along with the main variable.

```
*y.z = y.x;
```

The pointer structure variable 'y.z' receives value from y.x.

Program 16–9

This is a program on linked list. In this program a structure of normal variables and pointer variables is created and the values are supplied to the pointer and normal sub-variable. The values of pointer variables are modified and the printing of pointer of sub-variable is obtained.

```
/* structure of normal variable and pointer */
main ()
{
    struct e
    {
            int v;
            int *x;
    };
    struct e n1;
    int i=10;
    clrscr();
    n1.v=1;
    n1.x=&i;
    ++i;
    printf("i=%d,n1.v=%d,n1.x=%d\n",i,n1.v,*n1.x);
}
```

Output	:	i=11,n1.v=1,n1.x=11

16.10 NESTED STRUCTURE

This is declared with one structure inside another structure. The structure of a particular variable becoming a member of another structure is an example of nested structure. In this case the reference of structure inside is treated as member of another structure. This can be seen in the following program.

Program 16–10

```
/* Nested structures */
main()
{
      struct em
      {
            char name[10];
            int age;
            struct address
            {
                  char city[10];
                  long int pin;
            }a;
      }e = {"Jay", 30, "Nagpur", 440001};
      clrscr();
      printf("%s %d %s %ld", e.name,e.age,e.a.city,e.a.pin);
      return;
}
```

Output	:	Jay 30 Nagpur 440001

In this program a structure 'em' is created to maintain the records of the persons having their names, age and cities of permanent and temporary addresses and pin code numbers.

Program 16–11

This program finds the difference between the two days. In this case the structure of day is declared and it is referenced to today & nextday. Then the 'today' and 'nextday' is scanned and the difference between the two days is calculated by 'if–else' statement by counting the no. of days in between the two days.

```
/* Difference between two dates */
main()
{
      struct day
      {
            int date;
            int month;
            int year;
      };
      int sum=0,i;
      struct day today;
      struct day nextday;
      int a[12]={31,28,31,30,31,30,31,31,30,31,30,31};
      clrscr();
```

```
printf("Enter the starting date \n");
scanf("%d/%d/%d",&today.date,&today.month,&today.year);
printf("Enter the leaving date\n");
scanf("%d/%d/%d",&nextday.date,&nextday.month,&nextday.year);
if(today.year !=nextday.year)
{
        sum=a[today.month–1]–today.date+nextday.date;
        for(i=today.month+1;i<=12;++i)
        sum=sum+a[i–1];
        for(i=1;i<nextday.month;++i)
        sum=sum+a[i–1];
}
else
if(today.month!=nextday.month)
{
        sum=a[today.month–1]–today.date+nextday.date;
        for(i=today.month+1;i<nextday.month;++i)
        sum=sum+a[i–1];
}
else
sum=nextday.date–today.date;
printf("The no. of days beween two days = %d\n",sum);
}
```

Input	:	Enter the starting date 4 / 7 / 2000 Enter the leaving date 5 / 7 / 2000
Output	:	The no. of days betwen two days = 1

Program 16–12

In this program the age of the person is calculated by using the structure. In this case, the today & dob (date of birth) of the person is supplied and the difference between year and months of today and dob is calculated by using the 'if–else' statement.

```
/* To find the age of the person */
main()
{
    struct day
    {
        int date;
        int month;
        int year;
    };
    float sum,i,age;
    struct day today, dob;
```

```
    clrscr();
    printf("Enter the date of birth \n");
    scanf("%d/%d/%d",&dob.date,&dob.month,&dob.year);
    printf("Enter the current date\n");
    scanf("%d/%d/%d",&today.date,&today.month,&today.year);
    age=today.year – dob.year;
    sum=today.month – dob.month;
    if(sum<0)
    {
        —age;
        sum = abs(sum);
    }
    age=age+sum/12.0;
    printf("The age of the person is = %g\n",age);
}
```

Input	:	Enter the date of birth 22 / 5 / 1970 Enter the current date 22 / 5 / 2000
Output	:	The age of the person is = 30

Program 16–13

In this program, the salary bill of the employees is calculated by declaring the structure of the employee as employee number, basic pay, name and surname. It is referenced to the array and the data is scanned by using the 'scanf' statement. The salary of the employee is calculated in terms of DA, HRA, CLA and gross salary using the 'cal' function program.

```
/* Salary program of employees */
struct emp
{
    int e_no;
    int b_pay;
    char name[30];
    char s_name[30];
}
e[25];
int i,n;
main()
{
    clrscr();
    printf("\n enter the no. of employees\n");
    scanf("%d",&n);
    for(i=1;i<=n;++i)
    {
```

```
            printf("enter the employee  full name\n");
            scanf("%s%s", &e[i].name, &e[i].s_name);
            printf("enter the employee  emp no, basic pay\n");
      }
      for(i=1;i<=n;++i)
      cal();
}
cal()
{
      float da[100],cca[100],hra[100],g_salary[100];
      da[i]=0.60*e[i].b_pay;
      cca[i]=50.0;
      hra[i]=0.25*e[i].b_pay;
      if(hra[i]>=1000)
      {
            hra[i]=1000;
      }
      g_salary[i]=da[i]+cca[i]+hra[i]+e[i].b_pay;
      printf("************************************************\n");
      printf("————————————————————————————————————————————————\n");
      printf("  NAME   : %s  %s            EMPLOYMENT NO  %d        \n",
            e[i].name,e[i].s_name,e[i].e_no);
      printf("  BASIC PAY          : %d \n",e[i].b_pay);
      printf("  DA                 : %g \n",da[i]);
      printf("  CCA                : %g \n",cca[i]);
      printf("  HRA                : %g \n",hra[i]);
      printf("\n");
      printf("  GROSS  SALARY           :           %g \n",g_salary[i]);
      printf("————————————————————————————————————————————————\n");
      printf("************************************************\n");
}
```

```
Input     :     enter the no. of employees
                2
                enter the employees full name
                Anita Bakshi
                enter the employees emp no,basic pay
                2   2500
                enter the employees full name
                Vanita Sathe
                enter the employees emp no,basic pay
                2   3000
Output    :
                ****************************************************
```

```
-----------------------------------------------------------------------------------
    NAME                    : Anita Bakshi    EMPLOYMENT NO. 1
    BASIC PAY               : 2500
    DA                      : 1500
    CCA                     : 625
    GROSS SALARY            : 4675
-----------------------------------------------------------------------------------
*****************************************************


*****************************************************
-----------------------------------------------------------------------------------
    NAME                    : Vanita Sathe    EMPLOYMENT NO. 2
    BASIC PAY               : 3000
    DA                      : 1800
    CCA                     : 750
    GROSS SALARY            : 5600
-----------------------------------------------------------------------------------

*****************************************************
```

EXERCISE

1. Write a program to accept the elements of the structures
   (i) Emp– no and (ii) Basic pay and display and the same structure alongwith the A, HRA, CCA, and Gross salary. The DA and CCA are calculated as:
   DA = 51% OF Basic pay
   CCA = Rs. 100/–
   HRA = 15% of basic pay subject max^{M} Rs. 800/–
2. Write a program to prepare a list of holidays in a year.
3. Write a program to prepare Electricity bill as per following units
   For first100 units – Rs.11 per unit
   For next 300 units – Rs. 2/05 per unit
   beyond 300 units – Rs. 3/50 per unit
   All users have to pay 15% charge. The program should read units consumed, name, address and consumer no.
4. Wrirte a program to calculate the bill of a departmental store where customer no., name and list of items purchased are given to calculate cost of the items using structure.
5: Write a program to calculate number of sundays between two dates supplied to the program using structures.
6. If a column of length 'L' is loaded by an axial load 'P' at an eccentricity 'e' from the centroidal axis, the maximum stress σ_{max} is given by,

$$6\max = \frac{\sqrt{P}}{A}\left[1+\frac{e.c}{r^2} - \text{Sec}\left(\frac{1}{r}\sqrt{\frac{P}{4EA}}\right)\right]$$

Where,

$A = b.t$

$C = \frac{t}{2}$

$r = \frac{t}{\sqrt{12}}$

E = Young's modulus

Write a program to calculate 6_{max} for five sets of values P,b,t,e,E,L.

7. The roll numbers, marks in physics, chemistry and maths out of 100 of 135 students are known. Write a program which will calculate the following
   (i) No. of students in Dist, 1st, 2nd, 3rd, failed
   (ii) Marksheets of all students.
   (iii) Total number of students passed and failed and their percentage results. If the marks are below 40% in one subject then the student has failed in the subject.

   If his aggregate score is above 75%, he has scored distinction, if aggregate marks are above 60% , 50% and 40% . Then he has scored first, second and third division.

   Also print merit list of first three students.

8. Write a computer program which will calculate income tax and total tax for a group of 150 persons at following rates.
   (a) Taxable income upto 40,000 – no tax
   (b) Taxable income from 40,000 to 60,000
       income tax = 0.15 (Taxable income – 40000)
   (c) Taxable income from 60,000 to 1,20,000
       income tax = 3000 + 0.3 (Taxable income – 60000)
   (d) Taxable income over 1,20,000
       income tax = 21000 + 0.4 (Taxable income – 1,20,000)

   Surcharge on tax = 0.2 × income tax
   if income is above 1,50,000.

   The program should accept income tax no., name, address, the gross income and tax payable.

9. Write a program to calculate monthly interest to be payable to the fixed deposit holders of bank at following rates

No. of years	Interest rate
more 5	12%
3 to 5	11%
1 to 3	10%
½ to 1	8%

   If the amount exceeds above Rs. 50000/– additional interest of 0.5 for every 25,000 deposited.

   The program should accept the account no., name of customer, amount and no. of years for 20 customers.

10. In a departmental store the number of customers purchase variety of items. Prepare a program which accepts name of customer, date, no. of item purchase, name of items, it's cost per unit and no. of items purchased. The program should calculate total cost of items total bill of the customers with these rules:

Bill Amount	Discount
above Rs. 500/–	5%
above Rs. 1000/–	10%
above Rs. 2000/–	20%

11. Write a program to read the customer details from screen as name of customer address, pincode, due amount, due date and should calculate list of all customers with total due amount.
12. Write a program to calculate compound interest in an investment company using sructure for customer names, code, date of starting number of years, amount, interest payable, total amount to be paid.
13. Write a program to store the records in a hotel as customer name, address, company, period of stay, type of room alloted and the room charges.
14. Develop a program to allow users to perform operations on student records.
A student record should contain the below minimum information:
    - StudentID : 10 characters
    - Name : 30 characters
    - Gender : an enumerated type of male and female
    - DateOfBirth : date format in nested date type dd/mm/yyyy
    - DateJoined : date format in nested date type dd/mm/yyyy
    - SubjectsArray : array consisting of the 13 SubjectCodes and the 13 corresponding marks of the student

    The program should be able to store up to 100 students' records
    Program should at least perform the below operations:
    - Add student records in Student ID order
    - Find and display student information given the Student ID
    - Find and display student information given the Student Name
    - Display all students' information
    - Display Student information with highest average marks
    - Display Student information with lowest average marks
    - Find and display students' information who joined the school after a given date (use DateJoined field)
    - Find and display students' information who are born a given year (use DateOfBirth field)
    - Find and display all male students' information
    - Find and display all female student information
15. This program is to calculate the monthly payment of a loan. You will ask the user from the amount of the loan and the interest rate of the loan. You are to calculate the simple interest, add it to the amount of the loan and compute the monthly payment. You are to inform the user of the total amount to be repaid and the amount of the monthly payment. Note: The loan must be paid off in 12 months!
```
Loan Calculator
Enter the amount of the loan: 450.00
Enter the interest rate (Enter 7% as 0.07!): 0.05
You will repay $39.38 a month.
You will pay back a total of $472.50.
```
16. The example indicates that during a game, player number 3 was at bat four times and made 2 hits, 1 walk and 2 outs. For each player there are several lines in the file. Each player's batting average is computed by adding the player's total number of hits and dividing by the total number of at-bats. A walk does not count as a hit or a time at bat. Print a table showing the player id number, batting average (to 3 decimals), and number of walks. (Remember Id numbers are 1-20, but array indexes start at 0. Also, beware division by zero).

17
FILE OPERATION

AN OVERVIEW

In the last chapter you have studied the utilization of pointer in the structure. The pointers where used in the independently in the earlier chapter and in structure they are used as a member of structure. The pointer variable can become main variable of structure and it can be used with the sub variable of structure. The structure of pointers is a association of number of pointers. This type of analysis is very useful for creating transaction of values between two pointers.

In this unit we are going to study the operations on file. The files are utilizes for storage of data in the file. In software technology there are variety of files used for storing the data, storing graphics and for storing the text. The files can also store data in the binary format. The storage of data is very important because the data can be retrieved whenever it is required.

OBJECTIVES

* Explain the file operation.
* Define the file pointers
* Demonstrate opening and closing file.
* Describe reading and writing files.

17.1 CREATION OF FILES

The file operation in 'C' means execution of program using C–files. If the data is very large and fixed, then it can be stored in a data file and can be linked to program file, where the program file will read the data from the data file and execution of the program will be carried out. In case, if the results of the program are to be stored in a result file, then output values will be placed in result a file. If a file is to be copied from one file to another file, then the file operation is used to copy the characters from one file to another file. The file operation program provides instructions to open and close the required file after carrying out the desired execution. This program will also be stored in the file which will be executed by C–compiler.

The operation on files is a very important operation performed in all variety of the softwares . The storage of information of accounts in a bank, reservation record on railway station, maintenance of records of stores are various areas in which file operation is used.

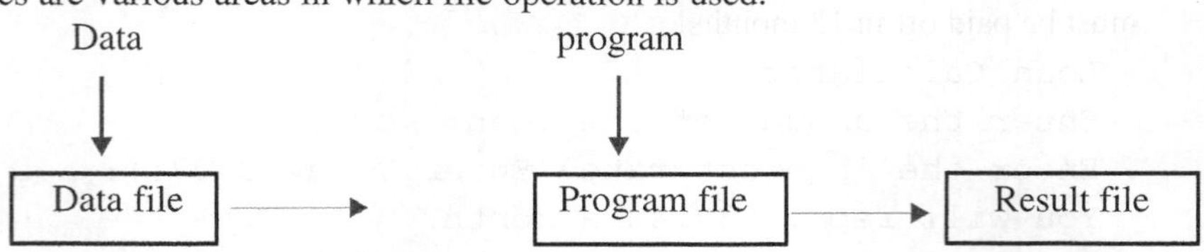

Fig. 17.1

The operation on file is carried out by a program file which contains the program. The program opens the given data file and then reads the data from data file which is utilized in the program to calculate the results which are written in a result file.

17.2 APPLICATIONS OF FILE OPERATION

The file operation is used in the different fields. Some examples are

1. Railway reservation system
2. Banking system
3. Salary system
4. Store record system

1. Railway reservation system

The railway reservation system maintains the record of the passengers travelling in the different trains on different dates reaching to different destinations. In this system the reservation of the passengers is made by supplying the train number or name of a train and the class in which the travelling to be done. The file is opened for the given train and the record is searched and if the vacancy exits then the name of person and his destination are entered and the berth number is allotted . The fare is calculated by using the fare table stored in the file.

2. Banking system

In the banking system the accounts of the customers are maintained in a file and the file is opened when the withdrawals or credits are made in the bank account. The file having a particular account is opened and the last the balance is read. The withdrawal or credits are submitted and a new balance is calculated. The new balance is stored in the file and when the next operation is performed the result written in the current file becomes the data next operations.

3. Salary system

In the salary software the salary of employees is calculated on the basis of the current basic pay which is acquired from the employees data file and the calculation are made for DA, HRA, CLA and other benefits. The deductions are calculated using the given procedure and the gross, net salary is prepared for every employee. The grand total amount required for payment of salary has been calculated and slip of every employee is prepared.

4. Store record system

In the store record system is a record of all the items stored in the store. This is known as inventory control system . In this system all the records of the item, their configurations, price and number items are stored in a data base format in the file. When the items are received in the store then the file is opened and these items are added to the record. If the items are supplied from the store then the record is updated by entering the delivered items.

17.3 FILE ORGANIZATION

A file is organized to ensure that records are available for processing. A file organization depends upon the nature of storage media. There are four methods of organizing files :

1. Sequential file
2. Direct file organization
3. Indexed sequential file organization
4. Random access file organization

17.3.1 Sequential file

In a sequential file, records are written and stored on a secondary storage device in the same sequence in which they were collected. The records are arranged in which they were collected. The records are arranged in order using a unique key as identity number. The Fig. shows sequential file

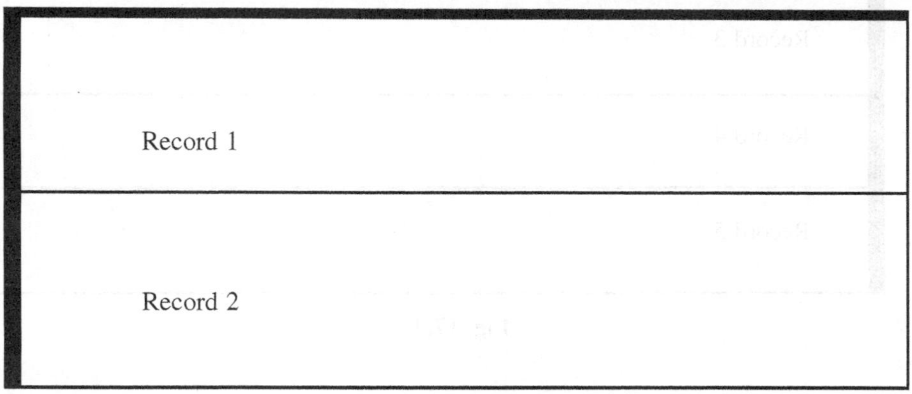

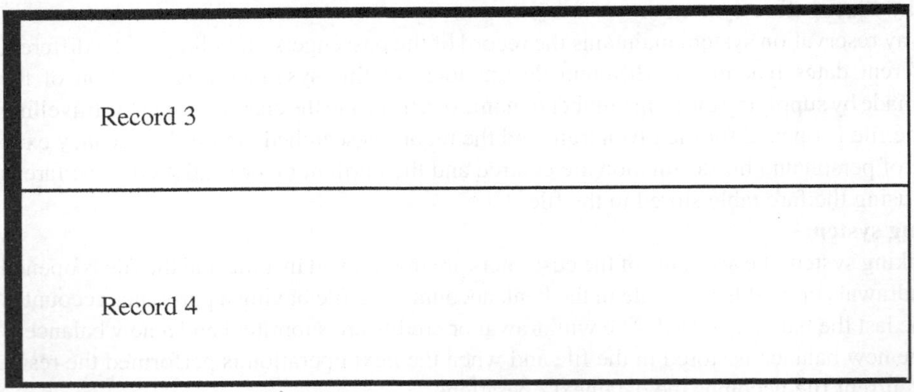

Fig. 17.2

Fig.17.2 Shows the sequential file in which the records are stored in sequence.In this file, if any record is required then all the records are read and then the specific record is selected.

17.3.2 Direct file Organization

This allows data to be retrieved quickly in a random manner irrespective of the manner in which the data is stored. A unique key is used to organize files as identity number which is converted directly to a memory address using a hashing algorithm.

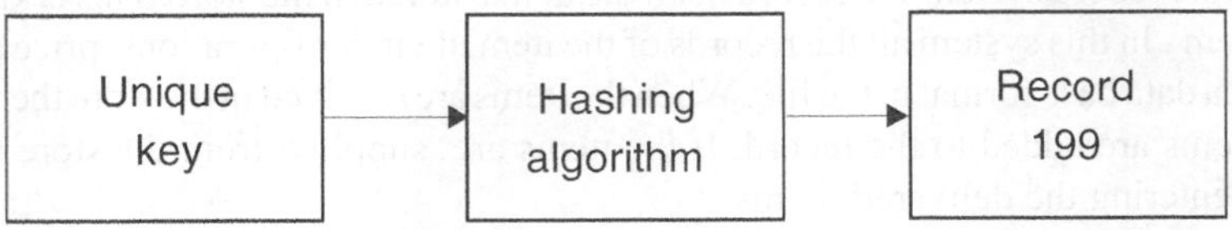

Fig. 17.3

Fig. 17.3 shows that the Key is used by hashing algorithm to search the record.

17.3.3 Indexed sequential file organization

In this method, the data is stored in a sequence but an index is created which shows the memory address of each data. A file index shows the memory address or physical location of each data which makes it easier and quicker to access the data.

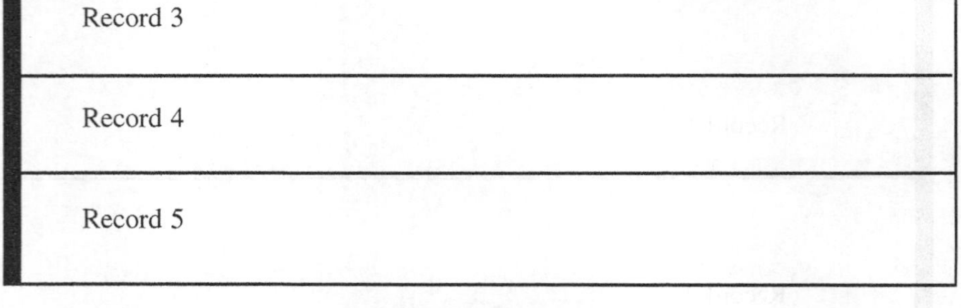

Fig. 17.4

17.3.4 Random access file organization

In these file organization, the data is accessed directly and this allows for random access of any record. Every record is allotted fixed number of bytes of memory irrespective of the memory required by the record. The access of record is almost easy because of counting of bytes by the record number.

100 bytes	Record 1
100 bytes	Record 2
100 bytes	Record 3
100 bytes	Record 4
100 bytes	Record 5
100 bytes	Record 6

Fig. 17.5

17.3.5 Limitations of file based system

The file based system has number of disadvantages

1. Data redundancy

   The data may be duplicated and can be present in large number of files.

2. Data Integrity
   The problems are present due to updating of one file while another file containing the dame record are not to be updated.
3. Data availability
   This problem arises due to non-uniformity in file design.
4. Management Control
   This problem arises because as the data values increases the files becomes complex and unreliable. A summary is given below :

File Organization Methods
A Summary

Method	Advantages	Limitations
Sequential	Simple to design Easy to program variable length and blocked records available Best use of storage space	Records cannot be added to middle of file
Indexed-Sequential	Records can be inserted or updated in middle of file Processing may be carried out sequentially or randomly.	Unique keys required Processing occassionally slow.
Direct File	Used in application requested specific data on multiple keys.	Periodic reorganization of file required
Random	Records can be inserted or updated in middle of file. Better control over record allocation.	Calculating address required for processing Variable-length records are not possible to process

Many applications by their nature are best done sequentially. Payroll is good example. In contrast, real time applications such as Railway booking, banking operations are examples of random - access design, where response requirements are critical.

17.4 FILE POINTERS

These are the pointers which can access the address of a file and can move on the file. They can be used for extraction of data from the file. The file name can be indicated by a file pointer and it can be used in place of name of file.

```
FILE *fptr;
```

Where, *fptr — File pointer variable declared by 'FILE' declaration.

17.5 OPENING OF FILE

When the data is to be read or stored on the file, then the file is accessed by the program by opening of the file on the memory device by use of opening commands in program .The program has to open the file on the memory , then the storage of data or retrieval of the data from the file is possible.

To open a file in the program , the function 'fopen' is used. This function returns a pointer to a file. It is used as follows :

```
file pointer = fopen ( "file name", "mode");
```

17.5.1 file name

A file is a format which allows for storage and retrieval of data. This is the physical file name for the data in the storage device.The file name can be indicated by the name and the extension name.The path of the file can also be supplied in the file as drive and directory.

Ex. data1.dat

file name extension name

17.5.2 mode

Any file in "C" can be opened in various ways and the mode decides the read/write operations with the data file.It is the purpose for which the file is really opened by the program. There are various types of modes used for opening of file.

The "mode" in fopen can be represented as :

Mode	*Purpose*
w	writes the data on new file or on old file.
a	if file is not available new file is created, if file exists then data is added to the file.
r	it allows only read operation of data.
w+	this reads data if file exists or fresh data is written in new file.
a+	it does not destroy the data if file already exists reads and appends.
r+	reads and writes operations without deleting data from file.

Ex.: The file pointer 'fptr' opens a file as

fptr = fopen("Data1.bmp", "r");

In this case, the file "Data1.bmp" is opened for the purpose of reading and the address of the file is supplied to the file pointer which will be representing the file in future.

17.6 FILE CLOSING

All the files that are opened in the program should be closed after all input and output operations are completed with the file.This has to be done to prevent the data from getting corrupted.

fclose(file-pointer);

or

fclose("file name");

After this, no Input / Output operations with the file are possible .

Ex : fclose(fptr);

or

fclose("Data1.bmp");

17.7 ERROR IN OPENING OF FILE

While opening a file it may be possible that the file pointer is unable to open a file, because of some error . This can be indicated after the execution of fopen operation. The errors in opening the file may occur due to following possibilities:

(a) The data file is not available on the disk

(b) The memory storage device is not available

(c) Storage device is not good and has bad sectors.

When such errors occur, then 'fopen 'function returns the 'NULL' character. To avoid the abrupt end of the program, the execution during the occurrence of the error, the program may be written with reference to 'NULL' character and to print a comment unable to open a given file.

In the following program where a reading file is opened and immediately closed, if the file pointer is unable to open a file then it returns 'NULL' character which means it was unable to open a file.

All the file functions are available in a library 'stdio.h' which must be included in the program.

Program 17–1

This program opens a reading file and closes the file.

```
/* To open a file */
# include < stdio.h>
main()
{
    FILE *fp;
    fp = fopen ("data.bmp","r");
    if (fp == NULL)
            printf("The file does not exist or error in reading the file\n");
    else
            printf("File is successfully opened\n");
    fclose(fp);
}
```

Output	:	File is successfully opened

This program opens file 'data.bmp' file and if file does not exist, then it indicates the error in opening the file or file is successfully opened.

17.8 FILE INPUT FUNCTION

The input function of the file is used for supply of data from the file to the program. The data written on a file is read by the file pointer from the file and is supplied to the variables in a program. The data can be in the form of numeric numbers or characters. There are two types of functions used for reading numeric data or character data. These are

(i) 'fgetc ' function
(ii) 'fscanf ' function

17.8.1 'fgetc' FUNCTION

This function has one parameter which is the file pointer declared or standard input device pointer. This function reads one character at a time from the file referenced by the file pointer.

```
fgetc (file_pointer);
```

Ex :

```
c = fgetc(fptr);
```

where, 'c' is a char variable.

This function reads one character from a file at the current position of the file pointer and supplies the character to 'c' char variable.

17.8.2 'fscanf' FUNCTION

This function works in the same way as 'scanf' statement ,but the only difference is that it reads the data from the given file referred by the file pointer. This function reads the data given in the file through the given format in sequence of specified variables. It is written as :

```
fscanf(file–pointer, "data formats", variable list);
```

Ex :

```
fscanf(fptr, "%d%d%d", &a, &b, &c);
```

Where, fptr — File pointer

In this statement, a, b and c are the variables of the program whose value is read from the file referred by file pointer in the given format list.

Program 17–2

This program reads data from a file. The file is opened by the file pointer. The data is read from the file using 'fscanf' statement by the variables in the program. The values of variables read from the file are printed on the user screen using 'printf' statement.

```
/* program to demonstrate reading from files */
# include<stdio.h>
main()
{
    FILE *inp_file;
    int i, beam [3]; float bm[3], sf[3];
    inp_file = fopen ("data.bm", "r");
    if (inp_file == NULL)
            printf("Unable to open a file\n");
    else
            printf("file is successfully opened\n");
            for (i = 0 ; i < 3;++ i)
            {
                    fscanf(inp_file," %5d %10f %10f',&beam[i],&bm[i],&sf[i]);
                    printf("beam=%5d, bm=%5d, sf=5d\n", beam[i], bm[i], sf[i];
            }
    fclose(inp_file);
}
```

17.9 FILE OUTPUT FUNCTION

These functions are used for printing of numeric or character values of the variable or arithmetic expression of the program. These are of two types :

(i) 'fputc' function

(ii) 'fprintf' function

17.9.1 'fputc' FUNCTION

This function is used for printing of characters on a given file from the given char variable. This function prints a character on a file at the current position of the pointer in the file.

```
fputc(variable, file_pointer);
```

Ex :

```
fputc(c, fptr);
```

Where, c — char variable whose value is to be printed on the file.

fptr — Pointer to which file is referred in which character is to be written.

17.9.2 'fprintf' FUNCTION

This function works similar to printf statement with the difference that the printing of values of variable is carried out on the file referred by the file pointer.

```
fprintf(file pointer, "Data formats", variable list);
```

Ex:

```
fprintf(fptr,"a = %d, b = %d, c = %d", a, b, c);
```

In this statement the values of a,b,c variables are printed on file referred by the file pointer 'fptr' through the given format along with the given comments.

Program 17–3

This program writes the values of variable to a given file. The variables are supplied with values using arithmetic statement in the program and these values are printed on a file using 'fprintf' statement by referring to a file given by file pointer.

```
/* to supply values to a file */
# include <stdio.h>
main()
{
      FILE * ptr; int a; float; char c;
      int a = 2;
      float b = 3.2;
      char c = 'c';
      ptr = fopen ("Data.Tc","w+");
      if(ptr = = NULL)
               printf("Unable to open file\n")
      else
               printf("File is successfully opened\n");
      fprintf(ptr,"a= %d, b=%f,c=%c\n", a,b,c);
      fclose (ptr);
}
```

In this program, the values of a,b,c are written on a file using the 'fprintf' statement in the given format .

Program 17–4

In this program , the function program analysis scans the values of input variables and supplies them to the main program. The values of variables are printed on a file using 'fprintf' statement.

```
/* Program to demonstrate file writing */
# include<stdio.h>
main()
{
      FILE *result_file;
      int i, beam [3];
      float bm [3], sf [3];
      analysis (beam, bm, sf);
      result_file = fopen ("Data1.bmp", "w");
      for (i = 0;  i < 3 ; ++ i)
      fprintf (result_file, "Beam No % d, bending moment = % 5.2f, shear force = % 5.2f\n", beam[i],
               bm[i],sf[i]);
      fclose (result_file);
}
analysis (beam_no, bm, sf)
int beam_no[3]; float bm[3], sf[3];
{
      int i ;
      for (i = 0;  i < 3; ++ i)
      scanf ( "%d%f%f", &beam_no[i], & bm[i], &sf[i]);
}
```

This program reads the data from the user screen by using analysis function and writes on a file.

17.10 END OF FILE

When a file pointer moves on a file, the file pointer reaches to the end of file. The end of file condition is necessary in programing. If the end of file is not specifically known, the end of file condition can be determined by the statements of the program if complete data on file is to be extracted.

There are two types of methods used to find end of file condition :

1. 'feof' function
2. EOF flag

17.10.1 'feof' FUNCTION

This function is used to find out whether the end of file condition has been reached, while reading the records. It is written as :

```
feof(fptr);
```

Where,

fptr – file pointer

The value of this function is a logical answer as true or false. If the 'feof' function supplies true value then it is the end of file else the pointer has not reached end of file condition.

Ex :

```
if(feof(fptr))
        printf("It is end of a file");
else
        printf("It is not end of file");
```

17.10.2 'EOF' FLAG

The end of data on a file is the end of file and the end of file condition exists ,when the last piece of data has been read from the file. An attempt to read ahead of end of file results in an error. Most of the functions from the standard I/O library which read data from a file returns a special flag to indicate when a program has reached the end of the file. This is called by a name 'EOF' which is defined in the standard I/O library.

Ex:

```
if(fptr == EOF)
        printf("It is end of a file");
        else
        printf("It is not end of file");
```

Program 17–5

```
Program on 'feof()' function
/*program 'feof' function */
# include < studio.h >
main()
{
    FILE *stream;char c;
    stream = fopen ("Data.dbf", "r");
    while(!feof(stream))
    {
            fgetc(c,stream);
            putc(c);
    }
    /* check for EOF */
    if(feof(stream))
            printf (" We have reached end of file\n");
    else
            printf ("We have not reached end of file\n");
    fclose (stream);
}
```

In this program a file is opened for reading and the file pointer is moved on the file by reading every character from the file using 'fgetc' function till the end of file is not reached. When the file reaches the end then the reading of characters is stopped. Then it is checked whether the file has reached the end of file condition or not.

Program 17–6

```
/* program to copy one file to another */
# include < stdio.h>
main()
{
    char in_name [25], out_name [25];
    FILE *in_file, *out_file;
    int c;
    *in_file = fopen("data.c", "r");
    if (in_file == NULL)
        printf ("could not open %s for reading \n", in-name);
    else
    *out_file = fopen ("result.c","w");
    {
    if (out_file == NULL)
        printf("could not open file for writing");
    while ((c = fgetc (in_file)) ! = EOF)
    fputc (c,out_file);
    printf ("file has been copied \n");
}
```

This program reads the content from one file and copies it in another file, where 'fgetc' and 'fputc' function are used to transfer the characters from one file to another file.

17.11 'fgets' AND 'fputs' FUNCTION

For reading and writing entire lines of the data from and to a file, the fputs and fgets functions can be used.

17.11.1 'fgets' FUNCTION

This function is used when the reading of lines consisting of bunch of words are to be read. In this statement, given number of characters are read from a file specified by the file pointer.

This is written as :

fgets(s,n,fptr);

where,

- s – character array where the line that is read will be stored.
- n – integer value that represents the number of values to be read from the given file.
- fptr – It identifies the file from which the line is to be read.

This function reads characters from the specified file until a new line character has been read (which will get stored into the 's') or until (n-1) characters have been read whichever occurs first. The function automatically places a NULL character after the last character in the 's' and returns the value of the 's' if the reading is successful and the value of 'NULL', if an error occurs in reading or an attempt is made to read past the end of the file.

Ex :

fgets(s,n,fptr);

where,

s – is a char array
n – number of characters to be read
fptr – is a file pointer

17.11.2 'fputs' FUNCTION

This function writes a line of characters to a specified file.

fputs(s,file-pointer);

where,

s – is a char array.

The characters stored in the array pointed to by the s are written to the file identified by file–pointer until the null character is not written to the file.

Ex :

fputs(s,fptr);

Where 'fptr' is file pointer to which the content of 's'char array will be written.

17.12 stdin, stdout AND stderr FILE POINTER

Wherever a C program is executed, three 'files' are automatically opened by the system for the user of the program. These files are identified by the constant FILE pointers 'stdin, stdout and stderr', which are defined in the standard I/O include files.

The FILE pointer 'stdin' identifies the standard input of the program and is associated with the terminal.

The 'scanf' function reads its input from 'stdin' and a call to this function is equivalent to a call to the fscanf function with stdin as the first argument.

It is written as

fscanf(stdin," %d", & i);

It will read the integer value from the standard input, which will normally be your terminal.

If input to your program has been redirected to a file, then this call will read the next integer value from the file that the standard input has been redirected.

Similarly,

fprintf(stdout, "hello there!\n");

This works similar to 'printf' statement of the program with 'stdout' as a output file pointer which refers to user screen.

The FILE pointer 'stderr' identifies the standard error file. The error messages can be printed where the normal output is written. This is particularly desirable wherever the program's output is redirected to a file. In such a case, the normal output will be written into the file, but in this case error message will appear at the terminal.

Ex.

```
if (( i_file == NULL)
{
fprintf(stderr, " could not open data for reading\n");
}
```

This statement will write the indicated error message to stderr if the file data cannot be opened for reading or standard output file had been redirected to a file.

Program 17–7

```
/*Program on stderr function.*/
#include <stdio.h>
main()
{
    FILE *in,*out;
    if ((in=fopen ("graph.cpp","rt"))==NULL)
```

```
    {
        fprintf(stderr,"cannot open input file\n");
    }
    if ((out=fopen("graph6.cpp","wt"))==NULL)
    fprintf(stderr,"cannot open output file \n");
}
    while (!feof(in))
    fputc(fgetc(in),out);
    fclose (in);
    fclose(out);
}
```

17.13 'exit' FUNCTION

Sometimes it may be desirable to force the termination of a program , such as when an error condition is detected by a program. The program execution is automatically terminated whenever the last statement in the 'main' program is executed. But in order to explicitly terminate a program, the 'exit' function can be called

exit(n);

Where,

n – condition code, non-zero when error condition occurs.

This function call has the effect of terminating the current program. Any of the opened files will be automatically closed by the system.

17.14 'fread' FUNCTION

This function reads data item from a file indicated by file pointer and stores it in a char array. It is written as :

fread(s,n1,n2,fptr);

where,

s	–	char array
n1	–	size of character
n2	–	number of such characters
fptr	–	file pointer referred by a file from which reading is to be done.

17.15 'rewind' FUNCTION

This rewinds the file back to its beginning position. It is written as :

rewind(fptr);

Where,

fptr – file pointer referred to a file.

17.16 'fwrite' FUNCTION

This function writes a string into a file.
It is written as :

fwrite (s,l, x, fptr)

where,

s	–	char array variable
l	–	length of string
x	–	number of times
fptr	–	file pointer for the writing file.

17.17 'fseek' FUNCTION

This function provides a new position in a file. It is written as :

fseek(fptr,os,y);

Where,

os – The new position relative to the position specified in the y

y – It indicates the position in the file by the following words

These are as below

SEEK_SET – seek from beginning of the file

SEEK_CUR – seek from current position

SEEK_END – seek from end of file

Ex : fseek(fptr,10,SEEK_SET);

This statement seeks a position 10 bytes ahead of the start position in the file .

17.18 'ftell' FUNCTION

This function is used to indicate the size of file in bytes.

It is written as :

ftell(fptr);

where, fptr – It is the file pointer.

Ex: i = ftell(fptr);

where, i – integer variable indicating length of the file.

Program 17–8

```
/*Program on fseek and ftell() function.*/
# include < stdio.h >
main()
{
    FILE *ptr;
    ptr = fopen ("Data.x", "w+");
    printf (ptr, "This is a test");
    printf ("Files size of file is %ld bytes\n", files_length
    (ptr));
}
long files_length ( FILE * ptr)
{
    long int c, length;
    c = ftell(stream);
    fseek (ptr, O,SEEK_END);
    length = ftell (ptr);
    return (length)
}
```

In this function program a file is opened by a file pointer in an append mode and the pointer is taken to the end of the file by giving a call to a function program files_length. This function program finds the length of a file in terms of character or bytes by using 'ftell' function.

Program 17–9

```
/*Program on fwrite, fseek and fgets functions.*/
#include < stdio.h >
```

```
main()
{
    FILE *fptr;
    char string[] = "C–Programing is exciting";
    char msg[20];
    fptr = fopen ("Data.x", "w+");
    /* write a string into the file */
    fwrite (string, strlen(string),1,fptr);
    /* seek to the start of the file */
    fseek(fptr,0,SEEK_SET);
    /* read a string form the file */
    fgets (msg, strlen (string), 1, fptr);
    /* display the string */
    printf ("%s", msg);
    fclose (ptr);
}
```

In this function program, a file pointer opens a file for writing and reading purposes. A string is written to a file by using 'fwrite' function. Then the pointer seeks the starting position in a file and reads a string from the file using 'fgets' function. This string is received by 'msg' char array. This char array is printed by 'printf' statement.

Program 17–10

This program prepares the Roll list of the students .In this program the names of students are supplied from data file and they are written on the file by allotting the roll numbers to the students name.

```
/*program to prepare roll list*/
#include <string.h>
#include <stdio.h>.
main()
{
    FILE *t;
    int i,n;
    char name[20],name2[20];
    clrscr();
    t=fopen("sh.dat","a+");
    printf("enter no of students\n");
    scanf("%d",&n);
    fwrite("————————————————————————\n",68,1,t);
    fputs("\n",t);
    fwrite("Roll no.        Name of student\n",40 ,1,t);
    for(i=1;i<=n;++i)
    {
            printf("enter name of student \n",i);
            scanf("%s%s",name,name2);
            fseek(t,10,SEEK_CUR);
            fprintf(t,"\n %d        ",i);
            fwrite(name,strlen(name),1,t);
            fprintf(t,"\t");
            fwrite(name2,strlen(name2),1,t);
            fputs("\n",t);
```

```
    }
    fseek(t,10,SEEK_END);
    fwrite("——————————————————————————————\n",68,1,t);
    fputs("\n",t);
    fclose(t);
    return;
}
```

Program 17–11

In this program ,numbers are supplied from the screen to an array and these numbers are scanned by finding their remainder and the numbers are then separated as odd or even numbers .The odd numbers are written in one file and even numbers are written in another file using file pointer by opening two ./* SORT OUT THE EVEN AND ODD NUMBERS */

```
#include <stdio.h>
FILE *fptr1;
FILE *fptr2;
main()
{
    int  n,i;char s1[20],s2[20];
    int a[20];
    int answer;
    int number;
    clrscr();
    printf("Enter the name of even no. file\n");
    scanf("%s",s1);
    printf("Enter the name of odd no. file\n");
    scanf("%s",s2);
    fptr2=fopen(s1,"w");
    fptr1=fopen(s2,"w");
    if((fptr1 == NULL) && (fptr2 == NULL))
            printf("file does not open\n");
    else
            printf("The file is successfully opened\n");
    printf("Enter the number \n");
    scanf("%d",&n);
    printf("The numbers are\n");
    for(i=1;i<=n;++i)
    {
            scanf("%d",&a[i]);
    }
    for(i=1;i<=n;++i)
    {
    if(a[i]%2 == 0)
            fprintf(fptr2,"%d\t",a[i]);
    else
            fprintf(fptr1,"%d\t",a[i]);
    }
    fcloseall();
    return(0);
}
```

Program 17–12

In this program, numbers are supplied to the program in array which is read from a file .These numbers are separated by using 'if–else' statement and the odd numbers are written to a file whereas the even numbers are written to another file using the file pointers.

```
/* SORT OUT THE EVEN AND ODD NUMBERS from a file*/
#include <stdio.h>
FILE *fptr1;
FILE *fptr2;
FILE *fptr;
main()
{
     int n,i;char s1[20],s2[20],s3[20];
     int a[20];
     int answer;
     int number;
     clrscr();
     printf("Enter the name of even no. file\n");
     scanf("%s",s1);
     printf("Enter the name of odd no. file\n");
     scanf("%s",s2);
     printf("Enter the reading file \n");
     scanf("%s",s3);
     fptr2=fopen(s1,"w");
     fptr1=f  open(s2,"w");
     fptr=fopen(s3,"r");
     if((fptr1 == NULL) && (fptr2 == NULL))
               printf("file does not open\n");
     else
               printf("The file is successfully opened\n");
               i=1;
               while(!(feof(fptr)))
               {
                         fscanf(fptr,"%d",&a[i]);
                         ++i;
               }
     n=i–2;
     for(i=1;i<=n;++i)
     {
     if(a[i]%2 == 0)
               fprintf(fptr2,"%d\t",a[i]);
     else
               fprintf(fptr1,"%d\t",a[i]);
     }
     fclose all();
     return(0);
}
```

Program 17–13

This program reads array of numbers from a file and then the array is sorted by using a 'sort' function program.This function program arranges all the elements of the array in the ascending order and then the numbers are separated by using a function program 'choice' which does the separation between the odd and even numbers.Then these numbers are written to two separate files using the file pointers.

```
/* SORT OUT THE EVEN AND ODD NUMBERS  IN ASCENDING ORDER */
#include <stdio.h>
FILE *fptr1;
FILE *fptr2;
FILE *fptr;
sort (s,n)
int s[30],n;
{
     int ii,j,temp;
     for(ii=1;ii<=n-1;++ii)
     {
     for(j=ii+1;j<=n;++j)
     {
     if(s[ii]>s[j])
     {
               temp  = s[ii];
               s[ii] =  s[j];
               s[j]  =  temp;
     }
     }
     }
     return(0);
}
choice(a,n)
int a[30],n;
{
     int i;
     for(i=1;i<=n;++i)
     {
     if(a[i] % 2 == 0)
               fprintf(fptr2,"%d\t",a[i]);
     else
               fprintf(fptr1,"%d\t",a[i]);
     }
     return;
}
main()
{
     int n,i;
     char s1[30],s2[30],s3[30];
     int j,ii;
     int a[30],s[30];
     int answer;
     int number;
```

```
        clrscr();
        printf("Enter the name of even no. file\n");
        scanf("%s",s1);
        printf("Enter the name of odd no. file\n");
        scanf("%s",s2);
        printf("Enter the reading file \n");
        scanf("%s",s3);
        fptr2=fopen(s1,"w");
        fptr1=fopen(s2,"w");
        fptr=fopen(s3,"r");
        if((fptr1 == NULL) && (fptr2 == NULL))
                printf("file does not open\n");
        else
                printf("The file is successfully opened\n");
        i=1;
        while(!(feof(fptr)))
        {
                fscanf(fptr,"%d",&a[i]);
                ++i;
        }
        n=i-2;
        printf("n=%d",n);
        sort(a,n);
        choice(a,n);
        fcloseall();
        return(0);
}
```

EXERCISE

1. Write a program to read five numbers from a file and calculate average of the numbers and print in another output file.
2. Write a program to prepare roll list of students in an alphabetical order in a file by supplying the roll number.
3. Write a program to prepare list of suppliers, their address, type of material available with the supplier and print this in a file.
4. Write a program to prepare bank account of the person by maintaining input/output file.
5. Write a program to prepare salary bill of company using an input data file to store the data and output file to store the pay slips of employees. The structure could be created as :

   (i) Emp– no and (ii) Basic pay and display and the same structure alongwith the A, HRA, CCA, and Gross salary. The DA and CCA are calculated as:

   DA = 51% OF Basic pay

   CCA = Rs. 100/–

   HRA = 15% of basic pay subject max^{M} Rs. 800/–

   The data of employee should be read from the file.
6. Write a program to search the name and address of persons having age more than 30 in the data list of persons.

7. Write a program to prepare electricity bill of different customers with their names, consumer numbers, addresses, units consumed and the amount charged according to the slab rate and print the data in a file.
   The rates of electricity bill as per following units
   For first100 units – Rs.1/- per unit
   For next 300 units – Rs. 2/05 per unit
   beyond 300 units – Rs. 3/50 per unit
   All users have to pay 15% charge. The program should read units consumed, name, address and consumer no.
8. Write a program to maintain the record of different parts available in the store using their part number, name, quantity rate and write it in a file.
   In a departmental store the number of customers purchase variety of items. Prepare a program which accepts name of customer, date, number of item purchase, name of items, it's cost per unit and number of items purchased. The program should calculate total cost of items total bill of the customers with these rules:

Bill Amount	Discount
above Rs. 500/–	5%
above Rs. 1000/–	10%
above Rs. 2000/–	20%

9. Write a program to find a particular part from a file containing record of store and read the quantity of part or rate of part and calculate the following
   (i) Total cost of inventory
   (ii) Parts having quantity more than 15
   (iii) Parts having quantity less than 3
10. Write a program to prepare analysis of a marketing department of company having 10 regions and their sales every month of each region is to be recorded in one file. Further the program should read the data from this file and calculate sales of every region in output file. The first and second in sales are to be indicated as best regions of the year.
11. Write a program to read a file until EOF and report the
    (i) Number of characters
    (ii) Number of words
    (iii) Number of lines
    (iv) Number of tabs
    (v) Number of new line characters.
12. Write a program to read customer details from screen and write it to file using structure of name, type of customer, address, pin-code, amount due, due date, and write the total amount due.
13. Write a program to store the information about the material supplier on a file for following items Sr. No., quantity, name of item, name of supplier, price, using structure.
14. Write a program on analysis of sales using following information on file week, name of sales man, area, product code, unit sold, price per unit. The program should produce output for total sales of product, area, salesman, total sales amount of individual salesman.
15. Write a program to calculate compound interest on fixed deposit in an investment company using structure and write the complete record in a file for customer name, code, date of starting, number of year, amount, interest payable, due date of interest payment, total amount payable.
16. The roll numbers, marks in physics, chemistry and maths out of 100 of 135 students are known. Write a program which will calculate the following

(i) Number of students in Dist, 1st, 2nd, 3rd, failed
(ii) Marksheets of all students.
(iii) Total number of students passed and failed and their percentage results. If the marks are below 40% in one subject then the student has failed in the subject.

If his aggregate score is above 75%, he has scored distinction, if aggregate marks are above 60% , 50% and 40% . Then he has scored first, second and third division.

Also print merit list of first three students.

17. Write a computer program which will calculate income tax and total tax for a group of 150 persons at following rates.
(a) Taxable income upto 40,000 – no tax
(b) Taxable income from 40,000 to 60,000
income tax = 0.15 (Taxable income – 40000)
(c) Taxable income from 60,000 to 1,20,000
income tax = 3000 + 0.3 (Taxable income – 60000)
(d) Taxable income over 1,20,000
income tax = 21000 + 0.4 (Taxable income – 1,20,000)

Surcharge on tax = 0.2 × income tax
if income is above 1,50,000.

The program should accept income tax number, name, address, the gross income and tax payable.

18. Write a program to calculate monthly interest to be payable to the fixed deposit holders of bank at following rates

No. of years	interest rate
more 5	12%
3 to 5	11%
1 to 3	10%
½ to 1	8%

If the amount exceeds above Rs. 50000/– additional interest of 0.5 for every 25,000 deposited.

The program should accept the account number, name of customer, amount and number of years for 20 customers.

19. Program written in C that will read 10 integers from a file. (You can use the numbers 1 - 10). Then turn these integers into an array and print them out backwards into another file. They should be this format:

1
2
3
4
5
6
7
8
9
10

If we change the 10 numbers in the input file, they should print out backwards in the output file.

18

C++ PROGRAMMING

AN OVERVIEW

In the previous chapter, we have seen the programming in C. The C-programming is the basic programming which allows for control, looping and cyclic operations. The function programs and arrays are the useful for preparing programs for complicated problems. The string operations and pointers are useful for memory compression and character operations.The file operation and structures allows storage of data in the structured form.

In this chapter, the extension of C to C++ has been covered. Some of the deficiencies of C-programming have been modified and C++ provides addtional functions and operations in C.

OBJECTIVE

In this unit , you will able study

* new statements in C++.
* Modification in the declaration of variables.
* input/output statement in C++.

18.1 INTRODUCTION

The C++ is an extensive version of C–language. The C++ is built on C because of C's suitability to complex programming situation. For better understanding of C++, the knowledge of C–language is necessary. Also C++ has more versatile and useful features as below :

(i) It provides function for input and output statement.
(ii) It allow single line comments.
(iii) The variables could be declared at the point of use.
(iv) It allows for declaration of constant.
(v) It has number of function program.
(vi) It provides techniques of object based programming.
(vii) It allow use of classes and objects to store large data.
(viii) It provides new simplified method for file operation.
(ix) It allows creation of new classes and objects.
(x) The database operation can be performed using array of objects.

18.2 RELATIONSHIP BETWEEN C AND C++

The relationship between C and C++ is shown in the following figure. All the function and commands of C-language can be utilized in C++. In addition C++ provides new methods and techniques of programming. It also provides object based programming which could be further extended to object oriented programming.

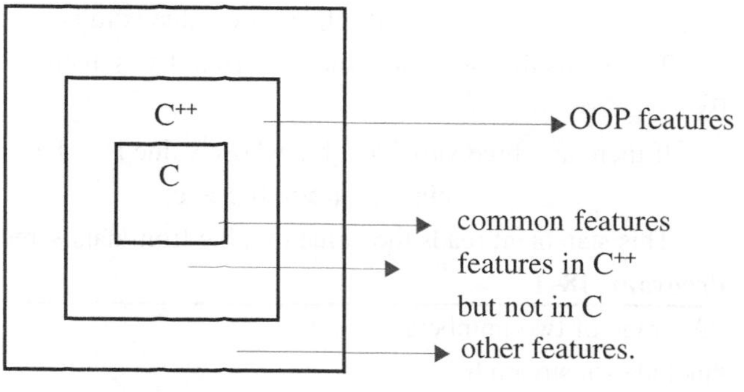

Fig.18.1

Fig.18.1 shows the features of C-language. The C^{++} language is based on C, but reduces C's traditional reliance on various functions and statements. Above Figures shows all function and command C-language which can be utilized in C^{++}. The C^{++} –language allows object oriented programming.

18.3 METHOD OF PROGRAMMING

In C^{++} language, to use C^{++} commands a header file "iostream.h" must be included in every program. The C^{++} functions are available in header file "iostream.h", which are accessible in the program.

```
# include < iostream.h>
```

Every file of C^{++} must be written with ".cpp" extension name.

18.4 COMMENT STATEMENT

The comment in C^{++} can be written by a new symbol '//'. The comment starts with a double slash symbol and terminates at the end of the line.

Ex : // THIS IS C^{++} PROGRAMMING

18.5 INPUT/OUTPUT STATEMENT

In C^{++}, 'cout' and 'cin' statement are used as input /output statement. There are no formats used in C^{++}.

18.5.1 Output statement

The results can be printed in C^{++} using 'cout' statement.

```
cout << x;
```

This statement prints the value of 'x' variable or an expression or a comment.

where,

x – comment enclosed in double inverted quotes or variable or arithmetic expression whose value is to be printed.

Ex :
```
cout << a << b << c;
cout << a + b;
cout << " Programming in c is fun \n ";
cout << "\n"
```

18.5.2 Input statement

The data can be read from data screen using 'cin' statement.

```
cin >> y;
```

Where,

y – variable whose value is to be read.

This reads the value of y variable from data screen.

Ex :

If there are three variable a,b,c whose value is to be read.

```
cin >> a >> b >> c;
```

This statement reads the value of a,b,c from data screen.

Program 18–1

```
//Average of two numbers
#include <iostream.h>
```

```
#include<conio.h>
main()
{
        float num1, num2, sum, ave;
        clrscr();
        cout <<"Enter two numbers";
        cin >> num1;
        cin >> num2;
        sum = num1+num2;
        ave = sum/2.0;
        cout << "sum="<<sum<<"\n";
        cout << "Average="<<ave <<"\n";
}
```

Input	:	Enter two numbers 5 6
Output	:	sum=11 Average=5.5

This program scans two number 'num1' and 'num2' and calculates their sum and average, which is printed by 'cout' statement.

18.6 DECLARATIONS OF VARIABLES

The C++ has similar declaration of variables as C, but it allows the declaration of a variable any where in the scope of the program. This means that the variable can be declared at the point of its use. This makes our program easier to use and write.

This can be seen in the following program where the variable are declared at the place of their use.

Program 18–2

```
// Average of any five given numbers.
#include <iostream.h>
#include<conio.h>
main()
{
        float x; float  sum=0;
        clrscr();
        cout<<"Enter five numbers\n";
        for (int i =0; i< 5; i++)
        {
                cin >> x;
                sum = sum + x     ;
        }
        float average;
        average = sum/i;
        cout << "Average="<<average;
}
```

Input	:	Enter five numbers
		1 2 3 4 5
Output	:	Average=3

In this program the five numbers are read and sum is calculated in the program. The variables in this program are declared at the point of their use. The average is calculated and printed. The'average' variable is declared at place of its use, which is permitted.

Program 18–3

This program finds whether the number is even or odd by finding the remainder of the number. If the remainder is found to be 0 then the number is even or otherwise it is odd. This is determined by if–else statement as in the C–language.

```
//program to determine whether number is even or odd
#include<iostream.h>
#include<conio.h>
main()
{
    clrscr();
    cout<<"Enter the value of n \n";
    int n;
    cin>>n;
    int rem = n % 2;
    if (rem==0)
    {
        cout<<"Number is Even\n";
    }
    else
    {
        cout<<"Number is Odd\n";
    }
}
```

Input	:	Enter the value of n
		4
Output	:	Number is Even

Program 18–4

This program utilizes 'if–else' construct statement to find whether the given character is alphabet or number or special character of a keyboard. The character is scanned by using char variable and it is checked by using 'if–else–construct' statement.

```
//program to find whether the given character is
//an alphabet,digit or special character
#include<iostream.h>
#include<conio.h>
main()
{
    clrscr();
```

```
    cout<<"Enter the character  \n";
    char y;
    cin>>y;
    if ((y>='a'&& y<='z')||(y>='A'&& y<='Z'))
            cout<<" The Character Is An Alphabet\n";
    else
    if (y>='0' && y<='9')
            cout<<" The Character Is A Digit\n";
    else
            cout<<" The Character Is A Special Character\n";
}
```

Input	:	Enter the character S
Output	:	The Character Is An Alphabet

Program 18–5

This program calculates the series of Fibonacci number using the for statement which performs the cycle such that every Fibonacci number is the sum of the two previous numbers. These numbers are created by generating numbers 'fa' and 'fb'. The Fibonacci number 'fc' is calculated by addition of 'fa' and 'fb'.

```
//PROGRAM TO PRINT  50 Fibonacci NUMBERS
#include<iostream.h>
#include<conio.h>
main()
{
    clrscr();
    cout<<"Enter the numbers of fa and fb\n";
    int fa,fb;
    cin>>fa>>fb;
    for(int n =3;n<=15;++n)
    {
            int fc = fa + fb;
            cout<<"Fabonacci Number is : "<<fc<<"\n";
            fa = fb;
            fb = fc;
    }
}
```

Input	:	Enter the numbers of fa and fb 1 2
Output	:	Fibonacci Number is : 3 Fibonacci Number is : 5 Fibonacci Number is : 8

Program 18–6

The following program calculates the value of g using 'if–else' statement enclosed in a 'for' statement. The value of 'g' is calculated for the various value of h using two formula's by choice of h using if else statement.

```
//TO CALCULATE VALUE OF 'g'
#include<iostream.h>
#include<conio.h>
main()
{
    clrscr();
    cout<<" Enter the value of hm,hs \n";
    float hm,hs;
    cin>>hm>>hs;
    float g;
    for(float  h=-10;h<=hm;h=h+hs)
    {
    if(h>0)
        g = 32.17 * (4390 / (4390 + h)) * (4390 / (4390 +h));
    else
        g = 32.17 * (1 + h / 4390 );
        cout<<" h = "<<h<<"\t g = "<<g<<"\ n";
  }
}
```

Input	:	Enter the value of hm,hs
		3 4
Output	:	h = –10 g = 32.096722
		h = –6 g = 32.126034
Output	:	h = –2 g = 32.155342
		h = 2 g = 32.140709

Program 18–7

This program prints the name of a person by scanning it from the screen. The name of person is stored in a char array and the char array is printed by using 'for' statement.

```
//A PROGRAM TO PRINT A NAME ARRAY USING AN ARRAY
#include<iostream.h>
#include<conio.h>
main()
{
    char name[20];
    int i,n=6;
    clrscr();
    cout<<" Enter a name upto 10 characters \n";
    for(i = 1;i<=n;++i)
    {
```

```
            cin>>name[i];  //SCANING THE CHARACTER
      }
      cout<<" Name read was \n";
      for(i = 1;i<=n;++i)
      cout<<name[i];
}
```

Input	:	Enter a name upto 10 characters Akshay
Output	:	Name read was Akshay

Program 18–8

This program calculates average of any given numbers by scanning of an array and the sum of all the numbers is calculated using 'for' statement. Then the average of the given number is calculated and the variance from the mean value is calculated and added and the total of variance is printed.

```
//A PROGRAM TO CALCULATE AVERAGE OF GIVEN NUMBERS USING
//ARRAYS AND VARIANCE OF THE NUMBER
#include<iostream.h>
#include<conio.h>
main()
{
      int i,n;
      clrscr();
      cout<<" Enter the maximum number for an array "<<endl;
      cin>>n;
      cout<<" Enter elements of an array"<<endl;
      float a[20];
      for(i=1;i<=n;++i)
      {
            cin>>a[i];
      }
      float sum = 0.0;
      float avg;
      for(i=1;i<=n;++i)
      {
            sum = sum + a[i];
      }
      avg = sum/n;
      float s;
      float z = 0;
      for(i=1;i<=n;++i)
      {
            s = (a[i] – avg) * (a[i] – avg);
            z = z + s;
```

```
    }
    float var;
    var = z / n;
    cout<<" Average : "<<avg<<"\n"<<" Variance : "<<var<<endl;
}
```

Input	:	Enter the maximum number for an array 5 Enter elements of an array 1 2 3 4 5
Output	:	Average : 3 Variance : 2

Program 18–9

```
// MULTIPLICATION OF THE COLUMN AND ROW
#include <iostream.h>
#include <conio.h>
main()
{
    int a[20][20];
    int i,j,m,n;
    clrscr();
    cout <<"Enter the max value m and n\n";
    cin >>m>>n;
    for(i=1;i<=4;++i)
    {
    for(j=1;j<=4;++j)
    {
        a[i][j] = i * j;
    }
    }
    cout <<"The matrix is  "<<endl;
    for(i=1;i<=m;++i)
    {
        for(j=1;j<=n;++j)
        cout <<'\t'<<a[i][j];
        cout <<"\n";
    }
}
```

Input	:	Enter the max value m and n 3 3
Output	:	The matrix is 1 2 3 2 4 6 3 6 9

Program 18–10

In this program the matrix is scanned in a two dimensional integer array and the matrix is printed by using nested 'for' statement.

```
//A PROGRAM TO SCAN AND PRINT A MATRIX
#include<iostream.h>
#include<conio.h>
main()
{
    int  s[20][20];
    int i,n,j,m;
    clrscr();
    //ENTERING THE ORDER OF MATRIX
    cout<<" Enter the order of matrix \n";
    cin>>m>>n;
    cout<<" Enter the elements of "<<m<<" x "<<n<<" matrix "<<endl;
    for(i = 1;i<=m;++i)
    {
    for(j = 1;j<=n;++j)
    {
            cin>>s[i][j]; //SCANNING THE ELEMENTS
    }
    }
    cout<<" The Matrix is "<<endl;
    for(i = 1;i<=m;++i)
    {
    for(j=1;j<=n;++j)
    cout<<'\t'<<s[i][j];
    cout<<"\n";
    }
}
```

Input	:	Enter the order of matrix 3 3 Enter the elements of3x3matrix 1 2 3 4 5 6 7 8 9
Output	:	The matrix is 1 2 3 4 5 6 7 8 9

Program 18–11

In this program sum of the diagonal elements of square matrix is calculated by scanning the matrix using 'nested for' statement. The diagonal elements having row number and column number same. Therefore, the elements which have the same row number and column number are added.

```
//A PROGRAM TO OBTAIN SUM OF THE DIAGONAL ELEMENTS
#include<iostream.h>
#include<conio.h>
main()
{
    int i,j,m;
    clrscr();
    //ENTERING THE ORDER OF MATRIX
    cout<<"Enter  only  order m of A matrix \n";
    cin>>m;
    cout<<"Enter the elements of "<<m<<" x "<<m<<" A matrix"<<endl;
    int a[20][20];
    for(i = 1;i<=m;++i)
    {
    for(j = 1;j<=m;++j)
    {
          cin>>a[i][j]; //SCANING THE ELEMENTS OF A MATRIX
    }
    }
    int sum = 0;
    for(i=1;i<=m;++i)
    sum = sum + a[i][i];
    cout<<"Sum of diagonal elements of a matrix is  "<<sum;
    cout<<endl;
}
```

Input	:	Enter only order m of A matrix
		3
		Enter the elements of3x3 A matrix
		1 2 3
		4 5 6
		7 8 9
Output	:	Sum of diagonal elements of a matrix is 15

18.7 'void' DECLARATIONS OF FUNCTION

The function can be declared void. This is used to

1. Specify the non return type of a function when it is not returning any value.
2. To indicate empty argument list to a function.

Ex : void compute();

This indicates void type of compute function. The function is declared in the main program void declaration of function.

18.8 'return' STATEMENT

In C++, the 'main()' program returns integer value to the operating system. Therefore, 'main()' program should end with

return (0);

statement otherwise a warning will occur in the program.

The function programs which are not declared as the 'void' programs are ended with 'return 0' statement.

Program 18–12

In this program the minimum and maximum numbers in the array are calculated by using function program as in the C–language. The array is supplied and scanned in the main program using 'for' statement. Then a call is given to a function program 'compute' which calculates minimum or maximum number in an array.

```
//A FUNCTION PROGRAM TO PRINT THE MIN OR MAX VALUE
#include<iostream.h>
#include<conio.h>
main()
{
    void compute(int a[],int n);
    clrscr();
    cout<<"Enter the number of array\n";
    int n;
    cin>>n;
    cout<<"Enter the elements of an array\n";
    int a[30];
    for(int i=0;i<n;++i)
    {
        cin>>a[i];
    }
    compute(a,n);
}
void compute(int a[30],int n)
{
    int max = a[0];
    int min = a[0];
    // CONSIDERING FIRST NUMBER MAX OR MIN
    for(int j=0;j<n;++j)
    {
    if(a[j]<=min)
    {
        min = a[j];
    }
    if(a[j]>=max)
```

```
    {
        max = a[j];
    }
    }
    cout<<"The maximum number is  "<<max<<endl;
    cout<<"The mimimum number is  "<<min;
}
```

Input	:	Enter the number of array 5 Enter the elements of an array 4 7 5 1 9
Output	:	The maximum number is 9 The minimum number is 1

Program 18–13

In this program an array is multiplied by the scalar by a function program scalar. In this program the array is supplied to the main program and the display function program shows the array. Then the elements of array are multiplied by the scalar using the function program scalar. Then the display function program is called to display the new array.

```
//PROGRAM TO MULTIPLY A ARRAY BY
//A SCALAR NUMBER 2
#include<iostream.h>
#include<conio.h>
int display(int a[5])
{
    for(int i=0;i<5;++i)
    {
        cout<<'\t'<<a[i];
    }
    return(0);
}
int scalar(int a[5],int s)
{
    for(int i=0;i<5;++i)
    a[i] *= s;
    return(0);
}
int display(int b[5]);
int scalar(int b[5],int s);
main()
{
     int b[5] = {2,3,4,5,6};
    clrscr();
     cout<<" Original Array is \n";
```

```
    display(b);
    cout<<"\n";
    scalar(b,2);
    cout<<"An Array Multiplied By 2 is \n"<<endl;
    display(b);
}
```

Input	:	Original Array is 2 3 4 5 6
Output	:	An array Multiplied By 2 is 4 6 8 10 12

Program 18–14

This function program uses mathematical function from math.h library to calculate logrithmic and exponent values by giving a call to a function program 'log_x' and 'expo'.

```
// program to calculate the values of x and y using
//following equation x = log,y=exp-5z
#include<iostream.h>
#include<conio.h>
#include<math.h>
float x,y,a,z;
log_x(float n)
{
    x = a * log(n);
    return(0);
}
expo(float e)
{
    y = a * exp( –5 * e);
    return(0);
}
main()
{
    clrscr();
    cout<<" enter the values of a and z\n ";
    cin>>a>>z;
    log_x(z);
    cout<<"x ="<<x<<endl;
    expo(z);
    cout<<" y ="<<y<<endl;
}
```

Input	:	Enter the values of a and z 2 3
Output	:	x = 2.197225 y = 6.118046e–07

Program 18–15

In this program the pointers are used in C++ which are similar to C. The pointers are declared and used in C++ as in the C–language. The following program shows the exchange of values of pointers using function program 'exchange'.

```
//PROGRAM ON EXCHANGE OF POINTER USING FUNCTION
#include<iostream.h>
#include<conio.h>
exchange(int *point1,int *point2)
{
    int temp = *point1;
    *point1 = *point2;
    *point2 = temp;
    return(0);
}
main()
{
    int i1,i2;
    int *p1 = &i1;
    int *p2 = &i2;
    cout<<"enter the values of i1,i2 \n";
    cin>>i1>>i2;
    cout<<" i1 = "<<*p1<<"\n i2 = "<<*p2<<endl;
    exchange(p1,p2);
    cout<<"The new values after the exchange"<<endl;
    cout<<"i1 = "<<*p1<<"\ni2 = "<<*p2;
}
```

Input	:	enter the values of i1,i2
		4 8
Output	:	i1= 4
		i2= 8
		The new values after the exchange
		i1= 8
		i2= 4

18.9 'enum' STATEMENT

In case of 'enum' statement in C++, the number attached to the list cannot be used but name can be used.

```
int colour;
enum colour { red, blue, green };
        colour = 2;        ——→ This is an error
        but
        colour = blue;
        is permitted.
```

When 'colour' variable is enumerated, the colour must be indicated by word rather than a number.

18.10 CHAR ARRAY

In C–language in case of char array, if the initialization is to be done, the size of array is the exact length of string.

```
char string [3] ={ "xyz"};
```

In this case '\0' (Null character) is automatically attached, but in case of C++ the char array size should be one larger than the number of characters in the string to account for null character.

```
char string [4] = {"xyz"};
```

18.11 SYMBOLIC CONSTANTS

There are two ways of creating symbolic constants in C++

(1) declaration of a constant :

The constant is a value which cannot be modified in the program. Such value are declared by the word 'const' or 'constant'.

It can be written as

```
constant int size = 10;
        or
  const size = 10;
```

This is same, because in default constant is integer.

The constants are similar variables, but their values cannot be changed.

(2) Using 'enum' statement :

Another method of specifying constant is

```
enum {x,y,z};
```

In this case, x has value of 1, y is 2 and z is 3.

```
enum { x = 100, y = 50, z = 200 };
```

In this case, x is made equal to 100, y equals to 50 and z equals to 200 by 'enum' statement.

Program 18–16

In this program the area of circle, volume of sphere and surface area of sphere is calculated by using function programs. A constant 'pi' is declared as a symbolic constant and is passed as an argument of function program to evaluate the value of volume surface area and area of circle.

```
//A PROGRAM TO CALCULATE AREA OF CIRCLE, VOLUME AND SURFACE
//OF A SPHERE BY DECLARING 'PI' AS CONSTANT
#include<iostream.h>
#include<conio.h>
float const pi = 22.0/7.0;
main()
{
    void area(float ,float);
    void volume(float ,float);
    void s_area(float ,float);
    clrscr();
    cout<<"Enter the radius \n";
    float r;
    cin>>r;
    area(pi,r);
    s_area(pi,r);
```

```
    volume(pi,r);
}
void  area(float pi,float r)
{
    float a1=pi * r * r;
    cout<<" Area = "<<a1<<endl;
}
void s_area(float pi,float r)
{
    float s_a1 = 4.0 * pi * r * r;
    cout<<" Surface area = "<<s_a1<<endl;
}
void volume(float pi,float r)
{
    float v1 = 4 / 3 * pi * r * r * r;
    cout<<" The volume = "<<v1;
}
```

Input	:	Enter the radius 3
Output	:	Area = 28.285713 Surfae area = 113.142853 The volume = 84.85714

18.12 REFERENCE VARIABLES

A reference variable provides an alternative name for a previously defined variable.It is written as

x &y = z;

where,

x – declaration of type

y – reference name

z – variable name.

Ex: float total = 100;

float &sum = total;

Here the 'total' is a float type variable, which has already been declared. But 'sum' is the alternative name declared to represent the 'total' variable.

Program 18–17

In this program the reference variable is used and a call is given to a function program. The reference variable receives the value from the normal variable in the call of function program and the value is modified by incrementing the value by 10.

```
#include<iostream.h>
#include<conio.h>
void f(int &x)
```

```
{
    x = x + 10;
}
main()
{
    int m = 10;
    f(m);
    cout<<m;
}
```

Output	:	20

18.13 MANIPULATORS

There are two types of manipulators used :

1. endl
2. setw

18.13.1 Endl Manipulator

This is used in output statement, which causes a new line feed to be inserted. It is similar to '\n' character of C-language.

Ex: Cout << "m = " << m << endl;

In this case after printing of value of 'n' 'endl' executes new line control.

18.13.2 setw Manipulator

This function set a field width for printing of numbers. It is written as

setw(w);

Where,

w – field width

Ex: cout << setw(5) << sum << endl;

The field width of 5 is set and then sum is printed.

These statements are defined in file 'iomanip.h' file ,which must be included in the program.

18.14 AUTOMATIC CONVERSION

In C++ automatic conversion of variables in expression from 'float', 'double', 'int' is carried out even if mixed expression is supplied.

Ex: m = 5 + 2.75 is permitted.

18.15 'void' POINTERS

These are the pointer variables declared as 'void' which makes them capable of accepting data from any type of pointer.

Ex. : void *gp

In this case 'gp' is a pointer variable of void type which can accept any type of value

If

```
int * ip;
ip = (int  *) gp;
```

This means that now 'gp' receives the address 'ip' and naturally the value of 'ip'.But the void variable can be given value by declaring it at the place of assignment.

18.16 CONSTANT POINTER

These are pointer utilized for the constants used in the program. These pointers can accept a value from constants and can access the address of the constant. The constant pointers and pointer to a constant are defined as

char * const ptr1 = {"GOOD"};

This is pointer constant 'ptr' whose value is 'GOOD'

int const * ptr1 = & m;

This is a pointer to a constant which accepts address of 'm' variable.The contents of such pointers can not be changed .

18.17 SCOPE RESOLUTION OPERATOR

The C++ – language differentiates the concept of global variable and internal variable of the program. In a program, same variable name can be used for a global variable and internal variable. Then in such a case a scope resolution operator specifies that the given variable is a global variable or internal variable. The internal variable is a variable which is valid for internal operation of the program but cannot be accessed outside the main or function program. The global variable is a variable which is declared as common variable and can be accessed by a main program or function program readily. But in the event of same variable name being global and internal the situation is confusing. This is solved by scope resolution operator.

In C++ language a scope resolution operator is used to indicate the scope of variable in the block. The '::' symbol is used for scope resolution operator. It is written as

:: x

where,

x – variable name

Then x is a global variable rather than local variable.

Ex :

:: count

'count' is a global variable and not a local variable.

Program 18–18

This program uses scope resolution operator to obtain global or local variable value. The global variable is declared outside the 'main' program and the local variable is declared inside the 'main' program. To access the value of global variable scope resolution operator is used.

```
//scope resolution operator.
# include <iostream.h>
int m = 10;
main ()
{
    int m = 20;
    {
        int k = m;
        int m = 30;
        cout << "k=" << k << "\n";
        cout <<"::m=" <<::m << "\n"
```

```
        cout << "m=" <<m<< "\n".
    }
}
```

Output : k = 20
:::m = 10
m = 30

In this program :: m is a global variable, whose value is 10 and m is a normal variable whose value is 30 .

18.18 RETURN BY REFERENCE

A function can be returned by a reference multiple values depending upon the condition found to be true or false. If in a function program multiple values are to be returned by choice of any one value.

Ex : The following is a function program on return by reference

```
int max (int & x, int & y)
{
if (x > y)
        return (x);
else
        return (y);
}
```

In this case the x & y are input values, if x > y, then x is returned or if x < y then y is returned. Hence multiple returns are available.

18.19 INLINE FUNCTION

These are small functions and can be used as micros.They are declared by a word 'inline'.

Ex :
```
inline double cube (double a)
        {return (a*a*a);}
```

This function program cube returns cube of a number to the main program.

18.20 DEFAULT ARGUMENTS

In C++, there are default arguments available i.e., if the argument of function program are not given, then default values will taken by it.

Ex : float amount (float principal, int period,float rate = 0.15);

This is the declaration of function. When a call is given to this function then only first two arguments are supplied, third is taken by default.

v = amount (5000,7);

In this call only principal amount and year are supplied, the interest rate is available in default.

18.21 FUNCTION OVERLOADING

This is used to carry out calculations of same quantity for different purposes. It means that, we can design a family of functions with one function name, but with different argument list.

Ex : There are two 'add' functions with different argument list.

```
int add (int a, int b);
int add (int a, float b, int c);
```

Then any one of them can be used for printing. The number of argument list decides which function has been called.

```
cout << add (5,10);
```

In second case another function call is given.

```
cout << add(5,0.1, 10);
```

In such a case, 'matching' function call matches argument list with their types and choose the function properly.

Program 18–19

In this program volume of cube, cylinder and a box is calculated by using the 'volume' function program. There are three function programs of the same name 'volume'. These function programs are called in the main program but their arguments are different, in case of cube only one argument is present, in case of cylinder arguments are present whereas in the case of box two and three arguments are present therefore the call of function program is decided by the number of arguments in the call.

```
//TO CALCULATE VOLUME OF CUBE , CYLINDER AND BOX
//USING FUNCTION OVERLOADING
#include<iostream.h>
#include<conio.h>
main()
{
    int volume(int);
    double volume(double,int);
    int volume(int,int,int);
    clrscr();
    cout<<"VOLUME OF SPHERE   :"<<volume(10)<<"\n";
    cout<<"VOLUME OF CYLINDER :"<<volume(2.5,8)<<"\n";
    cout<<"VOLUME OF BOX      :"<<volume(10,7,2)<<"\n";
}
int volume(int c)
{
    return(4.0/3.0 * 3.142 * c * c * c);
}
double volume(double r,int h)
{
    return(3.14519 * r * r * h);
}
int volume(int l,int b,int h)
{
    return(l * b * h);
}
```

```
Output    :    VOLUME OF SPHERE  : 4189
               VOLUME OF CYLINDER  : 80
               VOLUME OF BOX  : 140
```

18.22 'new' AND 'delete' OPERATOR

The 'new' and 'delete' operators are used in C–language to obtain the required memories and to delete the unrequired memories. The 'new' operator assists in opening of new memories and the delete operator deletes the created memories. This saves the memory required for execution of program by vacating unrequired memory.

Ex : int *p;

p = new int (20);

This statement results in assigning value of 20 to p.

delete p;

This results in deleting the memory of p.

p = new int [20];

This results in creating 20 memories and assigns the base address to p.

delete p ;

This deletes memory of p.

Program 18–20

In this program, new memories are created to an array by using 'new' operator and these memories are deleted by using 'delete' operator.

```
//NEW AND DELETE OPERATOR
#include<iostream.h>
#include<conio.h>
main()
{
    clrscr();
    int *p;
    p = new int(25); //allocate memory for integer
    cout<<" VALUE IS INTEGER AT p :- "<<*p<<endl;
    delete p; //release memory
    p = new int[20];
    *(p + 1) = 35;
    cout<<"VALUE IS "<<*(p+1);
    return 0;
}
```

Output	:	VALUES IS INTEGER AT p :- 25 VALUES IS 35

18.23 FILE OPERATION

The concept of file operation has already explained in the chapter 13. The file operation was carried out in C-language using file pointers. But in C++ it is performed by use of objects to access the address of file.

18.23.1 Opening and Closing of files

In C^{++} programming, file opening /closing is similar to C.The output files can be opened using 'ofstream' command.

ofstream outfile ("file name");

This statement opens a file with the given name.

The 'outfile' is name of the file,which is an object like pointer to file.

The input file can be opened using 'ifstream' command

ifstream infile ("file name");

where 'infile' is a pointer to given file name.

These file operations commands are available in a file "fstream.h",which must be included in every program.

Alternately, the files can be opened by using other commands

outfile.open("filename");

This opens an output file of the given name.

infile.open("filename");

This open input file of given name.

The file can be closed by using the pointer.

outfile.close();

This closes the 'outfile' file.

infile.close();

This closes the 'infile' file.

18.24 WRITING RESULT ON FILE

The results can be written on output file as below :

outfile << x;

Where,

x – variables, comments which are to be printed on the file opened by the 'outfile'.

18.25 READING DATA FROM FILE

The data can be read from input file as below :

infile >> x;

Where,

x – variable whose value is to be read from a file opened by the 'infile' .

18.26 END OF FILE

Similar to C–language, C^{++} has end of file function as 'eof()' function .

It is written as

outfile.eof()

This indicates end of a given file.

18.27 ERROR IN HANDLING THE FILE

Similar to Null character of C, a function is used in C^{++} as 'fail'.

'fail ()'

This function indicates failure while opening the file.

Ex. : if (infile.fail())

```
          cout<<"unable to open a file\n";
```

This reports the error in opening file.

Program 18–21

```
//program on file operation
#include<fstream.h>
main()
{
    ofstream outfile("xx.rr");
    cout<<"Enter the item name:";
    char name[30];
    cin>>name;
    outfile<<name<<"\n";
    cout<<"enter the cost\n";
    float cost;
    cin>>cost;
    outfile<<cost<<"\n";
    outfile.close();
    ifstream infile("xx.rr");
    infile>>name;
    infile>>cost;
    cout<<"name of item :"<<name <<"\n";
    cout<<"cost of item :"<<cost <<"\n";
    infile.close();
}
```

In this program, the output file is opened by using the 'outfile' object and the data as 'name of item' and 'cost' is scanned from the screen and are written on the output file "xx.rr".Then this file is closed. The file is further opened as the input file and the data is read from the file and written on the userscreen.

18.28 STRING OPERATION

In C++ there are operations available for reading and writing of the strings. These statement are

1. getline
2. write

These statements are used in C++ for reading and writing of a statement as

```
cin.getline(x,y);
```

This statement reads a line from the userscreen consisting of 'y' number of characters and stores in `x' char array.

```
cout.write(x,y);
```

This statement writes a line on the userscreen consisting of 'y'number of characters and stores in 'x' char array.

Program 18–22

In this program the name of the area of the person is scanned from the userscreen and using the getline function and this name is printed by the cout statement and then further by the use of the write statement.

```
//A PROGRAM TO PRINT NAME OF AREA USING 'getline() '
//AND ' write()'FUNCTIONS
#include<iostream.h>
#include<conio.h>
#include<string.h>  //for stirng operation
main()
{
    int size=20;
    clrscr();
    cout<<"enter CITY  name \n";
    char city[20];
    cin.getline(city,size);
    cout<<"\nCITY Name is \n"<<city<<"\n\n";
    cout.write(city,size);
}
```

Input	:	enter CITY name MAHABALESHWAR
Output	:	CITY Name is MAHABALESHWAR MAHABALESHWAR

18.29 COMMAND LINE ARGUMENT

In this case, the main program receives an argument from a DOS screen as the number of arguments 'argc' and the names of the arguments are supplied from the DOS screen. The program is run from a command line of DOS, where the first name supplied is the program file name and it is accepted as the argument 'argv[0]' which is a char array accepting first name. The subsequent names will be accepted by 'argv[1]' and 'argv[2]' etc. which may be the input file or the output file.

Program 18–23

```
// WRITE A PROGRAM TO RUN COMMAND LINE ARGUMENTS
#include <fstream.h>
#include <stdlib.h>
#include <conio.h>
main(int argc, char *argv[])
{
    clrscr();
    argc = 3;
    int number [9] = {11,22,33,44,55,66,77,88,99};
    if(argc!=3)
    {
        cout << " argc = " << argc << "\n";
        cout << " Error in arguments \n";
        exit(1);
    }
    ofstream fout1, fout2;
```

```
    fout1.open(argv[1]);
    if(fout1.fail())
    {
        cout << " Could not open file ! " << argv[1] << "\n";
        exit(1);
    }
    fout2.open(argv[2]);
    if(fout2.fail())
    {
        cout << " Could not open file ! " << argv[2] << "\n";
        exit(1);
    }
    for(int i=0; i<9; i++)
    {
        if(number[i] % 2 == 0)
            fout2 << number[i] << "  "; // Write to EVEN file
        else
            fout1 << number[i] << "  "; // Write to ODD file
    }
    fout1.close(); fout2.close();
    ifstream infile; char ch;
    for(int j=1; j<argc; j++)
    {
        infile.open(argv[j]);
        cout << " Contents of " << argv[j] << "\n";
        do
        {
            infile.get(ch);
            cout << ch;
        } while(infile);
        cout << "\n\n";
        infile.close();
    }
}
```

Input	:	C:\TC\BIN>cpp75 even.dat odd.dat
Output	:	Contents of even.dat 3 4 5 6 7 8 9 10 11 Contents of odd.dat 2 4 6 8 10 12 14 16 18

EXERCISE

1. Write a function to calculate average of 4 'n' given numbers using function program .
2. Write a function program to calculate the sum of series using function program .

   $S = 1 + x + x^2 + x^3$ .... UPTO n TERMS.
3. Write a program using function program to find minimum or maximum value in an array.
4. Write a program using function program to scan and print names of 'n' employees in the department.
5. Write a program using function program to join string using char array.
6. Write a program using function program to find surface area and cross section area of solid cylinder of radius 'r' and length 'l' using symbolic constant.
7. Write a program using function program to calculate interest and total amount payable as an principal amount 'p' for 'n' year with interest rate of 'i' compounded six monthly.
8. Write a function program to prepare a table containing the values of displacement 'x' at different time 't' in the S.H.M.

   $x = a \text{ Sin } (wt + f)$

   where,

   w – angular velocity

   f – phase angle

   a – maximum amplitude.
9. Write a program to use the function program to calculate volume of sphere using 'inline' function and symbolic constants .
10. Write a program using function program to multiply all element of array by a scalar .
11. What is a 'scope resolution operator' and how it can be used for global variable?.
12. What is meant by class and which are the two types of the members of the class ? How are they declared ?
13. Write a program using function program to arrange the elements of array in ascending order.
14. Write a program using function program for addition of two matrices
15. Write a program using function program to find average of all elements of matrix.
16. Write a program using function program to calculate sum of diagonal elements of matrix.
17. Write a program using function program to find length of string.
18. Write a program using function program to read elements of array from a file and calculate the average of all numbers.
19. Write a program using function program to separate even and odd numbers from an array and print them in given files.
20. Write a program using function program to calculate volume of box,cylinder and sphere using function over loading.
21. Write a program that asks the user to input two integers a and b and then states whether or not is divisible by b.
22. Write a program that reads the radius of a circle and determine its area, the area of largest square contained within it and the ratio of the two.
23. Write a program using function to swap the two numbers.
24. Prepare a program to calculate sum of all prime numbers between 1 and 100.

25. Write a program to determine sum of the integers from 1 to n with the added constant that five and integer divisible by five not included in the sum using 'continue ' statement.
26. Word FindPuzzle using two-dimensional arrays, character char arrays, string manipulation functions, user-defined types, and structures struct, dynamically allocated arrays using the new[] operator. Word Find is a puzzle where you are given a list of words that you must find in a rectangular matrix of letters. Words must be found in a straight line, and the letters of each word must be in exact sequence (do not skip over letters to form a word). Words may appear horizontally (left to right, or right to left), vertically (top to bottom, or bottom to top), or diagonally (at a 45° angle) in either direction. Words may begin or end at any location in the matrix, or even overlap.

19

OBJECT ORIENTED PROGRAMMING

AN OVERVIEW

In the previous chapter, we have seen the programming in C^{++}. The C^{++} is the extension of C. Some of the deficiencies of C-programming have been modified and C^{++} provides addtional functions and operations in C.

In this chapter you will study the object oriented programming in C^{++}. This is concept of the classes which creates objects and the objects have capacity to modify the value of variables of class using the function members of the class.

OBJECTIVE

In this unit , you will able study

* Necessity of object oriented programming
* Concept of classes
* Member of the class
* Creation of objects
* Inheritance and polymorphism

19.1 STRUCTURED PROGRAMMING AND OBJECT ORIENTED PROGRAMMING

There are two categories of programming techniques:

1. Structured programming
2. Object oriented programming

The *structured programming* is a system of programming in which the programming is performed by using the sequential commands. All the programming instructions are written in a structured format and executed in a sequence. The processing is performed in a systematic manner on the data very easily accessible in the class.

The object oriented programming is a technique which is performed in a manner that the data remains in a hiding format in the variables of the protected and public type. The operations in the object oriented programming are performed by the member functions using objects.

19.2 NEED FOR OBJECT ORIENTED PROGRAMMING

Object oriented programming is required for handling the complexities in programming due to the operation on data base system. In the structured programming, the data is maintained in the variables and can be very easily accessed in the program. It generally happens that the data values are defined for specific quantities and there are large number of such quantities. The data values are easily accessed in structured programming and the data values remain free either in the arrays or normal variables. Therefore, in this case it is not possible to protect the data values or hide them. The function programs access and transfer the values of variables very easily in structured programming. In case of object oriented programming, the access in function program can be protected to the data values and the data values can be maintained in a structured format under the objects. The access of function members is controlled by the objects and under the objects large number of values can be stored. The variables can be utilized as protected variables, public variables, private variables and global variables. The data values can be prevented from direct access by member functions and objects. This results in a creation of softwares with proper formats and operations.

19.3 CLASSES

A class is a way to bind the data and its associated functions together. It allows the data to be hidden for external use. When defining a class, we are creating a new abstract data type that can be treated like any other built in data type. The class specification has two parts :

1. Class declarations
2. Class function definitions.

The class declaration describes the type and scope of its members.The class function definitions describe how the class functions are implemented.

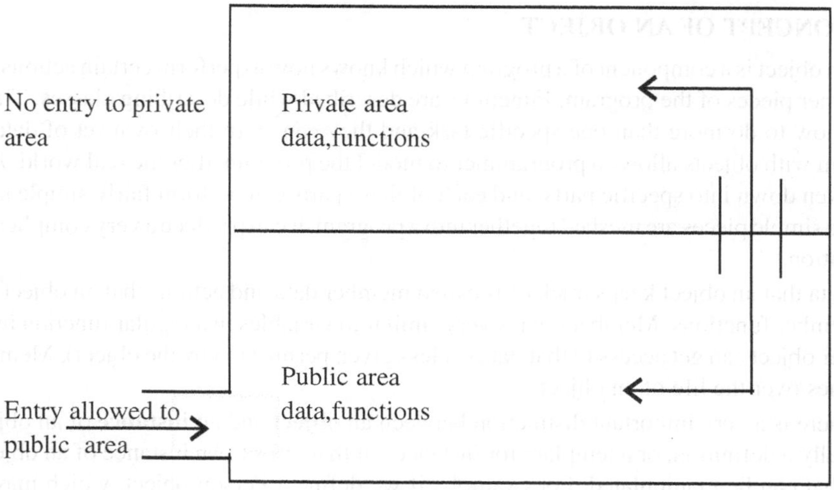

The general form of a class declaration is

```
class class_name
{
        Private :
                Variable declarations;     } Private member
                function declarations;
        Public :
                Variable declarations;     } Public member
                function declarations;
}
```

The functions and variables are members of the class. The private members can be accessed only from within the class, but the public member can be accessed from outside also. In default of declaration of public or private all the members of the class are private.

19.4 APPLICATIONS OF OBJECT ORIENTED PROGRAMMING

The object oriented programming technology has been used for

1. Computer Aided Engineering
2. Simulation and Modelling
3. Data system
4. Internet Application system
5. Artificial Intelligence and expert system

6. Operating system design
7. Graphic user interface
8. Multi media application
9. Design of support system
10. CAD/CAM systems

The object oriented technology improves the productivity of the programmer and also increases the quality of software system. It allows for communicating the messages and is capable of creating a network to access the data or the softwares of any other user at any other location.

19.5 CONCEPT OF AN OBJECT

An object is a component of a program which knows how to perform certain actions and to interact with other pieces of the program. Functions are described while describing classes. The objects can know how to do more than one specific task and they can store their own set of data. Designing a program with objects allows a programmer to model the program after the real world. A program can be broken down into specific parts, and each of these parts can perform fairly simple tasks. When all of these simple pieces are meshed together into a program, it can produce a very complicated and useful application.

Data that an object keeps track of is called member data and actions that an object knows how to call member functions. Member data is very similar to variables in a regular function in the sense that no other object can get access to that data (unless given permission by the object). Member data keeps its values over the life of an object.

There is a very important distinction between an **object** and an **instance** of an object. An object is actually a definition, or a template for instances of that object. An instance of an object is an actual thing that can be manipulated. For example, if we define a Person object, which may include such member data as hair color, eye color, height, weight, etc. An instance of this object could be "rajesh" and rajesh has values for hair color, eye color, etc. This allows for multiple instances of an object to be created.

Objects are ways of bundling parts of programs into small, manageable pieces. Objects are simply a definition for a type of data to be stored. An instance of an object contains meaningful information, these are manipulated by the program. There can be more than one instance of an object. Instances of objects keep track of information, called member data, or instance variables. This data is kept track of by the instance until it no longer exists. Object instances also know how to perform certain functions, called member functions, or class functions. Every instance of an object performs the same steps when carrying out a member function, although the steps can be influenced by the instances' present member data.

19.6 OBJECT DESIGN

The role that an object plays within a program should be able to be defined. For instance, good concise role's for an object would be:

- Manages all requests into a data structure
- Arbitrates turns in a multi-user game
- does all data type conversions within program
- easy interface to reading, writing, and parsing files.

Drawing pictures that describe the functionality of objects can be a big help when designing a program. Pictures can often describe the relationship between objects better than a paragraph of words.

19.7 DECLARING A CLASS

Once the object has been designed , writing the C++ code is simple. The hard part is designing objects that will interact well with each other, that will do everything which is needed. There is almost no new syntax we need to learn to write objects in C^{++}. It involves using the syntax for variables and functions

19.8 INSTANTIATION

The writing of a class declaration needed to instantiate an object. Instantiating an object which allows to actually use objects in the program. A class declaration is merely a template for an object should be configured. When you instantiate an object, C^{++} follows the class declaration as if it were a blueprint for how to create an instance of that object. The objects are exactly same as that of variable except they have multiple variable values.

19.9 CLASS PROGRAMS

In C^{++} the program which uses class are arranged in the following fashion. The include files are written in the beginning of the program. Then the classes are declared. The class functions are defined and then the 'main' program is written, which uses all these components.

Include files
Class declaration
Class functions definitions
Main function program

Ex :

class declaration item is as follows :

```
class item
{
        int number;                    variables declared
        float cost;                    are private by default
public :
        void getdata (int a, float b);
        void putdata (void);
};
```

This declaration of class item consists of number and cost variables as the members of the class. Since these variables are not declared to be private or public they are private members whereas the class has two public members which are functions 'getdata' and 'putdata'. The private members 'number' and 'cost' can be accessed by public members 'getdata' and 'putdata' function whereas the outside functions which are not members of the class can not access the private members.

The classes can be used to the main program to acquire the values by use of the objects. When a class is referred to an object, then the object can receive a value. The object automatically receives private and public members and can acquire the values by utilizing the public members. The private members are utilized for storage of values received by the object.

The class can be referred to the object as

```
item   i1;
```

In this case item class is received by the object i1, which means that all the private members and public members are accessible to the object. The objects can give a call to public members which may be supplied with input values and the object stores the values in private members.

Program 19–1

In this program the information about the names of the persons and their ages is maintained by use of class person.

```
// CLASSES PROGRAM
# include <iostream.h>
class person
{
        char name [30];
        int age;
    public :
        void getdata (void);
        void display (void);
};
void person :: getdata (void)
{
    cout << "Enter name:";
    cin >> name;
    cout << "Enter age:";
    cin >> age;
}
void person :: display (void)
{
    cout <<"\n Name : "<< name;
    cout <<"\n Age : "<< age;
}
main ()
{
    person p;              ——> declaration of object 'p' to class 'person'
    p.getdata ();          ——> call of member function by the objects
    p.display ();
}
```

Input	:	Enter name :Anita Enter age :24
Output	:	Name :Anita Age :24

In this program a class is declared as persons which consists of two private members and two public members. The private members consists of 'name' char array and 'age' as variable. The public members of the class consists of two function programs 'getdata' and 'display'. The class is referred to object 'p' and it gives call to 'getdata' function as

p.getdata();

This call receives the 'name' and 'age' of a person which is stored in private members of class. Then 'p' gives a call to 'display' function to display the 'name' and 'age' of person available with the object.

Program 19–2

This program is used for scanning and printing of numbers and cost of the item. It consists of a class 'item' having private members 'number', 'it_name' and 'cost'. The class has public members as 'getdata' and 'putdata'. The class is referred in the main program to an object x which gives a call to a 'getdata' function to receive values to the private members and it gives a call to 'putdata' function to display the values of private members.

```
//A PROGRAM TO SCAN AND PRINT NUMBER AND COST OF ITEM USING CLASSES
#include<iostream.h>
#include<conio.h>
class item
{
            int number;
            char it_name[20];
            float cost;
      public:
            void getdata(void);
            void putdata(void);
};
void item::getdata()
{
    cout<<"enter the No,Name and Cost of Item?\n";
    cin>>number>>it_name>>cost;
}
void item::putdata()
{
    cout<<" ITEM NUMBER    :"<<number<<endl;
    cout<<" NAME OF ITEM   :"<<it_name<<endl;
    cout<<" COST OF ITEM   :"<<cost<<endl;
}
main()
{
    clrscr();
    item x;
    x.getdata();
    x.putdata();
}
```

Input	:	enter the No., Name and Cost of item? 120 Tooth_Paste 25		
Output	:	ITEM NUMBER	:	120
		NAME OF ITEM	:	Tooth_Paste
		COST OF ITEM	:	25

Program 19–3

In this program a function program becomes a private member of the class and the class has another private member 'm'. There are two public members 'update' and 'write' functions. These functions are declared out of the class and the 'private member' function is also declared outside the class. The class sample is assigned to an object 'a' and a call is given by the object to 'update' function program. The 'update' program further gives a call to 'read' function which is a private member. The 'read' function reads the values of 'm' and it is modified by 'update'. Then the object is used for calling display function to display the value of 'm'.

```
//A PROGRAM FOR PRIVATE MEMBER FUNCTION IN OBJECT OF CLASS
#include<iostream.h>
#include<conio.h>
class sample
{
            int m;
            void read(void);  //private member function
    public:
            void update(void);
            void write(void);
};
void sample::update(void)
{
    read();
    m = 2 * m;
}
void sample::write(void)
{
    cout<<" m = "<<m;
}
void sample::read(void)
{
    cout<<"Enter number :";
    cin>>m;
}
main()
{
    clrscr();
    sample a;
    a.update();
    a.write();
}
```

Input	:	Enter number : 5
Output	:	m = 10

Program 19–4

In this function program class item uses 'item_code', 'item_name', 'item cost' variables which are array variables and 'count' variable as private members of the class. The class consists of public member functions as function programs. The public member function program are called by the object and the values of various 'itemcodes', 'names' and 'costs' are stored in array variables by use of the menu which allows storage of values, deletion of items or addition of items.

```
//A PROGRAM FOR ARRAY OF ELEMENTS OF OBJECT
#include<iostream.h>
#include<conio.h>
const m = 50;
class item
{
        int it_code[m];
        char it_name[m];
        float it_cost[m];
        int count;
    public:
        void cou(void){count = 0;}//initializes count 0
        void getdata(void);
        void dispsum(void);
        void remove(void);
        void dispitems(void);
};
void item::getdata(void)
{
    cout<<"enter item code : \n";
    cin>>it_code[count];
    cout<<"enter item name : \n";
    cin>>it_name[count];
    cout<<"enter item cost : \n";
    cin>>it_cost[count];
    count++;
}
void item::dispsum(void)
{
    float sum = 0;
    for(int i=0;i<count;i++)
    sum = sum + it_cost[i];
    cout<<" Total Value : "<<sum<<"\n";
}
void item::remove(void)
{
    int a;
    cout<<"Enter item code :";
```

```
cin>>a;
for(int i=0;i<count;i++)
if(it_code[i]==a)
it_code[i]=0;
}
void item::dispitems(void)
{
    cout<<"\n ITEM CODE  COST OF ITEM \n";
    for(int i=0;i<count;i++)
    {
            cout<<"\n"<<it_code[i];
            cout<<"\n"<<it_name[i];
            cout<<"   "<<it_cost[i];
    }
    cout<<"\n";
}
main()
{
    clrscr();
    item order;
    order.cou();
    int x;
    do
    {
            cout<<"Enter appropriate number \n";
            cout<<"\n1 : Add Item ";
            cout<<"\n2 : Display Total Value ";
            cout<<"\n3 : Delete Item ";
            cout<<"\n4 : Dispaly All Items ";
            cout<<"\n5 : Quit ";
            cout<<"\n\nWhat is your option ? ";
            cin>>x;
            switch(x)
            {
                    case 1 : order.getdata();
                     break;
                    case 2 : order.dispsum();
                     break;
                    case 3 : order.remove();
                     break;
                    case 4 : order.dispitems();
                     break;
                    case 5 : break;
                    default:
                    cout<<" Error in input ! check it \n";
            }
    }while(x!=5);
}
```

Input	:	Enter appropriate number 1 : Add Item 2 : Display total value 3 : Delete item 4 : Display all items 5 : Quit What is your option ? 1 enter item code : 23 enter item name : Tooth_paste enter item cost : 25 Enter appropriate number 1 : Add Item 2 : Display total value 3 : Delete item 4 : Display all items 5 : Quit What is your option ? 5

19.10 CONSTRUCTORS AND DESTRUCTORS

The constructors are the function of the class used by the objects of the class, but they are different from the normal functions of the class. The constructors are the function programs which performs work of construction means to build the value in the objects and variables. The constructors are the methods which have same name of the class. These methods are very easily recognized by there name which is same as the name of a class. The constructors comes into action when the objects are created. The constructor can be declared in the class as below :

```
class base
{
            int a, b;
      public:
            base(int, int);
            void print ();
            ~base();
}
```

In this case a class base has a function program which is member of class having name base. This base function program is a constructor of the class. This constructor is a function program having same name of class can be utilized to create the object of the class and can be called while declaring the objects.

```
base B (10, 20);
```

In this case B object is created from base class and a call to a constructor is given.

The constructor can be called in the manner used for calling other functions

```
base B ;
B = base (10,20);
```

The destructor is also a function member of a class which performs the work of destruction. It is a constructive destructor of the class which destroy assign values and deletes the unrequired memories. The destructor is indicated by ~.

The destructors are the function member of a class which performs a work of destruction of the assigned values and the memories. The destructors works reverse to the work of constructor. The constructors are basically the members which constructs the values in the software whereas the destructors acts in reverse of the decrement of values or deletion of values or deletion of memories. They are indicated by '~' with the same name of constructor. The destructors acts immediately after the work of constructor is over.

Program 19–5

```
//PROGRAM ON CLASSES WITH CONSTRUCTORS
#include<iostream.h>
#include<conio.h>
class con
{
            int m,n;
    public:
            con(int,int); //Declaration of constructor
            void display(void)
            {
                    cout<<"m = "<<m;
                    cout<<"\nn = "<<n;
            }
};
con::con(int x,int y)   //Definition of constructor
{
    m = x;
    n = y;
}
main()
{
    clrscr();
    con c1(0,100);
    con c2 = con(25,75);
    cout<<"\nObject1 "<<"\n";
    c1.display();
    cout<<"\nObject2 "<<"\n";
    c2.display();
}
```

```
Output    :    Object1
               m = 0
               n = 100
               Object2
               m = 25
               n = 75
```

In this program , a class ' con' uses a constructor 'con' which a method of the class. The main program declares the object 'c1' using 'con' class and the constructor is automatically evoked . Then a 'c2' object is declared and a call of 'con' constructor is given by supplying the arguments. The display method displays the content of the object by printing of the private variables.

Program 19–6

```
// Program on Constructor and Destructor
#include<iostream.h>
#include<conio.h>
int count=0;
class al
{
    public:
            al()
            {
                    count++;
                    cout<<"\n  matter created "<<count;
            }
            ~al()
            {
            cout<<"\n  matter destroyed "<<count;
            count—;
        }
};
main()
{
    clrscr();
    cout<<" Enter main ";
    al A1;
}
```

Output	:	Enter main matter created 1 matter destroyed 1

19.11 INHERITANCE

The inheritance the concepts of utilization of existing classes for creating new classes by way of modification of these classes. The inheritance provide a facilities of reusability of the existing classes. The object oriented programming allows modification of old class to form a new class which saves time and money. The original class is called base class and the derived class inherits from base class. When a class inherits from another class it is capable of utilizing the variables and function members of that class as well it can have its own member functions and variables.

The inheritance can be created as below :

Consider A is a base class from which class B can be derived by inheritance

```
class A
{
```

```
    private :
            ---------
    public:
            ---------
};
class B : public A
{
    private :
            ---------
    public:
            ---------
};
```

In this case base class A has public and private member functions and class B is derived from A. This means that B inherits from A. The public and private member function of class A becomes member of class B automatically. The class B can have its own member functions and variables.

Inheritance is the process by which object of one class acquires the properties of another class. Inheritance supports the concept of hierarchical classification. For example, the atlas is a part of class bicycle, which is again a part of the class cycle. As illustrated in the principal behind this sort of division is that each derived class shares common characteristics with the class from which it is derived. In OOP, the concept of inheritance provides the idea of reusability. This means that we can add additional features to an existing class without modifying it. This is possible deriving a new class from the existing one. The new class will have the combined features of both the classes. Thus the real appeal and power of the inheritance mechanism is that allows the programmer to reuse a class that is almost, but not exactly, what he wants, and to tailor the class is such a way that is does not introduce any undesirable side effects into the rest of the class. The drive class is knows as 'subclass'.

Program 19-7

```
#include<iostream.h>
#include<conio.h>
class one   // declare class one
{
public:
void test()
{
cout<<"Hello from class one";
}
};
class two : public one   // inherit class two by class one
{
public:
void test()
{
cout<<"Hello from class two";
one::test();  // calling function from class one
}
};
```

```
void main()
{
clrscr();
two t;   // declare a object for class two
cout<<"Hello from main function";
t.test();   // calling function from class two
getch();
}
```

Program 19–8

```
// inheritance and classes
#include <iostream.h>
#include <conio.h>
class A
{
            int a, b;
    public:
            int c;
            void getdata(void);
            void mul(void);
};
class B : public A
{
    public:
            void display(void);
};
void A :: getdata(void)
{
    cout << " Enter the values of a and b \n ";
    cin >> a >> b;
}
void B :: display(void)
{
    cout << " C = " << c << " \n ";
}
void A :: mul(void)
{
    c = b * a;
}
main()
{
    B d;
    clrscr();
    d.getdata();
    d.mul();
    d.display();
}
```

Input	:	Enter the values of a and b
		2 3
Output	:	C = 6

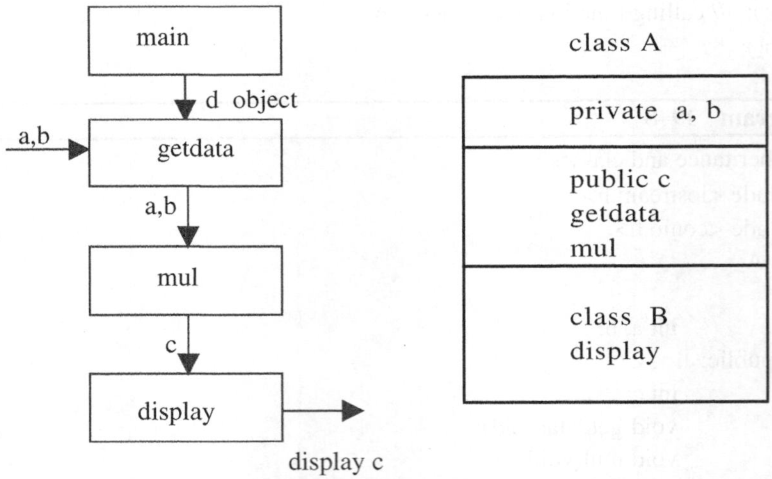

In this program, class 'A' has 'a' and 'b' as private member and 'c' variable is public member. The 'A' class has got 'getdata' and 'mul' as two public member functions. The class 'B' has a public member function and inherits from class 'A'. The object of class 'B' can utilize public member functions of class 'A' by virtue of inheritance. A public member variable of class 'A' becomes private member of class 'B' and can be accessed by public member function of 'B'. The private member functions of class 'A' can be accessed by public member functions of class 'A' which could called by object of class 'B'.

Program 19–9

```
// Single inheritance – PRIVATE
#include <iostream.h>
#include <conio.h>
class A
{
            int a, b;
    public:
            int c;
            void getdata(void);
            void mul(void);
};
class B : private A
{
    public:
            void display(void);
};
void A :: getdata(void)
{
    cout << " Enter the values of a and b \n ";
```

```
      cin >> a >> b;
  }
  void B :: display(void)
  {
      getdata();
      mul();
      cout << " C = " << c << " \n ";
  }
  void A :: mul(void)
  {
      c = b * a;
  }
  main()
  {
      B d;
      clrscr();
      d.display();
  }
```

Input	:	Enter the values of a and b 2 3
Output	:	C = 6

This program shows a reverse case of previous program, in this 'B' class inherits from 'A' class privately. Therefore, the public member functions of class 'A' becomes private member functions of class 'B'. The objects of class 'B' accesses the public member function of class 'B' and public member functions of class 'B' access public member function of class 'A'. Then private member functions of class 'A' accept the data by calling public member functions through public member functions of class 'B'. The public member variable of class 'A' can be accessed by public member functions of class 'B'.

19.12 PRIVATE AND PROTECTED MEMBERS

Specifying that a data member or member function is private means that it can only be accessed from within the class. For data members, this means that the data can be accessed or modified only while inside a member function of the class. For member functions, this means that the function can be called only while inside another member function of the class. This is the default, if no specifiers are used.

Specifying that a data member or member function is public means that it can be accessed from anywhere in the code. The public specifier is less restrictive than private.

Specifying that a data member or member function is protected means that it can only be accessed from within the class or a subclass. The protected specifier is less restrictive than private but more restrictive than public.

Specifiers allow a class to be very complex, with many member functions and data members, while having a simple public interface that other classes can use. A class which has number data members and member functions can be very complicated to write In general, it is good practice to make data members private. Member functions which must be called from outside the class should be public, and member functions which are only called from within the class (also known as "helper functions") should probably be private. These specifiers are especially useful in a large program involving more than one programmer.

19.13 ENCAPSULATION

Encapsulation is the mechanism that binds together code and the data if manipulates, and keeps both safe from outside interference and misuse. The encapsulation is as a protective wrapper that prevents the code and data from being arbitrarily accessed by other code defined outside the wrapper. Access to the code and data inside the wrapper is tightly controlled through a well-defined interface. It is the wrapping up of data and methods into a single unit (called class) is known as *encapsulation*.

Program 19-10

```
#include<iostream.h>
#include<conio.h>
class prd   // declare a class
{
private:
int a;
public:
void printdata()
{
a = 7;
cout<<"Value of a is "<<a;
}
};
void main()
{
clrscr();
prd a;   //declare a object for the class one
cout<<"Now I am in main function and going to call a function from class one";
a.printdata();  // calling function from class one
getch();
}
```

19.14 POLYMORPHISM

Polymorphism is a feature that allows one interface to be used for a general class of actions. The specific action is determined by the exact nature of the solution. Polymorphism means the ability to take more than one form. For example, consider the operation of addition. For two numbers, the operation will generate the sum. If the operands are three numbers, then the operation would produce the product of them. That a single function name can be used to handle different number and different arguments. This is something similar to a particular word having several different meanings depending on the context. Polymorphism plays an important role in allowing objects having different internal structures to share the same external interface. This means that a general class of operations may be accessed in the same manner even though specific actions associated with each operation may differ. Polymorphism is extensively used in implementing inheritance.

Program 19-11

```
#include<iostream.h>
#include<conio.h>
#include<graphics.h>
class poly
```

```
{
        private:
        int gd,gm;
        public:
    void graph()  // for initialize graphics
    {
        gd=DETECT;
        initgraph(&gd,&gm,"");
    }
    void draw(int a)  // function with one args
    {
        cleardevice();
        circle(getmaxx()/2,getmaxy()/2,a);
        getch();
    }
    void draw(int a, int b)   // function with two args
    {
        cleardevice();
        rectangle(getmaxx()/2-a/2,getmaxy()/2-b/2,
    getmaxx()/2+a/2,getmaxy()/2+b/2);
        getch();
    }
    };
void main()
{
        clrscr();
        poly p;
        p.graph();  // initialize graphics
        p.draw(50);   // calling one args function
        p.draw(50,50);  // calling two args function
        closegraph();  // closing graphics
    }
```

EXERCISE

1. What is means by class and which are the two types of members of the class? How they are declared ?
2. What is meant by members of the class ?
3. What is the difference between a C-structure and C^{++} class?
4. Write a program to accept the elements of the classes
   (i) emp–no. (ii) basic pay
   and display the salary slip along with the DA, HRA, CCA, and gross salary . The DA and CCA are calculated as:
   DA = 81% of basic pay for salary < 5000
   = 51% of basic pay for salary between 3000 to 7000

= 41 of basic pay for salary > 7000

CCA = Rs. 350/–

HRA = 15% of basic pay subject max^{m} Rs. 840/–

5. Write a program to prepare bill of electricity of electricity board as per following units

   for first 150 units – Rs. 1 per unit

   for next 350 units – Rs. 2 per unit

   beyond 350 units – Rs. 3/50 per unit

   all users are charge of 15% is charged. The program should read units consumed, name, address consumer no. use classes and objects for the program.

6. Write a program using classes to calculate the bill of a departmental store where customer no, name and list of items purchase and to calculate cost of the items.

7. If a column of length 'L' is loaded by an axial load 'P' at an eccentricity 'e' from the centroidal axis, the maximum stress σ_{MAX} is given by

$$\sigma_{max} = \frac{P}{A} 1 + \frac{e.c}{r^2} \text{ Sec } \frac{1}{r} - \frac{P}{4EA}$$

   Where,

   A = b.t

   C = t / 2

   r = t / 12

   E = Young's modulus

   Write a program to calculate σ_{MAX} for five sets of values P,b,t,e,E,L

8. The roll numbers, marks in physics, chemistry and maths out of 100 for 135 students are known. Write a program using classes and objects which will calculate the following

   (i) No. of students in distinction, 1st, 2nd, 3rd, failed

   (ii) Marksheets of all students.

   (iii) Total no. of students passed and failed and their percentage results.

   If the marks are below 40% in one subject then the student has failed in the subject .

   If his aggregate score is above 75%, he has scored distinction, if aggregate marks are above 60% , 50% and 40% then he has scored first, second and third division . Also print merit list of first three students.

9. Write a computer program using classes which will calculate income tax and total tax for a ground of 150 persons at following rates.

   (a) Taxable income upto 40,000 – no tax

   (b) Taxable income from 40,000 – 60000

   income tax = 0.15 (taxable income – 40000)

   (c) Taxable income from 60000 – 1,20,000

   income tax = 3000 + 0.3 (taxable income – 60000)

   (d) Taxable income over 1,20,000

   income tax = 21000 + 0.4 (taxable income – 1,20,000)

   Surcharge on tax = 0.2 x income tax if income above 1,50,000.

   The program should accept income tax – Pan – no, name, address, the gross income and tax payable.

10. Write a program using objects and classes to calculate monthly interest to be payable to the fixed deposit holders of bank at following rates if

Amount is deposited	Interest rate
more 5 years	12%
3 to 5 years	11%
1 to 3 years	10%
½ to 1 year	8%

If the amount exceeds above Rs. 50000/- additional interests of 0.5 for every 25,000 deposited.

The program should accept the account no., name of customer, amount, and number of years for 20 customers.

11. In a departmental store the no. of customers purchases variety of items.Prepare a class based program which accepts name of customer, date, no. of item purchase name of items, it's cost per unit and no. of items purchased . The program should calculate total cost of items and total bill of the customers with these rules:

Bill Above	Discount
Rs. 500/–	5 %
Rs. 1000/–	10%
Rs. 2000/–	20%

12. Write a program using classes to prepare list of suppliers, their address of type of material available with supplier and print this in a file.
13. Write a program to prepare bank account of the person using class in which the account number, name of the person and the file operation is to be used to store the transaction of the credit and debit are stored in input/output file.
14. Write a program with object oriented programming to store the names , age and address of the person using a class .Then to search the name and address of person having age more than 30 in the data list of persons from a file .
15. Write a class program to find a particular part from a file containing record of store and read the quantity of part or rate of part calculate following:
    (i) Total cost of inventory
    (ii) Parts having arts quantity more than15
    (iii) Parts having quantity less than 3
    (iv) Parts not available in store.
16. Write a program to prepare analysis of a marketing department of company having 10 regions and their sales every month of each regions to be recorded in one file. Further the program should read the data from this file and calculate average sales/month and total sales of year of every region in output file. The first and second in sales are to be indicated as best regions of the year.
17. The rate of interest offered by the bank on fixed deposits is

Period			Interest p.a.
(i)	< 6 months	–	8%
(ii)	between 6 months to 1 year	–	9%
(iii)	between 1 to 3 years	–	10%
(iv)	between 3 to 5 years	–	11%
(v)	above 5 years	–	12%

Write a program using classes to calculate the total interest and amount on maturity. The program should accept the account number , name ,address and the amount to deposited and the number of years.

18. Prepare a program using classes to prepare the list of the cricket team.The class should contain the information about the player name , team name and their batting average. The array of object is to be declared to read the information of 50 players and print the information teamwise containing names of play with their batting average .
19. What do you mean by constructor and destructors ?
20. Explain the advantages of inheritance and how the classes can be created by way of inheritance.
21. What is meant by inheritance ? How it is used in a classes ?
22. What is the difference between base class and inherited class ?
23. Write a program to maintain the information of the employees in the different department using base class and inherited class.
24. Write a program to calculate surface area, cross-sectional area and volume of a cylinder using base class and inherited class.
25. Write a program to calculate compound interest on a fixed deposit in a bank at the rate of 'i' percent interest and no. of years using base class to maintain the name and account number and inherited class to calculate the total amount of fixed deposit alongwith interest.
26. Write a program to maintain the records of the students in the college using base class to maintain their information and inherited class to calculate their results.
27. What are the different types of inheritance ? explain.
28. What is meant by polymorphism and where it is to be used?
29. What is difference between the protected , private and public variable in the class ?
30. Write a program to prepare bills of customer in a hotel using polymorphism in which the records of the customers are maintained in the file and the bill of the customer will prepared on the date of leaving the hotel.
31. Write a program to calculate and maintain the records of the customers of the chartered accountant filing income tax returns at the standard rates.
32. Write a program to calculate the bills of the items in the shop using inheritance and polymorphism.

20

OPERATIONS ON BIT

20.1 BIT OPERATORS

For operation on bits the bitwise operators are used. These are similar to the mathematical operators which operate on two numbers. The bit operators allows operation on binary numbers to construct a new binary number which has an equivalent decimal number.

Operators	*Meaning*
&	direct multiplication of bits
|	if both bits are zero, then result is zero, else one. (Bitwise inclusive)
^	if both bits are zero or one then result is zero, else one
~	compliment (gives reverse) bits of existing
<<	left shift
>>	right shift

20.2 BITWISE "&" "AND" OPERATOR

In this operator, the binary digits are multiplied at their corresponding locations and the result of the multiplication generates a new binary number which has equivalent decimal number.

If b1 and b2 are represented in binary form,then b1 & b2 is represented by b3.

Variables	binary form number	Decimal number
b1	0 0 1 1	-3
b2	0 1 0 1	5
b3 = b1&b2	0 0 0 1	1

If this operator is used with a constant then,

b3 = b2 & 3

This results in converting all bits of b2 except last two bits to zero.

20.3 BITWISE '| ' "OR" INCLUSIVE OPERATOR

In case of this operator, if both bits are 0, then result of bits is 0, otherwise the result of the bits is 1. The result of b1 | b2 generates a new number b3 which has a decimal equivalent

Variable	Binary form	Decimal No.
b1	0 0 1 1	3
b2	0 1 0 1	5
b3 = b1 | b2	0 1 1 1	07

If a constant is used with this operator, then

b3 = b2 |6

This results in setting 2 rightmost bits of b2 to 1.

20.4 BITWISE "^" `OR' EXCLUSIVE OPERATOR

In this case, if both the bits are equal, then the result is zero and if they are different, then result is 1. If b1 & b2 are two numbers then bitwise operation b1 ^ b2 results in generation of b3.

Variable	Binary form	Decimal No.
b b2 b3 = b1^ b2	0 0 1 1 0 1 0 1 0 1 1 0	3 5 6

20.5 COMPLIMENT '~' OPERATOR

This is a unary operator which produces compliment bits of given value and it is attached to the variable as '~' ,then it produces reverse bit of the number.

Variable Binary Number

b1 --------- 0 0 0 0 0 0 0 1

~b1 ---------- 1 1 1 1 1 1 1 0

20.6 LEFT SHIFT '<<' OPERATOR

In this case bits contained in value are shifted to left and the no. of spaces the value is shifted is specified.

If b1 is a binary number then b1 << 1 results in shifting of a bit 1 by 1 location.

Variable	Binary Number	Decimal Number
b1 b1 << 1	0 0 0 0 1 1 0 0 0 1 1 0	03 06

The 1 bit at right most location shift to third location from end.

20.7 RIGHT SHIFT ">>" OPERATOR

In this case the location bit is shifted to right side. If b1 is a binary number then b1 >> 1 results in shifting of bit by 1 location from starting.

Variable	Binary Number
b1 b1 >> 1	1 0 0 1 0 1 1 0 0 0 1 1 0 1 1 0

One bit at left most location shifts to third location from start.

Program 20-1

```
bitwise operation */
main()
{
    int b1=3,b2=5,b3;
    clrscr();
    b3=b1&b2;
    printf("AND b3=%u\n",b3);
    b3=b1;b2;
    printf("OR b3=%u\n",b3);
    b3=b1^b2;
    printf(EX-OR b3=%u\n",b3);
    b1=65534;
    b3=~b1;
```

```
        printf("COMPLIMENT b1=%u\n",b3);
        b1=03;
        b1=b1<<1;
        printf("LEFT SHIFT b1=%u\n",b1);
        b1=5;
        b1=b1>>2;
        printf("RIGHT SHIFT b1=%u\n",b1);
        return;
}
```

Output	:	AND b3 = 1 OR b3 = 3 EX–OR b3 = 6 COMPLIMENT b1 = 1 LEFT SHIFT b1 = 6 RIGHT SHIFT b1 = 1

20.8 MASKING

This is a process of extracting desired bits from a variable by using logical bitwise operation. The operand are variable or constant and constant or variable is used to perform masking.

```
Ex : y = x &mask;
     y = x |mask;
```

Program 20–2

```
#include <stdio.h>
#include <conio.h>
void bit_pattern(int u)
{
     int i, x, word;
     unsigned mask;
     mask = 1;
     word = 8 * sizeof(int);
     mask = mask << (word–1);
     for(i=1; i<=word; ++i)
     {
               x = (u &mask) ? 1:0;
               printf("%d",x);
               mask >> 1;
     }
}
main()
{
     clrscr();
     bit_pattern(10);
}
```

Output	:	0000000000000000

EXERCISE

1. Input two binary strings of length 1<= n <= 32
   Output: bitwise AND, OR and XOR strings.
   For example if the user enters
   1001
   1110
   Bitwise AND 1000
   Bitwise OR 1111
   Bitwise XOR 0111

21
C-GRAPHICS

21.1 COMPUTER GRAPHICS

Computer graphics is defined as creation, storage and manipulation of pictures and drawings by means of a digital computer. It enhances the power of communication between the computer and its users. It allows representation of huge set of numbers in the form of a graph or a picture which helps in better understanding of the characteristic and pattern of data.

21.2 IMAGES ON SCREEN

The representation of images in computer graphics is made by bits.

21.2.1 Converting Images into binary form

Any image is constructed by st.lines, curves and text matter. These are formed of set of dots. A line consists of a set of dots lying on the shortest path connecting its end points. An arc is a collection of dots lying on the trajectory of the arc. Hence an image can be represented as a set of dots at the appropriate locations. Most of CAD system use raster scan display for producing images.

21.2.2 Frame buffer

A viewing surface of a raster scan display is divided into an array of pixels. A CRT screen is made up of horizontal and vertical lines. Each horizontal line is made up of pixels. The memory of the computer is a collection of bits and a bit can take any value either 0 or 1. Each pixel can be represented by one bit in memory. This memory is called frame buffer.

21.2.3 Scan conversion

If a line has to be represented, then the pixel must be made bright to display the line. The pixel state of bit must be 1 in memory. This is known as scan conversion. The location of each pixel on the viewing surface and the corresponding memory location in the frame buffer is accessed by an (x,y) co-ordinate pair. The origin of co-ordinates system is fixed at the bottom –left corner.

Raster ------------>

600 × 400

A display unit of 600 × 400 pixels requires 24×10^4 bits in the frame buffer, which is equivalent of 240 kb. If the image to be displayed is composed of colours, or with different brightness levels, more bits should be provided to every pixels.

If there are 2 bits associated with each pixel then four different combinations are possible. The number of colours n that can be displayed is equal to

$$c = 2^n$$

where,

n = number of bit planes

c = number of colours

A display system with 8 bit planes require 240 KB of memory (resolution 600 × 400) in the frame buffer and can display 2^8 i.e. 256 colours simultaneously.

The current technology allows 24 bit planes with resolution upto 4096 × 4096 pixel.For engineering design applications, a resolution of 1280 × 1024 with 8 bit planes is sufficient. An enhanced graphics adapter (EGA) gives a resolution of 600 × 400 pixels with 16 colours.The display surface is given a two dimensional co-ordinate pair. The x value start at the origin and increases from left to right, while the y value starts at the top and increases towards bottom as in a standard Cartesian co-ordinate system.

In many CRT displays the pixels may not be square and no. of pixels per unit length in horizontal and vertical direction vary.

The lines are drawn on a raster scan display by turning on the pixels which lie lighter on or very close to the shortest path between the end points of the line. The lines drawn on the displays with lower resolutions will have more gaps between the pixels compared to one with high resolution display.

There are variety of languages which can be used in computer graphic's.But C-languages is a suitable language to produce difficult pictures effectively on screen.

21.3 GRAPHIC MODE

In a graphic mode it is possible to display text and graphical figures. The graphic mode uses the pixel which depends on the resolution of the monitor. The graphic functions are available in C–language in a library file "graphics.h" in Borland C++ which must be included in the program.

The following functions should be used to indicate graphic mode operations.These are available in Borland C++ library.

1. "initgraph" FUNCTION

This function is used to initialize the graphics system and load the appropriate specified graphic driver and the video mode used by the graphic function.

The general form

initgraph (& driver, & mode, "x");

where, driver and mode must be defined as integer.

The driver is specified as 0 to 10 representing the monitor type.

Monitor	Number
DETECT	0
CGA	1
MCGA	2
EGA	3
EGA 64	4
EGAMONO	5
IBM8514	6
HERCMONO	7
ATT 400	8
VGA	9
PC 3270	10

mode – specifies the resolution of the video which is normally "VGAHI".

x – path where the graphic driver files are to be searched which consist of the drive directory,subdirectory .

2. **"restorecrtmode" FUNCTION**

This function restores the screen to the mode that it had prior to the operation of initgraph() . restorecrtmode();

3. **"detectgraph" FUNCTION**

This function detects the driver and mode of the system. It is written as

detectgraph(&x,&y);

where, x – graphic driver

y – mode of the system.

4. **"closegraph" FUNCTION**

This function deallocates all the memory allocated by the graphic system. It restores the screen to the mode in which it was before execution of the initgraph.

closegraph();

5. **"getch" FUNCTION**

This function is used to obtain the view of the graphic screen when the program is being executed. It is written as :

getch();

This can be obtained by including the file 'conio.h' in program.

21.4 GRAPHIC FUNCTIONS

1. **"Setpalatte " FUNCTION**

This function closes an index for palette and matches the colour with the index and this color sets the background

setpalatte (0, GREEN);

2. **"Setcolor " FUNCTION**

This function sets the drawing colour specified by the variable.

setcolor(n);

where, n – number of colours.

3. **"putpixel" FUNCTION**

This function illuminates the pixel represented by x and y co-ordinates in the colour.

putpixel (10,20, RED);

4. **"get pixel " FUNCTION**

This function returns the colour in which the pixel (x,y) is illuminated.

i = getpixel (10,20);

where,

i – integer variable to store the colour.

The colour number of the pixel at 10,20 location is stored in i variable.

5. **"moveto" FUNCTION**

This function positions the current cursor into the pixel (x,y).

moveto (100, 150);

This moves the control of the pixel to a new location (100,150).

Program 21–1

/* This program taken the red colour screen present at the particular pixel.*/

```
# include < graphics.h >
main()
{
    int driver, mode, colr;
    driver = 9;
    mode = VGAMED;
    /* driver and modes are set */
    initgraph(&driver, &mode, "\\Tc");
    /* graphics mode is initialized */
    setpalette (O,GREEN);/* sets palette */
    moveto (75,100);/* moves to (75,100) */
    putpixel (75,100,RED); /* illuminates pixel (75,100) red */
    colr = getpixel (75,100);
    /* colr holds the colour number of RED which is the colour of the pixel (75,100) */
    setpallete(o,colr);
    getch();
    restorecrtmode();
}
```

This program brings the text mode screen to a graphic screen and resolves the screen to a resolution of 600 × 400 pixels and the dot is highlighted on the screen with a particular colour.

The screen is further converted to a screen of the dot colour.

21.5 DRAWINGS ON THE SCREEN

For preparing any type of drawing elements are used. The drawings are of two varieties as 2–D drawings and 3– drawings. The drawings are prepared by using the elements joined together to represent a picture of the object. There is a variety of applications of drawing such as machine drawing, arts drawing, isometric drawing, perspective drawing, civil drawing, layout drawing etc. All these drawings utilize the following elements:

(a) Line drawing
(b) Curve drawing
(c) Filling point
(d) Text

21.5.1 Line drawing

There are readymade functions available for drawing of line on the screen. The functions are also available for line related objects such as rectangle, polygon, triangle etc.

1. 'lineto' function

lineto(x,y)

This function draws a line from the current cursor position to (x,y)

Ex : lineto(150,175);

2. 'line' function

This function draws a line from (x1,y1) to (x2,y2) .

line(x1,y1,x2,y2);

3. 'bar' function

This function draws a filled rectangle with diagonal co-ordinates (x1,y1) to (x2,y2)

bar(x1,y1,x2,y2);

4. 'bar3d' function

This function provides a 3 dimensional view of a rectangular box with diagonal from (x1,y1) to (x2,y2), depth and top flag.

bar3d (x1,y1,x2,y2,h,x);

where,

h – depth

x – topflag if non-zero then it is provided.

5. 'drawpoly' function

This function draws a polygon outline with given points, line style and colour.It is written as

drawpoly(n,x);

where, n – no of points

x – array indicating position of points.

6. 'rectangle' function

This function draws a rectangle between two points as diagonal points.

rectangle (x1,y1, x2,y2);

(x1, y1) & (x2, y2) are the diagonal co-ordinates of rectangle

Program 21–2

This program draws a line from (100,200) pixel to (400,500)

```
# include < graphics.h >
# include < conio.h >
main()
{
    int driver, mode;
    driver = 9;
    mode = VGAMED;
    initgraph (&driver, &mode,"\\Tc");
    line (100, 200, 200, 300);
    getch();
    restorecrtmode();
}
```

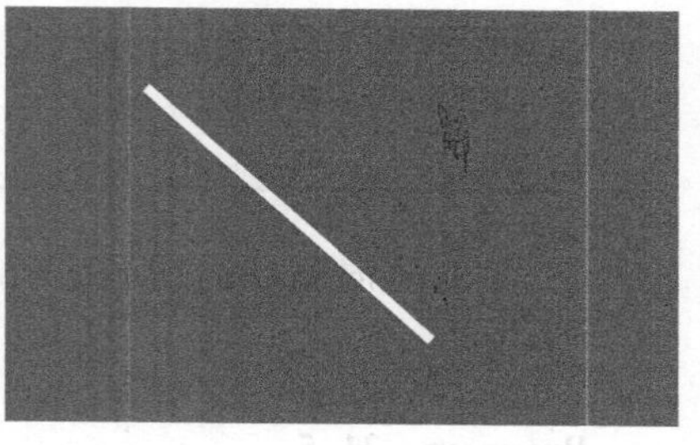

This program draws a line from (100,200) to (200,300) pixels location.

Program 21–3

This program draws a rectangle from (50,40) to (100,80) diagonal.

```
# include < graphics.h >
# include < conio.h>
main()
{
    int driver, mode;
    driver = 9;
    mode = VGAMED;
    initgraph(&driver, &mode,"\\Tc");
    line (50, 40, 50, 80);
    line (50, 80, 100, 80);
    line (100, 80, 100, 40);
```

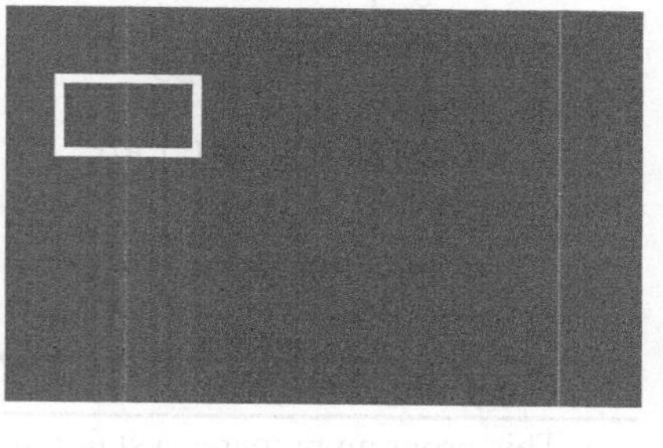

```
    line (100, 40, 50, 40);
    getch();
    restorecrtmode();
}
```

This program draws a rectangle using diagonal co-ordinates (50,40) and (100,80).

Program 21–4

This program draws a filled rectangle from (100,150) to (250,300)

```
#include < conio.h >
#include < graphics.h >
main()
{
    int driver, mode, colr;
    driver = 9;
    mode = VGAMED;
    initgraph (&driver, &mode, "\\Tc");
    /* Draws a rectangle (100,150) to (250,300) */
    bar (100,150,250,300);
    getch();
    restorecrtmode();
}
```

This program draws a filled rectangle with white colour using diagonal co-ordinates(100,150) to (250,300).

Program 21–5

```
# include <conio.h>
# include < graphics.h >
main()
{
    int driver, mode;
    driver = 9;
    mode = VGAMED
    initgraph (&driver, &mode,"\\Tc");
    set color (3);
    bar (10, 25, 100, 75);
    bar (125, 75, 200, 150);
    getch();
    restorecrtmode();
}
```

Program 21–6

This program prepares a staircase by using the rectangle drawn in sequence.

```
#include <conio.h>
#include <graphics.h >
```

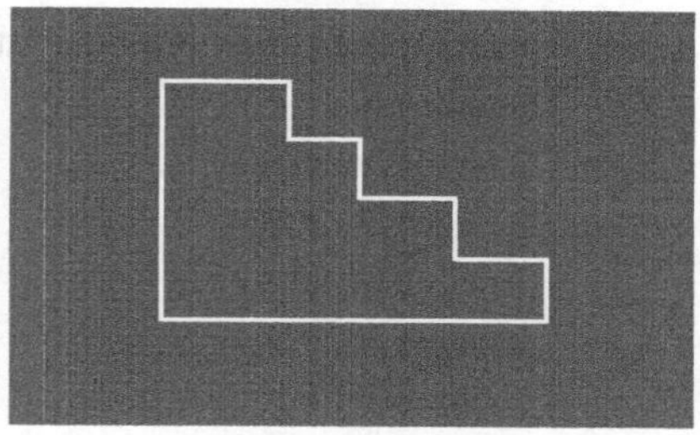

```
main()
{
      int driver, mode, colr, x,y,i;
      driver = 9;
      mode = VGAMED;
      initgraph(&driver, &mode,"\\TC");
      setcolor(5);
      x = 100; y = 150;
      for (i=1; i<=6; ++i)
      {
            bar(x, y, x+100, Y+150);
            x = x+50;
            y = y+50;
      }
      getch();
      restorecrtmode();
}
```

This program prepares a drawing of a staircase using line drawing function.

Program 21–7

This program prepares a 3-dimensional view of a box.

```
#include <conio.h>
#include < graphics.h >
main()
{
      int driver, mode;
      driver = 9;
      mode = VGAMED;
      initgraph (&driver, *mode, "\\Tc");
      setcolor(3);
      bar3d(100,150,300,50,2);
      getch();
      restorecrtmode();
}
```

Program 21–8

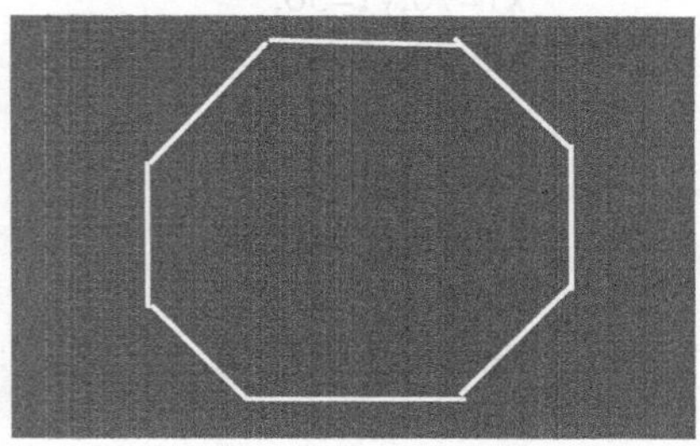

```
/* drawing of a hexagon */
#include<conio.h>
#include<math.h>
#include<graphics.h>
#define    PI     (22.0/7.0)
main()
{
      int driver,mode,x1,y1,x2,y2,theta,xs,xc;
      driver = 9;
      mode = VGAHI;
```

```
    initgraph(&driver,&mode,"\\tc");
    setcolor(7);
    x1=110;y1=200;
    x2=60;y2=200;
    line(x1,y1,x2,y2);
    moveto(x2,y2);
    theta=60*PI/180.0;
    xs=sin(theta);
    sc=cos(theta);
    lineto(x2=x2+50*xs,y2=y2-50*xc);
    moveto(x2,y2);
    lineto(x2=60,y2=y2-50*xc);
    moveto(x2,y2);
    lineto(x2=x2+50,y2=y2);
    moveto(x2,y2);
    lineto(x2=x2-50*xs,y2=y2+50*xc);
    moveto(x2,y2);
    lineto(110,200);
    getch():
    restorecrtmode();
}
```

Program 21-9

```
/* drawing of a box */
#include<conio.h>
#include<graphics.h>
main()
{
    void rect(int x1,int y1,int x2,int y2);
    int x1,x2,y1,y2;
    int driver,mode;
    driver = 9;
    mode = VGAHI;
    initgraph(&driver,&mode,"\\tc");
    setcolor(7);
    x1=70;y1=30;
    x2=70;y2=80;
    rect(x1,y1,x2,y2);
    x1=75;y1=50;
    x2=75;y2=100;
    rect(x1,y1,x2,y2);
    line(70,30,75,50);
    line(70,80,75,100);
    line(150,30,155,50);
    line(150,80,155,100);
```

```
        getch();
        restorecrtmode();
    }
    void rect(int x1,int y1,int x2,int y2)
    {
        line(x1,y1,x2,y2);
        moveto(x2,y2);
        lineto(x2=x2+80,y2);
        moveto(x2,y2);
        lineto(x2,y2=y2–50);
        moveto(x2,y2);
        lineto(x2=x2–80,y2);
    }
```

Program 21–10

```
/* drawing of triangle */
#include<conio.h>
#include<graphics.h>
main()
{
    int driver,mode,x1,y1,x2,y2;
    driver = 9;
    mode = VGAHI;
    initgraph(&driver,&mode,"\\tc");
    setpalette(0,3);
    setcolor(6);
    x1=100;y1=300;
    x2=250;y2=300;
    line(x1,y1,x2,y2);
    moveto(x2,y2);
    lineto(x2=x2–75,y2=y2–150);
    line(x2,y2,x1,y1);
    getch();
    restorecrtmode();
}
```

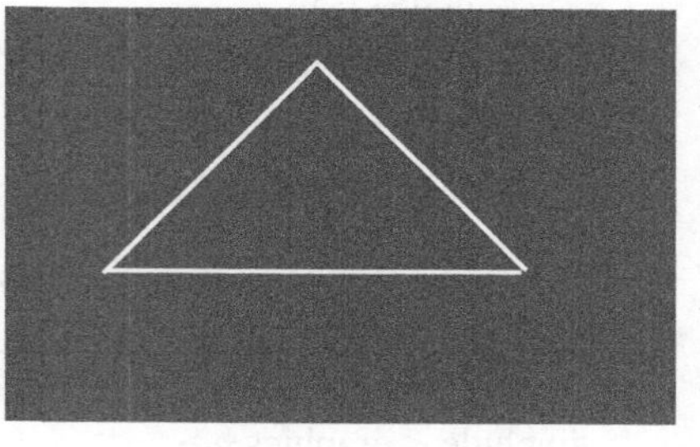

21.5.2 Curve Drawing

1. **'circle' function**

    This function draws a circle centered at (x,y) with radius specified

    circle (x,y,R);

    where,

    R – Radius of circle.

2. **'arc' function**

    This function draws an arc of the circle with radius.

    arc (x,y,a1,a2,R)

where,

x,y are co-ordinates of centre,
a1,a2 are angle representing the arc
R radius of circle.

3. 'pieslice' function

This function works similar to arc, but it provides 2 radii from centre to start and end.

pieslice (100,100,90,180,50);

Draws a pie with centre at (100,100) and radius 50 and from 90° angle to 180° angle.

Program 21–11

```
/*  This program draws a circle */
# include < conio.h>
# include < graphics.h >
main()
{
    int driver, mode, colr;
    driver = 9;
    mode = VGAMED;
    initgraph ( &driver, &mode,"\\Tc");
    /* draws circle of radius 25 pixel and centre
    at (50,50) in color 3 */
    setpalette(0,3);
    setcolor (5);
    circle (50,50,25)
    getch();
    restorecrtmode();
}
```

Program 21–12

```
/* This program draws a chain of circles */
#include < graphics.h >
#include < math.h >
#include < conio.h >
main()
{
    int driver, mode, i;
    driver = 9;
    mode = VGAMED;
    initgraph (&driver, &mode, "\\Tc");
    for(i=50;i<=200;i=i+30)
    circle (i,i+30,50);
    getch();
    restorecrtmode();
}
```

Program 21–13

```
/* This program draws concentric circle */
/* Program to display concentric circles */
# include < graphics.h >
main()
{
    int driver, mode, i;
    driver = 9;
    mode = VGAMED;
    initgraph(&driver, &mode, "\\Tc");
    setcolor(11);
    for(i=25;i<150;i+=25)
    circle (150,150, i);
    getch();
    /* draws concentric circle of radius i pixels and centre at (50,50,i) in color 3 */
    restorecrtmode();
}
```

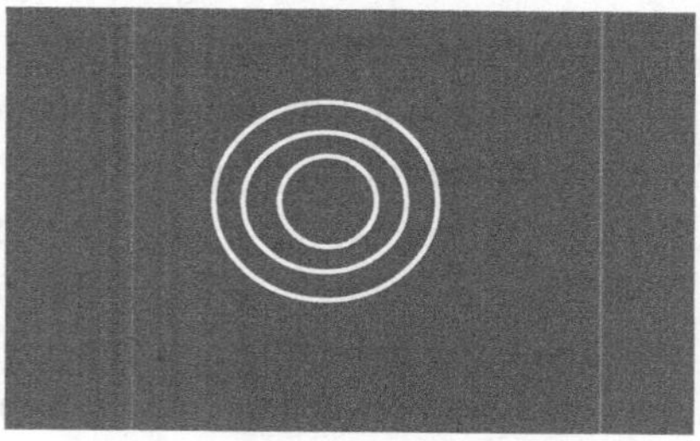

4. 'ellipse' function

This function prepares a drawing of vertical or horizontal ellipse.

ellipse(xc,yc, thi, the, a,b);

Where, xc, yc are center co-ordinates

thi, the are the start and end angle of ellipse

a, b are the major and minor axis of ellipse.

21.5.3 Filling point

This is used for filling of pictures and figures. Generally in drawing the objects are filled with different colours. The areas are filled by filling point. The filling may be of different varieties like solid fill, hatch fill, dash fill, dot fill etc. The process of colouring a definite area or region. The given area of the diagram or figure is completely filled with colour.

There are two methods of filling :

1. Flood filling

In this method the user generally provides initial pixel as starting point. The algorithm will inspect each of the surrounding eight pixels to determine whether the extent has been reached. The process is repeated until all pixels inside the region have been inspected.

2. Boundary filling

In this method starting pixel is supplied by user. The algorithm inspects the left and right side of pixel upto boundary points and a line is drawn till the boundary pixels are not hit. The process continues till all pixels in the boundary are not hit.

There are various functions available for filling of drawing in "C" language.They are as below:

(*i*) 'Setfillstyle' function

This sets the pattern in which the closed boundaries can be filled and the colour to fill the boundary.

setfillstyle (a,b);

where,

a – pattern being set

b – fills the colour.

(*ii*) **'setfillpattern' function**

This function helps the tiling and halftoning. It sets the filling pattern.

setfillpattern (p,q);

where,

p – pointer indicating the matter

q – colour

(*iii*) **'flood fill' function**

This function fills the area bounded by the color border

flood fill (x , y, n)

Where, (x,y) – are locations

n – colour number

The box can be filled by drawing the horizontal lines by varying the y co-ordinates of box and drawing lines between x1 and x2 co-ordinates.

For setting different line styles following function is used :

(*iv*) **'setlinestyle' function**

This function determines the way the subsequent lines should look.

setlinestyle (p, q, r)

Where,

p – Type of line as below

1. SOLID_LINE
2. DOTTED_LINE
3. CENTER_LINE
4. DASHED_LINE
5. USERBIT_LINE

r – width of line given as below

1. NORM_WIDTH
2. THICK_WIDTH

q – pattern

21.5.4 Text

The text can be printed in drawing to indicate dimensions, partlist , title of drawing, scale etc. The text funtion is used for printing of text.

1. 'outtext' function

The text can be printed at the specified location. given by co-ordinates (x,y)

```
gotoxy(x,y);
outtext ("dimensions are");
```

2. 'outtextxy' function

```
outtextxy (x,y, "dimensions are");
```

This displays "dimensions are" statement at x,y location.

3. 'settextstyle' function

This function sets font, direction and size of character for 'outtext' command.

settextstyle (f,d,s);

Where, f – type of font or character (0–11)

d – direction (0 – horizontal, 1 – vertical)

s – size of character

All the above functions in graphics for drawing of lines, text, curves , and styles of filling etc. are utilized for variety of drawings like

1. Machine Drawing
2. Artistic Drawing
3. Civil Drawing
4. Electrical Drawings
5. Isometric Drawings

The following programs shows applications of graphics :

Program 21–14

This program draws a dotted line style and prints a statement below the line.

```
#include<conio.h>
#include<graphics.h>
main()
{
    int driver, mode;
    driver = 9;
    mode = VGAMED;
    initgraph(&driver,&mode,"\\Tc");
    setlinestyle(DOTTED_LINE,3,NORM_WIDTH);
    line(100,150,200,150);
    outtextxy(100,151,"Dimension are");
    getch();
    restorecrtmode();
}
```

Program 21–15

```
/* PROGRAM TO FILL AN ELLIPSE BY REDUCING THE SIZE OF AN ELLIPSE */
#include <graphics.h>
#include <conio.h>
#include <math.h>
elli_R(xc,yc,rx,ry)
float xc,yc,rx,ry;
{
    while(rx>0.0 && ry>0.0)
    {
            ellipse(xc,yc,0,360,rx,ry);
            -- rx;
            ++ry;
            getch();
    }
    return;
}
main()
{
```

```
float xc,yc,rx,ry;
int i;
int driver,mode;
driver=9;
mode=VGAHI;
initgraph(&driver,&mode,"\\tc");
setpalette(0,23);
for(i=0;i<=7;++i)
{
        setcolor(1);
        getch();
        ellipse(250,250,0,360,140,80);
        getch();
        elli_R(250.0,250.0,140.0,80.0);
}
restorecrtmode();
return;
}
```

Program 21–16

```
/* PROGRAM TO FILL ELLIPSE BY LINE DRAWING */
#include <graphics.h>
#include <conio.h>
#include <math.h>
#define pi 22.0/7.0
elli_line(xc,yc,rx,ry)
float xc,yc,rx,ry;
{
    float th,thr,x,y,a,b;
    ellipse(xc,yc,0,360,rx,ry);
    for(th=0.0;th<=90.0;th=th+0.1)
    {
        thr=pi*th/180.0;
        x=rx*cos(thr);
        y=ry*sin(thr);
        line(xc,yc,x+xc,y+yc);
        line(xc,yc,–x+xc,y+yc);
        line(xc,yc,–x+xc,–y+yc);
        line(xc,yc,x+xc,–y+yc);
        getch();
    }
    return;
}
main()
```

```
{
    float xc,yc,rx,ry;
    int dr,mode;
    dr=9;
    mode=VGAHI;
    initgraph(&dr,&mode,"\\tc");
    setpalette(0,10);
    setcolor(12);
    getch();
    ellipse(250,250,0,360,180,80);
    getch();
    elli_line(250.0,250.0,180.0,80.0);
    restorecrtmode();
    return;
}
```

Program 21–17

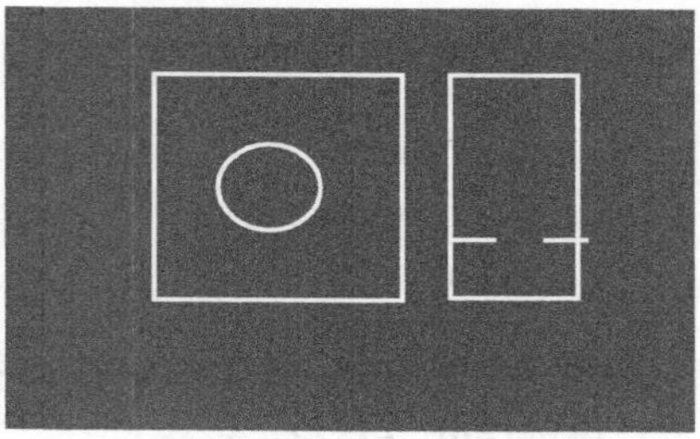

```
/* PREPARE A DRAWING OF PLATE WITH HOLE */
#include <graphics.h>
#include <conio.h>
main()
{
    int driver,mode;
    driver=9;
    mode=VGAHI;
    initgraph(&driver,&mode,"c:\tc\bgi");
    setpalette(0,12);
    getch();
    line(100,100,150,100);
    line(150,100,150,150);
    line(150,150,100,150);
    line(100,150,100,100);
    circle(125,125,10);
    line(175,100,200,100);
    line(200,100,200,150);
    line(200,150,175,150);
    line(175,150,175,100);
    setlinestyle(DOTTED_LINE,4,1);
    line(175,115,200,115);
    line(175,135,200,135);
    setlinestyle(CENTER_LINE,4,1);
    line(165,125,210,125);
    outtextxy(115,155,"F.V");
    outtextxy(177,155,"S.V");
    getch();
    restorecrtmode();
    return;
}
```

Program 21–18

```
/* PROGRAM  TO DRAW THE  SECTIONAL FRONT VIEW OF A HOLLOW SHAFT */
#include <graphics.h>
#include <conio.h>
main()
{
     int driver,mode;
    driver=9;
    mode=VGAHI;
    initgraph(&driver,&mode,"\\tc");
    setpalette(0,14);
    getch();
    setcolor(6);
    rectangle(100,100,200,150);
    rectangle(100,115,200,135);
    getch();
    setfillstyle(3,6);
    floodfill(103,103,6);
    floodfill(103,138,6);
    getch();
    restorecrtmode();
    return;
}
```

Program 21–19

```
/* PROGRAM TO FILL THE CONCENTRIC CIRCLES */
# include <graphics.h>
#include <conio.h>
main()
{
    int dr,mode;
    int i,j,k,l,m,n;
    dr = 9;
    mode = VGAHI;
    initgraph(&dr,&mode,"\\TC");
    getch();
    setpalette(0,BLUE);
    getch();
    setcolor(RED);
    for(i=100; i>=0; i– –)
    {
            circle(300,200,i);
            getch();
    }
```

```
    setcolor(YELLOW);
    for(j=80; j>=0; j– –)
    {
            circle(300,200,j);
            getch();
    }
    setcolor(GREEN);
    for(k=60; k>=0; k– –)
    {
            circle(300,200,k);
            getch();
    }
    setcolor(MAGENTA);
    for(l=40; l >=0; l– – )
    {
            circle(300,200,l);
            getch();
    }
    setcolor(WHITE);
    for(m=20; m>=0; m– –)
    {
            circle(300,200,m);
            getch();
    }
    setcolor(BLACK);
    for(n=10; n>=0; n– –)
    {
            circle(300,200,n);
            getch();
    }
    restorecrtmode();
    return;
}
```

Program 21–20

```
/* PROGRAM TO DRAW THE CARTOON */
#include <graphics.h>
#include <conio.h>
#include <math.h>
elli_R(xc,yc,rx,ry)
float xc,yc,rx,ry;
{
    while(rx>0.0 && ry>0.0)
    {
```

```
            ellipse(xc,yc,0,180,rx,ry);
            ++rx;
            – – ry;
            getch();
      }
      return;
}
main()
{
      floatxc,yc,rx,ry;
      int   j,k,l,m,x1=200,x2=170,y1=357,y2=380,x3=300,x4=330,y3=357,y4=380,x5=150;
      int  x6=350,y5=380,y6=380;
      int driver,mode;
      driver=9;
      mode=VGAHI;
      initgraph(&driver,&mode,"\\tc");
      setpalette(0,YELLOW);
      for(i=0;i<=7;++i)
      {
            setcolor(RED);
            getch();
            ellipse(250,250,0,360,120,100);
            getch();
            elli_R(250.0,250.0,120.0,100.0);
            setcolor(BLUE);
            circle(170,265,10);
            circle(320,265,10);
            setcolor(BLUE);
            for(k=3; k>=0;– –k)
            {
                  circle(170,265,k);
                  getch();
            }
            for(j=3; j>=0;– –j)
            {
                  circle(320,265,j);
                  getch();
            }
            setcolor(GREEN);
            for(l=8;l>=0;– –l)
            {
                  circle(250,280,l);
                  getch();
            }
```

```
            setcolor(RED);
            for(m=5;m>=0;--m)
            {
                    circle(250,280,m);
                    getch();
            }
            setcolor(RED);
            ellipse(250,300,180,360,15,10);
            getch();
            ellipse(250,350,160,20,50,20);
            getch();
            line(x1,y1,x2,y2);
            getch();
            line(x3,y3,x4,y4);
            getch();
            setcolor(MAGENTA);
            line(x5,y5,x6,y6);
            getch();
            setcolor(GREEN);
            circle(120,260,10);
            getch();
            setcolor(RED);
            circle(120,270,8);
            getch();
            setcolor(BLUE);
            circle(120,280,6);
            getch();
            setcolor(GREEN);
            circle(380,260,10);
            getch();
            setcolor(RED);
            circle(380,270,8);
            getch();
            setcolor(BLUE);
            circle(380,280,6);
            getch();
            setcolor(MAGENTA);
            circle(250,330,1);
            getch();
            circle(240,340,1);
            getch();
            circle(260,340,1);
            getch();
    }
    restorecrtmode();
    return;
}
```

21.6 TEXT MODE

This is used for customization of software to bring asthetic effect in the drawing. It also, provides a perfect finishing in the writing of text.

The graphic text can be displayed on the text screen using textmode .The text mode display can be in two forms as 25 rows of 80 columns or 25 rows of 40 columns. The text can be displayed in 16 colours on the colour monitor. This mode allows the data entry or display of results in coloured text with coloured background. This also asist in creation of menu and scrolling the menus using colours in software.

21.7 TEXT MODE FUNCTIONS

1. **"textmode" Function**

   This function sets the number of rows and columns of the screen.

   textmode(n);

   Where, n – represent number 0,1,2,3

2. **"clrscr" Function**

   This function clears the entire screen and locates the cursor in the top left corner (1,1)

   clrscr();

3. **"gotoxy" Function**

   This function positions the cursor to the location specified by x and y. representing row number and column number.

   gotoxy (3,4);

4. **"textbackground" Function**

   This function gives the facility to change the background color of the text by given colour.

   textbackground (4);

5. **"textcolor" Function**

   This function sets the color in which the subsequent text is to be displayed

   textcolor(6);

6. **"delline" Function**

   This function is used to delete a line of text and after the deletion all the subsequent lines will be pushed up by one line

   goto xy (5,4);
   delline();

7. **"insline" Function**

   This function is used to insert a line at the current cursor position.

   goto xy (3,5);
   insline();

8. **"cgets" Function**

   This function reads a string of characters from console ,storing the string in the location pointed by the pointer .It is written as

   cgets(x)

   Where,

   x – char array variable.

9. **"cputs" function**

   This function write a string of character terminated by a null character to the current text window.It is written as

   cputs (x);

10. "cscanf" Function

This function scans the variables through customized user screen . It is written as

cscanf("%d%d",&a,&b);

where,

a ,b – are the integer variables

11. "cprintf" Function

This function prints a series of characters or numeric data on screen at the current text position and window .

cprintf(" a = %d, b = %d", a, b);

12. "windows" Function

This function defines a text window on the screen. It is written as

windows (n1,n2,n3,n4);

where,

(n1,n2) – position of start of window.
n3 – position of terminating column of window.
n4 – position of terminating row of window.

13. "gettext" Function

This function reads the content of rectangle into the memory in char array sequentially from left to the right and top to the bottom.It is written as

gettext(n1,n2,n3,n4,x);

Where,

x – char array variable
n1,n2,n3,n4 – window position indicating the text.

14. "puttext" Function

This function writes the content in a char variable array on to the text screen. It is written as.

puttext(n1,n2,n3,n4,x);

15. "movetext" Function

This function moves the given text indicated by diagonal co-ordinates to a new location on the screen. It is written as.

movetext(n1,n2,n3,n4,n5,n6);

where,

(n1,n2) and (n3,n4) are the diagonal co-ordinates of row and column in which the text is located.

(n5,n6) are the co-ordinates of point to which the text is to be shifted.

Programs 21–21

```
#include <conio.h>
char b[40];
main()
{
    int i;
    for(i=0;i<=20;i++)
    cprintf("Line  %d \n",i);
    gettext (1,1,80,25,b);
```

```
    gotoxy(1,25)
    cprintf("Press any key to clear screen");
    getch()
    clrscr();
}
```

Program 21–22

```
#include <conio.h>
main()
{
    textmode (BW40);
    cprintf("ABC);
    getch();
    textmode(c40);
    getch();
    textmode(c80)
    cprintf("ABC");
}
```

P\rogram 21–23

```
#include <string.h>
#include <conio.h>
main()
{
    char *str = "This is a test string";
    cputs(str);
    getch();
    movetext(1,1,strlen(str),2,10,10);
    getch()
}
```

Program 21–24

```
#include <conio.h>
main()
{
    window(10,10,40,11);
    textcolour(BLACK);
    textbackground (WHITE);
    cprintf("This is c programming \n");
}
```

Program 21–25

```
#include <conio.h>
char b[40];
main()
```

```
{
    int i;
    for(i=0;i<=20;i++)
    cprintf("Line  %d \n",i);
    gettext (1,1,80,25,b);
    gotoxy(1,25);
    cprintf("Press any key to clear screen");
    getch();
    clrscr();
    gotoxy(1,25);
    cprintf("Press any key to restore screen");
    getch();
    puttext(1,1,20,25,b);
    gotoxy(1,25);
    cprintf("Press any key to quit");
}
```

21.8 APPLICATION OF OBJECT ORIENTED PROGRAMMING

The object oriented programming is a new approach for preparing the graphic programs. The concept of classes and objects can be utilized for generation of graphics. The object oriented programming approach is capable of handling complex situation involved in 3-D graphics and graphics of dynamic objects. The object oriented programming can be performed in C^{++} – language which allows us to create classes for graphic functions and variables storing the data. While preparing object oriented programs the following procedure is adopted.

1. A class must be created containing private members and public members.
2. A function member to evoke the graphic mode on the screen.
3. A function member to close the graphic mode.
4. Data members to store the co-ordinates of points of graphics.
5. A function member to read the values of co-ordinates.
6. Graphic member function to display the drawing on screen.

The following programs shows the application of object oriented programming approach to graphics.

Program 21–26

This program draw a line.

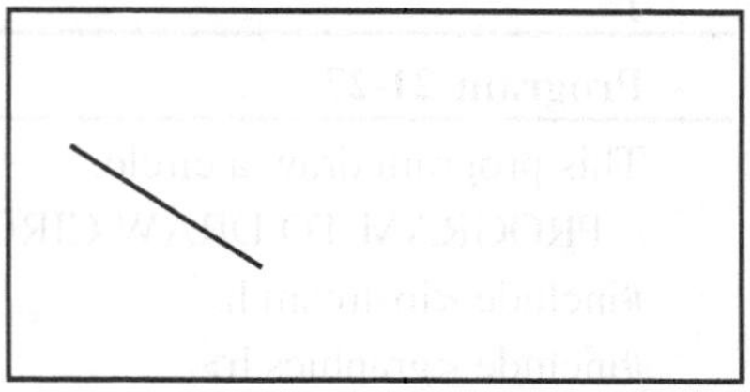

```
// PROGRAM TO DRAW LINE
#include <iostream.h>
#include <graphics.h>
#include <conio.h>
class Gra
{
    private:
            float x1, y1, x2, y2;
            int driver, mode;
    public:
            void line_dr(float x1,float y1,float x2,float y2);
```

```
            void gmode(void);
            void gomode(void);
};
void Gra::line_dr(float x1,float y1,float x2,float y2)
{
    line(x1,y1,x2,y2);
}
void Gra::gmode()
{
    driver = 9;
    mode = VGAHI;
    initgraph(&driver,&mode,"\\tc");
    setpalette(0,4);
    getch();
}
void Gra::gomode()
{
    getch();
    restorecrtmode();
    getch();
}
void main()
{
    Gra L;
    float xx1, yy1, xx2, yy2;
    cout << " Enter the co-ordinates x1, y1 and x2, y2 \n";
    cin >> xx1 >> yy1 >> xx2 >> yy2;
    L.gmode();
    L.line_dr(xx1, yy1, xx2, yy2);
    getch();
    L.gomode();
    getch();
}
```

Program 21-27

This program draw a circle.

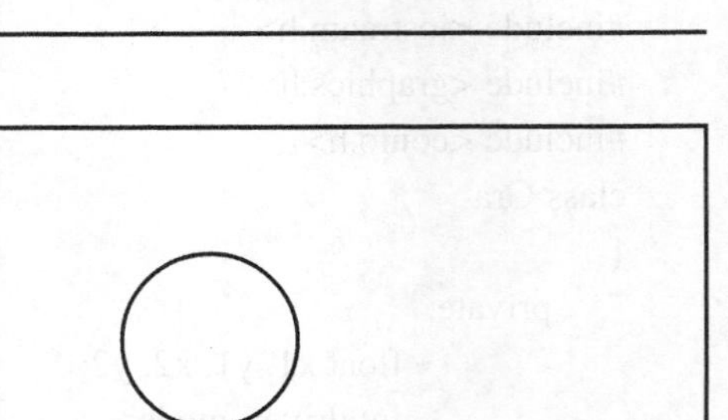

```
// PROGRAM TO DRAW CIRCLE
#include <iostream.h>
#include <graphics.h>
#include <conio.h>
class Gra
{
    private:
            int driver, mode;
```

```
public:
        void circ_dr(float x1, float y1, float r);
        void gmode(void);
        void gomode(void);
};
void Gra::gmode()
{
    driver = 9;
    mode = VGAHI;
    initgraph(&driver, &mode," \\tc ");
    setpalette(0, 5);
    getch();
}
void Gra::gomode()
{
    restorecrtmode();
    return;
    getch();
}
void Gra::circ_dr(float x1, float y1, float r)
{
    circle(x1, y1, r);
}
void main()
{
    Gra C;
    float x1, y1, r;
    cout << " Enter the co-ordinates and radius \n ";
    cin >> x1 >> y1 >> r;
    C.gmode();
    C.circ_dr(x1, y1, r);
    putpixel(x1, y1, WHITE);
    getch();
    C.gomode();
    getch();
}
```

Program 21-28

This program draw a ellipse

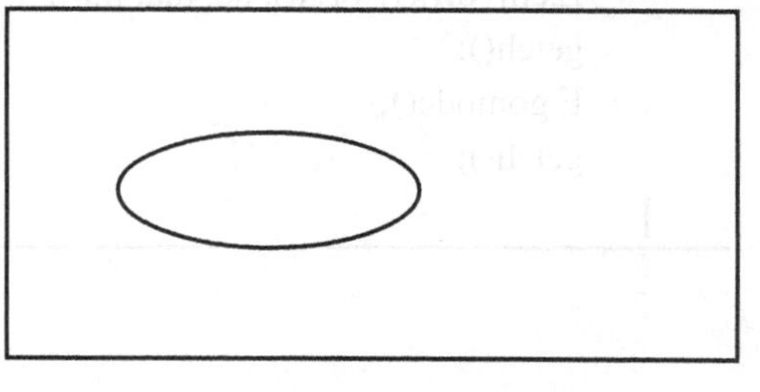

```
// PROGRAM TO DRAW THE ELLIPSE
#include <iostream.h>
#include <graphics.h>
#include <conio.h>
class Gra
{
```

```
    private:
            int driver, mode;
    public:
            void elli_dr(float x1, float y1, float as, float ae, float ma, float mb);
            void gmode(void);
            void gomode(void);
};
void Gra::gmode()
{
    driver = 9;
    mode = VGAHI;
    initgraph(&driver, &mode," \\tc ");
    setpalette(0, 6);
    setcolor(4);
    getch();
}
void Gra::gomode()
{
    restorecrtmode();
    return;
    getch();
}
void Gra::elli_dr(float x1, float y1, float as, float ae, float ma, float mb)
{
    ellipse(x1, y1, as, ae, ma, mb);
}
void main()
{
    Gra E;
    float x1, y1, as, ae, ma, mb;
    cout << " Enter the co-ordinates \n ";
    cin >> x1 >> y1;
    cout << " Enter the start angle and end angle \n ";
    cin >> as >> ae;
    cout << " Enter the major axis and minor axis \n ";
    cin >> ma >> mb;
    E.gmode();
    E.elli_dr(x1, y1, as, ae, ma, mb);
    getch();
    E.gomode();
    getch();
}
```

Program 21-29

This program draw arc.

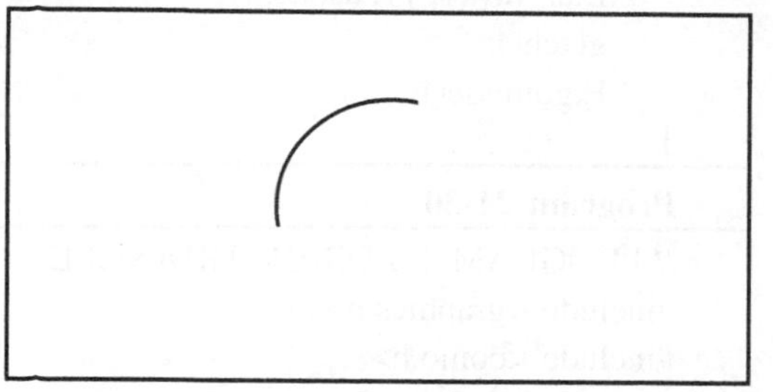

```
// PROGRAM TO DRAW THE ARC
#include <iostream.h>
#include <graphics.h>
#include <conio.h>
class Gra
{
    private:
            int driver, mode;
    public:
            void ar_dr(float x1, float y1, float as, float ae, float r);
            void gmode(void);
            void gomode();
};
void Gra::gmode()
{
    driver = 9;
    mode = VGAHI;
    initgraph(&driver, &mode," \\tc ");
    setpalette(0, 7);
    setcolor(4);
    getch();
}
void Gra::gomode()
{
    restorecrtmode();
    return;
    getch();
}
void Gra::ar_dr(float x1, float y1, float as, float ae, float r)
{
arc(x1, y1, as, ae, r);
}
void main()
{
    Gra E;
    float x1, y1, as, ae, r;
    cout << " Enter the co-ordinates \n ";
    cin >> x1 >> y1;
    cout << " Enter the start angle and end angle \n ";
    cin >> as >> ae;
    cout << " Enter the radius of arc \n ";
    cin >> r;
```

```
    E.gmode();
    E.ar_dr(x1, y1, as, ae, r);
    getch();
    E.gomode();
}
```

Program 21-30

```
// PROGRAM TO DRAW TRIANGLE
#include <graphics.h>
#include <conio.h>
#include <iostream.h>
double x, y, h, v, sx, sy;
float l, m, n;
class Gra
{
private:
            int dr, mode;
            float b[20][20], c[20][20];
            float a[3];
public:
            void gmode(void);
            void gomode(void);
            void tri_draw(Gra p[5]);
            void getpoint(void);
};
void Gra::gmode()
{
    dr = 9;
    mode = VGAHI;
    initgraph(&dr, &mode," \\tc ");
    setpalette(0, 16);
    setcolor(WHITE);
    getch();
}
void Gra::gomode()
{
    restorecrtmode();
    return;
    getch();
}
void Gra::tri_draw(Gra p[5])
{
    line(p[0].a[0],p[0].a[1],p[1].a[0],p[1].a[1]);
    line(p[1].a[0],p[1].a[1],p[2].a[0],p[2].a[1]);
    line(p[2].a[0],p[2].a[1],p[0].a[0],p[0].a[1]);
    getch();
    return;
```

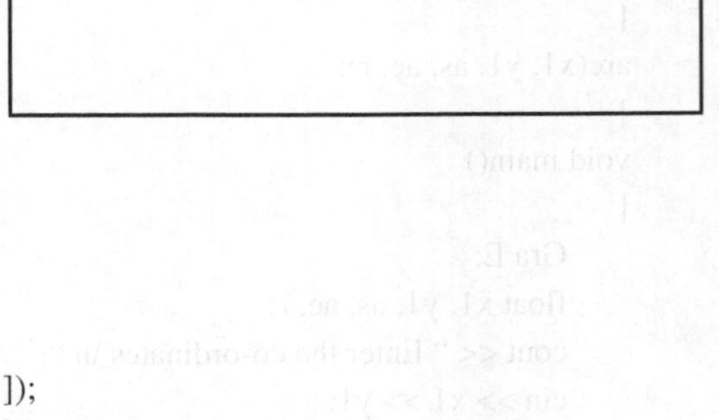

```
}
void Gra::getpoint(void)
{
     cin >> a[0] >> a[1] >> a[2];
}
void main()
{
     Gra p[5],T;
     for(int i=0; i<3; ++i)
     {
               cout << " Enter the co-ordinates " << i << " of point \n ";
               p[i].getpoint();
     }
     T.gmode();
     T.tri_draw(p);
     getch();
     T.gomode();
}
```

EXERCISE

1. Explain the method of generating image on the screen.
2. Explain the memory requirement for a coloured image to be produced on the screen.
3. Write a program to draw line from point (100, 100) of length 50 units at an angle 30° to horizontal.
4. Explain the advantages and disadvantages of bresamham algorithm over DDA algorithm for drawing of line.
5. Write a program to draw a half circle.
6. Write a program to draw a circle passing through a point (200, 150) with a centre (100, 100).
7. Write a program to draw an ellipse with centre (100, 100) and ratio major and minor axis is 1.5. The ellipse passes through a point whose x co-ordinate is 150.
8. Write a program to draw an arc with varying radius from 25 to 50 units with angle between 30° to 95° at centre (100, 100).
9. Prepare a program to draw a circle passing through the two points (x1,y1) and (x2,y2).
10. Write a program to draw a circle passing through the points (x1,y1) , (x2, y2) and (x3, y3) .
11. Write a program to draw an ellipse at the centre (xc,yc) passing through a point (x1,y1) inclined at an angle of theta (θ).
12. Write a program to draw a filled rectangle and circle inside it with given colour.

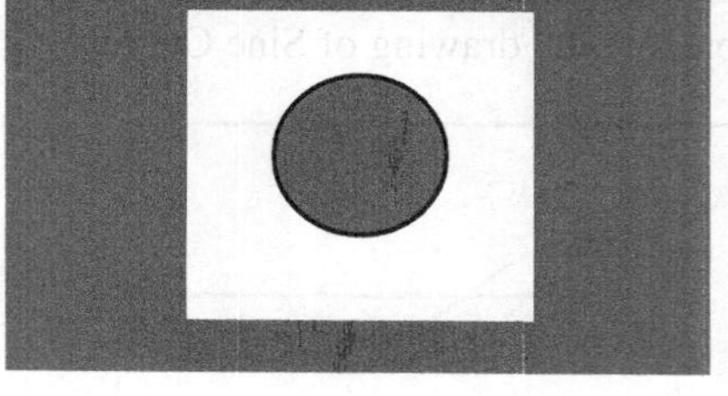

13. Wrtie a program to fill arc.
14. Write a program to fill a circle.

15. Explain the object oriented programming used in graphic drawing.
16. Write a program to prepare a drawing of a rectangle using object oriented programming.
17. Write a program to prepare drawing of polygon using object oriented programming.
18. write a program to prepare a drawing of Belt Drive.

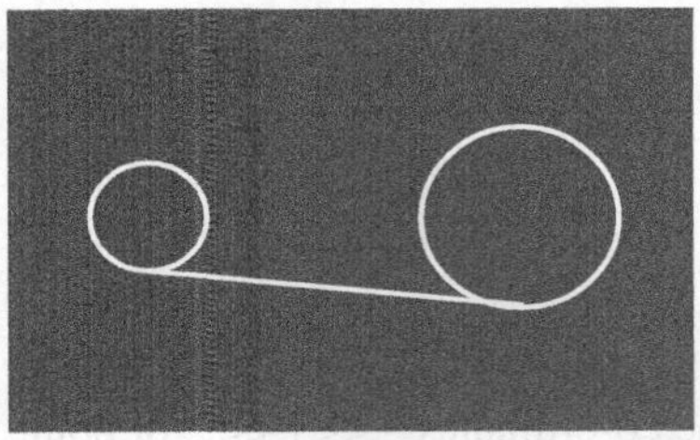

19. Write a program to draw the F.V. and T.V. of the V – Block.

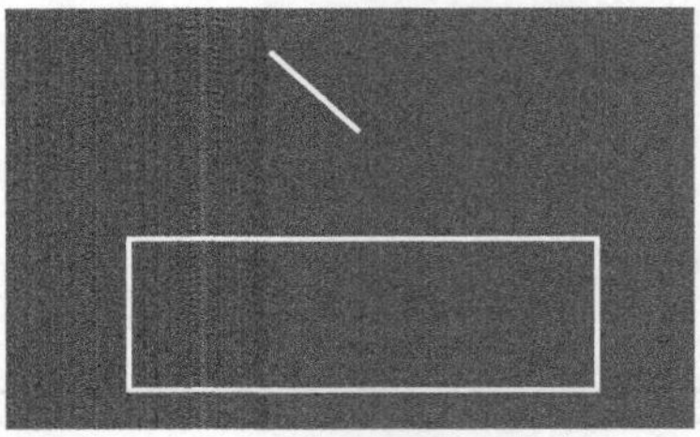

20. Write a program to prepare a drawing of plate with four holes.

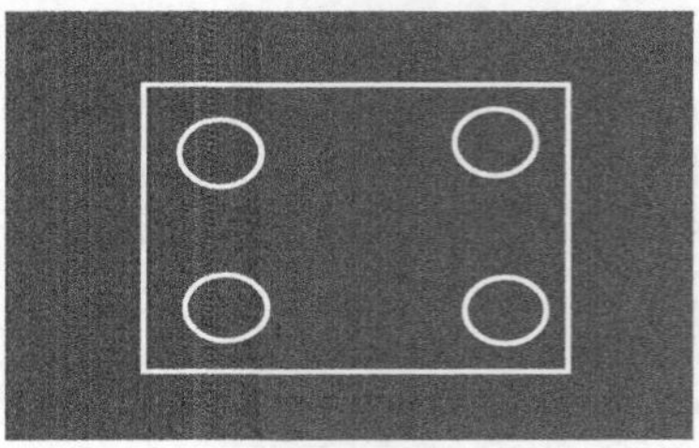

21. Write a program to prepare a drawing of Tapered Shaft.
22. Write a program to draw the polygon.

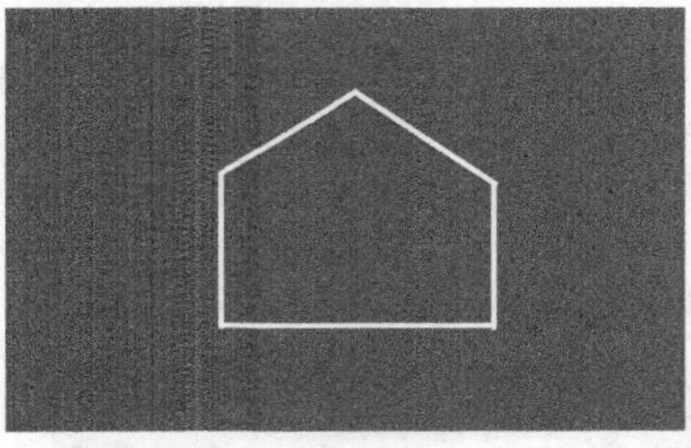

23. Write a program to prepare the drawing of Sine Curve.

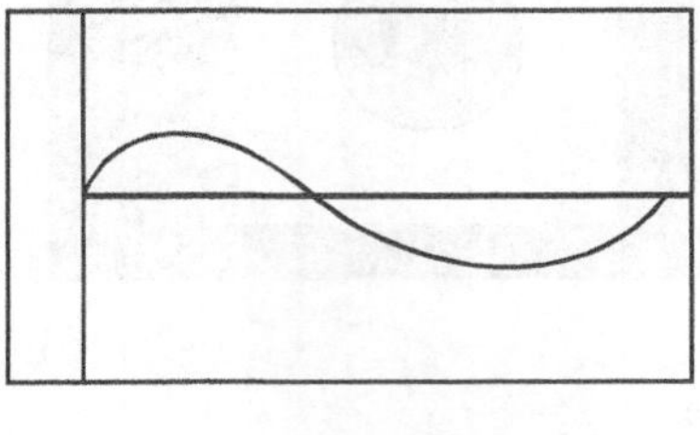

22
PROJECTS IN C & C++

This is the chapter on application of C & C++ programming in various fields. These are projects presented on different areas to apply the techniques of C-programming.

Project 22–1

22.1 AREA OF A TRAPEZOID

This program calculates the area of a trapezoid where (x1,y1),(x2,y2) and (x3,y3),(x4,y4) are the co-ordinates of four points of trapezoid.

```
/*To calculate the area*/
#include<math.h>
float area(x1,y1,x2,x3,y3,x4,y4)
float x1,y1,x2,x3,y3,x4, y4;
{
    float a;
    if(y3 > y4)
            a=(x2 – x1) * (y4–- y1) + .5 * (x2–x1) * abs(y4–y3);
    else
            a= (x2 – x1) * (y3–- y1) + .5 * (x2–x1) * abs(y3–y4);
    return(a);
}
main()
{
    float area1;
    float x1,x2,y1,y2,x3,y3,x4,y4;
    clrscr();
    printf("enter the values for x1,y1,x2,y2,x3,y3,x4,y4 \n");
    scanf("%f%f%f%f%f%f%f%f",&x1,&y1,&x2,&y2,&x3,&y3,&x4,&y4);
    printf("AREA = %g ",area(x1,y1,x2,x3,y3,x4,y4));
}
```

Project 22–2

22.2. RECORDS OF INVENTORY IN A STORE

This software is used for maintaining the records of the inventory in a store. The software allows the entry of the number of items to be stored in the store. The items present in the store their quantity, price etc. is stored in a file through the software. The editing of the record and the retrieval of the record is possible through software.

```
#include "process.h"
#include "ctype.h"
#include "alloc.h"
#include "dos.h"
#include "stdlib.h"
#include "stdio.h"
#include "conio.h"
struct cust
```

```
{
      char name_item[40];
      float cost;
      int code_no,no_item,l_lel_rec,h_lel_rec;
} c[20];
 FILE *fp;
 int a[10][10];
float i,n;
char another ;
main()
{
     char ans;
     char fa   r*vid_mem;
     clrscr();
      printf("Enter the  mode of operation 'w' or 'r' :\n");
     scanf("%c",&ans);
     fp=fopen("record.dat","a+");
     if(ans == 'w')
                 writefromfile();
     else
     if(ans=='r')
                readfromfile();
     else
     fclose(fp);
      return 0;
}
cal()
{
     fwrite("Code No.          :",17,1,fp);
     fprintf(fp,"     %d",      c[i].code_no);
     fputs("\n",fp);
     fseek(fp,0,SEEK_CUR);
     fwrite("No. Of Item        :",17,1,fp);
     fprintf(fp,"     %d",      c[i].no_item);
     fputs("\n",fp);
     fwrite("Name Of Item       :",17,1,fp);
     fprintf(fp,"     %s ",     c[i].name_item);
     fputs("\n",fp);
     fwrite("Cost Of Item       :",17,1,fp);
     fprintf(fp,"     %5.2f",      c[i].cost);
     fputs("\n",fp);
     fwrite("Law Level Record   :",17,1,fp);
     fprintf(fp,"     %d",       c[i].l_lel_rec);
     fputs("\n",fp);
```

```
        fwrite("High Level Record   :",17,1,fp);
        fprintf(fp,"    %d",       c[i].h_lel_rec);
        fputs("\n",fp);
        fwrite("_____________________________________________",45,1,fp);
        fputs("\n",fp);
        return;
    }
    writefromfile()
    {
        printf("Enter Record no.");
        scanf("%f",&n);
        for(i=1.0;i<=n;++i)
        {
                printf("Code No.          \n");
                scanf("%d",&c[i].code_no);
                printf("No.OfItem         \n");
                scanf("%d",&c[i].no_item);
                printf("Name Of Item      \n");
                scanf("%s",&c[i].name_item);
                printf("Cost Of Item      \n");
                scanf("%f",&c[i].cost);
                printf("Low Level Record  \n");
                scanf("%d",&c[i].l_lel_rec);
                printf("High Level Record \n");
                scanf("%d",&c[i].h_lel_rec);
        }
        for(i=1.0;i<=n;++i)
        {
                cal();
        }
        return ;
    }
    readfromfile()
    {
        int q=80;  int i;
        char s[100];
        char ch[20];
        long int pos,c[200];
        char prt;
        char far *vid_mem;
        int choice,lh,pg;
        int getkey();
        int  up(),down(),left(),right();
        clrscr();
```

```
fp = fopen("record.dat", "r");
if(fp==NULL)
{
        printf("Unable to open file");
        fclose(fp);
}
fseek(fp,0,SEEK_SET);
while(!(feof(fp)))
{
        ch[0]=getche();
        pg=atoi(ch);
        fseek(fp,ch[pg],SEEK_SET);
         for(i=0;i<=20;i++)
        {
                //getch();
                fgets(s,q,fp);
                fputs(s,stdout);
        }
         //gotoxy(1,1);
         printf("Press arrow key to move ");
         while(1)
        {
                getch();
                lh=getkey();
                 switch(lh)
                {
                        case 72:
                        choice=72;
                        while(choice == 72)
                        {
                                up();
                                if(a[1][1]<=0)
                                a[1][1]=0;
                                gotoxy(a[1][2],a[1][1]);
                                choice=getkey();
                        }
                        case 80:
                        choice=80;
                        while(choice == 80)
                        {
                                down();
                                if(a[1][1]>=25)
                                a[1][1]=25;
                                gotoxy(a[1][2],a[1][1]);
                                choice=getkey();
```

```
                                }
                                case 77:
                                choice = 77;
                                while(choice == 77)
                                {
                                        right();
                                        if(a[1][2]>=80)
                                        a[1][2]=80;
                                        gotoxy(a[1][2],a[1][1]);
                                        choice=getkey();
                                }
                                case 75:
                                choice = 75;
                                while(choice == 75)
                                {
                                        left();
                                        if(a[1][2]<=0)
                                         a[1][2]=0;
                                         gotoxy(a[1][2],a[1][1]);
                                        choice=getkey();
                                }
                                default:
                                {
                                if((choice >='A' && choice <= 'Z')||(choice >='a' && choice
                                                <='z')||(choice>='0' && choice<='9'))
                                        writechar();
                                }
                        }/*end of swich*/
                } /*end of while*/
        }/*end of while*/
    return;
    } /*end of function*/
    /* Moving Subroutines*/
    up()
    {
        a[1][1]--= 1;
        return;
    }
    down()
    {
        a[1][1] += 1;
        return;
    }
    right()
```

```
{
    a[1][2] += 1;
    return;
}
left()
{
    a[1][2] -= 1;
    return;
}
int getkey()
{
    union REGS i,o;
    while(!kbhit());
    i.h.ah= 0;
    int86(22,&i,&o);
    return(o.h.ah);
}
writechar(r,c,ch,attb)
int r,c,attb;
char ch;
{
    char *v;
    v=vid_mem+r*160+c*2;/* calculate address corresponding to row r & column c*/
    *v=ch;/*store ascii value of character*/
    v++;
    *v=attb;/*store attribute of character*/
}
getname(row,col,p)
int row,col;
char *p;
{
    int i=0;
    char str[30];
    size(5,7);
    if(i!=0)
    {
        i--;
        writechar(row,col+i,' ',47);
        return;
    }
}
```

Project 22–3

22.3 SALARY BILL OF THE EMPLOYEES IN A COMPANY

This software is used for preparing the salary bill of the employees in a company. The name of the employee, basic pay , department etc. is supplied to the software by the user. This software calculates the allowances, deductions, and gross salary of the employees and store the record of the formated salary slip in a file.

```
/*Program on Salary Bill*/
#include<string.h>
#include<stdio.h>
struct emp
{
    char name1[30];
    char name2[30];
    char name3[30];
    float bas;
    int emp_no;
}
e[100];
FILE *t;
float da[100],cca[100],hra[100],grs[100],total[100],deduct[100];
int i,n;
long position[10];
char ptr[512];
main()
{
    char ans;
    clrscr();
    t = fopen("salary.dat","w");
    clrscr();
    work();
    fclose(t);
    return 0;
}
cal()
{
    dadecide();
    hra_decide();
    cca[i]=110;
    grs[i]=e[i].bas+da[i]+hra[i]+cca[i];
    total[i]=grs[i];
    deducting();
    fseek(t,0,SEEK_END);
    fwrite("_____________________________________________\n",45,1,t);
    fputs("\n\n",t);
```

```
fprintf(t,"EMP.NO: ");
fprintf(t,"      %5d",e[i].emp_no);
fputs("\n",t);
fseek(t,0,SEEK_CUR);
fwrite("Name            ",17,1,t);
fwrite(e[i].name1,strlen(e[i].name1)+1,1,t);
fwrite(e[i].name2,strlen(e[i].name2)+1,1,t);
fwrite(e[i].name3,strlen(e[i].name3)+1,1,t);
fputs("\n\n",t);
fwrite("Basic pay    :",13,1,t);
fseek(t,0,SEEK_CUR);
fprintf(t,"%5.1f",e[i].bas);
fputs("\n",t);
fwrite("DA           :",13,1,t);
fseek(t,0,SEEK_CUR);
fprintf(t,"%5.1f",da[i]);
fputs("\n",t);
fwrite("Hra          :",13,1,t);
fseek(t,0,SEEK_CUR);
fprintf(t,"%5.1f",hra[i]);
fputs("\n\n",t);
fwrite("Cca          :110",19,1,t);
fseek(t,0,SEEK_CUR);
fputs("\n\n",t);
fwrite("TOTAL        :",13,1,t);
fseek(t,0,SEEK_CUR);
fprintf(t,"%5.1f",total[i]);
fputs("\n\n",t);
fwrite("Deduction    :",13,1,t);
fseek(t,0,SEEK_CUR);
fprintf(t,"%5.1f\n\n",deduct[i]);
fwrite("             \n",15,1,t);
fwrite("Net Pay      :",13,1,t);
fseek(t,0,SEEK_CUR);
fprintf(t,"%5.2f",grs[i]);
fputs("\n",t);
return;
}
work()
{
    char ans;
    printf("How Many Number of Employees ?\n");
    scanf("%d",&n);
    for(i=1;i<=n;++i)
```

```
    {
            printf("enter SUR_name of the employee\n");
            scanf("%s",e[i].name1);
            printf("enter_name of the employee\n");
            scanf("%s",e[i].name2);
            printf("enter the fathers name of the employee\n");
            scanf("%s",e[i].name3);
            printf("enter  employment no. and basic salary of the employee\n");
            scanf("%d%f",&e[i].emp_no,&e[i].bas);
    }
     for(i=1;i<=n;++i)
    {
            cal();
    }
    return;
}
dadecide()
{
    if(e[i].bas<=500)
    {
            da[i] = 0.40 * e[i].bas;
    }
    else
    {
    if(e[i].bas<=3500)
    {
            da[i] = 0.25 * e[i].bas;
    }
    else
    {
    if(e[i].bas<=6000)
    {
             da[i] = e[i].bas * 0.11;
     }
    else
    {
             da[i] = e[i].bas * 0.07;
    }
    }
    }
    return 0;
}
hra_decide()
{
```

```
    if(e[i].bas<=3500)
    {
            hra[i] = 650;
    }
    else
    {
    if(e[i].bas<=6000)
    {
            hra[i] = 850;
    }
    else
    {
            hra[i] = 1000;
    }
    }
    return;
}
deducting()
{
    if(grs[i]<3000  &&  grs[i]>2000)
    {
            deduct[i]  =  (grs[i] * 0.0833);
            /*grs[i] = grs[i]-(grs[i]*0.0833);*/
    }
    else
    {
    if(grs[i]<=5000  &&  grs[i]>3000)
    {
            deduct[i] = (grs[i] * 0.10);
            /*grs[i]=grs[i]-(grs[i]*0.1);*/
    }
    else
    {
    if(grs[i]>5000)
    {
            deduct[i] = (grs[i] * 0.5);
            /* grs[i]=grs[i]-(grs[i]*0.5);*/
    }
    else
    {
            if(grs[i]<=2000)      /*keep grs constant*/
            deduct[i]=0;
    }
    }
```

```
    }
    grs[i] = grs[i] - deduct[i];
    /*printf("deduction = %g,gross =  %g\n",deduct[i],grs[i]);    */
    return 0;
}
```

Project 22–4

22.4 SOFTWARE ON ROLL LIST OF THE STUDENTS

This software maintains the record of the students in a school or college. It stores the record of the student i.e. name,roll no., address, class, section etc. in a file. The data is supplied to the software by the user.

```
/* PROGRAM  TO MAINTAIN THE RECORDS OF STUDENTS */
#include <stdio.h>
struct Student
{
    char ron[20];
    char cla[20];
    char std[20];
    char dob[20];
    char add[20];
    char cit[20];
    char lr[20];
    char name1[20];
}
e[10];
FILE *t;
int i,n;
int no;
read_name()
{
    printf("Enter the roll no\n");
    scanf("%s",e[i].ron);
    printf("Enter the class of the student\n");
    scanf("%s",e[i].cla);
    printf("Enter the standard of student\n");
    scanf("%s",e[i].std);
    printf("Enter the name of student\n");
    gets(e[i].name1);
    gets(e[i].name1);
    printf("Enter the date of birth\n");
    scanf("%s",e[i].dob);
    printf("Enter the address of the student\n");
    gets(e[i].add);
    gets(e[i].add);
    printf("Enter the city\n");
```

```
        scanf("%s",e[i].cit);
        printf("Enter the last result\n");
        scanf("%s",e[i].lr);
        printf("\n");
        return;
    }
    main()
    {
        clrscr();
        t=fopen("std1.dat","w");
        student_rec();
        fclose(t);
    }
    student_rec()
    {
        clrscr();
        printf("Enter the total no. of students\n",i);
        scanf("%d",&no);
        for(i=1;i<=no;++i)
        {
                read_name();
        }
        for(i=1;i<=no;++i)
        {
                print_name();
        }
        return;
    }
    print_name()
    {
        fprintf(t," No  Roll No Class Std Name Dob add city last result \n");
        for(i=1;i<=no;++i)
        {
                fprintf(t,"%3d    ",i);
                fprintf(t,"%3s    ",e[i].ron);
                fprintf(t,"%3s  ",e[i].cla);
                fprintf(t,"%4s  ",e[i].std);
                fprintf(t,"%8s  ",e[i].name1);
                fprintf(t,"%8s  ",e[i].dob);
                fprintf(t,"%8s  ",e[i].add);
                fprintf(t,"%8s  ",e[i].cit);
                fprintf(t,"%8s  ",e[i].lr);
                fputs("\n",t);
        }
        return;
    }
```

Project 22–5

22.5 SOFTWARE ON TELEPHONE DIRECTORY

This software maintains the record of the telephone numbers and the names of the subscribers. The records can be supplied to the software by the user and the software can be utilized for the retrieval of the telephone number of a person. The software also allows the modification of the records of the name or telephone number.

```
/*Telephone Directory*/
#include<fstream.h>
#include<conio.h>
#include<stdlib.h>
#include<string.h>
#include<iomanip.h>
int strcm(char *x,char *y)
{
    int j=0;
    while(*x==*y && *x!='\0' && *y!='\0')
    {
            *x++;
            *y++;
            if(*x!='\0' && *y!='\0')
            {
            if(*x==*y)
            {
                    j=1;
            }
            else
            {
                    j=0;
            }
            }
    }
    return(j);
}
class phone
{
            char name1[10];
            char name2[10];
            long int num;
            int count;
    public:
            void getdata(void)
            {
                    cout<<"Enter firstname     :\n";cin>>name1;
                    cout<<"Enter surname       :\n";cin>>name2;
                    cout<<"Enter phone number  :\n";cin>>num;
```

```
        }
    void putdata(void)
    {
            cout.width(10);cout<<name1;
            cout.width(10);cout<<name2;
            cout.width(10);cout<<num;
            cout<<endl;
    }
    int readdata(char c[],char s[])
    {
            int found;
            found=strcm(name1,c);
            if(found==1)
            {
                    strcmp(name2,s);
                    if(found==1)
                    {
                            cout<<num;
                            getch();
                    }
            }
            return(found);
    }
};
main()
{
    clrscr();
    phone ph[10];
    int i=0;
    fstream file;
    while(1)
    {
            clrscr();
            gotoxy(30,2);
            cout<<"MAIN MENU\n";
            gotoxy(20,4);
            cout<<"********************************\n";
            gotoxy(30,6);
            cout<<"1.ADD RECORD  ";
            gotoxy(30,8);
            cout<<"2.LIST RECORD ";
            gotoxy(30,10);
            cout<<"3.FIND NUMBER ";
            gotoxy(30,12);
```

```
cout<<"0.EXIT\n";
gotoxy(20,14);
cout<<"******************************\n";
gotoxy(30,16);
cout<<"YOUR OPTION ?\n";
gotoxy(44,16);
char opt=getche();
gotoxy(44,16);
cout<<opt;
switch(opt)
{
        case'1':
        clrscr();
         file.open("mru.txt",ios::app|ios::binary);
          cout<<"ADD RECORDS...\n";
        cout<<" How many records are entered ? ";
        int n;
         cin>>n;
          for(i=0;i<n;i++)
        {
                 file.seekg(ios::end);
                ph[i].getdata();
                 file.write((char *)&ph[i],sizeof(ph[i]));
        }
        file.close();
        break;
        case'2':
        i=0;
        clrscr();
        file.open("mru.txt",ios::in);
        file.seekg(0,ios::beg);
        cout<<" CONTENTS OF THE FILE \n";
        cout<<"————————————————————————\n";
        while(file.read((char  *)&ph[i],sizeof(ph[i])))
        {
                ph[i].putdata();
                i++;
        }
        getch();
        file.close();
        break;
        case'3':
         i=0;
        clrscr();
```

```
                file.open("mru.txt",ios::in|ios::binary);
                cout<<"Enter name :\n";
                char fnm[10],snm[10];
                cin>>fnm>>snm;
                int z=0;
                file.seekg(ios::beg);
                while(file.read((char  *)&ph[i],sizeof(ph[i])))
                {
                        z=ph[i].readdata(fnm,snm);
                        if(z==1)
                        goto bot;
                }
                if(z==0)
                cout<<" Name is not Found,Please check!";
                getch();
                file.close();
                bot:
                break;
                case'0':
                exit(0);
                default:
                cout<<"\nEnter proper number!";
                getch();
                continue;
        }//end of switch
    }//end of while
}
```

Project 22–6

22.6 SOFTWARE TO MAINTAIN THE RECORDS OF HOTEL

This software maintains the records of the customers staying in the hotel and prepares the bill of the customers staying in the hotel with different taiffs of the room. It also maintains the details of the customer staying in the hotel like name,age, address, arrival date, date of leaving etc.

```
/* PROGRAM  TO MAINTAIN THE RECORDS OF HOTEL */
#include <stdio.h>
struct Hotel
{
    char rmn[20];
    char name1[20];
    char add[20];
    char age[20];
    char std[20];
    char dol[20];
    char tor[20];
    int chr;
```

```
        int no1;
        int tob;
        int exb;
        int tot;
    }
    e[10];
    FILE *t;
    int i,n;
    int no;
    int b[4]={1200,700,870,550};
    char a[20][20]={"A.C.","NON A.C.","DOUBLE BEDROOM","SINGLE BEDROOM"};
    int ii,k;
    read_name()
    {
        printf("Enter the room no\n");
        scanf("%s",e[i].rmn);
        printf("Enter the name of the customer\n");
        gets(e[i].name1);
        gets(e[i].name1);
        printf("Enter the no. of days\n");
        scanf("%d",&e[i].no1);
        printf("Enter the address of the customer\n");
        gets(e[i].add);
        gets(e[i].add);
        printf("Enter the age of the customer\n");
        scanf("%s",e[i].age);
        printf("Enter the starting date\n");
        scanf("%s",e[i].std);
        printf("Enter the date of living\n");
        scanf("%s",e[i].dol);
        printf("Enter the type of room\n");
        gets(e[i].tor);
        gets(e[i].tor);
        for(ii=0;ii<4;++ii)
        {
                if(strcmp(e[i].tor,a[ii])==0)
                {
                        k=ii;
                        e[i].chr=b[k];
                        break;
                }
        }
        printf("The type of the room is=%s\n",e[i].tor);
        printf("The charges of the room is=%d\n",b[k]);
```

```
    e[i].tob = e[i].no1 * e[i].chr;
    printf("Enter the extra bill of the room\n");
    scanf("%d",&e[i].exb);
    e[i].tot = e[i].tob + e[i].exb;
    printf("\n");
    return;
}
main()
{
    clrscr();
    t=fopen("std2.dat","w");
    hotel_rec();
    fclose(t);
    return;
}
hotel_rec()
{
    clrscr();
    printf("Enter the total no. of customers\n",i);
    scanf("%d",&no);
    for(i=1;i<=no;++i)
    {
            read_name();
    }
    for(i=1;i<=no;++i)
    {
            print_name();
    }
    return;
}
print_name()
{
    fprintf(t," No  Room No Name   No  add   age std  Dol  tor   char tob exb  tot\n");
    for(i=1;i<=no;++i)
    {
            fprintf(t,"%3d    ",i);
            fprintf(t,"%3s    ",e[i].rmn);
            fprintf(t,"%3s  ",e[i].name1);
            fprintf(t,"%3d  ",e[i].no1);
            fprintf(t,"%4s  ",e[i].add);
            fprintf(t,"%8s  ",e[i].age);
            fprintf(t,"%8s  ",e[i].std);
            fprintf(t,"%8s  ",e[i].dol);
            fprintf(t,"%8s  ",e[i].tor);
```

```
            fprintf(t,"%8d  ",e[i].chr);
            fprintf(t,"%8d  ",e[i].tob);
            fprintf(t,"%8d  ",e[i].exb);
            fprintf(t,"%8d  ",e[i].tot);
            fputs("\n",t);
        }
        return;
    }
```

Project 22–7

22.7 SOFTWARE ON GRAPHICS OF STEPPED SHAFT

This software prepares a drawing of a stepped shaft in 3-dimensional graphics system. It prepares the graphic by using line and ellipse functions to obtain a three dimensional view of shaft using oblique projection method.

```
/* PROGRAM TO DRAW 3-D VIEW OF A STEPPED SHAFT */
#include <graphics.h>
#include <conio.h>
#include <math.h>
#define pi 22.0/7.0
float a[20][4],xx1[20][4],b[4][4],c[20][4];
int m=19,n=4,l=4;
main()
{
    int dr,mode;
    detectgraph(&dr,&mode);
    initgraph(&dr,&mode,"\\tc");
    setpalette(0,16);
    setcolor(58);
    a[1][1]=100;   a[1][2]=100;  a[1][3]=100;  a[1][4]=1;
    a[2][1]=100;   a[2][2]=200;  a[2][3]=100;  a[2][4]=1;
    a[3][1]=300;   a[3][2]=100;  a[3][3]=100;  a[3][4]=1;
    a[4][1]=300;   a[4][2]=200;  a[4][3]=100;  a[4][4]=1;
    a[5][1]=100;   a[5][2]=150;  a[5][3]=100;  a[5][4]=1;
    a[6][1]=75;    a[6][2]=150;  a[6][3]=100;  a[6][4]=1;
    a[7][1]=125;   a[7][2]=150;  a[7][3]=100;  a[7][4]=1;
    a[8][1]=275;   a[8][2]=150;  a[8][3]=100;  a[8][4]=1;
    a[9][1]=325;   a[9][2]=150;  a[9][3]=100;  a[9][4]=1;
    a[10][1]=300;  a[10][2]=150; a[10][3]=100; a[10][4]=1;
    a[11][1]=300;  a[11][2]=125; a[11][3]=100; a[11][4]=1;
    a[12][1]=300;  a[12][2]=175; a[12][3]=100; a[12][4]=1;
    a[13][1]=287;  a[13][2]=150; a[13][3]=100; a[13][4]=1;
    a[14][1]=312;  a[14][2]=150; a[14][3]=100; a[14][4]=1;
    a[15][1]=400;  a[15][2]=150; a[15][3]=100; a[15][4]=1;
    a[16][1]=387.5; a[16][2]=150; a[16][3]=100; a[16][4]=1;
    a[17][1]=412.5; a[17][2]=150; a[17][3]=100; a[17][4]=1;
```

```
        a[18][1]=400;   a[18][2]=175; a[18][3]=100; a[18][4]=1;
        a[19][1]=400;   a[19][2]=125; a[19][3]=100; a[19][4]=1;
        equi();
        shaft();
        getch();
        equi();
        shaft();
        getch();
        restorecrtmode();
        return;
    }
    equi()
    {
         float i;
         float theta=10;
        double atheta;
        atheta=pi*theta/180.0;
        for(i=1;i<=19;++i)
        {
                xx1[i][1]=a[i][1]+a[i][3]*cos(atheta);
                xx1[i][2]=a[i][2]-a[i][3]*sin(atheta);
        }
        return;
    }
    shaft()
    {
          float zz1,zz2;
         void ellip(float h,float k,float a,float b);
        line(xx1[1][1],xx1[1][2],xx1[3][1],xx1[3][2]);
        getch();
        line(xx1[2][1],xx1[2][2],xx1[4][1],xx1[4][2]);
        getch();
        zz1=(xx1[7][1]–xx1[6][1])/2.0;  zz2=(xx1[2][2]–xx1[1][2])/2.0;
          ellip(xx1[5][1],xx1[5][2],zz1,zz2);
        getch();
          putpixel(xx1[5][1],xx1[5][2],4);
        zz1=(xx1[9][1]–xx1[8][1])/2.0;  zz2=(xx1[4][2]–xx1[3][2])/2.0;
        ellip(xx1[10][1],xx1[10][2],zz1,zz2);
        getch();
        putpixel(xx1[10][1],xx1[10][2],4);
        line(xx1[11][1],xx1[11][2],xx1[19][1],xx1[19][2]);
        getch();
        line(xx1[12][1],xx1[12][2],xx1[18][1],xx1[18][2]);
        getch();
```

```
        zz1=(xx1[14][1]-xx1[13][1])/2.0; zz2=(xx1[12][2]-xx1[11][2])/2.0;
        ellip(xx1[10][1],xx1[10][2],zz1,zz2);
        getch();
        putpixel(xx1[10][1],xx1[10][2],4);
        zz1=(xx1[17][1]-xx1[16][1])/2.0; zz2=(xx1[19][2]-xx1[18][2])/2.0;
        ellip(xx1[15][1],xx1[15][2],zz1,zz2);
        getch();
        putpixel(xx1[15][1],xx1[15][2],4);
        getch();
        return;
}
void ellip(float h,float k,float a,float b)
{
        float x,y,theta;
        double atheta;
        float theta1=360.0;
        for(theta=0.0; theta<=theta1; ++theta)
        {
                atheta= theta*pi/180.0;
                x=a*cos(atheta)+h;
                y=b*sin(atheta)+k;
                putpixel(x,y,RED);
        }
        return;
}
```

Project 22–8

22.8 SOFTWARE ON THE FLAG

This software prepares a drawing of the flag . It uses basic functions of graphics and prepares a filled drawing of the flag .

```
/* PROGRAM TO DRAW THE FLAG*/
#include <graphics.h>
#include <conio.h>
#include <math.h>
main()
{
        int driver,mode;
        float x1,y1,x2,y2,th1,th,x;
        driver = 9;
        mode = VGAHI;
        initgraph(&driver,&mode,"\\TC");
        getch();
        setpalette(0,200);
        getch();
        moveto(0,0);
```

```
setlinestyle(SOLID_LINE,5,THICK_WIDTH);
setcolor(RED);
getch();
rectangle(0,0,640,165);
getch();
for(x=0; x<=640; ++x)
{
        line(x,0,x,165);
        getch();
}

setcolor(WHITE);
rectangle(0,165,640,315);
for(x=0; x<=640; ++x)
{
        line(x,165,x,315);
        getch();
}
setcolor(GREEN);
rectangle(0,315,640,465);
for(x=0; x<=640; ++x)
{
        line(x,315,x,465);
        getch();
}
setcolor(0);
circle(320,237,70);
getch();
circle(320,237,20);
getch();
for(th1=0; th1<360; th1+=15)
{
        th = (3.14 / 180) * th1;
        x1 = 20 * cos (th);
        y1 = 20 * sin (th);
        x2 = 70 * cos (th);
        y2 = 70 * sin (th);
        line(320+x2,237+y2,320+x1,237+y1);
}

getch();
setcolor(18);
getch();
moveto(200,300);
```

```
outtext("THIS IS THE  FLAG");
getch();
restorecrtmode();
return;
}
```

Project 22–9

22.9 SOFTWARE ON DRAWING OF FLYWHEEL

```
/* PROGRAM  TO  DRAW A  FLYWHEEL */
#include <graphics.h>
#include <conio.h>
#include <math.h>
#define pi 22.0/7.0
main()
{
    float th[9]={0,10,80,100,170,190,260,280,350};
    double a[20][3],i,thr;
    int driver,mode;
    driver=9;
    mode=VGAHI;
    initgraph(&driver,&mode,"\\tc");
    setpalette(0,8);
    setcolor(YELLOW);
    circle(100,100,20);
    getch();
    circle(100,100,50);
    getch();
    circle(100,100,70);
    getch();
    setcolor(GREEN);
     for(i=1;i<=8;++i)
    {
            thr=pi*th[i]/180.0;
            a[i][1]=20*cos(thr);
            a[i][2]=20*sin(thr);
            a[i+9][1]=50*cos(thr);
            a[i+9][2]=50*sin(thr);
    }
    for(i=1;i<=8;++i)
    {
            line(a[i][1]+100,a[i][2]+100,a[i+9][1]+100,a[i+9][2]+100);
            getch();
    }
    getch();
    restorecrtmode();
    return;
}
```

Project 22–10

22.10 SOFTWARE ON DRAWING OF MONOGRAM

This software prepares a monogram which is having seven colours ellipse attached to the 'R' . This is a monogram which could be prepared through software.

```
/* PROGRAM TO DRAW A MONOGRAM */
#include <graphics.h>
main()
{
    float w,h,wd,hd,m,n,i;
    int driver,mode;
    driver=9;
    mode=VGAHI;
    clrscr();
    printf("ENTER WIDTH 'w' AND HEIGHT 'h' of  monogram \n");
    printf("==========================================\n");
    scanf("%f%f",&w,&h);
    initgraph(&driver,&mode,"\\tc");
    setpalette(0,0);
    setcolor(20);
    getch();
    wd=w*1.0/7;
    hd=h*1.0/7;
    m=w;
    n=h;
    while(m>=0||n>=0)
    {
            ellipse(325,225,90,270,m,n/2);
            getch();
            m=m–wd;
            n=n–hd;
    }
    getch();
    line(325,225–h/2,325,225+h/2);
    setfillstyle(1,21);
    floodfill(325–6*wd–2,225,20);
    setfillstyle(1,27);
    floodfill(325–5*wd–2,225,20);
    setfillstyle(1,41);
    floodfill(325–4*wd–2,225,20);
    setfillstyle(1,26);
    floodfill(325–3*wd–2,225,20);
    setfillstyle(1,14);
    floodfill(325–2*wd–2,225,20);
    setfillstyle(1,60);
```

```
        floodfill(325–wd–2,225,20);
        setfillstyle(1,4);
        floodfill(325–2,225,20);
        wd=(3*1.0)/5*w;
        hd=h/4.0;
        m=wd;
        i=0;
        while(i<=1.0)
        {
                ellipse(325,225-h/4,270,90,m,hd);
                getch();
                m=wd–w/7;hd=hd–h/14.0;
                ++i;
        }
        setfillstyle(1,22);
        floodfill(325+wd–4,225–h/4,20) ;
        moveto(325,225);
        lineto(325+wd,225+h/2);
        lineto(325+m,225+h/2);
        lineto(325,225+h/14.0);
        setfillstyle(1,22);
        floodfill(325+m+2,225+h/2–2,20);
        getch();
        restorecrtmode();
        return;
    }
```

Project 22–11

22.11 SOFTWARE ON DESIGN OF BOX

This software prepares a drawing of the sheet to be cut to prepare a box of given dimensions. The dimensions of the box could be supplied to the software by the user and the drawing is prepared by the software.

```
    /*PROGRAM FOR SHEET DESIGN */
    #include <graphics.h>
    #include <conio.h>
    #include <math.h>
    float a[50][50],l,b,h;
    main()
    {
        int dr,mode;
        dr=9;
        mode=VGAHI;
        initgraph(&dr,&mode,"\\TC");
        setpalette(0,19);
        setcolor(7);
```

```
    supply();
    rawdraw();
    draw();
    getch();
    restorecrtmode();
    return;
}
supply()
{
    printf("enter the values of l,b,h\n");
    scanf("%f%f%f",&l,&b,&h);
    a[1][1]=50;a[1][2]=50;
    a[2][1]=50+h;a[2][2]=50;
    a[3][1]=50+l+h;a[3][2]=50;
    a[4][1]=50+2*h+l;a[4][2]=50;
    a[5][1]=50+h;a[5][2]=50+b;
    a[6][1]=50+h+l;a[6][2]=50+b;
    a[7][1]=50;a[7][2]=50+b+h;
    a[8][1]=50+h;a[8][2]=50+b+h;
    a[9][1]=50+l+h;a[9][2]=50+b+h;
    a[10][1]=50+2*h+l;a[10][2]=50+b+h;
    a[11][1]=50;a[11][2]=50+h+2*b;
    a[12][1]=50+h;a[12][2]=50+h+2*b;
    a[13][1]=50+l+h;a[13][2]=50+h+2*b;
    a[14][1]=50+2*h+l;a[14][2]=50+h+2*b;
    a[15][1]=50;a[15][2]=50+(2*h)+(2*b);
    a[16][1]=50+h;a[16][2]=50+(2*h)+(2*b);
    a[17][1]=50+l+h;a[17][2]=50+(2*h)+(2*b);
    a[18][1]=50+2*h+l;a[18][2]=50+(2*h)+(2*b);
    return;
}
rawdraw()
{
    line(a[1][1],a[2][2],a[4][1],a[4][2]);
    line(a[4][1], a[4][2], a[18][1], a[18][2]);
    line(a[18][1], a[18][2], a[15][1], a[15][2]);
    line(a[15][1], a[15][2], a[1][1], a[1][2]);
    getch();
    return;
}
draw()
{
    setcolor(4);
    line(a[2][1],a[2][2], a[5][1], a[5][2]);
```

```
        line(a[5][1], a[5][2], a[6][1], a[6][2]);
        line(a[6][1], a[6][2], a[3][1], a[3][2]);
        line(a[3][1], a[3][2], a[17][1],a[17][2]);
        line(a[17][1], a[17][2], a[16][1], a[16][2]);
        line(a[16][1], a[16][2], a[2][1], a[2][2]);
        line(a[7][1],a[7][2], a[10][1], a[10][2]);
        line(a[10][1], a[10][2], a[14][1], a[14][2]);
        line(a[14][1], a[14][2], a[11][1], a[11][2]),
        line(a[2][1], a[2][2], a[3][1], a[3][2]);
        line(a[7][1],a[7][2],a[11][1], a[11][2]);
        getch();
        return;
    }
```

Project 22–12

22.12 SOFTWARE ON COST ESTIMATION

This software estimates the cost of the package made up of a paper of the given size specified by the GSM of the paper. The GSM of the paper and its cost are stored in a file and the data is read from a file and the cost of the package is estimated.

```
/* PROGRAM  ON COST ESTIMATION OF PACKAGE */
#include <stdio.h>
#include <math.h>
main()
{
    FILE *fptr;float gsm,cost,tcost;
    int v,i;
    clrscr();
    fptr=fopen("gsm.r","r");
    if(fptr==NULL)
            printf("the file does not exist\n");
    else
            printf("the file is opened successfully \n");
    for(i=1;i<=10;++i)
    {
            fscanf(fptr,"%f%f",&gsm,&cost);
            printf("gsm=%g , cost=%g\n",gsm,cost);
            tcost=tcost+gsm*cost;
            printf("tcost=%g\n",tcost);
    }
    fclose(fptr);
    return;
}
```

Project 22–13

22.13 SOFTWARE ON GEAR DESIGN

This software is on analysis and design of the mechanical component gear which is used for transmission of power. This software calculates the face width, module, number of teeth and PCD of gear. The material for the gear is selected from the standard values.

```
#include"stdio.h"
#include"conio.h"
#include"math.h"
#include"string.h"
#define pi 3.14

float mat_stress(char c[20])
{
    char m_name[15][20]=
    {"CIO","CIM","CIH","SAE1020","SAE1030","SAE1035","SAE1040","SAE1045",
    "SAE1045HT","SAE2320","SAE3245","SAE6145"};
    char backup[20];
    float s[15]={56,70,105,126,140,161,175,210,240,350,456,473};
    int i,flag;
    float choice;
    for(i=0;i<15;i++)
    {
    flag=strcmp(c,m_name[i]);
    if(flag==0)
    {
    choice=s[i];
    break;
    }
    }
    if(flag!=0)
    {
    printf("can not find material in database\n");
    printf("Enter new material\n");
    scanf("%s",backup);
    mat_stress(backup);
    }
    return(choice);
}
float mod_select(float m)
{
    float mod[18]={1,1.25,1.5,2,2.5,3,4,5,6,8,10,12,16,20,25,32,40,50};
    float m1;
    int i,j=0;
    for(i=0;i<18;i++)
```

```
    {
    if(mod[i]>m)
    {
     j=1;m1=mod[i];
    break;
    }
    }
    if(j==0)
    {
    printf("No module is available\n");
    m1=m;
    }
    return(m1);
}
cust()
{
    textmode(C40);
    textcolor(YELLOW+BLINK);
    gotoxy(10,10);
    cprintf("GEAR DESIGN SOFTWARE");
    getch();
    textmode(C80);
    clrscr();
}
main()
{
    FILE *fptr;
    float Pr,Vr,Np,Ng,Pa,m,Cv,Yp,Yg,tp,tg,Pcdp,Pcdg,C,q,e,Adp,Ddp,Adg,Ddg,Sop,
    Sog,Bb;
    float Ft,Fw,Fd,Fb,Fenp,Feng,K,Kl,Vp,Pd,Sebp,Sebg;
    float n1,n2,n3,n4,n5,n6,a1,b1,zz,xx,Gr;
    int temp=0;
    char Mk;char s[20]; char sh;
    char mat_name1[20],mat_name2[20];
    float a[4][3]= { {0.8,1,1.25}, {1,1.25,1.5}, {1.25,1.5,1.8}, {1.5,1.8,2.0} };
    float def_fact[3][3]={ {5700,5900,6100}, {7800,8100,8500}, {15000,11800,12300}};
    cust();
    clrscr();
    printf("\tEnter the value of power,speed of pinion and velocity ratio\n");
    scanf("%f %f %f",&Pr,&Np,&Vr);
    printf("\tEnter the type of load as 1,2,3,4(table XVI-2)\n");
    scanf("%f",&n1);
    printf("\tEnter the type of service as 1,2,3\n");
    scanf("%f",&n2);
```

```
Kl = a[n1-1][n2-1];
Pd = Pr*Kl;
printf("\tEnter the number of teeth on pinion tp\n");
scanf("%f",&tp);
if(Vr>1)
        Gr = Vr;
else
        Gr = 1.00/Vr;
tg = Gr*tp;
temp = tg;
if((tg-temp)!=0.00)
        tg = temp+1;
Ng = Np/Gr;
top:
printf("\tEnter the material for pinion\n");
scanf("%s",mat_name1);
Sop = mat_stress(mat_name1);
printf("\tEnter the material for gear\n");
scanf("%s",mat_name2);
Sog = mat_stress(mat_name2);
printf("\tEnter the value of pressure angle Pa\n");
scanf("%f",&Pa);
if(Pa == 14.5)
{
a1=0.39,b1=2.16;}
if(Pa==20)
{
printf("\tIs full depth Y/N \n");
fflush(stdin);
scanf("%c",&Mk);
if(Mk=='y'|| Mk=='Y')
{
a1=0.485,b1=2.87;
}
else
{
a1=0.551,b1=2.9;}
}
Yp=a1-b1/tp;
Yg=a1-b1/tg;
Cv=0.3;
if(Sop*Yp<=Sog*Yg)
        zz=(1000.00*60.00*Pd)/(pi*tp*Np*Sop*Cv*10.00*Yp);
else
```

```
        zz= (1000.00*60.00*Pd)/(pi*tg*Ng*Sog*Cv*10.00*Yg);
m = pow(zz,(1.00/3.00));
m = mod_select(m);
Pcdp = m*tp; Pcdg = m*tg;
Adp = m; Adg = m;
Ddp = 1.157*m; Ddg=1.157*m;
Vp = (pi*Pcdp*Np)/(1000.00*60.00);
Ft = Pd/Vp;
Bb = 10*m;

if(Vp>=2.5&&Vp<=7.5)
        Cv = 3.00/(3.00+Vp);
else
if(Vp>7.5&&Vp<=15)
        Cv = 4.5/(4.5+Vp);
else
if(Vp>15&&Vp<=20)
        Cv=6.00/(6.00+Vp);
else
        Cv=5.5/(5.5+sqrt(Vp));
if(Sop*Yp<=Sog*Yg)
        Fb=Sop*Cv*Bb*Yp*m;
else
        Fb=Sog*Cv*Bb*Yg*m;
if(Ft>Fb)
{
printf("\tThe design is not safe in bending\n");
getch();
goto top;
}
else
{
printf("\tDesign is safe in bending\n");
getch();
}
printf("\n Fb=%f Ft=%f",Fb,Ft);
begin:
printf("\n\tEnter the value of load stress factor K\n");
scanf("%f",&K);
q = (2*tg)/(tg+tp);
Fw = Pcdp*Bb*K*q;printf("\nFw=%f",Fw);
if(Ft>Fw)
{
printf("\n\tDesign is not safe in wear\n");
```

```
getch();
printf("\tIncrease the value of load stress factor K\n");
getch();
goto begin;
}
else
printf("\tDesign is safe in wear\n");
printf("\tEnter the value of design profile error\n");
scanf("%f",&e);
printf("\tEnter the materials of gear in mesh(table XVI-4) as 1,2,3\n");
scanf("%f",&n5);
if(Pa==14.5)
        n6 = 1;
if(Mk=='y'||Mk=='Y')
        n6 = 2;
else
        n6 = 3;
C = def_fact[n5-1][n6-1];
xx = (21.00*Vp*(C*e*Bb+Ft))/(21.00*Vp+sqrt(C*e*Bb+Ft));
Fd=Ft+xx;
printf("\nFd=%f",Fd);
if(Fd>Fw)
{
printf("\n\tDesign is not safe in dynamic load\n");
getch();
goto top;
}
else
{
printf("\n\tDesign is safe in dynamic load\n");
getch();
}
printf("\tEnter the vlues of endurance strengths of pinion and gear\n");
scanf("%f %f",&Sebp,&Sebg);
Fenp=Sebp*Bb*Yp*m;
Feng=Sebg*Bb*Yg*m;
printf("\n\tFenp=%f Feng=%f",Fenp,Feng);
if(Fd>Fenp && Fd>Feng)
{
printf("\n\tDesign is not safe in endurance\n");
getch();
goto top;
}
else
```

```
{
printf("\n\tDesign is safe\n");
getch();
}
printf("                PINION                  GEAR\n");
printf("\nMaterial       %10s                  %10s",mat_name1,mat_name2);
printf("\nt              %10g                  %10g",tp,tg);
printf("\nNrpm           %10g                   %10g",Np,Ng);
printf("\nDiameter       %10g                  %10g",Pcdp,Pcdg);
printf("\nModule         %10g",m);
printf("\nFace width      %10g",Bb);
printf("\nAdd            %10g                  %10g",Adp,Adg);
printf("\nDdd            %10g                  %10g",Ddp,Ddg);
printf("\n\tDo you want to store the results in a file Y/N");
fflush(stdin);
scanf("%c",&sh);
if(sh=='y'|| sh=='Y')
{
printf("\n\tEnter the file name\n");
scanf("%s",s);
fptr=fopen(s,"w+");
if(fptr==NULL);
{
printf("\tUnable to open the file\n");
getch();
exit();
}
fprintf(fptr,"------------------------------------------------------------\n");
fprintf(fptr,"m=            %g\n",m);
fprintf(fptr,"Bb=   %g\n",Bb);
fprintf(fptr,"------------------------------------------------------------\n");
fprintf(fptr,"         PINION          GEAR\N");
fprintf(fptr,"\nt        %10g          %10g\n",tp,tg);
fprintf(fptr,"\nNrpm     %10g           %10g\n",Np,Ng);
fprintf(fptr,"\nDiameter  %10g          %10g\n",Pcdp,Pcdg);
fprintf(fptr,"\nAll Dimensions In mm");
fclose(fptr);
}
}
/*End of main()*/
```

Project 22–14

22.14. INCOME TAX CALCULATION SOFTWARE

This is a software for calculation of income tax for the salaried employees. This software displays the menu and allows calculation of income tax for employees. It stores the results into a file. The record in the file could be viewed or displayed.

```
# include<stdio.h>
/*Program to write income sheet for CA  */
# include <string.h>
# include <stdio.h>
# include <conio.h>
char word[40][40]={"ZERO","FIRST","SECOND","THIRD ","FOURTH","FIFTH ","SIXTH ",
"SEVENTH ","EIGHTH ","NINETH ","TENTH ","ELEVENTH ","TWELFTH
","THIRTEENTH", "FOURTEENTH ","FIFTEENTH ","SIXTEENTH ","SEVENTEENTH
","EIGHTEENTH ","NINETEENTH", "TWENTYTH ","TWENTYFIRST
","TWENTYSECOND","TWENTYTHIRD ","TWENTYFOURTH", "TWENTYFIFTH ",};/
*"TWENTYSIXTH ","TWENTYSEVENTH ","TWENTYEIGHTH ","TWENTYNINETH,
"THIRTYTH" ,}; */
    float sd[30],tpa[30],sume[30],sum[30],sum1[30],sum2[30],sum3[30],sum4[30],i;
    float nt[ 30],nt1[30],nt2[30],nt3[30];
    char g,x[30];
struct data
{
    char name[30];char addr[30],addr1[30],addr2[30];
    char  pan[30];float sal;float pt;float hp;float hra;
    float con;char text[6][30];float texti[6];char texte[6][30];
    float textei[6];char text1[6][30];float text1i[6];
    float textd[6];float tp;char tr[10][30];
    float tri[10];char td[10][30];float tdi[10];
    float nti[10];} inc[30];
    FILE *t;
    float n,n1,n2,n3,n4,n5,t_reb[40];
    char fn[12];
main()
{
    char ans ;clrscr();
    textmode(C40);textbackground(GREEN);
    textcolor(RED+BLINK);clrscr();
    gotoxy(10,10);
    printf("INCOME TAX SOFTWARE");
    getch();clrscr();
    textmode(C80);
    textbackground(GREEN);
    textcolor(RED);
    while(1)
    {
      clrscr();
      menu();
```

```
    }
    fclose(t);
    return 0;
}
menu()
{
    char ans1;g=' ';
    gotoxy(25,8);
    printf(" MAIN MENU");
    gotoxy(25,9);
    printf("=================");
    gotoxy(25,11);
    printf(" 1. ENTER NEW RECORD  ");
    gotoxy(25,13);
    printf(" 2. ADD RECORD  ");
    gotoxy(25,15);
    printf(" 3. PRINT  ");
    gotoxy(25,17);
    printf(" 4. SHOW FILE");
    gotoxy(25,19);
    printf(" 5. EXIT  ");
    gotoxy(25,21);
    printf(" ENTER YOUR CHOICE  :  %c    ",g);
    gotoxy(48,21);
    g=getche();
    clrscr();
    switch(g)
    {
    case '1':
            oper();
            call();
    break;
    case '2':
            add();
            call();
    break;
    case '3':
            fclose(t);
            pr();      /*          FOR PRINTING ON PRINTER*/
    break;
    case '4':
            fclose(t);
            list();
    break;
```

```
    case '5':
        exit();
    break;
  }
  return;
  }
  call()
  {
  char ans ;ans= ' ';clrscr();
    while(1)
    {
      gotoxy(25,12);
      printf(" 1. ADD RECORD  ");
      gotoxy(25,14);
      printf(" 2.DELETE RECORD  ");
      gotoxy(25,16);
      printf(" 3.SHOW RECORD ");
      gotoxy(25,18);
      printf(" 4. MODIFY RECORD  ");
      gotoxy(25,20);
      printf(" 5. EXIT  ");
      gotoxy(25,22);
      printf(" ENTER YOUR CHOICE  :  %c    ",ans);
      gotoxy(48,22);
      ans=getche();
      clrscr();
      switch(ans)
      {
        case '1':
            add_rec();
            getch();
            clrscr();
        break;
        case '2':
            del();
            getch();
            clrscr();
        break;
        case '3':
            show();
            getch();
            clrscr();
        break;
        case '4':
```

```
                    modi();
                    getch();
                    clrscr();
            break;
            case '5':
                    goto bot;
                    getch();
            }
    }
    bot :
    return;
}

    oper()
    {
    printf("Enter the name of new file : ");
    scanf("%s",fn);
    t=fopen(fn,"a+");
    if(t == NULL)
    {
    printf("UNABLE TO OPEN THE FILE\n");
    getch();
    }
    clrscr();
    printf("enter  the no of the persons maximum upto 30 ");
    scanf("%f",&n);
    i=1;
    while(i<=n)
    {
       enter();
       cal();
       tax_c();
       res_prn(t);    /*FOR WRITING IN FILE*/
       ++i;
    }
    return;
    }
    modi()
    {
            float k;
            fclose(t);
            t=fopen(fn,"w+");
            fseek(t,0,SEEK_SET);
            clrscr();
```

```
            printf("Enter the rec nowhich is to be modified\n");
            scanf("%f",&i);
            enter();
            cal();
            tax_c();
            while(i<=n)
            {
                res_prn(t);    /*FOR WRITING IN FILE*/
                ++i;
            }
            getch();
            return;
}

del()
{
      float k,j;
      fclose(t);
      t=fopen(fn,"w+");
      fseek(t,0,SEEK_SET);
      clrscr();
      printf("Enter the rec no which is to be deleted\n");
      scanf("%f",&j); i=1;
      while(i<=n)
      {
          if(j != i)
                    res_prn(t);    /*FOR WRITING IN FILE*/
          ++i;
      }
      getch();
return;
}
list()
{
      char fi[100],fs[30];
      printf("Enter the name of file which you want to see : ");
      scanf("%s",fs);
      t=fopen(fs,"r");
      if(t == NULL)
      {
      printf("UNABLE TO OPEN THE FILE\n");
      getch();
      }
      else
```

```
        {
            clrscr();
            fseek(t,0,SEEK_SET);
            while(!(feof(t)))
            {
                    fseek(t,0,SEEK_CUR);
                    fread(fi,1,100,t);
                    fwrite(fi,1,100,stdout);
                    getch();
            }
        }
        return;
    }
    show()
    {
        clrscr();
        printf("Enter rec no which you want to see\n");
        scanf("%f",&i);
        res_prn(stdout);
        getch();
    }
    add_rec()
    {
        float nn;
        printf("Enter no of rec to be added\n");
        scanf("%f",&nn);
        i=n;n=n+nn;
        while(i<=n)
        {
            enter();
            cal();
            tax_c();
            res_prn(t);    /*FOR WRITING IN FILE*/
            ++i;
        }
        return;
    }
    add()
    {
        fseek(t,0,SEEK_END);
        oper();
        return;
    }
    res_prn(xt)
```

```
FILE *xt;
{
    float k;
    fseek(xt,0,SEEK_END);
    fwrite("————————————————————————————————————
\n",77,1,t);
    fputs("\n\n",xt);
    fprintf(xt," NAME : ");
    fputs(inc[i].name,xt);
    fputs("\n",xt);
    fseek(xt,0,SEEK_CUR);
    fwrite(" ADDRESS          : ",21,1,xt);
    fwrite(inc[i].addr,strlen(inc[i].addr)+1,1,xt);
    fputs("\n                 ",xt);
    fwrite(inc[i].addr1,strlen(inc[i].addr)+1,1,xt);
    fputs("\n                 ",xt);
    fwrite(inc[i].addr2,strlen(inc[i].addr)+1,1,xt);
    fputs("\n",xt);
    fwrite(" STATUS           : INDIVIDUAL",32,1,xt);
    fputs("\n",xt);
    fwrite(" ACCOUNTING PERIOD : 1-4-97 TO 31-03-98",40,1,xt);
    fputs("\n",xt);
    fwrite(" Asstt. YEAR      : 97-98",26,1,xt);
    fputs("\n",xt);
    fwrite(" PAN / GIR        : ",20,1,xt);
    fwrite(inc[i].pan,strlen(inc[i].pan)+1,1,xt);
    fputs("\n",xt);
    fwrite(" STATEMENT OF TAXABLE INCOME   ",30,1,xt);
    fputs("\n",xt);
    fwrite("————————————————————————————————————\n",76,1,xt);
    fputs("\n",xt);
    fwrite(" 1. INCOME FROM SALARY        :      ",36,1,xt);
    fseek(xt,0,SEEK_CUR);
    fprintf(xt," %10g ",inc[i].sal);
    fputs("\n",xt);
    fwrite("        LESS STD DEDUCTION :      ",36,1,xt);
    fseek(xt,0,SEEK_CUR);
    fprintf(xt," %10g ",sd[i]);
    fputs("\n",xt);
    fwrite("        LESS  PROF TAX      :     ",36,1,xt);
    fseek(xt,0,SEEK_CUR);
    fprintf(xt," %10g ",inc[i].pt);
    fputs("\n",xt);
    fwrite(" 2.NET INCOME FROM SALARY     :     ",46,1,xt);
```

```
    fseek(xt,0,SEEK_CUR);
    fprintf(xt," %10g ",nt[i]);
    printf("NETSAL= %10g\n ",nt[i]);
    fputs("\n",xt);
    fwrite(" 3. INCOME FROM HOUSE PROPERTY:              ",46,1,xt);
    fseek(xt,0,SEEK_CUR);
    fprintf(xt," %10g ",inc[i].hp);
    fputs("\n",xt);
    fwrite("  NET TOTAL INCOME          :              ",46,1,xt);
    fseek(xt,0,SEEK_CUR);
    fprintf(xt," %10g ",nt1[i]);
    fputs("\n",xt);
    fwrite(" 4. INCOME FROM OTHER SOURCES :        ",46,1,xt);
    fseek(xt,0,SEEK_CUR);
    for(k=1.0;k<=n1;++k)
    {
      fputs("\n\t\t\t",xt);
      fprintf(xt,"%10s",inc[i].text[k]);
      fprintf(xt,"\t");
      fprintf(xt,"%10g",inc[i].texti[k]);
    }
  for(k=1.0;k<=n2;++k)
  {
    fputs("\n\t\t\t",xt);
    fprintf(xt,"%10s",inc[i].text1[k]);
    fprintf(xt,"\t");
    fprintf(xt,"%10g",inc[i].text1i[k]);
    fprintf(xt,"\n");
    fwrite("\t\t\tDEDUCTIONS : ",13,1,xt);
    fputs("\t",xt);
    fprintf(xt,"%10g",inc[i].textd[k]);
  }
    fputs("\n",xt);
    fwrite("     TOTAL GROSS OTHER INCOME      :        ",46,1,xt);
    fseek(xt,0,SEEK_CUR);
    fprintf(xt," %10g ",sum[i]+sum1[i]);
    fputs("\n",xt);
    if(xt==stdout)
          getch();
    fwrite(" 5. EXEMPTED INCOME          :        ",46,1,xt);
    fseek(xt,0,SEEK_CUR);
    for(k=1.0;k<=n5;++k)
    {
    fputs("\n\t\t\t",xt);
```

```
fprintf(xt,"%10s",inc[i].texte[k]);
fprintf(xt,"\t");
fprintf(xt,"%10g",inc[i].textei[k]);
fprintf(xt,"\n");
}
fputs("\n",xt);
fwrite("    TOTAL  EXEMPT     INCOME       :      ",46,1,xt);
fseek(xt,0,SEEK_CUR);
fprintf(xt," %10g ",sume[i]);
fputs("\n",xt);
fwrite(" 6.TAXABLE TOTAL INCOME          :              ",46,1,xt);
fseek(xt,0,SEEK_CUR);
fprintf(xt," %10g ",nt2[i]);
fputs("\n",xt);
fwrite(" 7. TAX PAYABLE                  :              ",46,1,xt);
fseek(xt,0,SEEK_CUR);
fprintf(xt," %10g ",inc[i].tp);
fputs("\n",xt);
fwrite(" 8.TAX REBATE                    :              ",46,1,xt);
fseek(xt,0,SEEK_CUR);
for(k=1.0;k<=n3;++k)
{
fputs("\n\t\t\t" ,xt);
fprintf(xt,"%10s",inc[i].tr[k]);
fprintf(xt,"%10g",inc[i].tri[k]);
}
fputs("\n",xt);
fprintf(xt," 9. Total Amount Invested     :           %10g\t",sum3[i]);
fputs("\n",xt);
fprintf(xt," 10. Tax Rebate obtained      :           %10g\t", t_reb[i]);
fputs("\n",xt);
fprintf(xt," 11.The net tax payable       :           %10g \t",nt3[i]);
fputs("\n",xt);
fprintf(xt," 12. Tax Deducted             :\n");
for(k=1.0;k<=n4;++k)
{
fprintf(xt," \t\t\t%s      %10g \n",inc[i].td[k],inc[i].tdi[k]);
}
fputs("\n",xt);
fprintf(xt," 13. Tax  which is  paid   :              %10g ",sum4[i]);
fputs("\n",xt);
fprintf(xt," 14.Tax to be  paid or refund(-) :        %10g ",tpa[i]);
fseek(xt,0,SEEK_CUR);
fputs("\n",xt);
```

```
    fwrite("——————————————————————————————————————————————",77,1,xt);
    fputs("\n",xt);
    fprintf(xt,"\f");
    return;
}
cal()
{
    float stext1i,j;
    sd[i]=0.33*inc[i].sal;
    if(sd[i] >= 20000)
    sd[i]=20000;
    nt[i]=inc[i].sal-sd[i]-inc[i].pt+inc[i].hra + inc[i].con;
    nt1[i]=nt[i]+inc[i].hp;
    sum[i]=0.0;
    for(j=1.0;j<=n1;++j)
            sum[i] +=inc[i].texti[j];
    sum1[i]=0.0;
    for(j=1.0;j<=n2;++j)
    {
      stext1i=inc[i].text1i[j]-inc[i].textd[j];
     sum1[i] += stext1i;
    }
    sume[i]=0.0;
    for(j=1.0;j<=n5;++j)
    {
     sume[i] += inc[i].textei[j];
    }
    nt2[i]=nt1[i]+sum[i]+sum1[i]-sume[i];
    return;
}
tax_c()
{
    float j;
    if(nt2[i] <= 40000)
    inc[i].tp=0.0;
    if(nt2[i] >= 40000 && nt2[i] <= 60000)
            inc[i].tp=0.1*(nt2[i]-40000);
    if(nt2[i] >= 60000 && nt2[i] <= 120000)
            inc[i].tp=2000+0.2*(nt2[i]-60000);
    if(nt2[i] >= 120000)
            inc[i].tp=14000+0.3*(nt2[i]-120000);
    sum3[i]=0.0;
    for(j=1.0;j<=n3;++j)
            sum3[i]=sum3[i]+inc[i].tri[j];
```

```
        t_reb[i]=sum3[i]*0.2;
        nt3[i]=inc[i].tp-t_reb[i];
        sum4[i]=0.0;
        for(j=1.0;j<=n4;++j)
                sum4[i]=sum4[i]+inc[i].tdi[j];
        tpa[i]=nt3[i]-sum4[i];
        return;
}
enter()
{
        float j;
        textmode(C80);textbackground(GREEN);
        textcolor(RED);clrscr();
        textbackground(3);textcolor(BLUE);
        printf("enter  name of the %s person :     ",word[i]);
        gets(inc[i].name);
        gets(inc[i].name);
        printf("enter  address of the %s person upto 3 lines \t:",word[i]);
        gets(inc[i].addr);
        gets(inc[i].addr1);
        gets(inc[i].addr2);
        printf("enter  pan no of the %s person \t:",word[i]);
        scanf("%s",inc[i].pan);
        printf("enter  GROSS SALARY of the %s person \t:",word[i]);
        scanf("%f",&inc[i].sal);
        printf("enter  PROFESSION TAX of the %s person \t:",word[i]);
        scanf("%f",&inc[i].pt);
        printf("enter  HOUSE PROPERTY of the %s person \t:",word[i]);
        scanf("%f",&inc[i].hp);
        printf("enter  HRA RECEIVED of the %s person \t:",word[i]);
        scanf("%f",&inc[i].hra);
        printf("enter  CONVEYANCE RECEIVED of the %s person \t:",word[i]);
        scanf("%f",&inc[i].con);
        printf("How many non deductable other income sources ?    ");
        scanf("%f",&n1);
        for(j=1.0;j<=n1;++j)
        {
         printf("enter  name of the income source %s\n",word[j]);
         gets(inc[i].text[j]);
         gets(inc[i].text[j]);
         printf("enter  amount of the %s income source \n",word[j]);
          scanf("%f",&inc[i].texti[j]);
        }
        printf("How many  deductable other income sources ?    ");
```

```
        scanf("%f",&n2);
        for(j=1.0;j<=n2;++j)
        {
        printf("enter  name of the %s income source \n",word[j]);
        gets(inc[i].text1[j]);
        gets(inc[i].text1[j]);
        printf("enter  amount and deduction %s income source \n",word[j]);
        scanf("%f",&inc[i].text1i[j]);
        scanf("%f",&inc[i].textd[j]);
        }
        printf("How many  exempted income sources ?    ");
        scanf("%f",&n5);
        for(j=1.0;j<=n5;++j)
        {
        printf("enter  name of the %s exempt income source \n",word[j]);
        gets(inc[i].texte[j]);
        gets(inc[i].texte[j]);
        printf("enter  amount of the %s exempt income source \n",word[j]);
        scanf("%f",&inc[i].textei[j]);
        }
        printf("\nHow many  tax rebate ?    ");
        scanf("%f",&n3);
        for(j=1.0;j<=n3;++j)
        {
        printf("enter  name of the %s investment  \n",word[j]);
        gets(inc[i].tr[j]);
        gets(inc[i].tr[j]);
        printf("enter  amount of the %s investment  \n",word[j]);
        scanf("%f",&inc[i].tri[j]);
        }
        printf("\nHow many  sources at which tax deducted ?    ");
        scanf("%f",&n4);
        for(j=1.0;j<=n4;++j)
        {
        printf("enter  name of the %s place \n",word[j]);
        gets(inc[i].td[j]);
        gets(inc[i].td[j]);
        printf("enter  %s tax deducted \n",j);
        scanf("%f",&inc[i].tdi[j]);
        }
        return;
}
pr()
{
```

```
    char fi[100];
    t=fopen(fn,"r");
    if(stdprn == NULL)
            printf("Printer not ready");
    else
    {
    fseek(t,0,SEEK_SET);
    while(!(feof(t)))
    {
    fseek(t,0,SEEK_CUR);
    fread(fi,1,100,t);
    fwrite(fi,1,100,stdprn);
    /*                      getch();*/
    }
    }
}
```

Project 22-15

22.15 SOFTWARE ON PACKAGES

```
/*Programme to calculate weight of triangular, rectangular and circular package*/
#include<math.h>
#define pi 22.0/7.0
main()
{
    char oper;
    float b,h,l,t,Vs, Ws,d,A,c,a,D;
    clrscr();
    printf("enter the values of oper\n");
    scanf("%c", &oper);
    switch(oper)
{
    case 'R' :
/*programme to calculate the weight of the sheet required for rectangular shaped package*/
{
    printf("enter the values of breadth b in cm height h in cm length l in cm =   \n");
    scanf("%f%f%f",&b,&h,&l);
    printf("enter the thickness t of the sheet in mm = \n");
    scanf("%f",&t);
    Vs=((2*b*h)+(2*b*l)+(2*l*h))*t;
    printf("the volume of the sheet= %5f \n",Vs );
    printf("enter the density of the sheet=  \n");
    scanf("%f",&d);
    Ws=(d*Vs);
    printf("the weight of the sheet= %5f    \n",Ws);
}
break;
```

```
case 'T' :
/* Programme to calculate the weight of the sheet required for triangular shaped package*/
{
      printf("enter the area A of triangular shaped box cm =      \n");
      scanf("%f",&A);
      printf("enter the three sides a b c of the box in cm =      \n");
      scanf("%f%f%f", &a, &b, &c);
      printf("enter the thickness t and height h of the of the box in cm     \n");
      scanf("%f%f", &t,&h);
      Vs = ((a*h)+(b*h)+(c*h))+(2*A);
      printf("the volume of sheet =  %f  \n");
      printf("enter the density d of the package      \n");
      scanf("%f", &d);
      Ws = (d*Vs);
      printf("the weight of the sheet =%5f",Ws);
}
break;
case 'C':
/* Programme to calculate the weight of the sheet required for cylindrical shaped package*/
{
     clrscr();
     printf("enter the height h and diameter D of the box       \n");
     scanf("%f%f",&h,&D);
     printf("enter the thickness t of the box      \n");
     scanf("%f",&t);
     Vs =((pi*d*h)+2*(pi/4*(D*D)))*t;
     printf("the volume of the sheet required for the box= %6f  \n",Vs);
     printf("enter the density d of the box      \n");
     scanf("%f", &d);
     Ws = Vs * d;
     printf("the weight of the sheet required= %6f  \n",Ws);
     }
break;
default :
{
     printf("PLEASE EXCUSE ME , UNABLE TO OBTAIN THE DIMENSIONS\n");
}
break;
}
}
```

Project 22-16

22.16 STUDENT RECORD SOFTWARE

```
// NESTED CLASS OF OBJECTS
#include <iostream.h>
```

```
#include <conio.h>
#include <string.h>
class student
{
    private:
            char name[20];
            long int rollno;
            char sex;
    public:
            void st(char *na,long int rn,char sx);
            void display();
    class date
    {
    private:
            int day;
            int month;
            int year;
    public:
            void dt(int dy,int mh,int yr)
            {
            day = dy;
            month = mh;
            year = yr;
    }
    void show_date()
    {
    cout << day << "/" << month << "/" << year << endl;
    cout << "____________________________________________________" << endl;
    }
    };
};
void student :: st(char *na,long int rn,char sx)
{
    strcpy(name,na);
    rollno = rn;
    sex = sx;
}
void student :: display()
{
    cout << " Student's Name   RollNo   Sex    Date-of-birth (dd-mm-yr) \n";
    cout << " ____________________________________________________" << endl;
    cout << name << "            ";
    cout << rollno << "      ";
    cout << sex << "         ";
}
```

```
void main(void)
{
    clrscr();
    student s1;
    s1.st("Ravi",2,'M');
    date s2;
    s2.dt(13,7,94);
    s1.display();
    s2.show_date();
}
```

EXERCISE

Project 1 : Attendance programm

Design an attendance program. It needs to accept an arbitrary number of students up to 30 and attendance for each up to 16 days. The attendance can be Present(P), Absent(A), or Excused(X). It needs to save this information to disk, since each item above could be entered at a different time.

It needs to print(upon request), the results for each student. These results should include a % present days present/(total days so far-days excused). Program should check for disk files. If it does not find it, it should go into "ask for student name" mode and get class list. Otherwise it should accept input form operator indicating what type of data is being inserted (for example S for student, A for attendance, etc.) or that a report is wanted (e.g. R). When asking for attendance input, the program should task for what date (e.g. 1,2,...), the program should display the name of the student and accept the attendance code. It should be possible to add students and correct attendance results. After handling any of the requests above, program should re-ask for type of data until it gets a flag value indicating quit (e.g. Q or X). Program should not use global variables and should have multiple functions. It probably would be best if the student data was placed in an array of structures.

Report form should be something like:

Name 1 2 3 4 5 6 7 8 9 10 11 12 13
14
15 16 %
Prakash Dave P P
A
67

Vivek Singh P P
P
100
Suresh Dube A A
A
0

Project 2 : Loon repayment

```
#include<iostream>
#include<cmath>
struct Loan // Loan is called structure tag
```

```
{
int ID; // assume an unique integer between 1111-9999
float amount; // $ amount of the loan
float rate; // annual interest rate
int term; // number of months, length of the loan
};
float payment(float amount, float rate, int term);
int main( )
{
Loan loan1;
float monthly_payment;
// Initialize the loan1 object
cout << "Enter the ID of this loan \n";
cin >> loan1.ID;
cout << "Enter the amount of this loan \n";
cin >> loan1.amount;
cout << "Enter the annual interest rate of this loan (in %) \n";
cin >> loan1.rate;
cout << "Enter the term (number of months, length of the loan) \n";
cin >> loan1.term;
monthly_payment = payment(loan1.amount, loan1.rate, loan1.term);
cout << "The monthly payment for loan " << loan1.ID << " is: " << monthly_payment
<< endl;
return 0;
}
float payment(float amount, float rate, int term)
{
rate = rate/1200; // To convert % yearly rate to monthly fraction
return amount*rate*( pow( (rate+1), term)/ (pow( (rate+1), term) - 1) );
}
```

A struct can be passed to a function as a parameter. The rule for passing a struct as a parameter is the same as that of a simple variable. If you are modifying any of the **members** of the struct, then you need to pass the struct as call-by-reference. In the above program, we do not modify the members, so we can pass the struct to a function as call-by-value. Here is the modified version of the above program with a function that has the struct as its parameter.

```
// defines a structure for loan, creates an object from it,
// initializes the object from the keyboard, then displays the object.
#include<iostream>
#include<cmath>

struct Loan // Loan is called structure tag
{
int ID; // assume an unique integer between 1111-9999
float amount; // $ amount of the loan
float rate; // annual interest rate
int term; // number of months, length of the loan
};
```

```
float payment(Loan l);
int main( )
{
Loan loan1;
float monthly_payment;
// Initialize the loan1 object
cout << "Enter the ID of this loan \n";
cin >> loan1.ID;
cout << "Enter the amount of this loan \n";
cin >> loan1.amount;
cout << "Enter the annual interest rate of this loan (in %) \n";
cin >> loan1.rate;
cout << "Enter the term (number of months, length of the loan) \n";
cin >> loan1.term;
monthly_payment = payment(loan1);
cout << "The monthly payment for loan " << loan1.ID << " is: " << monthly_payment
<< endl;
return 0;
}
float payment(Loan l)
{
l.rate = l.rate/1200; // To convert % yearly rate to monthly fraction
return l.amount*l.rate*( pow( (l.rate+1), l.term)/ (pow( (l.rate+1), l.term) - 1) );
}
```

(1) Modify program so it asks user to enter 2 different loans and uses a function called *initialize_loan* to initialize each loan object. Compute and display payment for each individual loan and total monthly payment. Use a separate object for each loan.

(2) Complete program by defining member functions *display* and *payment* for class *loan*. *display* function will display all the information about loan

Example:

ID:
Amount:
Rate:
Term:

Display monthly payment in main prog by assigning returned value from the *payment* function to variable of type float. If we declare in main segment:

```
.....
float p;
Loan loan1;
loan1.set( );
.....
loan1.display( ) // will display the data members of loan1
p = loan1.payment( ) // will return the monthly payment of loan1
.....
#include<iostream>
#include<cmath>
class Loan // loan class definition
```

```
{
public:
        int ID; // assume an unique integer between 1111-9999
        float amount; // $ amount of the loan
        float rate; // annual interest rate
        int term; // number of months, length of the loan
};
float payment(Loan l);
int main( )
{
Loan loan1;
float monthly_payment;
// Initialize the loan1 object
cout << "Enter the ID of this loan \n";
cin >> loan1.ID;
cout << "Enter the amount of this loan \n";
cin >> loan1.amount;
cout << "Enter the annual interest rate of this loan (in %) \n";
cin >> loan1.rate;
cout << "Enter the term (number of months, length of the loan) \n";
cin >> loan1.term;
monthly_payment = payment(loan1);
cout << "The monthly payment for loan " << loan1.ID << " is: " << monthly_payment
<< endl;
return 0;
}
float payment(Loan l)
{
l.rate = l.rate/1200; // To convert % yearly rate to monthly fraction
return l.amount*l.rate*( pow( (l.rate+1), l.term)/ (pow( (l.rate+1), l.term) - 1) );
}
```

Need three functions:

void set( )

// This function will initialize the data members of an object

float payment( )

// This function will compute the monthly payment for a loan object

void display()

// This function will display a loan object

Functions should be included in public part of class definition

```
class Loan // Loan is called class tag
{
public:
        void set( );
        float payment( );
        void display( );
private:
        int ID; // assume an unique integer between 1111-9999
        float amount; // $ amount of the loan
```

```
float rate; // annual interest rate
int term; // number of months, length of the loan
};
```

Write functions by using **scope resolution operator (::)** to distinguish between member function and regular function. For example function *set* is now a member of class *Loan*. Thus, we use :: to identify it.

```
void Loan::set( )
{
// Initialize the loan1 object
cout << "Enter the ID of this loan \n";
cin >> ID;
cout << "Enter the amount of this loan \n";
cin >> amount;
cout << "Enter the annual interest rate of this loan (in %) \n";
cin >> rate;
cout << "Enter the term (number of months, length of the loan) \n";
cin >> term;
}
```

No need to specify whose data members we are initializing because function will be called with a **dot operator, as any_object.set( ),** which tells compiler that it is the data members of the any_object that you are initializing. For example, to call set function in main, we first define object of type *Loan*, by:

Loan loan1;

then call set as:

laon1.set( );

Driver that can be used to test set function:

```
#include<iostream>
using namespace std;
class Loan // Loan is called class tag
{
public:
void set( );
float payment( );
void display( );
private:
int ID; // assume an unique integer between 1111-9999
float amount; // $ amount of the loan
float rate; // annual interest rate
int term; // number of months, length of the loan
};
int main( )
{
Loan loan1;
loan1.set( );
return 0;
}
void Loan::set( )
```

```
{
// Initialize the loan1 object
cout << "Enter the ID of this loan \n";
        cin >> ID;
cout << "Enter the amount of this loan \n";
        cin >> amount;
cout << "Enter the annual interest rate of this loan (in %) \n";
        cin >> rate;
cout << "Enter the term (number of months, length of the loan) \n";
        cin >> term;
}
```

(1) Modify class *loan* to include *monthly_payment* as a data member in that class. Add new function called *add_loans,* defined as: *float add_loans(Loan loan1, Loan loan 2);* You still have *payment* function that computes the payment. Since you include *monthly_payment* as a member, instead of returning a value from the function, directly set value for *monthly_payment* in that function. The new function, *add_loans,* takes two loan objects and computes the total monthly payment, i.e., the sum of monthly payments of the two loans.

Project 3 : Investment plan

This program will track an investment plan to determine the amount that will accumulate over a period of time. The inputs to the program are:

iAmount	Initial amount invested
mAmount	Monthly amount invested
rate	Yearly interest rate
nCompound	Number of times per year the interest is compounded
nYears	Number of years for the investment.

The program should prompt the user for these values, then produce a table that shows yearly values for the total amount invested and the current value of the investment. The table should have three columns -the Year number, the Amount Invested and the Current Value. Make sure that the columns are aligned properly. Dollar amounts should be output with two decimal places.

The formula to compute the balance of the investment is:

$$\text{balance} = \text{amount} * (1.0 + \text{rate/nCompound})^{\text{nPeriods*nCompound}}$$

where *amount* is the balance at the start of the period, *rate* is the interest rate for one period of the investment, *nCompound* is the number of times the investment is compounded per period, and *nPeriods* is the number of periods for which the amount is invested. To keep things simple, assume that the monthly amounts that are invested are all added at the beginning of each year. Write a value function to compute the balance. Your program will call this function for each year of the investment. *(This means that the call to the Balance() function will be made with* nPeriods *of 1 each time).*

The input is going to be this

0.00	Initial amount invested
500.00	Monthly amount invested
10	Yearly interest rate
12	Number of times per year the interest is compounded
35	Number of years for the investment

Project 4 : Database of University

Assume that a university has hired you to design a database to store information about all persons studying or working for the university. Each person has an id , name, address, work and home phone numbers. Persons are either faculty or students (no staff other than faculty).

For students, the database must store the GPA, the list of courses that are currently taken and for every course, the location where it is taken(we suppose that a student can take up to 5 courses) . Students may be undergraduate or graduate. If graduate, the database must contain the degree (MS, MBA or PhD) and the advisor id (the id of the faculty member who is directing the thesis of the graduate student).

For faculty, the database must store department, specialty, rank and annual salary. Rank is one of : lecturer, assistant professor, associate professor or professor.

In the university, graduate students may teach, in this case they are students and faculty in the same time. They are called teaching assistant (TA). TAs are classified by lecturers.

Write a C++ program to support the following class hierarchy. Classes PERSON and STUDENT should be abstract classes in where you put all common functionality and data that derived classes inherit. Then you declare four arrays, one for faculty, one for undergraduate students, one for graduate students and one for TAs. These arrays are used to store the data.

In order to manage the database, you provide the user of a menu like:

Press one of the following options:

a. Adding Student or Faculty
b. Searching
c. Deleting[1]
d. Sorting
e. List
x. Exit.

And for every option, you'll have a submenu:

Submenu for a- Adding Student or Faculty

Choose from the following options to add a

1. Undergraduate Student
2. Graduate Student
3. Faculty Member
4. TA
5. Return Main Menu

Submenu for b- Searching

Choose from the following to Search for a

1. Undergraduate Student
2. Graduate Student
3. Faculty member
4. TA
5. In the Entire database
6. Return Main Menu

If the user chooses between 1 and 5, then you prompt to search by id or name…

Submenu for c- Deleting

Choose from the following to delete a

1. Undergraduate Student
2. Graduate Student
3. Faculty Member
4. TA
5. Return Main Menu

Then you prompt the user to enter the id of whom you want to delete.

Submenu for d-Sorting

Choose from the following to Sort

1. Undergraduate Students
2. Graduate Students
3. Faculty Members
4. TAs
5. Return Main Menu

Then you prompt the user to sort by id or by name.

Submenu for e-List

Choose from the following to have the list of

1. Undergraduate Students
2. Graduate Students
3. Faculty Members
4. TAs
5. Return Main Menu

[1] Deletion is done by assigning 0 to the id

Project 5 : PC management System

You are to develop a computer (PC) management system. For each computer, the system stores the following information:

Brand/Model	(a string)
Inventory ID#	(a unique integer value for each computer)
Date of Service	(day, month, and year put into service)
Location	(a string)
Processor Speed	(a floating point number (Ghz) ranging from .500 – 3.0)
Memory	(.25 (256 MB), .5 (512 MB), 1 (1 GB), 2 (2 GB))
Disk Space	(30 GB, 40 GB, 60 GB, 80 GB, 120 GB)
Program Description:	The program collects and reports data for the company's computer tracking system. The options are:

(1) A list of all computers within the organization sorted by inventory #

(2) A list of all computers within the organization sorted by location

(3) A list of all computers matching a user specified brand/model

(4) A list of all computers matching a user specified location

(5) Exit processing

Project 6 : Saving Bank database

1. You will develop an application program that implements a savings account database. The assignment covers basic object-oriented programming implementation in C++ including: class definitions, constructors, constructor initializers, private data members, member functions, static members, and operator overloading as member, non-member

and friend functions. In addition, random access (binary) file I/O is addressed in the assignment.

2. The SavingsAccount class will have the variables and member functions shown in the class definitions attached at the end of this assignment. These include functions for modifying the account number and balance, accessing the account number and balance, calculating monthly interest, etc. Overloaded <= and == operators are used for comparing two savings account objects, e.g. **sa1 <= sa2**, or **sa1 == sa2**. The **= = operator** is overloaded as a **member function** and the **<= operator** is overloaded as a **nonmember** function. Both functions will compare the **account balances** of the objects. The << operator for use with **cout** is overloaded as a **friend** function. This function allows printing of savings account data directly to the standard output. A summary of the member, friend and non-member functions is shown below.
   a. **void enterAccountNo(long acctno)** modifies a savings account number.
   b. **void enterBalance(float bal)** modifies a savings account balance.
   c. **void computeMonthlyInterest()** calculates interest for the month based on the current annual interest rate and adds interest to account balance.
   d. **long returnAccountNumber()** provides access to private account number member.
   e. **float returnBalance()** provides access to private balance member. This member function is already implemented with an inline definition in the class definition.
   f. **static float returnInterestRate()** provides access to private static interest rate member. This member function is already implemented with an inline definition in the class definition.
   g. **static void changeInterestRate(float rate)** modifies static interest rate member.
   h. **bool operator==(const SavingsAccount & sa)** overloaded == operator implemented as a member function
   i. **bool operator<=(const SavingsAccount & lhs, const SavingsAccount & rhs)** overloaded <= operator implemented as a non-member function.
   j. **friend ostream& operator <<(ostream & os, SavingsAccount& sa)** overloaded << operator implemented as a friend function.

3. In addition to the SavingsAccount class you will also develop a class called SavingsDb which will encapsulate an array of savings account records to create a database. The database is implemented as a static array of SavingsAccount objects. The SavingsDb class will have the following functionality:
   a. `void enterRecord (const SavingsAccount & rec)` add a savings account record to the database array (at the end of the array).
   b. `SavingsAccount retrieveRecord (int accountNumber)` retrieve a savings account record from the database by <u>**account number**</u>. If the record is found the data is printed to the screen and the record is returned. If the record is not found an appropriate message is printed and a literal record with an account number of -1 is returned.
   c. `void displayDb()` print out all savings account records in the database in an appropriate format using the SavingsAccount << operator.
   d. `bool openDbFile()` read database records from a binary (random access) format file into the database array. Returns true if file read is successful and false if file read fails.

e. **`bool saveDbFile()`** write database records to a binary (random access) format file from the database array. Returns true if file write is successful and false if file write fails.

f. The database files will be written and read in binary mode (versus text mode), i.e., using the **`ifstream::read()`** and **`ofstream::write()`** functions. Reading in records from a file will overwrite the existing database records (if any) and update the number of records in the database.

4. Use the class definitions in the attachment at the end of this assignment. Place each definition in its own header (.h) file. You will create separate implementation source (.cpp) files for each class. Therefore, you will have 5 code files in all: three .cpp files and two .h files.

5. Name your application (driver) program source file **asmt1.cpp** and your executable **asmt1.exe**. Your driver program should demonstrate the basic functionality of both the savings account class and the savings database class, e.g.:

   a. create several savings account objects with appropriate data, demonstrate printing data, assignment, and comparisons (<= and ==).

   b. create a savings account database object and populate it with several savings account records, i.e. add savings account records to the database.

   c. retrieve a **user specified** record from the database file using the account number as a search key, print the account data to the screen if found, or an appropriate message if not.

   d. perform interest calculations with individual account objects and with objects in the database. Each call to the **computeMonthlyInterest** function computes the monthly interest and adds it to the account balance.

   e. print out all records in the database using an appropriate format.

   f. write a database to a **user specified** file using binary file mode. Only the actual account records stored should be written to the file – not the entire database array (unless it is full).

   g. read a database from a **user specified** file. The file contents overwrite the existing database and the number of account records is updated.

Project 7 : Bank account

A mini- bank holds 20 accounts out of which there are 10 general accounts and the remaining 10 are special accounts. The Bank has a single cash-machine. The cash machine takes the account number and a password from an account holder. It then asks how much money the account holder wants to withdraw. If there is that much of money then it prints a message that the transaction has succeeded and shows the remaining balance on the screen: otherwise it tells that the transaction has failed. An account holder can also query the mini-bank about his balance(without asking for money). The cash-machine asks a single password from the general accountholder whereas it asks two passwords from the special account holder. A special account must always have a minimum balance of Rs.1000 whereas there is no such limitation for a general account.

The important things to do:

1. A general account holder withdrawing some money.
2. A general account holder wants to withdraw but there is not enough balance in the account.

3. A special account holder wants to withdraw some money but the transaction is refused because the transaction would violate the restriction that the account must hold a minimum amount.
4. A special account holder queries about his balance.

Project 8 : Video store

I need a working program that simulates a small video store. It has to have an order entry, inventory control and tracking and tape profitability forecasting system which could optimize the profitability of the store.

Customer file contains: name, address, telephone, credit card # and expiration and a customer number. Tape checkout file contains: cust. #, tape #, and copy #, checkout date and time & expected return date and actual return date. Tape inventory file contains: title, cost, price, tape and copy number & date first received.

The order should be input by typing the last 4 digits of the phone #, to get the customer, the tape # and copy using the 5 digits and a copy letter (instead of a bar code) and code should read your system clock for the date & time. Print a receipt for a due date and time & price for all rentals of customer. When tape is checked out the tape checkout & inventory files are updated. When tape is returned enter the tape & copy number to update the tape checkout & inventory files.

The program needs to be able to forecast the tape sales for each tape and decide if you should get more copies of a given tape and how profitable such an investment will be.

Project 9 : Person class

(1) Create a class Person that contains only a constructor and a virtual print function. The constructor should only accept a string for a persons name.

(2) Create 3 classes that inherit from the Person class and implement the print function. The 3 classes are Student, Teacher and Administrator. Their print functions should print the persons name and whether they are student, teacher or Administrator.

(3) Create a mainline program that creates an array of 4 pointers to the base class Person and prompts the user for names and if they are a Student, Teacher or Administrator. Instantiate the correct object and place it in the array. When the array is full, use the print function to print out the information on the people.

Project 10 : Zoo program

Write a program (call it Zoo) that initializes an instance of the class you wrote for homework 8, containing pointers to animals. It should then display a menu to the user allowing for the following options:

1. Add an animal (type selected by user, ie. Horse or Dog).
2. Print information about an animal (selected by the user).
3. Print information about all the Horses in the zoo.
4. Print information about all the Dogs in the zoo.
5. Remove an animal from the Zoo.
6. Print information about all the animals in the zoo.

Project 11 : Rainfall program

The Following arrays show the average monthly rainfall for a given year:
Double rainfall[]= {6.2,7.2,9.5,10.8,8.1,7.5,7.7,11.3,12.4,15.9,12.5};
String[]= {“Jan”, “Feb”,”Mar”,”Apr”,”May”,”Jun”,”Aug”,”Sep”,”Oct”,”Nov”,”Dec”};
Write appropiate codes that would:

(*a*) Print array values in reverse order the rainfall reading for each endinf quarter.
(*b*) Sum the rainfall readings.
(*c*) Find the average of the rainfall reading.

(d) List all of the readings above or below the average reading.
(e) Find the standard deviation of the rainfall readings.
(f) Find the highest or the lowest rainfall reading for the year.
(g) Make a horizontal bar graph of the rainfall readings.
(h) Search the array of readings for a specific reading.
(i) Sort the reading in ascending or descending order.

This program has to have two classes one call Rainfall and the other one is TestRainfall.

sample code:

```
class Rainfall
}
String months[];
Double rainfall[];
Rainfall (String Double R[]M[],)
month=M;
rainfall=R;
```

```
class testRainfall
{
public Static void main (Stringsrg[])
{
String months[]={"Jan","Feb"....};
Double Rainfall[]={9.5,2.4,........};
Rainfall R= new Rainfall(months,Rainfall);
R.reverse();
}
```

23

TRIAL PROGRAMS

In this chapter, some trial programs are provided for practice to understand the basics of C– programming. These programs are prepared by using the various alternative commands available in C–programming .

In the programming technique the programmer makes use of the various options available in C–language to create logics or algorithm useful to obtain the desired result from the program. Sometimes the logics are useful for creating cycles of execution to reach final value.

The programmers can enhance their capacity to understand the various options, operations and system available in C–language and the limitations of various statement.

The following programs create fun or a game for the programers to make variations in C–language.

Program 23–1

```
/*increament operator*/
main()
{
    int a,b,c,d;
    clrscr();
    a = 7;
    b = 18;
    c = (a++) – b;
    c++;
    d = (++a) – b;
    ++d;
    printf("c = %d , d = %d\n",c,d);
}
```

Program 23–2

```
/*arithmetic statement*/
main()
{
    int p,x,y;
    clrscr();
    x = 3;
    y = 4;
    p = x * 100 / y * 20;
    x = p * 2;
    p = p / 30;
    printf("x = %d , y = %d,p = %d \n",x,y,p);
}
```

Program 23–3

```
/*if statement*/
main()
{
    int a,b ,c;
    clrscr();
    printf("enter values of a & b\n");
    scanf("%d%d",&a,&b);
    if(a>b);
    {
            c = a + b;
    }
    printf("c = %d \n",c);
}
```

Program 23–4

```
/*if statement*/
main()
{
    int a,b,c;
    clrscr();
    printf("enter the value of a & b\n");
    scanf("%d%d",&a,&b);
    if(a>b)
            c = a + b;
    else
            c = a – b;
            c = a * b;
    printf("c = %d \n",c);
}
```

Program 23–5

```
/*DO....WHILE   STATEMENT*/
main()
{
    int a=15,b = 13,c=1;
    clrscr();
    do
    {
            ++a;
            b += 2;
            printf("Value :- %d %d\n",a,b);
    }while(++c<15);
}
```

Program 23–6

```
/*EXPLAIN THE  RESULTS  OF  THE  PROGRAM*/
/*FOR STATEMENT*/
main()
{
    int i,n=5;
    for(i=0;i<=n;++i);
    {
            printf("i = %d\n",i);
    }
}
```

Program 23–7

```
/*EXPLAIN  THE  RESULTS  OF  THE  PROGRAM*/
/*FOR STATEMENT*/
main()
{
    int i,n = 15;
    clrscr();
    for(i=1;i<=n;++i)
    {
            i +=2;
            printf("i = %d\n",i);
    }
}
```

Program 23–8

```
/*EXPLAIN  THE  RESULTS  OF  THE  PROGRAM*/
/*FOR  STATEMENT*/
main()
{
    int i;
    clrscr();
    for(i=1;i<=20;i=i*2)
    {
            printf("i = %d\n",i);
    }
}
```

Program 23–9

```
/*FIND THE  RESULTS  OF  THE  PROGRAM*/
main()
{
    int i=5,x=2;
    clrscr();
```

```
    for(;i<15;i=i+2)
    {
            x = x * i;
    }
     printf("x = % d\n",x);
}
```

Program 23–10

```
/*FIND THE   RESULTS   OF THE   PROGRAM*/
main()
{
    int i,sum=0;
    clrscr();
    for(i=1;i==5;i+=2)
    {
            sum = sum + i;
    }
     printf("sum = %d\n",sum);
}
```

Program 23–11

```
/*FIND THE   RESULTS    OF THE    PROGRAM*/
main()
{
    int i,sum=0;
    clrscr();
    for(i=1;i!=5;i+=2)
    {
            sum = sum + i;
    }
     printf("sum = %d\n",sum);
}
```

Program 23–12

```
/*WRITE    OUTPUT    OF THE    PROGRAM*/
main()
{
    int i,sum=0;
    clrscr();
    for(i=1;i<10;)
    {
            sum = sum + i;
            printf("sum = %d\n", sum);
    }
}
```

Program 23–13

```
/*WRITE OUTPUT OF THE PROGRAM*/
main()
{
    int i,sum=0;
    clrscr();
    for(i=1;i>10;++i)
    {
        sum = sum + i;
    }
    printf("sum = %d\n",sum);
}
```

Program 23–14

```
/*WRITE OUTPUT OF THE PROGRAM*/
main()
{
    int p=1,sum=0;
    clrscr();
    while(p < 20)
    {
        p++;
        sum += p++;
    }
    printf("sum = %d\n",sum);
}
```

Program 23–15

```
/*WRITE OUTPUT OF THE PROGRAM*/
main()
{
    int i=0;
    clrscr();
    while(1)
    {
        printf("i = %d\n",i+1);
        if(i++ == 15)
            break;
    }
}
```

Program 23–16

```
/*WRITE OUTPUT OF THE PROGRAM*/
main()
{
```

```
    int a,b;
    clrscr();
    printf("enter two values of a & b\n");
    scanf("%d%d",a,b);
    printf("a =%d,b =%d\n",a,b);
}
```

Program 23–17

```
/*WRITE OUTPUT OF THE PROGRAM*/
main()
{
    int i=0;
    clrscr();
    while(0)
    {
            printf("i = %d\n",i+1);
            if(i++ == 15)
                    break;
    }
}
```

Program 23–18

```
/*WRITE OUTPUT OF THE PROGRAM*/
main()
{
    int a=17,b=13;
    int c,d,e;
    clrscr();
    c = a > b;
    d = a==b;
    e = a<=b;
    printf("c = %d,d = %d,e = %d",c,d,e);
}
```

Program 23–19

```
/*WRITE OUTPUT OF THE PROGRAM*/
main()
{
    int i=3;
    clrscr();
    do
    {
            i += 2;
            printf("i = %d\n",i-=0.5);
    }while(i!=15);
}
```

Program 23–20

```
/*WRITE  OUTPUT  OF THE  PROGRAM*/
main()
{
    int a,b,c,d;
    clrscr();
    a = 198;
    b = 22;
    c = a / b + 2;
    b = b / 3;
    a = ++a/4;
    d = a/++b;
    printf("a = %d,b = %d,c = %d, d= %d \n",a,b,c,d);
}
```

Program 23–21

```
/*WRITE  OUTPUT  OF THE  PROGRAM*/
main()
{
    int sum=0,i,n=4;
    clrscr();
    for(i=1;i<=n;++n)
    {
            sum +=2;
            printf("i = %d,sum = %d\n",i,sum);
    }
}
```

Program 23–22

```
/*WRITE  OUTPUT  OF THE  PROGRAM*/
main()
{
    int sum=0,i,n=20;
    clrscr();
    for(i=1;i<=n;i+=2)
    {
            sum +=i++;
            – –n;
            printf("i = %d,sum = %d\n",i,sum);
    }
}
```

Program 23–23

```
/*WRITE  OUTPUT  OF THE  PROGRAM*/
main()
```

```
{
    int sum=0,i,n=20;
    clrscr();
    for(i=1;i<=n;++i)
    {
            sum +=2;
            – – n;
            ++i;
    }
    printf("i = %d,sum = %d\n",i,sum);
}
```

Program 23–24

```
/*WRITE OUTPUT OF THE PROGRAM*/
main()
{
    int a;
    char c;
    clrscr();
    c = 'a';
    for(a = c;a<='z';a+=2)
    {
            c=a;
            printf("%10d  %10c\n",c,c);
    }
}
```

Program 23–25

```
/*WRITE OUTPUT OF THE PROGRAM*/
main()
{
    int i=0;
    char c[]={"he is good"};
    while(c[i] != ' ')
    {
            printf("%c",c[i]);
            ++i;
    }
}
```

Program 23–26

```
/*WRITE OUTPUT OF THE PROGRAM*/
main()
{
    int a[5]={6,–2,13,22,9};
```

```
    int i;
    clrscr();
    for(i=1;i<=3;++i)
    {
            printf("%d ",a[i]*=2);
    }
}
```

Program 23–27

```
/*WRITE OUTPUT OF THE PROGRAM*/
main()
{
    int a[20],i,j;
    clrscr();
    i = 1;
    j = i++;
    a[i] = 5,a[j]=++a[i];
    printf("a = %d ",a[i] * a[j]);
}
```

Program 23–28

```
/*WRITE OUTPUT OF THE PROGRAM*/
main()
{
    int a[20],i,j;
    clrscr();
    i = 1;
    j = i++;
    a[i] = 5,a[j]=++a[i];
    printf("a = %d ",a[i] * a[j]);
}
```

Program 23–29

```
/*WRITE OUTPUT OF THE PROGRAM*/
main()
{
    int a[10] = {-2,13,4,19,6,2};
    int i=1,y,z,j=1;
    clrscr();
    a[i] = a[i++];
    y = ++a[j];
    z = a[j+1]++;
    printf("y = %d ,z = %d\n",y,z);
    for(i=0;i<5;++i)
    printf("a[%d] = %d\n",i+1,a[i]);
}
```

Program 23–30

```
/*WRITE  OUTPUT  OF  THE  PROGRAM*/
main()
{
    int a[5] = {–5,6,9,13,2};
    int b[5] = {2,6,1,3,7};
    int i;
    clrscr();
    for(i=0;i<5;++i)
    {
            a[i] += b[i];
    }
    for(i=1;i<=5;++i)
    printf("%d  ",--a[i]);
}
```

Program 23–31

```
/*WRITE  OUTPUT  OF  THE  PROGRAM*/
main()
{
    char c[ ] = {"good"};
    int i;int j=1;
    clrscr();
    for(i=0;i<4;++i)
    c[i] = c[i]+++j;
    puts(c);
}
```

Program 23–32

```
/*WRITE  OUTPUT  OF  THE  PROGRAM*/
calculate(a,b,c)
int a[1], b[1], c[1];
{
    a[1] = ++a[1];
    b[1] = a[1] + 3;
    c[1] = a[1] * b[2]++;
}
main()
{
    int x[1],y[1],z;
    x[1]=4,y[1]=13;
    calculate(x,y,z);
    printf("x = %d,y = %d,z = %d\n",x,y,z);
}
```

Program 23–33

```
/*WRITE  OUTPUT  OF THE  PROGRAM*/
int x,y,z;
cal()
{
    int x = 2,y = 3;
    y = y++;
    z = x + y;
}
main()
{
    clrscr();
    cal();
    printf("x = %d,y = %d,z = %d\n",x,y,z);
}
```

Program 23–34

```
/* WRITE THE OUTPUT OF THE PROGRAM*/
main()
{
    int a = 9, b,*ptr1,*ptr2;
    *ptr1=a;
    ptr2=ptr1;
    ptr1=&b;
    (*ptr2)++;
    a += 3;
    printf("a = %d, *ptr1 = %d, *ptr2 = %d,b= %d\n",a,*ptr1,*ptr2,b);
}
```

Program 23–35

```
/* WRITE  THE OUTPUT OF THE PROGRAM */
main()
{
    int a = 9, b,*ptr1,*ptr2;
    clrscr();
    *ptr1=++a;
    ptr2=ptr1;
    ptr1=&b;
    b = *ptr1;
    b++;
    (*ptr2)++;
    printf("a = %d, *ptr1 = %d, *ptr2 = %d,b= %d\n",a,*ptr1,*ptr2,b);
}
```

Program 23–36

```
main()
{
    int a = 9, b,*ptr1,*ptr2;
    clrscr();
    *ptr1 = a;
    ptr2 = ptr1;
    b = *ptr1 ;
    ptr1=&b;
    b +=2;
    (*ptr2)++;
    a += 3;
    printf("a = %d, *ptr1 = %d, *ptr2 = %d,b= %d\n",a,*ptr1,*ptr2,b);
}
```

Program 23–37

```
main()
{
    int a = 9, b,*ptr1,*ptr2;
    clrscr();
    *ptr1 = ++a;
    b=*ptr1 ;
    ++b;
    ptr2=&b;
    (*ptr2)++;
    a += 3;
    printf("a = %d, *ptr1 = %d, *ptr2 = %d,b= %d\n",a,*ptr1,*ptr2,b);
}
```

Program 23–38

```
f(i)
int *i;
{
    (*i)++;
    *i+= 5;
}
main()
{
    int a = 9,*ptr1;
    clrscr();
    *ptr1 = a;
    ++(*ptr1);
    f(ptr1);
    printf("a = %d, *ptr1 = %d\n",a,*ptr1);
}
```

Program 23–39

```
/* WRITE THE OUTPUT OF THE PROGRAM*/
f(int *i)
{
    int z,z1;
    z = *i++;
    z1 = *i++;
     printf("z = %d, z1 = %d\n",z,z1);
}
main()
{
    int a[5] = {-6,9,10,5,4};
    clrscr();
    f(a);
}
```

Program 23–40

```
/*WRITE  OUTPUT OF THE  PROGRAM*/
main()
{
    char c[] = {"good"};
    int i;int j=1;
    clrscr();
    for(i=0;i<4;++i)
    c[i] = c[i]+++j;
    puts(c);
}
```

Program 23–41

```
/*WRITE  OUTPUT OF  THE PROGRAM*/
main()
{
    int c[4] = {12,34,2,7};
    int i;int j=1;
    clrscr();
    for(i=0;i<4;++i)
    {
            c[i] = c[i]+ ++j;
            printf("%d  ",c[i]);
    }
}
```

Program 23–42

```
/*WRITE  OUTPUT  OF  THE PROGRAM*/
main()
```

```
{
    int c[4] = {12,34,2,7};
    int i;int j=1;
    clrscr();
    for(i=0;i<4;++i)
    {
            c[i] = c[i] – ++j;
            printf("%d  ",c[i]);
    }
}
```

Program 23–43

```
/*WRITE  OUTPUT OF  THE  PROGRAM*/
calculate(a,b,c)
int a[1], b[1], c[1];
{
    a[1] = ++a[1];
    b[1] = a[1] + 3;
    c[1] = a[1] * b[1]++;
}
main()
{
    int x[1],y[1],z[1];
    clrscr();
    x[1]=4,y[1]=13;
    calculate(x,y,z);
    printf("x = %d,y = %d,z = %d\n",x[1],y[1],z[1]);
}
```

Program 23–44

```
/*WRITE THE OUTPUT OF THE PROGRAM*/
f(i)
int *i;
{
    (*i)++;
    *i+++= 5;
}
main()
{
    int a = 9,*ptr1;
    clrscr();
    *ptr1 = a;
    ++(*ptr1);
    f(ptr1);
    printf("a = %d, *ptr1 = %d\n",a,*ptr1);
}
```

Program 23–45

```
/* WRITE THE OUTPUT OF THE PROGRAM */
f(int *i)
{
    int z,z1;
    z += *i++;
    z1 = *i++;
     printf("z = %d, z1 = %d\n",z,z1);
}
main()
{
    int a[5] = {-6,9,10,5,4};
    clrscr();
    f(a);
}
```

Program 23–46

```
/* WRITE THE OUTPUT OF THE PROGRAM */
/*find the results*/
int a=4;
compute()
{
    int c;
    c = ++a * a * 2;
    printf("value is %d",c);
}
main()
{
    int a = 5;
    ++a;
    clrscr();
    compute();
}
```

Program 23–47

```
/* WRITE THE OUTPUT OF THE PROGRAM */
/*static & automatic*/
compute()
{
    int a=5;
    static int b=3;
    b = b+3;
    printf("value is %d,%d,%d\n",a,b,a* b++);
}
```

```
main()
{
    int k;
    clrscr();
    for(k=1;k<=4;++k)
    compute();
}
```

Program 23–48

```
/* WRITE THE OUTPUT OF THE PROGRAM */
/*register varibles*/
main()
{
    register int x=9;
    int i;
    clrscr();
    for(i=1;i<=20;i++)
    printf("value is %d\n",x++);
}
```

Program 23–49

```
/* WRITE THE OUTPUT OF THE PROGRAM */
/*string*/
main()
{
    char c='*';
    int i,j;
    clrscr();
    for(i=1;i<=10;i++)
    {
     for(j=i;j>=1;– –j)
    {
            printf("%c",c);
    }
    printf("\n");
    }
    for(i=10;i>=1;–  – i)
    {
    for(j=i;j>=1;– –j)
    {
    printf("%c",c);
    }
    printf("\n");
    }
}
```

Program 23–50

```
/* WRITE THE OUTPUT OF THE PROGRAM */
/*string*/
main()
{
     int c=0;
     int i,j;
     clrscr();
     for(i=1;i<=10;i++)
     {
      c– –;
       for(j=i;j>=1;– –j)
     {
               printf("%c",c++);
     }
     printf("\n");
     }
     for(i=10;i>=1;– – i)
     {
               c– –;
                for(j=i;j>=1;– –j)
               {
                         printf("%c",– – c);
               }
               printf("\n");
     }
}
```

Program 23–51

```
/* WRITE THE OUTPUT OF THE PROGRAM */
/*DO....WHILE STATEMENT*/
main()
{
     int a=15,b = 13,c=1,n=15;
     clrscr();
     do
     {
               ++a;
               b– –;
               printf("Value :- %d %d\n",a,b);
     }while(c++ <= – –n);
}
```

Program 23–52

```
/* WRITE THE OUTPUT OF THE PROGRAM */
/*DO....WHILE STATEMENT*/
main()
{
    int a=15,b = 13,c=1,n=15;
    clrscr();
    do
    {
        ++a;
        ++a;
        b– –;
        printf("Value :- %d %d\n",a,b);
    }while(c++ <=– ––n);
}
```

Program 23–53

```
/* WRITE THE OUTPUT OF THE PROGRAM */
main()
{
    static int a[3] = {2,4,6};
    int *ptr[3];
    int i;
    clrscr();
    for(i=0;i<=2;i++)
    *ptr[i]=++a[i];
    printf("\n");
    for(i=0;i<=2;i++)
    printf("%d\t",*ptr[i]);
}
```

Program 23–54

```
/* WRITE THE OUTPUT OF THE PROGRAM */
main()
{
    static int a[5]={2,4,6,8,10};
    static int b[5]={1,3,5,7,9 };
    int i;
    clrscr();
    for(i=1;i<5;++i)
    {
        a[i] = ++a[i] * b[i-1];
    }
    for(i=0;i<5;++i)
    {
```

```
            printf("a[%d] = %d\n",i,a[i]);
    }
}
```

Program 23–55

```
/* WRITE THE OUTPUT OF THE PROGRAM */
main()
{
    static int a[3] = {2,4,6};
    int *ptr[3];
    int i;
    clrscr();
    for(i=0;i<=2;i++)
    *ptr[i]=++a[i];
    printf("\n");
    for(i=0;i<=2;i++)
    printf("%d\t",*ptr[i]);
}
```

Program 23–56

```
/* WRITE THE OUTPUT OF THE PROGRAM */
disp(int x[15],int n)
{
    int i;
    for(i=0;i<n;++i)
    printf("%5d",x[i]);
}
main()
{
     int a[5]={2,4,6,8,10};
     int b[6]={1,2,4,2,3,1};
    int i;
    clrscr();
    a[++b[2]] = 9;
     i=4;
    a[b[++i]]=22;
    printf("The array A  is\n");
    disp(a,5);
    printf("\nThe array B  is\n");
    disp(b,6);
}
```

Program 23–57

```
/* WRITE THE OUTPUT OF THE PROGRAM */
main()
```

```
{
int i=4,j=5,k=6;
clrscr();
 i -= –j– –   – – –k;
printf("i= %d,j=%d,k=%d\n",i,j,k);
}
```

Program 23–58

```
/*input argument*/
int i;
modify(a)
int a[5];
{
   for(i=0;i<=4;i++)
   {
         a[i] *= 2;
   }
   return(a);
}
main()
{
   int a[]={2,4,6,8,5},x;
   clrscr();
   printf("The original matrix is \n");
    for(i=0;i<=4;i++)
   printf("%5d",a[i]);
    for(i=0;i<=4;i++)
   x = modify(a);
   printf("\nThe new matrix is \n");
   for(i=0;i<=4;i++)
   printf("%5d",a[i]);
}
```

Program 23–59

```
/*to accept a string and change the beginning letter of a string*/
main()
{
   char *string = "this is a string.";
   clrscr();
   *string—= 32;
    printf("%s",string);
   return 0;
}
```

Program 23–60

```
/*a program to convert a string from lowercase to uppercase*/
main()
{
    char *string = "this is a string";
    int length, i;
    length = strlen(string);
    for (i=0; i<length; i++)
    {
            string[i] = toupper(string[i]);
    }
    printf("%s",string);
    return 0;
}
```

Program 23–61

```
/*to read set of lines and find char,line,tabs,*/
/*new line character in the given text*/
#define MAX 20
main()
{
    char line[MAX];
    char ln1[MAX];
    int nch;
    int nl;
    char ch;
    int number(char line[]);
    int count (char ln1[]);
    cout<<"Enter a set of lines and terminated with @ \n";
    cout<<endl;
    cin.get(line,MAX,'@');//reading string
    cin.get(ln1,MAX,'\n');
    nch=number(line)-1;
    nl=number(ln1)-1;
    cout<<"output from the array "<<endl;
    cout<<line<<endl;
    cout<<"output from the array "<<endl;
    cout<<ln1<<endl;
    cout<<"number of characters ="<<nch<<endl;
    cout<<"number of lines = "<<nl<<endl;
}
int number (char a[])
{
    int i;
```

```
    i=0;
    while(a[i]!='\0')
            ++i;
    return(i);
}
int count (char b[])
{
    int j;
    j=0;
}
```

Program 23–62

```
main()
{
    int i = 2;
    clrscr();
    while(– –i >0)
    {
            printf("%d",i– –);
    }
}
```

Program 23–63

```
#define SQR(x) x*x
#define CUBE(x)x*SQR(x)
main()
{
    int i = 3,j=2;
    clrscr();
    printf("%d\n%d",SQR(i+j),CUBE(i–j));
}
```

Program 23–64

```
# include "conio.h"
# include "dos.h"
# include "ctype.h"
main()
{
    int c;
    clrscr();
    printf("Go on pressing space bar to get acquiated character set !\n\n\n");
    for(c=0;getch()&&c<128;c++)
    {
            if(c==26) continue;
                    printf("The chracter %d i.e. %c is a ",c,c);
```

```
            if(isdigit(c))
                    printf("DIGIT !\n");
            else
            if(islower(c))
                     printf("LOWER ALPHABET !\n");
            else
            if(isupper(c))
                    printf("UPPER ALPHABET !\n");
            else
            if(isspace(c))
                    printf("WHITE SPACE CHARACTER !\n");
            else
            if(iscntrl(c))
                    printf("CONTROL CHARACTER !\n");
            else
            if(ispunct(c))
            printf("PUNCTUATION MARK !\n");
            else
                    printf("E R R O R  ! \n");
    }
    printf("\n\n N O W    S T O P  ! ");
}
```

Program 23–65

```
# include "conio.h"
# include "dos.h"
# include "ctype.h"
main()
{
    int c;
    clrscr();
    printf("Go on pressing space bar to get acquiated  character set !\n\n\n");
    for(c=0;getch()&&c<128;c++)
    {
    if(c==26) continue;
            printf("The chracter %d i.e. %c is a ",c,c);
    if(isdigit(c))
             printf("DIGIT !\n");
    else
    if(islower(c))
             printf("LOWER ALPHABET !\n");
    else
    if(isupper(c))
            printf("UPPER ALPHABET !\n");
```

```
	else
	if(isspace(c))
		printf("WHITE SPACE CHARACTER !\n");
	else
	if(iscntrl(c))
		printf("CONTROL CHARACTER !\n");
	else
	if(ispunct(c))
		printf("PUNCTUATION MARK !\n");
	else
		printf("E R R O R  ! \n");
	}
	printf("\n\n N O W    S T O P  ! ");
}
```

Program 23–66

```
main()
{
	int num;
	clrscr();
	printf("enter two digit number\n");
	scanf("%d",&num);
	printf("converted to character is %c",num);
}
```

Program 23–67

```
/*input a number and display it an reverse order*/
main()
{
	int num;
	long int revnum,digit;
	clrscr();
	printf("enter number\n");
	scanf("%d",&num);
	revnum = 0;
	while(num>0)
	{
		digit = num%10;
		num= num/10;
		revnum = revnum * 10 + digit;
	}
	printf("Reverse order is %ld",revnum);
}
```

Program 23–68

```
/*a program to swap the given number*/
exchange(int x,int y)
{
    int temp;
    temp = x;
    x = y;
    y = temp;
}
main()
{
    int a,b;
    clrscr();
    printf("enter values for a & b\n");
    scanf("%d%d",&a,&b);
    exchange(a,b);
    printf("%d  %d",a,b);
}
```

Program 23–69

```
main()
{
    long int num,sum=0;
    for(num=0;num<=num;++num)
    {
        sum=sum+num;
        printf("%ld\n",sum);
        getch();
    }
}
```

Program 23–70

```
main()
{
    long int num,sum=0;
    for(num=1000;num>=num;– –num)
    {
        sum=sum+num;
        printf("%ld\n",sum);
        getch();
    }
}
```

Program 23–71

```
main()
{
    long int num,sum=0;
    for(num=1000;num>=num;– –num)
    {
        sum=sum+num;
        printf("%ld\n",sum);
        getch();
    }
}
```

Program 23–72

```
main()
{
    long int num,sum=0;
    for(num=1000;num>=num;– –num)
    {
        sum=num – sum;
        printf("%ld\n",sum);
        getch();
    }
}
```

Program 23–73

```
main()
{
    long int num,sum=0;
    for(num=0;num<=num;++num)
    {
        sum=num – sum;
        printf("%ld\n",sum);
        getch();
    }
}
```

Program 23–74

```
// A PROGRAM TO DISPLAY THE NUMBERS BETWEEN 0 TO 9 AS WELL AS 9 TO 0
// SIMULTANEOUSLY ONE BY ONE
#include <iostream.h>
#include <conio.h>
void main(void)
{
    clrscr();
    for(int i=0, j=9; i<=9; i++, j– –)
```

```
	{
		cout << " i = " << i << '\t' << " j = " << j << endl;
	}
}
```

Program 23–75

```
// PROGRAM TO FIND SQUARE OF NUMBERS FROM 1 TO 100
#include <iostream.h>
#include <conio.h>
void main(void)
{
	clrscr();
	int sum = 0;
	for(int i=0; i<=10; i++)
	{
		sum += i * i;
		cout << " i = " << i << '\t' << " sum = " << sum << endl;
	}
}
```

Program 23–76

```
// PROGRAM TO FIND SQUARE OF NUMBERS FROM 1 TO 100
#include <iostream.h>
#include <conio.h>
void main(void)
{
	clrscr();
	for(int i=0, j=0; i<=10; i++,j *= 2)
	{
		cout << " i = " << i << '\t' << " j = " << j << endl;
	}
}
```

Program 23–77

```
// USING SETW MANIPULATOR
#include <iostream.h>
#include <iomanip.h>
#include <conio.h>
void main(void)
{
	int a,b,c,d;
	a = 100;
	b = 200;
	c = 200;
	d = 100;
	clrscr();
	cout << setw(5) << a << setw(5) << b << setw(19) << c << setw(5) << d << endl;
	cout << setw(6) << a << setw(6) << b << setw(14) << c << setw(6) << d << endl;
	cout << setw(7) << a << setw(7) << b << setw(9)  << c << setw(7) << d << endl;
	cout << setw(8) << a << setw(8) << b << setw(4)  << c << setw(8) << d << endl;
}
```

Program 23–78

```
#include<iostream.h>
double const pi=22.0/7.0;
class volume
{
    float v;
    public :
            volume(){v=0;};
            volume(float r){v=4.0/3.0*pi*r*r*r;};
            volume(float r,float l){v=2.0*pi*r*r*l;};
            volume(float l,float b,float h){v=l*b*h;};
            void show(){cout<<v<<endl;};
};
main()
{
    float r,l,b,h;
    volume v1;
    cout<<"Enter the radius of the sphere\n";
    cin>>r;
    volume v2(r);
    cout<<"Enter the radius and length of cylinder\n";
    cin>>r>>l;
    volume v3(r,l);
    cout<<"Enter the length ,breadth and height of the box\n";
    cin>>l>>b>>h;
    volume v4(l,b,h);
    cout<<"The volume is initialized  ";
    v1.show();
    cout<<"The volume of the sphere is  ";
    v2.show();
    cout<<"The volume of the cylinder is  ";
    v3.show();
    cout<<"The volume of the box is  ";
    v4.show();
}
```

Program 23–79

```
// Long - term fixed deposite system
#include <iostream.h>
class fixed_deposit
{
        long int p_amount;
        int years;
        float rate;
```

```
            float R_value;
    public:
            fixed_deposit(){ };
            fixed_deposit(long int p,int y=5,float r = 0.12);
            void display(void);
};
fixed_deposit :: fixed_deposit(long int p,int y,float r)
{
    p_amount = p;
    years = y;
    rate = r;
    R_value = p_amount;
    for(int i=1; i<=y; ++i)
            R_value = R_value * (1.0 + r);
}
void fixed_deposit::display()
{
        cout<<" \n " << " Principal amount = " << p_amount << " \n "
              << " Return value    = " << R_value  << "          \n ";
}
main()
{
    //fixed_deposit  fd1,fd2,fd3;
    long int p,p1,p2;
    int y,y1;
    float r;
    int R;
    cout << " Enter amount,period,interest rate(in percent)" << " \n ";
    cin >> p >> y >> r;
    fixed_deposit  fd1(p,y,r);
    cout << " Enter amount,period" << "\n";
    cin >> p1 >> y1 ;
    fixed_deposit  fd2(p1,y1);
    cout << " \nEnter amount " << " \n ";
    cin >> p2 ;
    fixed_deposit  fd3(p2);
    cout << " \n Deposit 1 ";
    fd1.display();
    cout << " \n Deposit 2";
    fd2.display();
    cout << " \n Deposit 3";
    fd3.display();
}
```

additions to trial program

Program 23–80

```
//EXPLAIN THE RESULTS OF THE PROGRAM FOR STATEMENT
#include<iostream.h>
#include<conio.h>
main()
{
        int i,n = 15;
        clrscr();
        for(i=1;i<=n;++i)
        {
                i += ++i;
                cout<<"i =  "<<i<<endl;
        }
}
```

Program 23–81

```
//EXPLAIN THE RESULTS OF THE PROGRAM FOR STATEMENT
#include<iostream.h>
#include<conio.h>
main()
{
        int i,n = 15;
        clrscr();
        for(i=1;i<=n;++i)
        {
                i += i++;
                cout<<"i =  "<<i<<endl;
        }
}
```

Program 23–82

```
#include<iostream.h>
#include<conio.h>
main()
{
        float x[2][3] ={ {1.1,1.2,1.3},{2.1,2.2,2.3} };
        clrscr();
        cout<<"value  is "<<*(*x+1);
}
```

Program 23–83

```
//WRITE OUTPUT OF THE PROGRAM
#include<iostream.h>
```

```
#include<conio.h>
main()
{
          int i=0;
          char c[]={"she is good"};
          clrscr();
          while(c[i] != '\0')
          {
                    cout<<c[i];
                    ++i;
          }
}
```

Program 23–84

```
#include<iostream.h>
#include<conio.h>
main()
{
          union test
          {
                    int x;
                              char ch[2];
           };
  union test t;
  t.x = 10;
  t.ch[0] = 3;
  t.ch[1] = 2;
  cout<<"value of ch[0] is "<<t.ch[0]
             <<" \n and ch[1]is "<<ch[1]<<" \n x is "<<x;
}
```

Program 23–85

```
//pointer to type void
#include<iostream.h>
#include<conio.h>
main()
{
          int intvar;
          float flovar;
          clrscr();
          int *ptrint;
          float *ptrflo;
          void *ptrvoid;
          ptrint = &intvar; //right int* to int* variable
          ptrflo = &flovar; //right float* to float * variable
          //  ptrint = &flovar; this is incorrect
```

```
        // ptrflo = &intvar; this is incorrect
        ptrvoid = &intvar;
        ptrvoid = &flovar;
        cout<<"value of integer pointer is : "<<*ptrint<<endl;
        cout<<"value of float   pointer is : "<<*ptrflo<<endl;
        cout<<"value of void    pointer is : "<<ptrvoid<<endl;
}
```

Program 23–86

```
//testing using 'this' pointer
#include<iostream.h>
#include<conio.h>
class test
{
        private:
                int alpha;
        public:
                void testdata()
                {
                        this->alpha = 12;
                        cout<<this->alpha;
                }
};
main()
{
        test t;
        clrscr();
        t.testdata();
}
```

Program 23–87

```
//overloading function
#include<iostream.h>
#include<conio.h>
void funct();
void funct(char);
void funct(char,int);
main()
{
        clrscr();
         funct();
         funct('@');
         funct('$',15);
}
void funct()
{
```

```
        for(int i=5;i<15;i++)
                        cout<<'*';
  cout<<endl;
}
void funct(char ch)
{
        for(int i=0;i<20;i++)
                        cout<<ch;
  cout<<endl;
}
void funct(char ch,int n)
{
        for(int i=5;i<n;i++)
                        cout<<ch;
  cout<<endl;
}
```

Program 23–88

```
//use of void pointer for array
#include<iostream.h>
#include<conio.h>
main()
{
        int num[3]={11,22,33};
        void *ptrarr;
        for(i=0;i<3;i++)
        {
                ptrarr = &num[i];
        }
        cout<<"pointer array \n";
        for(i=0;i<3;i++)
        {
   cout<<ptrarr<<endl;
        }
}
```

Program 23–89

```
#include<iostream.h>
#include<conio.h>
main()
{
        float const pi = 22.0/7.0;
        clrscr();
        enum {rho=8300,h=20};
        cout<<"Enter the inner and outer diameter \n";
        int d1,d2;
```

```
        cin>>d1>>d2;
        float w = rho * pi * h * (d2 * d2 - d1 * d1);
        cout<<" Weight of cylinder = "<<w;
}
```

Program 23–91

```
#include<iostream.h>
main()
{
        int sum = 0;
        for(int i=1;i<=10;i++)
        {
                if(i==5)
                        continue;
                        sum += i;
        }
        cout<<sum<<endl;
}
```

Program 23–92

```
#include<iostream.h>
main()
{
        int sum = 0;
        cout<<"enter value of j \n";
        int j;
        cin>>j;
        for(int i=1;i<=10;i++)
        {
                if(j<5)
                {
                        cout<<"value is less then 5 ";
                        break;
                }
                sum += i+j;
                cout<<" i is  "<<i<<endl;cout<<"sum is "<<sum<<endl;
        }
}
```

Program 23–93

```
#include<iostream.h>
#define PASS 1
#define FAIL 0
main()
{
```

```
        cout<<"enter marks \n";
        int m;
        cin>>m;
        int ans;
        if(m>35)
        {
          ans = PASS;
          cout<<ans;
        }
        else
        {
        ans = FAIL;
        cout<<ans;
        }
}
```

Program 23–94

```
#include<iostream.h>
main()
{
        int sum = 0;
        for(int i=0;i<=5;i++)
        {
        sum += i;
        if(i==2)
                        continue;
        }
        cout<<sum<<endl;
}
```

Program 23–95

```
#include<iostream.h>
float compute(float p,float q)
{
        float c = p * q;
        return(c+10);
}
main()
{
        float p,q;
        cout<<"enter values of p , q\n";
        cin>>p>>q;
        float z = compute(p,q);
        cout<<"result is "<<z;
```

```
}
```

Program 23–96

```
#include<iostream.h>
#include<conio.h>
main()
{
        clrscr();
        int a=15,*ptr,b;
        ptr = &a;
        b = *ptr;
        ++a;
        cout<<"value of a  = "<<a<<"\nvalue of *ptr ="<<*ptr
           <<"\nvalue of b ="<<b;
}
```

Program 23–97

```
#include<iostream.h>
#include<conio.h>
main()
{
        clrscr();
        char ch = '$';
        char *cptr = &ch;
        cout<<ch<<*cptr<<endl;
        ch = '#';
        cout<<ch<<*cptr<<endl;
        ch = '?';
        cout<<ch<<*cptr<<endl;
}
```

Program 23–98

```
#include<iostream.h>
#include<conio.h>
main()
{
        clrscr();
        int a,b;
        int *ptr1;
         a = 5;
         ptr1 = &a;
         b = (*ptr1) * 5;
         cout<<"value of a "<<a<<"\nvalue of b = "<<b;
         cout<<"\nvalue of *ptr1 "<<*ptr1;
```

```
}
```

Program 23–99

```
#include<iostream.h>
#include<conio.h>
exchange(int *ptr1,int *ptr2)
{
        int temp;
        temp = *ptr1;
        *ptr1 = *ptr2;
        *ptr2 = temp;
        return(temp);
}
main()
{
        clrscr();
        int a = 5,b=99;
        int *pt1 = &a;
        int *pt2 = &b;
        exchange(pt1,pt2);
        cout<<"value of a = "<<a<<"\nvalue of b = "<<b;
}
```

Program 23–100

```
#include<iostream.h>
#include<conio.h>
        int i;
class array
 {
                int num[10];
        public:
                array();
                void set(int n[10]);
                void show();
                array operator+(array ob2);
                array operator-(array ob2);
                int operator==(array ob2);
};
array::array()
{
        for(i=0;i<10;i++)
                        num[i]=0;
}
void array::set(int *n)
{
```

```
        for(i=0;i<10;i++)
                        num[i] = n[i];
}
array array::operator+(array ob2)
{
        array temp;
        for(i=0;i<10;i++)
                        temp.num[i] = num[i] + ob2.num[i];
        return temp;
}
array array::operator-(array ob2)
{
        array temp;
        for(i=0;i<10;i++)
                temp.num[i] = num[i] - ob2.num[i];
        return temp;
}
void array::show()
{
        for(i=0;i<10;i++)
                        cout<<num[i]<<' ';
        cout<<"\n";
}
int array::operator==(array ob2)
{
        if(num[i]==ob2.num[i])
                        return 1;
        else
                        return 0;
}
main()
{
        clrscr();
        array o1,o2,o3;
        int i[10]={1,2,3,4,5,6,7,8,9,10};
        o1.set(i);
        o2.set(i);
        o3 = o1 + o2;
        o3.show();
        o3 = o1 - o3;
        o3.show();
        if(o1==o2)
                cout<<" o1  equals o2\n";
        else
                cout<<" o1 not equals o2\n";
```

```
        if(o1==o3)
                cout<<" o1 equals o3\n";
        else
                    cout<<" o1 not equals o3\n";
        return 0;
}
```

Program 23–101

```
#include<iostream.h>
#include<conio.h>
class coord
{
                        int x,y;
        public:
                        coord() { x = 0;y = 0;}
                        coord(int i,int j){ x = i;y = j;}
                        void getval(int &i,int &j){i=x;j=y;}
                        coord operator++();
                        coord operator--();
};
coord coord::operator++()
{
                x++;
                y++;
                return *this;
}
coord coord::operator—()
{
                x--;
                y--;
                return *this;
}
main()
{
                clrscr();
                coord o1(10,10);
                int x,y;
                o1++;
                o1.getval(x,y);
                cout<<" x: "<<x<<" y: "<<y<<"\n";
                o1--;
                o1.getval(x,y);
                cout<<" x: "<<x<<" y: "<<y<<"\n";
                return 0;
```

```
}
```

Program 23–102

```
#include<iostream.h>
#include<conio.h>
class triangle
{
		int height,base;
	public:
			triangle(int h,int b)
			{
				height = h;base = b;
			}
			void draw();
};
void triangle::draw()
{
	int i,j,h,k;
	i = j = base-1;
	for(h=height-1;h;h--)
	{
  for(k=i;k;k--)
			cout<<' ';
	cout<<'*';
  if(j!=i)
		{
		for(k=j-i-1;k;k--)
		cout<<' ';
		cout<<'*';
		}
	   i--;
		cout<<'\n';
		}
		for(k=0;k<base;k++)
					cout<<'*';
		cout<<'\n';
}
main()
{
	clrscr();
	triangle t1(5,5),t2(10,10),t3(12,12);
	t1.draw();
	cout<<"press key to continue\n";
	getch();
	t2.draw();
	cout<<"press key to continue\n";
```

```
        getch();
        t3.draw();
        cout<<"press key to return \n";
        getch();
}
```

Program 23–103

```
//nested while loop
#include<iostream.h>
#include<conio.h>
#include<stdio.h>
main()
{
        int count = 3;
        char ch = '\0';
        while(count—>= 0)
        {
        while(ch=(char)getch()!='q')
        {
                cout<<"ch = "<<ch;
                if(ch=='x')
                        break;
         }
         puts("inner loop ends !");
        }
        puts("outer loop ends !");
}
```

Program 23–104

```
//switch statement
#include<iostream.h>
#include<conio.h>
main()
{
        clrscr();
        cout<<"enter any two number & operator\n";
        float a,b;
        char opr;
        cin>>a>>b>>opr;
        float c;
        switch(opr)
        {
                case '+' :
                case '-' :
                case '*' :
                case '/' :
```

```
            c = a / b;
            cout<<"value of c is :- "<<c<<endl;
        }
}
```

Program 23–105

```
//switch statement
#include<iostream.h>
#include<conio.h>
main()
{
        clrscr();
        cout<<"enter any two number & operator\n";
        float a,b;
        char opr;
        cin>>a>>b>>opr;
        float c;
        switch(opr)
        {
                case '+' :
                  c = a + b;
                case '-' :
                  c = a - b;
                case '*' :
                  c = a * b;
                case '/' :
                  c = a / b;
        }
        cout<<" value of c is :- "<<c<<endl;
}
```

Program 23–106

```
//switch statement
#include<iostream.h>
#include<conio.h>
main()
{
        clrscr();
        cout<<"enter any two number & operator\n";
        float a,b;
        char opr;
        cin>>a>>b>>opr;
        float c,e,f,d;
        switch(opr)
        {
```

```
            case '+' :
              c = a + b;
            case '-' :
              d = a - b;
            case '*' :
             e = a * b;
            case '/' :
             f = a / b;
    }
    cout<<" value of c is :- "<<c<<endl;
    cout<<" value of d is :- "<<d<<endl;
    cout<<" value of e is :- "<<e<<endl;
    cout<<" value of f is :- "<<f<<endl;
}
```

Program 20–61

```
//switch statement
#include<iostream.h>
#include<conio.h>
main()
{
    clrscr();
    cout<<"enter any two number & a / b\n";
    float a,b;
    char opr;
    cin>>a>>b>>opr;
    float c,d,p,q,x,y,o,k;
    char xor,yor;
    cout<<"enter the char of x / y "<<endl;
    cin>>xor;
    cout<<"enter the char of p / q "<<endl;
    cin>>yor;
    switch(opr)
    {
            case 'a' :
      c = a + b;
      switch(xor)
      {
             case 'x' :
                              d = a + b / c;
             break;
             case 'y' :
                              d = a * b / c;
             break;
      }
      case 'b' :
```

```
                k = a - b;
        switch(yor)
            {
                case 'p' :
                        o = a + b / d;
                break;
                case 'q' :
                        o = a * b / d;
                break;
            }
        }
    cout<<" value of c is :- "<<c<<endl;
    cout<<" value of d is :- "<<d<<endl;
    cout<<" value of k is :- "<<k<<endl;
    cout<<" value of o is :- "<<o<<endl;
}
```

Program 23–107

```
#include<iostream.h>
class  base
{
    protected:
                int x;
};
class dshow : private base
{

    private :
                int y;
    public :
                void showdata();
};
void dshow::showdata()
{
    cout<<x<<endl;
    cout<<y<<endl;
}
main()
{
    dshow ds;
    ds.showdata();
}
```

Program 23–108

```
#include<iostream.h>
#include<conio.h>
```

```
main()
{
        int x,y;
        clrscr();
  cout<<"Enter value of x\n";
  cin>>x;
          y = (x > 5 ? 3 : 4);
  cout<<" The value of y "<<y;
}
```

Program 23–109

```
#include<iostream.h>
#include<conio.h>
main()
{
        clrscr();
        float *p;
        p = new float (20);
        cout<<" value of p is = "<<*p;
        delete p;
        p = new float (30);
        cout<<" \n value of p is = "<<*p;
}
```

Program 23–110

```
#include<iostream.h>
#include<conio.h>
        main()
        {
                clrscr();
                char c;int i;
                c = 1;
                for(i=1;i<=50;i++)
                {
                        cout<<'\t'<<c;
                }
}
```

Program 23–111

```
#include<iostream.h>
#include<conio.h>
main()
{
        clrscr();
        char c;int i;
        c = 'A';
```

```
        int a;
        a = c;
        cout<<c<<'\t'<<a<<endl;
        for(i=1;i<=255;i++)
        {
                c =i;
                cout<<i<<'\t'<<c<<endl;
        }
}
```

Program 23–112

```
#include<iostream.h>
#include<conio.h>
main()
{
        clrscr();
        char ch1[] = {'M','E','E','T'};
        for(int i=0;i<=4;i++)
        {
                cout<<ch1[i];
        }
        cout<<endl;
        getch();
        for(i=0;i<=1;i++)
        {
                cout<<ch1[i];
        }
        getch();
}
```

Program 23–113

```
#include<iostream.h>
#include<conio.h>
main()
{
        clrscr();
        char ch1[] = {'A','G','A','I','N','S','T'};
        for(int i=0;i<7;i++)
        {
                cout<<ch1[i];
        }
        cout<<endl;
        getch();
        for(i=1;i<=4;i++)
        {
                cout<<ch1[i];
```

```
        }
        getch();
}
```

Program 20–114

```
#include<iostream.h>
#include<conio.h>
main()
{
        clrscr();
        char ch1[] = {'S','E','R','V','I','C','E'};
        for(int i=0;i<7;i++)
        {
                cout<<ch1[i];
        }
        cout<<endl;
        getch();
        for(i=3;i<7;i++)
        {
                cout<<ch1[i];
        }
        getch();
}
```

Program 23–115

```
#include<iostream.h>
#include<conio.h>
main()
{
        clrscr();
        int a = 100,*b,**c;
                b = &a;
                c = &b;
        cout<<a<<"\n"<<*b<<"\n"<<**c;
}
```

Program 23–116

```
#include<iostream.h>
#include<conio.h>
main()
{
        clrscr();
        int a,b,*ptr;
        ptr = &a;
                a = 9;
                b = *ptr;
```

```
            a++;
      cout<<"value of a = "<<a<<"\nvalue of b = "<<b
        <<"\nvalue of *ptr = "<<*ptr;
}
```

Program 23–117

```
#include<iostream.h>
#include<conio.h>
main()
{
      clrscr();
      int a,b,*ptr;
            ptr = &a;
            a = 9;
            b = *ptr;
            *ptr += 5;
      cout<<"value of a = "<<a<<"\nvalue of b = "<<b
        <<"\nvalue of *ptr = "<<*ptr;
}
```

Program 23–118

```
#include<iostream.h>
#include<conio.h>
main()
{
      int x = 5,y = 8;
      while(y < 10)
      {
            ++x;
            --y;
      }
      cout<<x<<y;
}
```

Program 23–119

```
//inline function
#include<iostream.h>
#include<conio.h>
inline multi(float a, float b)
{
            return(a * b);
}
inline div(float a , float b)
{
            return(a / b);
}
```

```
main()
{
        clrscr();
        cout<<"Enter Two Values "<<endl;
        float num1,num2;
        cin>>num1>>num2;
        cout<<multi(num1,num2)<<endl;
        cout<<div(num1,num2)<<endl;
}
```

Program 23–120

```
//default argument function
#include<iostream.h>
#include<conio.h>
void sum(int num1,int num2,int num3 = 10,int num4= 20);
main()
{
        clrscr();
        cout<<"Enter two values "<<endl;
        int num1,num2;
        cin>>num1>>num2;
        sum(num1,num2);
}
void sum(int a,int b,int c,int d)
{
        int temp = a + b + c + d;
        cout<<"sum = "<<temp;
}
```

Program 23–121

```
//friend function
#include<iostream.h>
#include<conio.h>
class first
{
        private:
                int x;
    int y;
        public :
                void getdata()
          {
                        x = 25;
                        y = 20;
          }
                friend void disp(first f);
```

```
};
void disp(first f)
{
        int sum;
        sum = f.x + f.y;
        cout<<" Value is : "<<sum<<endl;
}
main()
{
        clrscr();
        first obj;
        obj.getdata();
        disp(obj);
}
```

Program 23–122

```
//virtual function
#include<iostream.h>
#include<conio.h>
class base1
{
        public :
                virtual void disp()
                {
                cout<<" This is virtual function of base1  class\n";
                }
};
class base2 : public base1
{
        public :
                virtual void disp()
                {
                cout<<" This is virtual function of base2  class\n";
                }
};
class base3 : public base2
{
        public :
                virtual void disp()
                {
                cout<<" This is virtual function of base3  class\n";
                }
};
main()
{
```

```
        clrscr();
        base1 b1;
        base2 b2;
        base3 b3;
        base1 *ptr[3];
        ptr[0] = &b1;
        ptr[1] = &b2;
        ptr[2] = &b3;
        for(int i = 0;i<=2;i++)
        {
                ptr[i]->disp();
        }
}
```

Program 23–123

```
//union
#include<iostream.h>
#include<conio.h>
main()
{
        union
        {
                int x;
                float y;
                char ch;
        };
        cout<<"enter values in x , y & character in c "<<endl;
        cin>>x>>y>>ch;
        cout<<" Value of x  = "<<x<<endl;
        cout<<" Value of y  = "<<y<<endl;
        cout<<" Value of ch = "<<ch<<endl;
}
```

Program 23–124

```
//typedef
#include<iostream.h>
#include<conio.h>
main()
{
        clrscr();
        typedef int int1;
        typedef float dec1;
        typedef char ch1;
        int1 x,y;
        dec1 dec;
        ch1 ch;
```

```
        x = 10;
        y = 30;
        dec = 35.55;
        ch ='$';
        cout<<"Using Typedef\n";
        cout<<"Value of x   = "<<x<<endl;
        cout<<"Value of y   = "<<y<<endl;
        cout<<"Value of dec = "<<dec<<endl;
        cout<<"Value of ch  = "<<ch<<endl;
}
```

Program 23–125

```
//enumeration constant declaration
#include<iostream.h>
#include<conio.h>
main()
{
        clrscr();
        enum days{mon=1,tue=2,wed=3,thus=4,fri=5,sat=6,sun=7};
        enum days day1;
        enum days day2;
        enum days day3;
        enum days day4;
        enum days day5;
        enum days day6;
        enum days day7;
        day1 = mon;
        day2 = tue;
        day3      = wed;
        day4 = thus;
        day5 = fri;
        day6 = sat;
        day7 = sun;
        cout<<"Monday    = "<<day1<<endl;
        cout<<"Tuesday   = "<<day2<<endl;
        cout<<"Wednsday  = "<<day3<<endl;
        cout<<"Thursday  = "<<day4<<endl;
        cout<<"Friday    = "<<day5<<endl;
        cout<<"Saturday  = "<<day6<<endl;
        cout<<"Sunday    = "<<day7<<endl;
}
```

Program 23–126

```
//overloading function with different arguments
#include<iostream.h>
#include<conio.h>
```

```
main()
{
        int cal(int a);
        int cal(int x,int y,int z);
        cout<<"Enter value of a "<<endl;
        int a;
        cin>>a;
        cout<<"Enter three numbers for addition "<<endl;
        int x,y,z;
        cin>>x>>y>>z;
        int c1 = cal(a);
        int c2 = cal(x,y,z);
        cout<<"Squre of number is "<<c1<<endl;
        cout<<"Adition of numbers "<<c2<<endl;
}
int cal(int a)
{
        return(a*a);
}
int cal(int x,int y,int z)
{
        return(x+y+z);
}
```

Program 23–127

```
//write function
#include<iostream.h>
#include<conio.h>
#include<string.h>
main()
{
        clrscr();
        char *ch = "object";
        int len = strlen(ch);
        for(int i=1;i<=len;i++)
        {
                cout.write(ch,i);
                cout<<endl;
        }
}
```

Program 23–128

```
//getline
#include<iostream.h>
#include<conio.h>
main()
```

```
{
        clrscr();
        cout<<" Enter small sentence "<<endl;
        char ch[20];
        cin.getline(ch,20);
        cout<<" Re-Enter  sentence "<<endl;
        char ch1[20];
        cin>>ch1;
        clrscr();
        cout<<"\nSee The Difference\n";
        cout<<ch<<endl;
        cout<<ch1<<endl;
}
```

Program 23–129

```
//this pointer
#include<iostream.h>
#include<conio.h>
class ptr {
                int x;
                int y;
        public:
                void setval()
                {
                        x = 20; y = 50;
                }
           void getval()
                {
                 this-> x;
                 this-> y;
                 cout<<" Values are "<<x<<"\t"<<y<<endl;
                }
};
main()
{
        clrscr();
        ptr p1;
        p1.setval();
        p1.getval();
}
```

Program 23–130

```
//constructor
#include<iostream.h>
#include<conio.h>
```

```
class account
{
                float balance;
                float rate;
                float amount;
        public:
                account()
                {
                        balance = 2000;
                        rate = 4.5 ;
                }
                void createacct()
                {
                        amount = balance * rate;
                        cout<<"Amount is "<<amount<<endl;
                }
};
main()
{
        clrscr();
        account acct;
   acct.createacct();
}
```

Program 23–131

```
#include<iostream.h>
void main()
{
        int a =10,b=20;
        char x =1,y = 2;
        if(a,b,x,y)
        {
                cout<<"ERROR\n";
        }
}
```

Program 23–132

```
#include<iostream.h>
main()
{
        int value;
        cout<<"enter value  \n";
        cin>>value;
        cout<<"decimal"<<dec<<'\t'<<value<<endl;
        cout<<"haxadecimal"<<hex<<'\t'<<value<<endl;
        cout<<"octal"<<oct<<'\t'<<value<<endl;
}
```

Program 23–133

```
#include<iostream.h>
void main()
{
        int i = 1;
        for (; i + + ;)
                        cout<<i;
}
```

Program 23–134

```
#include<iostream.h>
void main()
{
        int x = 3, y, z;
        z = y = x;
        z * = y | = x;
        cout<<"x="<<x<<"y="<<y;
}
```

Program 23–135

```
#include<iostream.h>
main()
{
        int a = 3, b = 2, c = 1, d;
        d = a | b & c;
        cout<<"d="<<d;
        d = a | b & ~c;
        cout<<"d="<<d;
}
```

Program 23–136

```
#include<iostream.h>
main()
{
        int a = 0xff;
        if (a < < 4 > > 12)
                        cout<<"left";
        else
                        cout<<"right";
}
```

Program 23–137

```
#include<iostream.h>
main()
{
        int i = + 1;
```

```
        while (~i)
                        cout<<"Happy New Year";
}
```

Program 20–93

```
#include<iostream.h>
main()
{
        static int b[ ] = {1,2,3,4,5};
        int i;
        for (i = 0; i < = 4; i + +)
                cout<<b[i]<<'\t';
}
```

Program 23–138

```
#include<iostream.h>
main()
{
        static int b[ ] = {10,20,30,40,50};
        int i, *K;
        K = & b[4] – 4;
        for (i = 0; i < = 4; i + +)
        {
                cout<<*K<<'\t';
                K++;
        }
}
```

Program 23–139

```
#include<iostream.h>
main()
{
        int i = 45;
        float C;
        C = check(i);
                        cout<<C<<'\t';
        }
check (int Ch)
{
                (Ch> = 45?return(3.14); return (6.28));
}
```

Program 23–140

```
#include<iostream.h>
main()
{
```

```
        int i = 400  * 400/400;
        if (i==400)
                        cout <<"students\n";
        else
                        cout <<"staff\n";
}
```

Program 23–141

```
//A PROGRAM FOR ARRAY OF ELEMENTS OF OBJECT
#include<iostream.h>
#include<stdlib.h>
#include<conio.h>
        const m = 50;
        class item      {
                        int it_code[m];
                        char it_name[m][20];
                        float it_cost[m];
                        int count;
         public:
                        void CNT(void){count = 0;}//initializes count 0
                        void getdata(void);
                        void dispsum(void);
                        void remove(void);
                        void dispitems(void);
};
void item::getdata(void)
{
        cout<<"enter item code : \n";
        cin>>it_code[c    ount];
        cout<<"enter item name : \n";
        cin>>it_name[count];
        cout<<"enter item cost : \n";
        cin>>it_cost[count];
        count++;
}
void item::dispsum(void)
{
        float sum = 0;
        for(int i=0;i<count;i++)
                                sum = sum + it_cost[i];
        cout<<" Total Value : "<<sum<<"\n";
}
void item::remove(void)
{
        int a;
        cout<<"Enter item code :";
```

```
        cin>>a;
        for(int i=0;i<count;i++)
                if(it_code[i]==a)
                                it_code[i]=0;
}
void item::dispitems(void)
{
        cout<<"\n ITEM CODE  COST OF ITEM \n";
        for(int i=0;i<count;i++)
        {
        cout<<"\n"<<it_code[i];
        cout<<"\n"<<it_name[i];
        cout<<"  "<<it_cost[i];
        }
        cout<<"\n";
}
main()
{
        clrscr();
        item order;
        order.CNT();
        int x;
        do
        {
        //clrscr();
        cout<<"Enter appropriate number \n";
        cout<<"\n1 : Add Item ";
        cout<<"\n2 : Display Total Value ";
        cout<<"\n3 : Delete Item ";
        cout<<"\n4 : Dispaly All Items ";
        cout<<"\n5 : Quit ";
        cout<<"\n\n What is your option ? "<<endl;
        cin>>x;
        switch(x)
        {
                case 1 : order.getdata();
        break;
                case 2 : order.dispsum();
        break;
                case 3 : order.remove();
        break;
                case 4 : order.dispitems();
        break;
                case 5 : break;
                default: cout<<" Error in input ! check it \n";
    }
```

```
} while(x!=5);
}
```

Program 23–142

```
// Remainder operator
#include <iostream.h>
#include <conio.h>
main()
{
	int c=0;
	clrscr();
	for(int i=0; i<30; ++i)
	{
		c = (c + 1) % 30;
		cout << " C = " << c << " \n ";
		getch();
	}
}
```

Program 23–143

```
//PROGRAM TO FILL AN ARC BY REDUCING THE SIZE OF AN ARC
#include <graphics.h>
#include <iostream.h>
#include <conio.h>
#include <math.h>
class arcdr
{
	public:
		void arc_R(float xc,float yc,float r);
};
void arcdr::arc_R(float xc,float yc,float r)
{
	while(r>0.0)
	{
		arc(xc,yc,0,90,r);
		--r;
		getch();
	}
	return;
}
main()
{
	arcdr A;
	int driver=9;
	int mode=VGAHI;
	initgraph(&driver,&mode,"\\tc");
	setpalette(0,112);
```

```
        setcolor(YELLOW);
        getch();
        arc(250,250,0,90,200);
        getch();
        A.arc_R(250.0,250.0,200.0);
        restorecrtmode();
}
```

Program 23–144

```
//PROGRAM TO FILL AN ARC BY REDUCING THE SIZE OF AN ARC
#include <graphics.h>
#include <iostream.h>
#include <conio.h>
#include <math.h>
class arcdr
{
        public:
                void arc_R(float xc,float yc,float r);
};
void arcdr::arc_R(float xc,float yc,float r)
{
        while(r>0.0)
        {
                arc(xc,yc,0,90,r);
                --r;
                getch();
        }
        return;
}
main()
{
        arcdr A;
        int driver=9;
        int mode=VGAHI;
        initgraph(&driver,&mode,"\\tc");
        setpalette(0,112);
        setcolor(YELLOW);
        getch();
        arc(250,250,0,90,200);
        getch();
        A.arc_R(250.0,250.0,200.0);
        restorecrtmode();
}
```

Program 23–145

```
// PROGRAM TO GENERATE THE SERIES
#include <iostream.h>
```

```
#include <conio.h>
main()
{
        clrscr();
        int i,j;
        for(i=9;i>=1;--i)
        {
        for(j=1;j<=i;++j)
        {
                cout << "   " << j;
        }
        cout << endl;
        }
}
```

Program 23–146

```
// PROGRAM TO READ POSITIVE INTEGER NUMBER N
#include <iostream.h>
#include <conio.h>
main()
{
        int i,j,n;
        clrscr();
        cout << " Enter the value of n\n";
        cin >> n;
        for(i=n; i>=1; --i)
        {
                cout << " " << i;
        }
        for(i=0; i<=n; ++i)
        cout << " " << i;
}
```

Program 23–147

```
// PROGRAM TO GENERATE THE SERIES
#include <iostream.h>
#include <conio.h>
main()
{
        clrscr();
        int i,j;
        for(i=1;i<=9;++i)
        {
        for(j=1;j<=i;++j)
        {
                cout << "   " << i;
                cout << "   " << j;
```

```
        }
        cout << endl;
        }
}
```

Program 23–148

```
// PROGRAM TO FIND THE SUM OF SERIES
// S = 1 + 2 + 5 + 8 + - - - - + N
#include <iostream.h>
#include <conio.h>
main()
{
        clrscr();
        int sum = 1,i,j;
        int n;
        cout << " Enter the no. of series \n";
        cin >> n;
        for(i=2,j=0; i<=n; ++i,j+=2)
        {
                sum = sum + j + i;
        }
        cout << " The sum of series = " << sum << endl;
}
```

Program 149

. What value is returned by the call F(3) where F is the recursive function given by the following code?

```
int FUN (int N)
{
   if (N == 0)
      return 1;
   else
      return (2 * FUN(N - 1));
}
```

Program 150

Consider the following recursive function:

```
int ms(int number) {
      if (number == 1)
           return 1;
      else
           return number * ms(number -1 );
}
```

a) What value does function 'ms' return when called with a value of 4?

b) What is the base case for function 'ms'?

24

DATA STRUCTURES IN C

24.1 INTRODUCTION

It is the way of organizing data in proper format. The data is in a complex format which is difficult to store in normal way. The data structure allows creation of complex structure of data and the retrival of data becomes more easier.

If data is arranged in form of link or structure then the operation could performed by computer program on the structure very easily by accessing the links of the data. This is called data structuring.

24.1.1 Types of data structure

There are two types of data structures

1. Simple linear data structure
2. Complex data structure

The complex data structures include stacks, queues, lists, trees and graphs.

24.1.2 Data Items

These are the values which we want store in the data structure.

24.1.3 Modular programming

The programming related to data structure when creating of data structure and processing on the structure is done by programming techniques using the logics of the program.

24.1.4 Algorithm

These are the logics of the program by these logics the processing of data is performed and desired results are obtained.

24.1.5 Entity

These are quantities stored under a memory area.

24.1.6 Keys

These are the quantities used for identifying given records.

24.1.7 Field

It is the space in which the values can be stored.

24.1.8 Record

It is an information about the given quantity. The record consist of number of fields.

24.1.9 Function

It is a program which performs a particular function.

24.1.10 Procedure

It is a program which repeats a particular procedure.

24.1.11 Sub-routine

It is a sub-program to perform a particular type of function.

24.1.12 Applications of data structure

The data structures can be used for

1. Data base management system
2. Data ware houses
3. Data mining
4. Compiler design
5. Statistical analysis
6. Numerical methods

7. Artificial intelligence
8. Simulation and network analysis

24.1.13 Data abstraction

It is arrangement of storage of data values and sets of operations to be performed for to operate on these values.

24.1.14 Data encapsulation

It is a protection of data values from the application to which the data is being used.

24.1.15 Classification of data structures

There are two type of data structures :

1. Linear
2. Non-linear.

24.1.16 Types of data

There are five type of data :

1. Integer
   This type of data stores only integer values.
2. Boolean
   This data type stores only boolean values as true or false.
3. Real
   This data type stores the character or decimal values.
4. Character
   This data type stores the character or string values.
5. Label
   This data type stores comments or non-executable strings.

24.1.17 Operations of data structure

There are various operations performed on the data structure such as

1. Sorting
2. Traversing
3. Searching
4. Inserting
5. Deleting
6. Merging.

24.1.18 Mathematical function

There are various types of mathematical function which can be performed on data structure

1. Square root
2. Exponent
3. Logrithm
4. Trignometric
5. Power
6. Hyperbolic

24.2 CONTROL STRUCTURE

The various types of control structures used are

1. Sequential flow
2. Conditional flow
3. Repetitive flow.

24.2.1 Sequential flow

The instruction are executed in a sequential models.

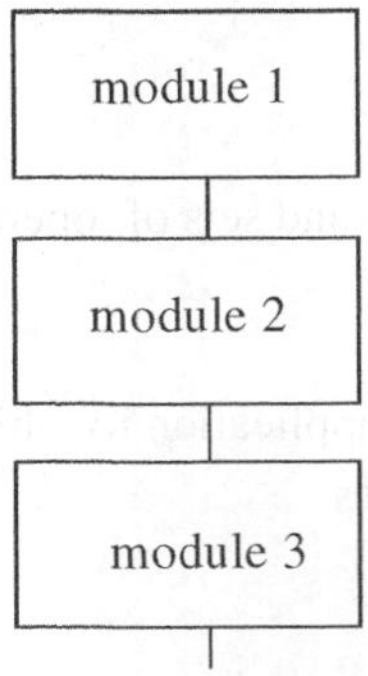

24.2.2 Coditional flow :

In this case, the logic is developed to contain number of conditions out of number of alternatives.

```
if(condition)
    then
        statement 1
    else
        statement 2
```

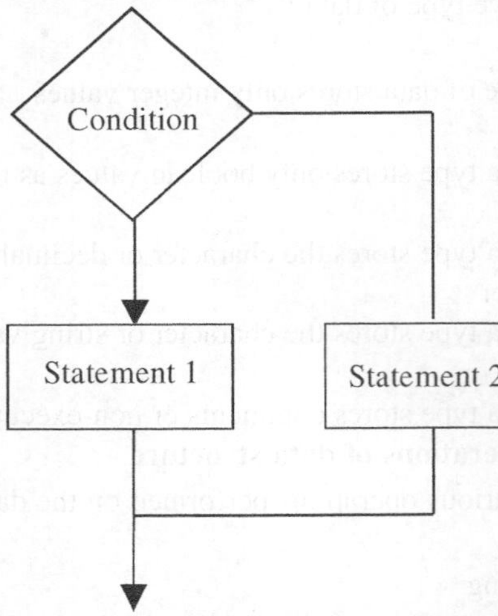

24.2.3 Repetitive flow

This is used to repeat steps for sequence of statements or modules whose values are taken successively by index till a logical expression is ture.

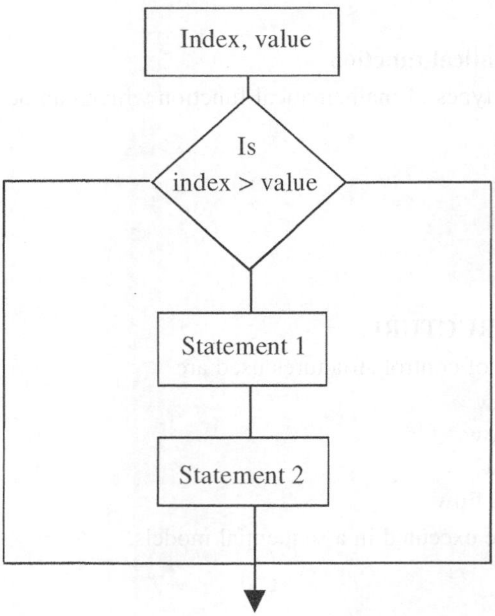

24.3 LINEAR DATA STRUCTURE

The data element in the structure can be easily identified by referencing any element in the structure. This simple and straight structures in which the element are inter related to each other and can be located by knowing its position.

24.3.1 Address

It is the memory location number in the memory

24.3.2 Address function

The selection operation associated with the structure is addressing function.

24.4 LIST

This is ordered arrangement of data items in an order. The list may contain number of data items where its length can vary and they are logically linked.

The list could be created if the data type are known. The structure in C-language allows creation of list where as classes in C^{++} allows creation of list.

For example

```
struct em
{
        int eno;
         int area;
         int volume;
        int weight;
};
```

Above is a structure of list of 'em' containing data items

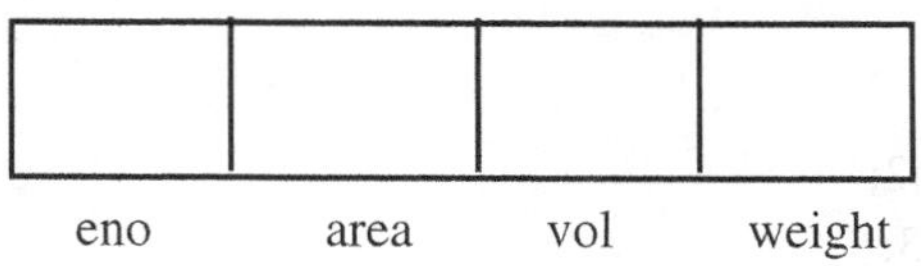

Every element in the list will have five members.

The classes can also be used to create list in C^{++} language.

The list can be implemented by use of

1. Contiguous data object
2. Linked data object

1. Contiguous data object : In these cases, the access to element is direct and any element can be accessed by simple compulation. The arrays are used in the list leads to easy detection of elements in the list.

2. Linked data object : In these cases, the elements in the list are linked and every element is interconnected to each other by link.

Program 24-1

```
/* Linked list program*/
main ( )
 {
   struct en
    {
          int v;
          struct en *n;
```

```
    };
struct en n1, n2, n3;
    int i;
    n1.v = 100;
    n2.v = 200;
    n3.v = 300;
    n1.n  = & n2;
    n2.n  = & n3;
    i = n1.n  — v;
    printf("%d", i);
    printf("%d\n", n2.n — v);
}
```

Program 24-2

```
/* Movement on link list */
main ( )
 {
    struct en
    {
            int v;
            struct en * n;
    };
struct en n1, n2, n3;
struct en *  lp = & n1;
n1. v  = 100;          n1.n  = & n2;
n2.v = 200;            n2.n = & n3;
n3.v = 300;            n3.n = 0;
while (lp ! = 0)
 {
    printf("%d/n" ,  lp  = v);
    lp  =  lp  = n;
 }
}
```

24.5 STACK

It is an ordered list into which new items or elements may be inserted and the items or elements may be deleted at one end. The stack has access only to the top of the list and operation can take place at top.

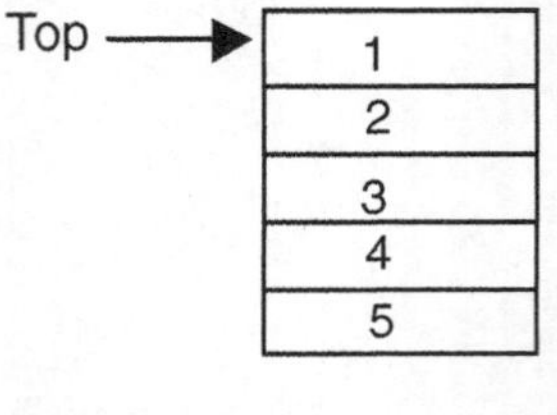

Push : It is operation of insertion in which the element is inserted by pushing the other element. The push operation adds an element n to the stack. In this case insertion operation occurs at top.

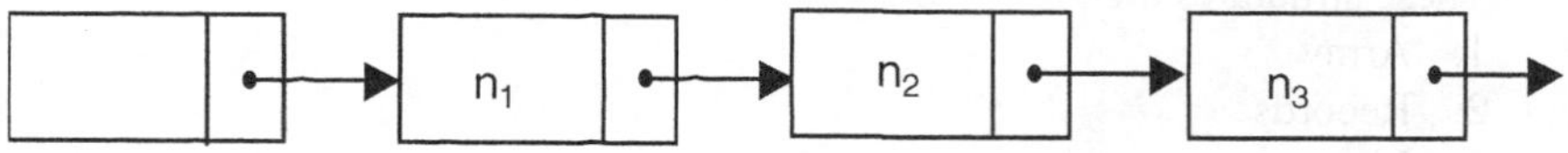

Original stack

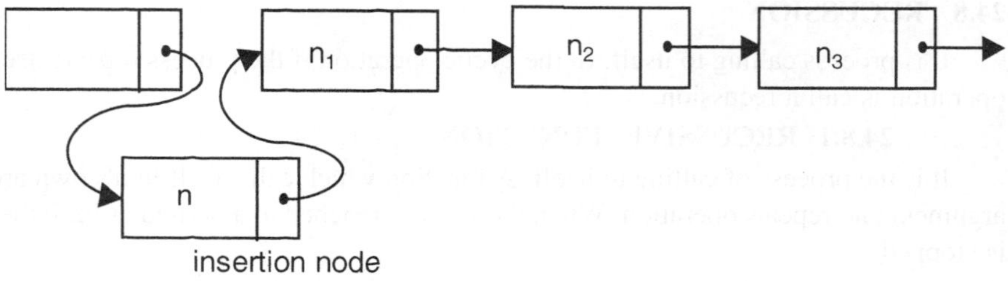

Insertion in the stack

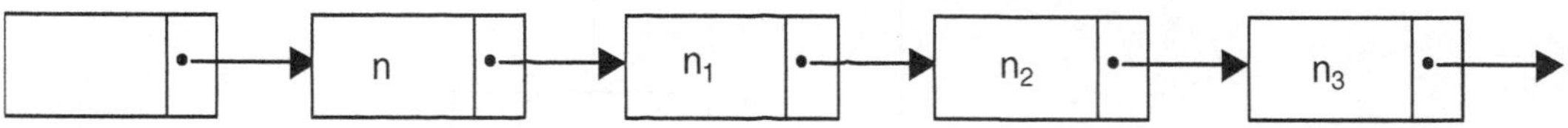

POP : It is operation of deletion in which any element is deleted by removing the elements from the list. This operation is deletion of element from stack which is carried out at the top node.

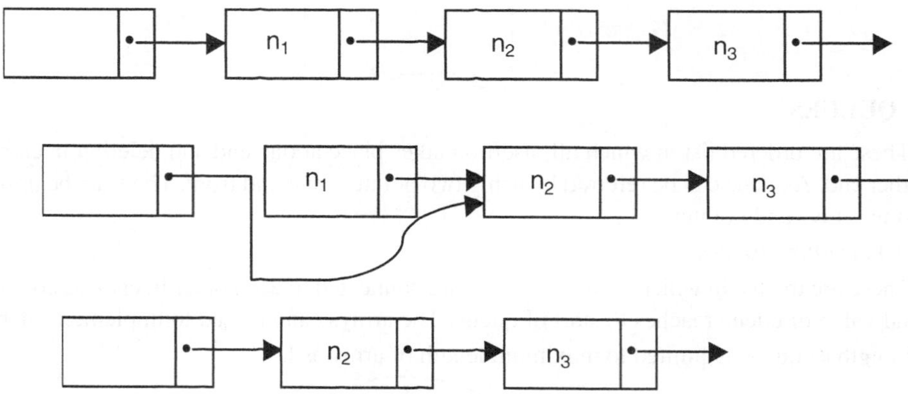

24.6 TYPES ADDRESSING METHODS

1. Address obtained by description of the data
2. Address obtained by storing address in computer memory

24.7 CLASSIFICATION OF DATA STRUCTURE

(a) Primitive data structure

The data structure operated directly by the machine level instructions. These are :

1. integer
2. real
3. character
4. pointer

(b) Non-primitive data structure

These are created by user using primitive data.

These structures are :

1. Array
2. Records
3. List
4. Files

24.8 RECUSSION

It is process calling to itself. In the cyclic operation if the process repeats itself during the cycle operation is call a recussion.

24.8.1 RECUSSIVE FUNCTION

It is the process of calling to itself. A function which calls itself in it's own area by reducing the argument and repeats operation. When the value is reached to a particular limit the recussion process is stopped.

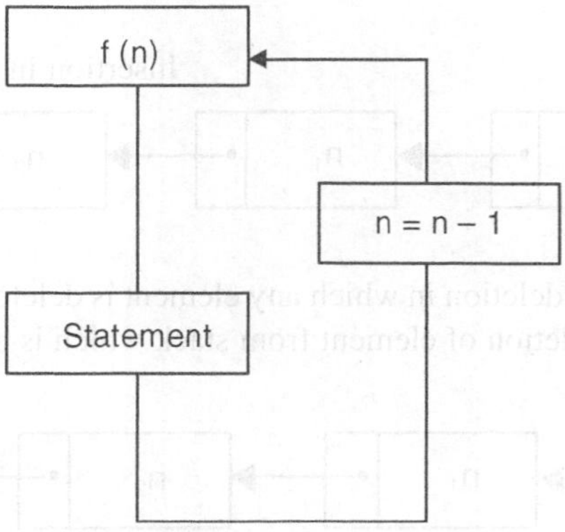

24.9 QUEUES

These are ordered list in which all insertion takes place at one end and deletion in carried out at the other end. A queue can be referred by using two pointers rear and front. They can be implemented by using arrays and pointers.

24.9.1 Circular Queues

These are the list in which all the elements are connected to each other in endless conditions and the end value of queue reaches to start of queue. The arrays can be used to implement such queues.

Length of queue is limited to maximum length of array as l.

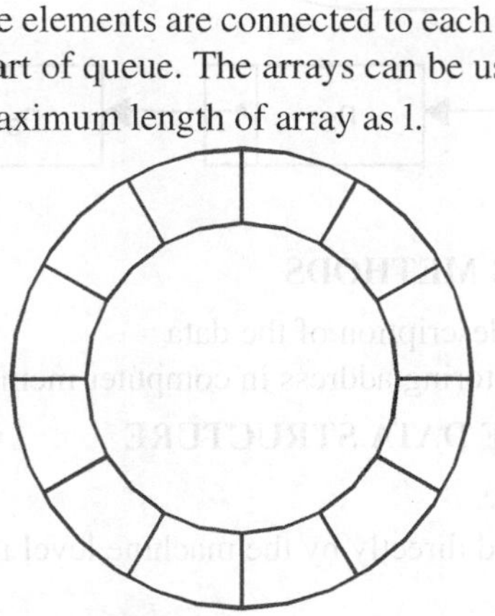

Double ended queue :

In these types of queues the insertion and deletion operation is performed from both the sides

deletion operation is performed from both the sides.

Priority Queues

These are the queues in which it is possible to insert items or remove items from any position.

24.10 ARRAY

These are the memories created under a variable name. The array variable has number of memories in which the data can be stored in the memory.

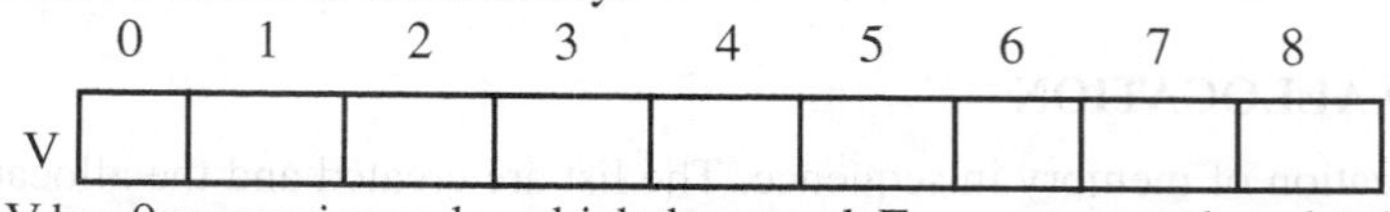

The variable V has 9 memories under which the stored. Every memory location is indicated by the index number.

There are two types of arrays

1. Single dimensional
2. Multi dimensional

1. Single dimensional

The single dimensional array variables are the variables having memories inform columns and only one row of data is used.

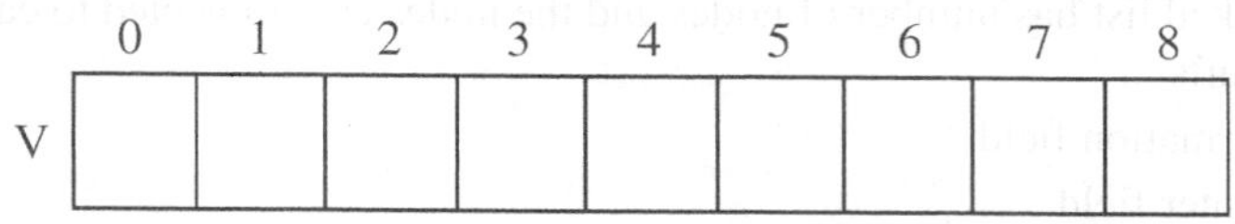

2. Multi dimensional

These are the arrays having memories in two or three dimension. A matrix is an example of two dimensional memories.

The two dimensional array has memories in row and column form. The elements are arranged in row and every row has memories in column. The element from the memory is extracted by row number and column number.

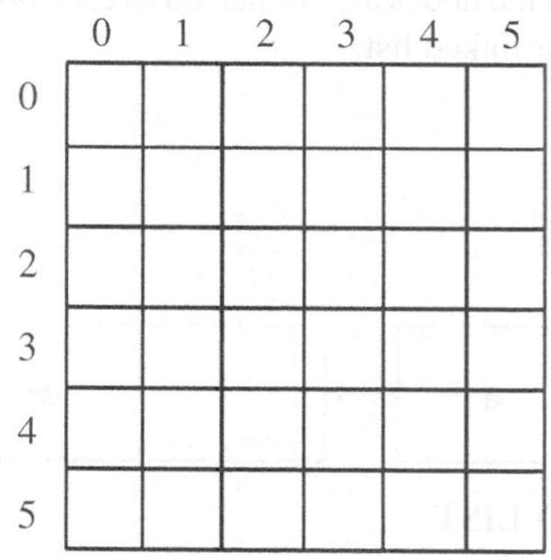

24.11 STRUCTURE

It is association of large number of variable or data type to store the data values

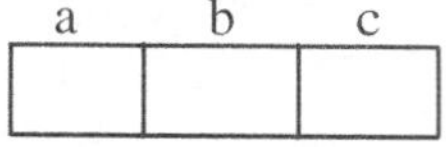

The variables a, b, c are associated together to form a structure.

24.11.1 ARRAY OF STRUCTURE

The arrays of structure are number of values of structure stored in array forms.

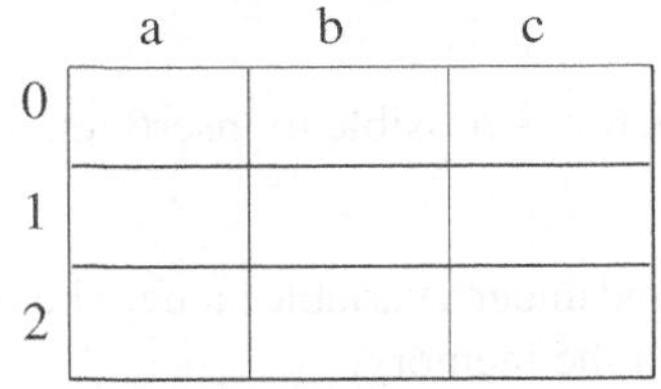

24. 12 LINKED ALLOCATION

It is the allocation of memory in sequence. The list are created and the allocation is carried out linking of element of list to each other.

24.12.1 Null and empty list

The list containing no elements is called null or empty list.

24.13 LINKED LIST

The list in which elements are linked by pointers is called linked list.

The linear linked list is list consisting of number of nodes or element in an order which may vary in number linked by pointer or link.

The linked list has number of nodes and the nodes are connected to each other. Every node consist of two parts

(i) Information field

(ii) Pointer field

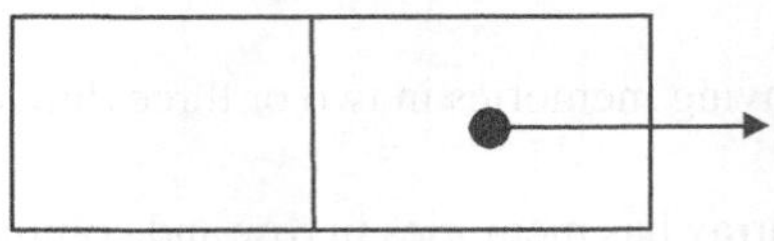

24.14 SINGLY LINEAR LIST OR CHAIN LINKED LINEAR LIST

The linked list in which all the nodes are connected to each other by a pointer. The chain of nodes is created is called singly linear linked list.

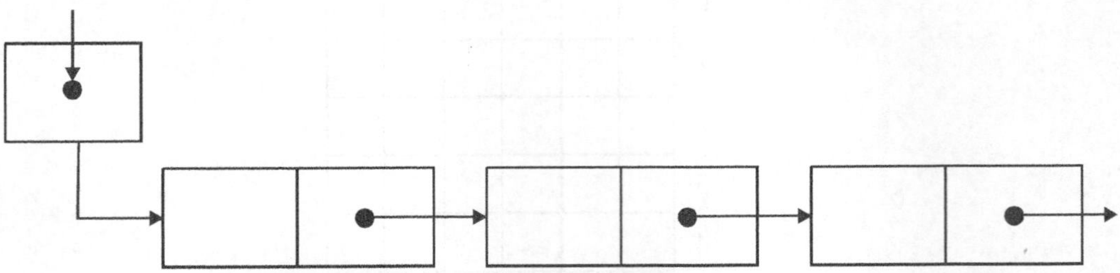

24.15 CIRCULAR LINKED LIST

The list in which nodes are inter connected to each other. The end of list is connected to start of list

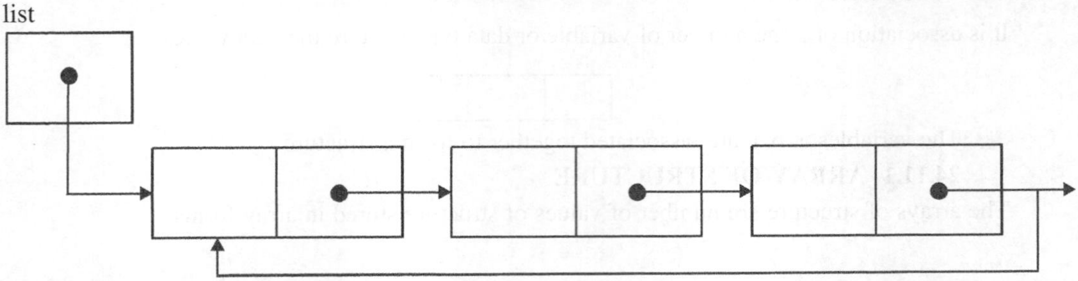

24.16 DOUBLY LINKED LINEAR LIST

The linked list in which the elements are interconnected to each other in forward and reverse direction.

24.17 NON-LINEAR DATA STRUCTURE

The non-linear data structure are trees. The trees indicate the structure of data by indicating the main system and various subsystem connected to main system by leaves.

24.18 BINARY TREE

The tree having two leaves

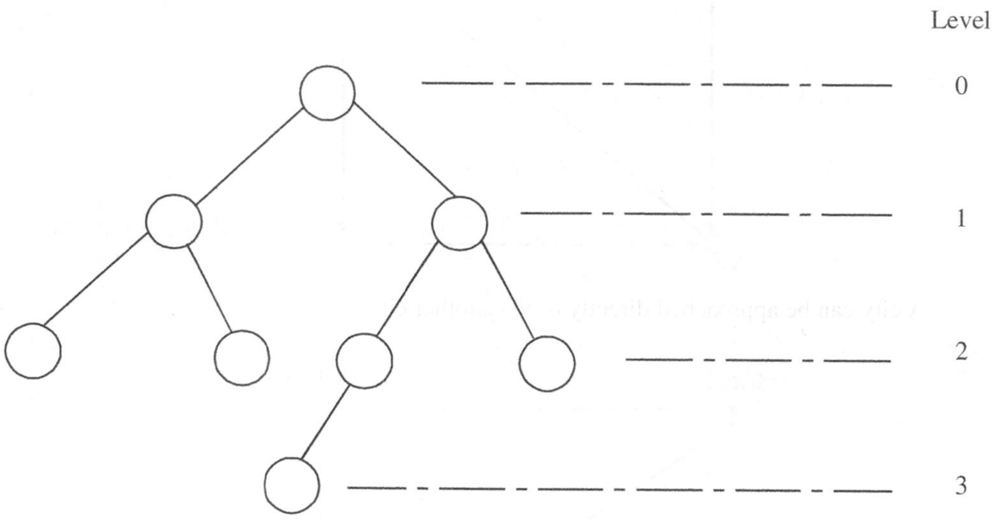

Depth of tree

It is the maximum level of any leaf node in the tree.

Root

It start point of the tree, level 0 is the root of the tree.

Node

It is the item of information in the tree.

Degree of tree

These are the number of sub-trees in the tree. They are regarded as level of the tree.

Types of tree

There are three types of tree

1. Direct tree
2. Ordered tree
3. Strictly binary tree

1. Direct tree

It is an cyclic graph which has one node as its root.

2. Ordered tree

The tree in which ordering node may be from left to right.

3. Strictly binary tree

If every non-leaf mode in a binary tree has non-empty left and right subtree, the tree is strictly binary tree.

24.19 GRAPH

A graph is a non-linear data structure defined as a collection of a set of nodes and set of edges. The example of graph is a road map

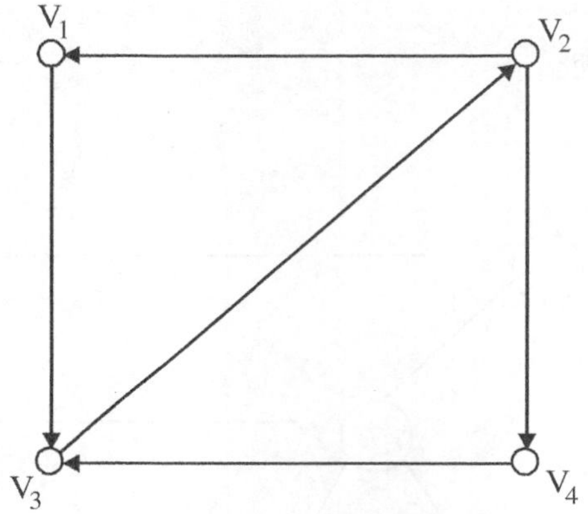

A city can be approached directly or via another city.

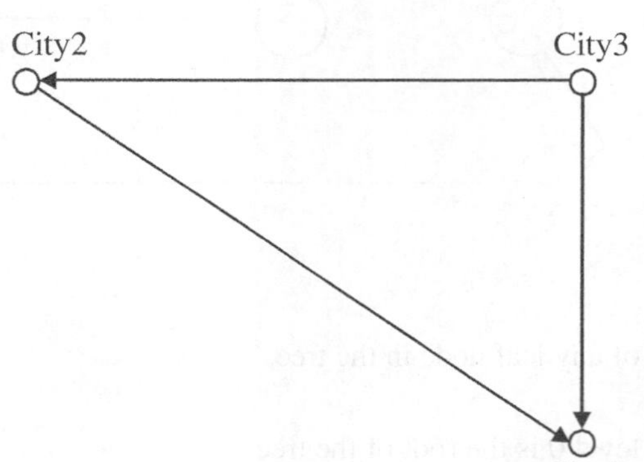

The city1 can be approached from city2 directly or via city3 is a representation of graph. The city becomes the node of the graph and arrows are the edges of the graph.

Outdegree of node

The maximum number of edges leaving from the node is called out degree of the node.

Indegree of node

The maximum number of edges entering into the node is indegree of node.

Sink node

The node whose outdegree is zero is a sink node.

Source node

The node whose indegree is zero is a source node.

Degree of node

These are the number of edges connected directly to the node is called degree of node.

24.20 TYPE OF DEGREE OF NODE

There are two types of degree of nodes :

1. Indegree of node
2. Outdegree of node

24.21 TYPES OF EDGES

There are different types of edges of graph :

1. Sling or loop edge

An edge of a graph which joins & node to itself is called sling or loop

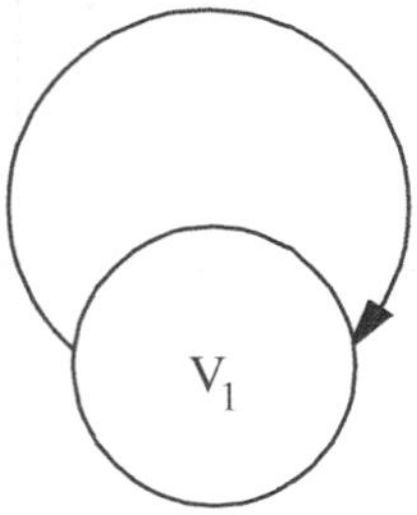

2. Multiple edge

These are number of distinct edges connected to the same node- is called multiple edges.

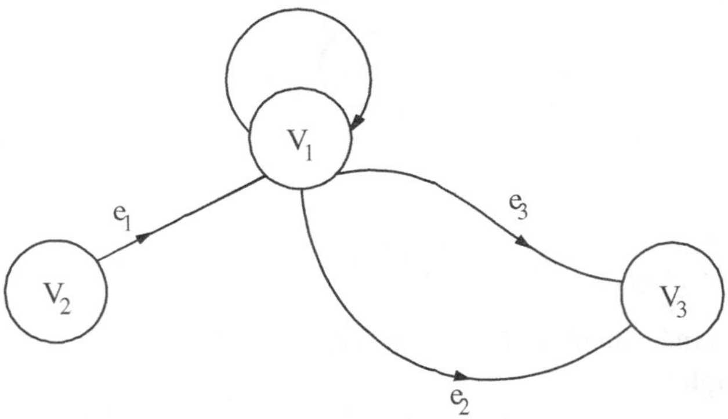

3. Parallel edges

In this case two edges flow from one node to another node parallel to each other are called parallel edges.

4. Weighted edge

An edge which has any numerical value is called weighted edge.

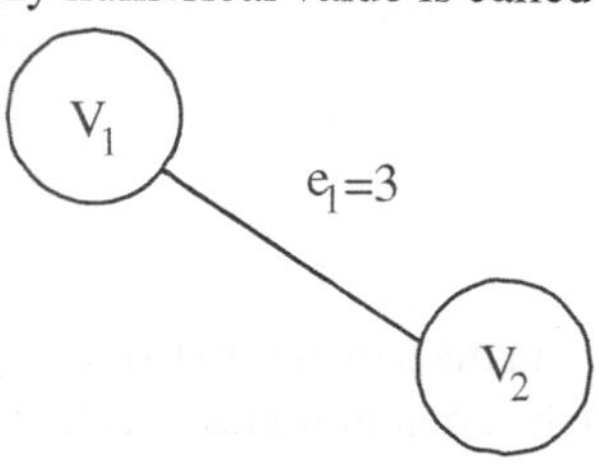

Isolated node

A node which has not been attached to an adjacent neighbour or attachment to any other node by an edge is called isolated node.

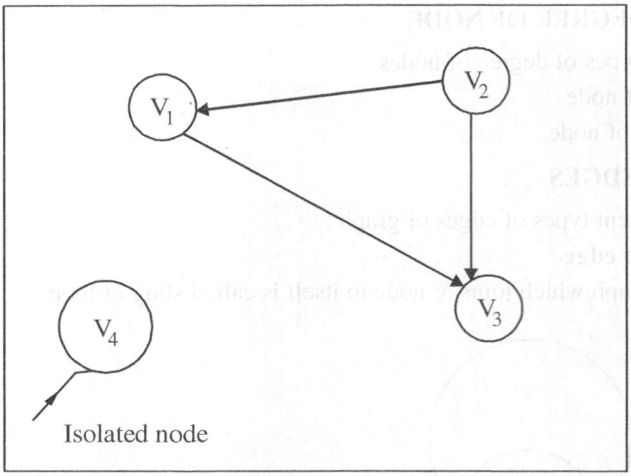

24.22 TYPES OF GRAPHS

There are different types of graphs :

1. Isolated graph

A graph which has set of empty edges or containing only isolated nodes is called a null graph or Isolated graph.

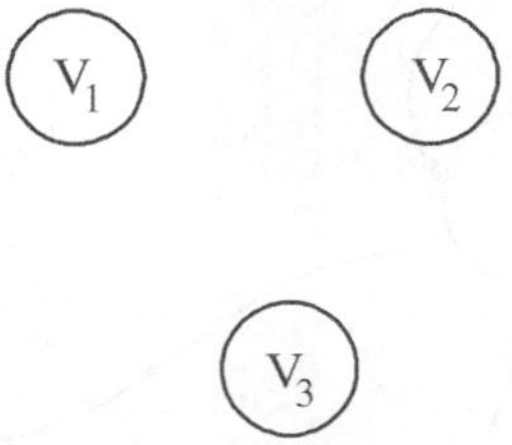

2. Finite graph

A graph which has finite number of nodes and edges.

3. Connected graph

A graph which has a path between pair of nodes is called connected graph.

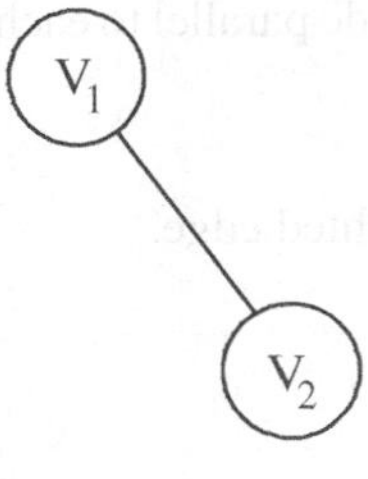

4. Complete graph

The graph which originates from one node and the path return to the originating node and the path return to the originating node by passing through series of nodes is called complete graph.

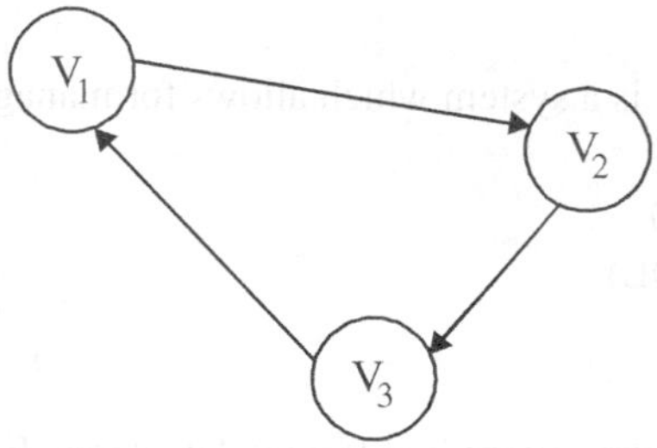

5. Weighted graph

A graph in which each and every edge has a numerical value assigned to it is called weighted graph.

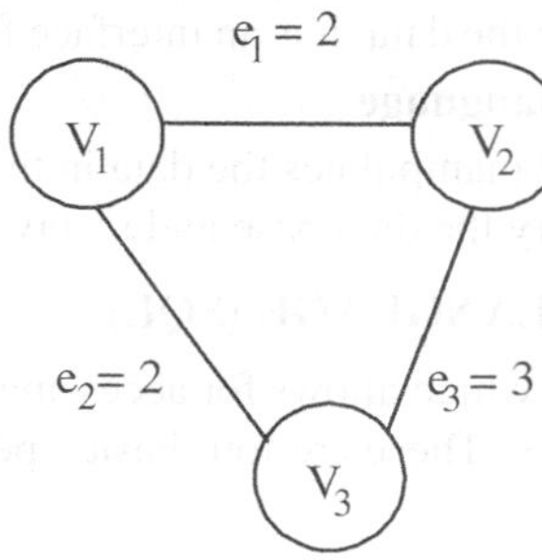

6. Multi-graph

A graph which contains some paralled edge is called multi-graph.

24.23 FILE STRUCTURES

The files and the data they store must be organized according to user requirements and the constraints of hardware and Operating System (OS). Some applications are processed daily and affect each record in the file.

An integrated approach to file design is the data base. The general theme is to handle information as an integrated whole, with minimum of redundancy and improved performance. Software languages are used to manipulate, describe and manage data.

There are basic terms used to describe the file hierarchy :

1. Byte

Byte is the smallest addressable unit in the computer. A byte is a set of eight bits that represent a character.

2. Data Item or element

One or more bytes are combined to form a data item . It describes an attribute of an object. For example, object is employee, attributes may be name, age etc. A data item is also called as a field.

3. Record

The data items related to an object are combined into a record. For example an Employee record having as its fields as employee's attributes.

4. File

A collection of related records make up a file. For example records of all employees in the organization makes a file.

5. Data base

The highest level in the hierarchy is the data base. It is a set of interrelated files for processing. It contains the necessary data for problem solving and can be used by several users accessing data concurrently.

24.24 COMPONENTS OF DBMS

The data base management system is a system which allows for management of the database. It has three main components.

1. Data dictionary system (DDS)
2. Data defination language (DDL)
3. Data manipulation language

24.24.1 Data dictionary system

It is a dictionary which stores the information in different data items. It describes the data and its characteristics

24.24.2 Data definition language

It is used to create and describe the data. It is an interface for application programs to we the data.

24.24.3 Data Manipulation language

A language that processes and manipulates the data in the database is called manipulation language. It allows the user to query the data base and receive the reports.

24.25 STRUCTURED QUERY LANGUAGE (SQL)

It is a non-procedure language which allows for accessing the data and manipulation on the data. It allows for data query and security. These are four basic operations in SQL :

1. Select the data base
2. Update the database
3. Insert the database
4. Delete the database

24.26 DATABASE MODELS

It is a method of organizing data which represents the logical relationships among the data elements in the database. There are three types of models

1. Hierarchical database
2. Network database
3. Relational database.

24.26.1 Hierarchical Database

In this model main database is connected to other databases arranged at the lower level.

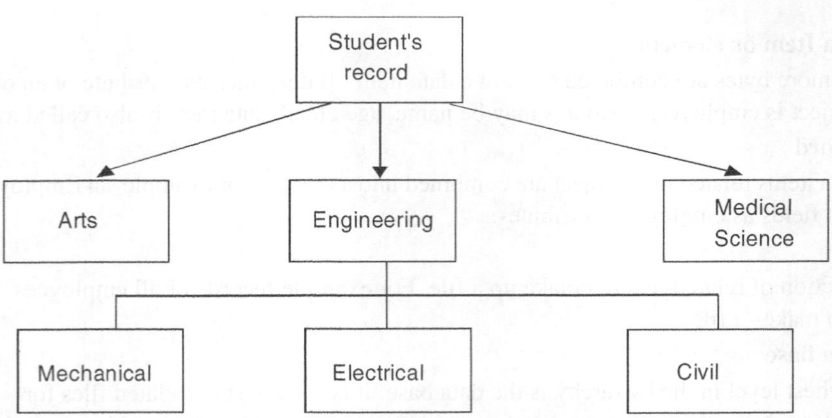

Fig.24.10

Fig.24.10 show hierarchical model of data bases in which students are connected to three other databases as Arts, Engineering and Medical Science. The Engineering database is connected to three other databases as Mechanical, Electrical and Civil.

24.26.2 Network databases

In this case, the main database is connected to number of databases in a network, where all other databases can be connected to the main database.

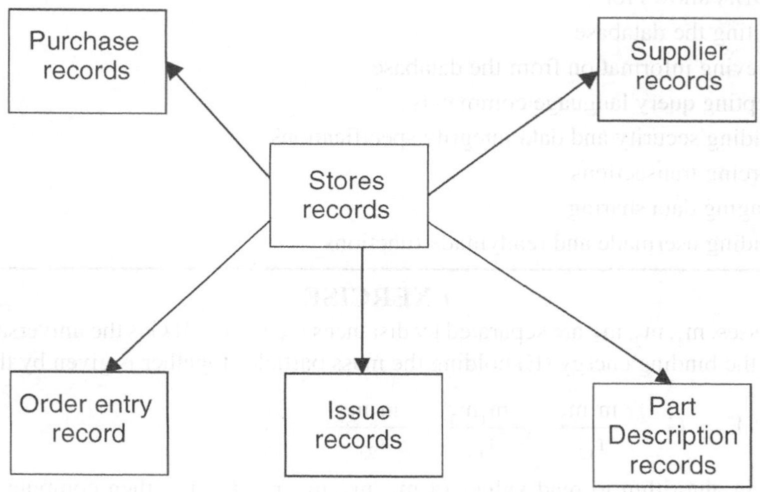

Fig.24.11

24.26.3 Relational databases

The database which are inter related to each other by relational data bases.

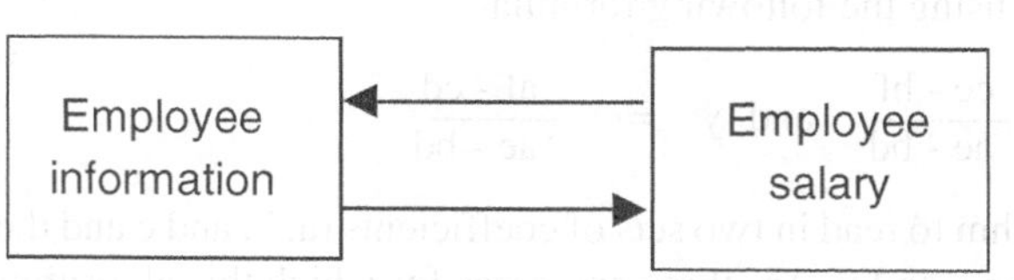

Fig.24.12

Fig.24.12 shows relational data base system of salary of employees and their information records.

24.27. RECENT DEVELOPMENT IN DATABASES

There are new varieties of databases being used in the information technology.

1. Distributed databases

It is a database distributed over the single or multi-vendor computer network located in different geographic areas. These are banking system,corporate companies, payroll system etc.

2. Client-Server databases

These data bases are used in the networking system. The network user can initiate several client and the server provide database which can be accessed by different clients

3. Object oriented databases

These databases are the databases which provide hiding of data values and allows modification of data members by assisting program. Some of the data values are protected and some of the values are easily modified.

4. Multi-media databases

These data bases can handle complex data objects like scanned images,map,drawing , pictures etc.The object oriented programming technology can handle complex databases.

24.28 DATABASE ADMINISTRATOR SYSTEM

It is the administrator used in the software which allows for administration of a database. The database administration system is a block of code loaded from the hard disc for operation of the system. The DBA allows for

1. Updating the database
2. Retrieving information from the database
3. Accepting query language commands
4. Providing security and data integrity specifications
5. Enforcing transactions
6. Managing data sharing
7. Providing usermade and readymade functions

EXERCISE

1. Three masses, m_1, m_2, m_3 are separated by distances r_{12}, r_{13}, r_{23}. If G is the universal gravitational constant, the binding energy (E) holding the mass particles together is given by the formula.

$$E = G \quad \frac{m_1 m_2}{r_{12}}, \frac{m_1 m_3}{r_{13}}, \frac{m_2 m_3}{r_{23}},$$

Design an algorithm to read values of m_1, m_2, m_3, r_{12}, r_{13}, r_{23}, then compute and print the binding energy with the initial data values. For mass in kilograms and distance in meters $G - 6.67 \times 10^{-11}$ N-m² /Kg². Assume that all input of real type.

2. A system of linear equations of the form

$ax + by = c \qquad dx + ey = f$

can be solved by using the following formulas

$$X = \frac{ce - bf}{ae - bd} \quad \text{and } y = \frac{af - cd}{ae - bd}$$

Design an algorithm to read in two sets of coefficients (a, b, and c and d,e and f) and print out the solution values for x and y. Are three any cases for which this algorithm will not work.

3. A car is traveling down a road approaches an intersection and slows down from a speed of 55 Km/hr to 30K/hr in 5 sec. Write an algorithm that calculates both the caris constant rate of acceleration and how long will take for the car to stop.

4. A utility company takes meter reading each month and charges its customers on the following basis: Write an algorithm that reads in last month's meter reading and this month's reading and calculations the customer's bill

Kilowatt hour	Rate
0 – 500	Rs 400
501 – 1000	Rs 400 + Rs 6 per K wh above 500
1001 and over	Rs 700 + Rs per K wh above 1000

5. Design an algorithm to read the length of the three sides of a triangle (S_1, S_2, S_3) and determine what type of triangle it is, on the basis of the following cases. Let A denote the largest of S_1, S_2, S_3 and B and C the other two, then

If	$A \geq b + C$	No Triangle formed
If	$A^2 = B^2 + C^2$	A right angled Triangle formed
If	$A^2 > B^2 + C^2$	A obtuse Triangle formed
If	$A^2 < B^2 + C^2$	A acute Triangle formed

6. Design an algorithm to compute and tabulate the values for the function

$$f(X, Y) = \frac{X^2 - Y^2}{X^2 + Y^2}$$

for x = 2, 4, 6, 8 and y = 6, 9, 12, 15, 18, 21

7. Design an algorithm to compute the number of points with integer valued co-ordinates that are contained within ellipse.

$$\frac{X^2}{16} + \frac{Y^2}{15} = 1$$

The range of co-ordinate is limited by the major and minor axes of the ellipse

8. Write the Algorithm and program for finding an equation of a line passing through the points having co-ordinates (x_1, y_1) & (x_2, y_2).
9. Write Algorithm and program which accepts two number and prints sum, product, difference and quotient of the two numbers.
10. Prepare Algorithm and program to read radius of circle and print diameter, circumference and area of circle.
11. If a,b,c are three points whose co-ordinates are (x_1, y_1), (x_2, y_2), (x_3, y_3)
    Write Algorithm and program to find whether points are colinear and if they are colinear then find and equation of a line.
12. If R is a radius of a circle and co-ordinates of any points are supplied to the program as (x_1, y_1) then write a Algorithm and a program to determine whether the point lies on circumference of circle or inside the circle or outside the circle.
13. If (x_1, y_1), (x_2, y_2) and (x_3, y_3) are co-ordinates of three apex points of triangle write Algorithm and program to find whether they form equilateral, iso sceles or scalene triangle.
14. The rate of interest offered by the Bank on fixed deposit is

Period	Interest %
< 9 months.	7
9 to 18 months	8
1.5 to 3 years	9
3 to 5 years	10
5 years or more	11

Write Algorithm and program to calculate monthly interest of customers.

15. Write an algorithm and program to interchange three numbers A, B, C.
16. Write algorithm and program to find prime factors of given number.
17. Write recursive sub-algorithm to find GCD (Greatest Common Division) of two integers.
18. Write an algorithm for addition of two matrices of order m × n.
19. Write an algorithm to search an item in the binary tree.
20. Write a algorithm and program to find products of diagonal elements of square matrix.
21. Define and explain concept of linked list.
22. Explain various types of list.

23. Explain the following terms :
    (i) NULL (ii) Empty list
    (iii) Header value (iv) Tailer node
24. Explain advantages and disadvantages of linked list.
25. Explain various operations performed on linked list.
26. Explain what do you mean by stack.
27. Write algorithm for creation of stack.
28. Explain PUSH and POP operation and write their algorithm.
29. Explain what is meant by queue.
30. Explain differences between circular queue and double ended queue.
31. What are the different types of variations of dequeue ?
32. What is priority queue ?
33. Explain various operations performed on queue.
34. Differentiate between singly linked list and doubly linked list.
35. Write sub-algorithm for singly linked linear list
    (i) Initialize (ii) Addition node
    (iii) Deletion of node at last (iv) Count number of nodes in a list.
36. Write algorithm insert and remove to implement queue such that head of the queue is always in the first position of a linear array.
37. Write algorithm to remove an item from circular queue such that all elements are moved by one position.
38. Write recursive functions to count number of nodes is singly linked list.
39. Two singly linked list are given whose elements are in ascending order. Merge them to yield a list whose elements are in descending order.
40. Write recursive function to count number of nodes in singly linked list.
41. Write a representation for a list where insertion and deletion of an element can be made at either end.The structure of dequeue.
42. Using an array representation of a stack formulate an algorithm to obtain its ith element without deleting it.
43. Explain the structure of tree.
44. Explain the terms used for tree
    (i) Depth of tree (ii) root
    (iii) node (iv) degree of tree (v) level of tree
45. What are the different types tree? explain.
46. Explain the different operations which can be performed on the tree.
47. Explain the insertion in the binary tree.

25

SUBJECTIVE & OBJECTIVE QUESTIONS

25.1 FILL IN THE BLANKS

1. The compilations is a process of ____________.
2. The semi colon ; is a _____________.
3. The constant is a quantity which do not _____________and the variable is a quantity_____________.
4. The double variable has ____________.
5. The variable name can be written by alphabet,number and ___________.
6. The arithmetic operators are used for _____________.
7. The modulus operator % is used for________________.
8. The arithmetic expression is a combination of variables, constants and __________.
9. The comment statement is a ________________.
10. The scanf statement is used for ____________.
11. The results are printed by using____________ statement.
12. The if statement is a ______________ statement.
13. The logical expression is used for __________.
14. The switch statement considers _____________and ___________.
15. The for statement is a ____________.
16. The while statement checks the condition at _____________.
17. The do while statement checks the condition at______________.
18. The breaks statement _____________the block.
19. The array variables are the variables having ______________.
20. The single dimensional array variable has ____________ row.
21. The array variable can be scanned by using __________ statement.
22. The two dimensional array variable has ______________rows.
23. The matrix can be stored in the ____________ variable.
24. The ___________ for statement can be used for scanning of 2-D array variable.
25. The string is ______________ characters.
26. The single dimensional char array stores ___________.
27. The two dimensional char array stores the ________ strings.
28. The function program is ________________.
29. The function program can have ________ name.
30. The function program is written ____________ main program.
31. The input to the function program is called ____________ of function program.
32. Function program is __________ in the main program.
33. The returnable function program __________ value to the main program.
34. The global variable are ______________ variables.
35. The static variable is declared by a word________________.
36. The c-preprocessor starts with ___________ sign.
37. The c-preprocessors are written __________ the main program.
38. The typedef statement is used for ___________.
39. The unions are association of _________________ variables.
40. The enum statement is used for _______________ of data.
41. A constant in C-language is quantity whose value __________ .
42. A variable in C-language is quantity whose value ___________.

43. A int variable stores the ___________ value .
44. The double variable has ____________ precision.
45. A long int variable stores a number upto__________.
46. The comment statement is ___________ statement.
47. The braces are used in C-language for____________.
48. The input statement is used for ____________.
49. The output statement is used for ____________.
50. The format are used for _____________.
51. The \n character is used for ___________.
52. The control statements are used for ___________.
53. The ++i statement _________ value of i by 1.
54. The i+=2 ___________ the value of i by 2.
55 The == operator is a _____________
56. && operator is a _____________.
57. ! operator is used for _____________.
58. The iteration statement is used for ____________.
59. The do-while statement is used for ____________.
60. break statement is used for _____________ cycle.
61. continue statement is used for ___________ cycle.
62. goto statement is used for _______________.
63. array variable have __________ memories.
64. The two dimensional array variable have memories in _____________
65. The char array is capable of storing _______________.
66. A string consists of ____________ characters.
67. function programs are _____________.
68. The returnable function programs are __________ value.
69. The non-returnable function programs are ___________ value.
70. recursive function program call __________.
71. The global variables are __________ variables.
72. The static variable ____________ .
73. The automatic variables ___________.
74. The register variables are used for ___________.
75. The C-preprocessor are used for ____________.
76. The strlen function is used for ___________.
77. The null character is indicated by ____________
78. The pointer variable is represented by __________.
79. The structure is a ____________ variables.
80. The file pointer is capable of accessing __________ .

25.2 STATE TRUE OR FALSE

1. Compilation of program do not detect any errors in the program.
2. Every program must be compiled.
3. C++ is an extension of C.
4. Every statement of C-language must be written on single line.
5. A constant always vary during the execution of program.
6. The variable value can remain constant during execution of program.
7. The under score should not be used during the writing of variable name.
8. The float variable is capable of storing integer value.
9. The double variable store value with 24 decimal accuracy.
10. The % operator calculates the division of two numbers.

11. The modulus operator finds the remainder between two floating values.
12. The arithmetic statement allows arithmetic expressions on lefthand side.
13. +, - operators receive first preference in operation.
14. The braces are used in arithmetic statement.
15. The braces creates a bunch and attaches to previous statement.
16. The comments statement is non executable statement of the program.
17. The d format is used for printing of integer variables.
18. The double variables are printed by g format.
19. The logical expression are used for creating a condition.
20. The arithmetic statement can be a decision statement.
21. The function programs are sub-programs.
22. The array variable can be of int,float or char type.
23. The element of array variable can be indicated by index number.
24. The two dimensional array variable store the values in the rows.
25. The array variables are not declared in the program.
26. The two dimensional array variables are printed by using printf statement.
27. The two dimensional array variables can not be scanned statement.
28. The elements of 2-D array can be supplied by arithmetic statement.
29. A string can be stored in the char array.
30. A string do not contain blank character.
31. It is possible to store number of words of English language in the char array.
32. The string can be terminated by null character.
33. The null character is indicated by a blank space.
34. The function program are written inside main program.
35. The function programs can have the output arguments.
36. The returnable function program returns only one value.
37. The recursive function gives a call to other function program.
38. The global variables are declared inside the main program.
39. The variable of same name can be global as well as local variable.
40. The static variable remains static.
41. The global variables are declared by word global.
42. The register variables are declared by word register.
43. The c-preprocessor are written at the end of the file.

25.3 OBJECTIVE QUESTIONS :

1. The C-language is language
   - (a) simple in construction
   - (b) advance functions available
   - (c) useful for database system
   - (d) all of the above

2. The C-language is based on
   - (a) English language
   - (b) French language
   - (c) Greek letters
   - (d) Hindi characters

3. A constant is a quantity
   - (a) Whose value varies
   - (b) Whose value remains to be constant
   - (c) converts value to a constant
   - (d) none of the above

4. A variable is quantity
   - (a) Whose value varies
   - (b) Whose value remains to be constant
   - (c) converts value to a constant
   - (d) none of the above

5. int variable stores
   - (a) decimal value
   - (b) integer value

(c) exponent value (d) none of the above

6. float variable is used for
   (a) decimal values (b) integer values
   (c) character values (d) none of the above
7. double variable is used for
   (a) 12 decimal accuracy (b) 24 decimal accuracy
   (c) 40 decimal accuracy (d) 20 decimal accuracy
8. char variable is used for
   (a) storage of single characters (b) storage of two characters
   (c) storage of word (d) storage of numbers
9. long int variable has memory range of
   (a) -1×10^{21} to 1×10^{21} (b) -1×10^{12} to 1×10^{12}
   (c) -1×10^{10} to 1×10^{10} (d) none of the above
10. long double variable has capacity of
   (a) 12 decimal accuracy (b) 24 decimal accuracy
   (c) 40 decimal accuracy (d) 20 decimal accuracy
11. unsigned variable accept value of
   (a) decimal type (b) positive integer number
   (c) negative integer number (d) none of the above
12. Arithmetic operators are used for
   (a) arithmetic operations (b) alphanumeric operations
   (c) character operations (d) none of the above
13. Arithmetic expressions are
   (a) combinations of characters and alphabets
   (b) combinations of arithmetic operators and variables
   (c) combinations of arithmetic operators, constants and variables
   (d) none of the above
14. Arithmetic statement
   (a) It is statement between variable and constant
   (b) It is statement between variable and variable
   (c) It is statement between variable and arithmetic expression
   (d) all of the above
15. Scanf statement is used for
   (a) Printing of result (b) alphanumeric operations
   (c) scanning of data (d) none of the above
16. The printf statement is used for
   (a) arithmetic operations (b) Printing of results
   (c) character operations (d) none of the above
17. The if statements are used for
   (a) arithmetic operations (b) Decision making
   (c) character operations (d) none of the above
18. The for statement is used for
   (a) arithmetic operations (b) Printing of results
   (c) Looping or cyclic operation (d) none of the above
19. The array variables store
   (a) A single value (b) Multiple values
   (c) character operations (d) none of the above

20. The function programs are used for
    (a) arithmetic operations (b) Printing of results
    (c) perform a function (d) none of the above
21. The recursive function is
    (a) arithmetic operations (b) Function calls to itself
    (c) character operations (d) none of the above
22. A void function is
    (a) Non returnable function (b) Function calls to itself
    (c) character operations (d) none of the above
23. The static variable is a variable
    (a) value initialized first time (b) Value cannot be modified
    (c) Value continuously changes (d) none of the above
24. The global variables are
    (a) unconventional variables (b) Common variable
    (c) Conventional variable (d) none of the above
25. The register variable is variable
    (a) which is registered (b) which is called frequently
    (c) character operations (d) none of the above
26. The enum statement is used for
    (a) Enumeration of data (b) Function calls to itself
    (c) Declaration of data (d) none of the above
27. The type -def statement is used for
    (a) arithmetic operations (b) Equivalence declaration
    (c) character operations (d) none of the above
28. The #define statement is
    (a) arithmetic operations (b) Function calls to itself
    (c) pre-preprocessor (d) none of the above
29. The %c format is used for
    (a) arithmetic operations (b) Function calls to itself
    (c) character operation (d) none of the above
30. A char array can store
    (a) A word (b) A line
    (c) Number of lines of word (d) all of the above
31. The %s format is used for
    (a) arithmetic operations (b) Scanning of word
    (c) character operations (d) none of the above
32. gets function is used for
    (a) arithmetic operations (b) Scanning of word
    (c) character operations (d) none of the above
33. The Pointer variable is
    (a) arithmetic operations (b) Scanning of word
    (c) A broker (d) none of the above
34. The *ptr
    (a) Indicate value of pointer (b) Scanning of word
    (c) character operations (d) none of the above
35. A structure is
    (a) arithmetic operations (b) Scanning of word

(c) Bunch of variables (d) none of the above

36. The file operation is used for
    (a) arithmetic operations (b) Storage of data on files
    (c) character operations (d) none of the above
37. The scope resolution operator is used for
    (a) arithmetic operations (b) Global variable
    (c) character operations (d) none of the above
38. Function overloading is used for
    (a) arithmetic operations (b) Scanning of word
    (c) Function of same name (d) none of the above
39. A class consist of
    (a) Private and public member (b) Scanning of word
    (c) character operations (d) none of the above

25.4 SUBJECTIVE QUESTIONS

1. What is a computer ?

   It is an electronic machine composed of the parts made up electronic circuit and mechanical components.

2. What are the functions of the computer?

   The computer performs following functions
   (i) It is capable of storing large amount of the data.
   (ii) It is able to retrieve the data at very fast speed .
   (iii) It is capable of performing the calculations at very fast speed.
   (iv) The accuracy of calculations is very high.
   (v) It can take the decisions according to the given conditions.

3. What are the advantages of computerization?

   The computerization provides large number of advantages to the user:
   (i) It performs calculations at very fast speed.
   (ii) The results obtained are very accurate.
   (iii) large amount of data can be stored.
   (iv) It is capable of retrieving the data at very fast speed.
   (v) The modifications can be very easily done.
   (vi) The errors are minimized.
   (vii) The results can be printed in the formatted form.
   (viii) The use of colours is possible.
   (ix) The results can be stored in file.
   (x) It allows graphics operation in addition to numeric operation.

4. Explain the difference between hardware and software.

   The hardware is a science related to the study of components and circuits of the computer.

   The software is a study of the translator or interpreter between the machine and the human operator.

5. Explain the hardware of the computer.

   The hardware of computer consists of six main components
   1. Input unit
   2. Output unit
   3. Temporary memory unit

4. Permanent memory or library unit
5. Arithmetic logic unit
6. Control unit

6. Explain the function of input and output unit.

The input and output unit is used for reading the data and printing of the results. The input unit assist in reading of the data from the user or it can be used for controlling the functions and operations on the screen.The output unit can be used for printing of the results or view of the results on the screen.

7. Explain the different types of input devices used.

The keyboard is a primary input device used.The other input devices used are

(i) Magnetic disc/tape
(ii) MICR- Magnetic ink character recognition
(iii) OCR/OMR - optical character or mark reader
(iv) Scanner
(v) Voice data entry terminal
(vi) cursur control devices

8. Explain the function and different types of cursor control devices used .

The major function of cursur control device is to control the positions of the different points on the screen and to actuate the graphic user interfaces available on the screen. The interfaces used are menu, buttons, check list, dialog boxes etc.

There are different types of cursur control devices used

1. mouse
2. track ball
3. thumb wheel
4. light pen
5. joy stick

9. What are the different types of output devices used ?

There are different types of output devices used such as

(i) Monitor
(ii) Magnetic disc/tape
(iii) printers
(iv) plotters

10. What is the operating system ?

The operating system is a system which makes computer capable of accepting the input supplied by the user. The operating system interconnects all the components of the computer , load the translator files, provides a text screen and allows user to feed the required commands for further execution of the software. It also loads basic components such fonts, printer and other devices.

11. What is the difference between a constant and variable?

A quantity whose value remains to be constant during execution is called constant. A quantity whose value varies during the execution is called variable.

12. What are the types of constants used in C-language?

There are three types of constants used

(i) Integer constant
(ii) Float constant
(iii) Exponent constant

13. Explain the difference between float and double variable.
The float variable accepts the values with 6 decimal accuracy and double variable accepts 12 decimal accuracy for the variables.

14. Explain the difference between long int and int variable.
The long int variable enhances the capacity of int variable from ± 32000 to ± IX10[21]. The int variable has a capacity of ± 32000.

15. What is a modulus operator?
The modulus operator is a operator which finds the remainder offer division of two number. It operates on only integer values. It is represented by % sign. This operates on integer values only.

16. Explain the arithmetic expression.
It is a combination of constant, variable and arithmetic operators to represent algebraic equations. For example

(a+b)/(c+d)

17. Explain what is meant by comment statement.
It is a non-executable statement written for purpose of
(i) Title of program
(ii) descriptions of variable
(iii) Explaining logics
The comment statement is written using /* and */ in which the text is enclosed.
For example
/* This is C-programming */

18. What is the use of 'printf' and 'scanf' statement is a output statement which prints results ?
The values of variable or arithmetic statements is printed by printf statement. The 'Scanf' statement is an input statement which reads the data values. The values of variable are read from data screen by are of this statement.

19. What are the different types of format conversion characters used ?
The format conversion characters used are
d — Integer variable
f — float variable
e — exponent variable
g — float variable with minimum space
c — character variables.

20. What are the different type of conversion modifier & used ?
The different types of modifier used are
n — field width number
l — long variable
n1 — decimal precision
- — To obtain printing from start of field

21. Explain the various types of white space characters.
These are different types of white space characters used
\t — tab character which leaves five blank spaces
\n — new line character. This shifts control to a new line
\r — Carriage return character. This shift control to start of line
\f — form feed character. This shifts control to new page

22. Explain what do you mean by post-script and pre-script increment ?

The C++ statement results in incrementing value of i by 1 where are i++ results in incrementing value of i by 1 mean ++i and i++ are same, but they differ as pre-script and post-script increments. In the first case, the increment is done initially and then operation is performed whereas in second case operation is performed and then value is incremented.

23. What is the concept of character ?

In C-language, any character of keyboard can be character of C-Language . A character of keyboard can be made character of C-language by writing it in a right side colon ' '.

Ex : 'A' — A is a character of C-language.

24. Which format is used for scanning and printing of character?

The '%c' format is used for scanning and printing of characters.

25. What is meant by integer division?

If a integer number is divided by another integer number then the value available is also an integer like 5/2 results in value of 2 because it is a division of two integers .

26. What is the use of braces in C-language.

The braces are used for bunching of statement and the bunch of statement is attached to the previous statement.

For example

```
if(a>b)
    {
        c=a+b;
        d=a/c;
    }
```

In this case the two statement are bunched by braces and attached to if statement.

27. What do you mean by looping?

These are the repetitive operation or cyclic operation performed by modifications of value in every cycle.

28. What are the different type of control statement ?

The 'if' statements are used as control statement. There are five types of 'if' statements

(i) simple 'if' statement

(ii) 'if-else' statement

(iii) compound 'if' statement

(iv) rested 'if' statement

(v) if-else construct statement

29. What is the purpose of control statement?

The control statements are used for purpose decision making. The decisions are made by control statement on the basis of satisfaction of the given conditions.

30. What is meant by logical expression ?

The logical expression creates a condition and it is formed by joining two variables or one variable and one constant by a logical operator.

Ex: a >= b

31. What is meant by decision statement?

Any statement of the program is a decision making statement like arithmetic statement, input/ Output statement, iteration statement can be decision statements to the control statements.

32. What is the difference between 'if' and 'if-else' statement?

In the 'if' statement, if the condition is satisfied then decision is executed where as in 'if-else' statement 'if' condition is satisfied the first decision is executed otherwise second decision is executed.

33. What are the compound logical operators ?

The compound logical operators are the operators which consider two or more logical condition simultaneously. These are two types of operators

1. and operator which is written as '&&'
2. or operator which is written as ||

The '&&' operators creates a compulsory condition where as || creates a optional condition.

34. What do you mean by nested if' statement?

It is the nesting of statement one inside the other statement. If a situation arises that a decision depends on two conditions but the second condition is checked if first condition is satisfied then 'nested f' statement are used.

35. What is the purpose of 'if-else' construct statement?

The statement consider multiple conditions and corresponding multiple decisions. But only are decision is executed on satisfaction of are condition.

36. Explain the difference between the 'for' statement and 'while' statement.

The 'for' statement has an index variable which performs cycles operations. The index variable has initial value and final value. The increment in the cycle are also specified

Ex:
```
for (i = 0 ; i < = 10 ; ++i)
{
__________
__________
}
```

where i is a index variable

The value of 'i' varies from 0 to 10 in step of 1.

In case of 'while' statement the value of index can vary independently. The final condition if satisfied then cycles are executed.

Ex:
```
i = 0;
while ( i < = 10)
{
++i ;
________
________
________
}
```

In this case, if value of 'i' is below or equal to 10, then the cyclic operations are performed.

37. What is the difference between 'while' and 'do-while' statement ?

The 'while' statement checks the condition initially and cycle is executed if condition is satisfied. In the case of 'do-while' statement the condition is checked at the end of first cycle. The first cycle is performed and then the condition is check. It means that the condition is checked at the end of every cycle.

38. Explain the use of 'goto' statement.

This statement shifts the control to any point. It is written as

```
goto x ;
______
________
________

x :
```

where x — Lable name

39. Explain the difference between 'break' and 'continue' statement.

The 'break' statement breaks a block or cyclic operation where as 'continue' statement breaks the current cycle and start next cycle.

40. Explain the nested 'for' statement.

In the nested 'for' statement is one 'for' statement inside another 'for' statement

Ex:
```
for (i = 1 ; i < = 3 ; ++i)
{
for (j = 1 ; j < = 3 ; ++j)
{
________
________
__________

}
```

41. What do you mean by array variable ? explain.

The variable which allows storage of multiple values in different memories is called array variable. It is declared as

```
int a[10];
```

This declares array variable of integer type having name 'a' with memory of 10. The array variable can be integer, float, character type. The array variable is single or two dimensional variable.

42. How an array variable is declared ?

It is declared by indicating nature, name and no. of memories of variable

```
int a [10];
```

This statement declares array variable and opens 10 memories under 'a' variable.

43. Explain how an array variable can be read from userscreen.

```
for (i = 0 ; i < = 5 ; ++i)
{
scanf ("%d", & a [c]);
}
```

The 'scanf' statement is executed in a 'for' statement and various elements of array are read by changing index of 'a' array variable.

44. Explain the concept of 2-D array.

The 2-D dimensional array variable is variable having memories arranged in rows and columns. These memories are designated by its row number and column number.

45. How a 2-D array is declared

The 2-D array variable is declared by

```
int x [5] [5]
```

This creates a 2-D array variable memory of size 5×5.

46. Explain what do you mean by initialization of array variable ?

An array variable which is declared and supplied with value at the same moment is called initialization of array variable

int a [5] = {5, 6, 10, 9, 42};

0 1 2 3 4

This declares 'a' array variable with 5 values supplied from index locations 0 to 4.

47. What is the concept of char array ?

The character array is an array having memories to store characters rather than numeric value. These are declared as

Char C [10] ;

This declares a char array 'C' having 10 memories to store 10 characters.

48. Can a char array store a string?

The char arrays are created for storing string consisting of number of characters. A sentence of english language consisting of number of words can be treated as string .

49. What is the use of 2-D char array?

The 2-D char arrays are used for storage of characters in rows and column. The char array has memory in 2-dimension in which the characters can be stored. Every row of char array store number of characters or one string. The char array stores number of strings in its memory.

50. What is the concept of function program?

The concept of function is a sub-program which is called in the main program. The function program are sub-programs performing certain function. The function programs are called by main program or function programs are called by another function program. The function programs have argument which forms an in put to function program and they are used to calculate the values of function program.

51. What are the different types of function program?

There are four types of function programs used

1. Returnable function
2. non-returnable function
3. Input/Output argument function
4. Recursive function.

52. Explain the difference between returnable and non-returnable function program.

The returnable function program is a program in which the value is returned to the call of function program . This function program is declared according to the value returned by function program.The value being returned is enclosed in a statement 'return ()'.This function returns only one value to the call.

The non-returnable function programs are the function program which do not return a value to the call of function. These function programs performs calculations and print the value.

53. Explain the recursive function program.

The function program which calls to itself in the function body is a recursive function. The call to itself result in a cyclic call and in every call the argument reduces it value. The recursive call must be terminated at certain condition or value of argument.

54. What is meant by call by value and call by reference in function program ?

When an array becomes argument of function program, then there are two situation possible

1. Complete array is argument of function program
2. One element of array is argument of function program.

If the complete array is argument of function program, then it is call reference to the array. If an element of array is argument of function program. Then it is call by value.

55. What do you mean by 'static' and 'automatic' variable ?

The static variable is declared by a 'static' word and this variable can be initialized for the first time and subsequent execution of the statement is not possible. The automatic variable can be declared either by ;auto' word or no declaration. Every variable declared in default is automatic variable .This variable has to be initialized in every cycle of execution.

56. What is a global variable ?

It is common variable which can be accessed in the main or any function program. These variable are declared in the beginning of file before writing main and function program.

57. Explain the use of register variable.

These variables are declared by a word 'register'. The variables are stored in the register memory where only few variables are stored. These variable can accessed at very fast speed. The register variables are used only int, char or pointer variables.

58. What do you mean by 'enum'statement ?

This statement enumerates the given string i.e. the supplied string are assigned numeric values which allow the variables to acquire the values by using the above string.

Ex: enum colour {RED, BLUE,GREEN,YELLOW};

This statement enumerates the four string as 0,1,2,3.

Colour = RED;

mean

Colour = 0 ;

This is because the value of RED as String is 0.

59. Explain the use of type def statement.

This statement is used to define equivalance of two strings.

Ex: type def float REAL;

This indicates that 'float' is equivalent to REAL. Then if the REAL word is written it is replace by float as both are equivalent.

60. What is the concept of Union ?

The union are used when the single variable is to be utilized to store the values of different nature. For example x variable is to be used to store multiple variety of values like float, int and char values.

```
union xx
    {
            int a;
            float b;
            char c;
    }
```

This is union of three dis-similar variable a,b,c having single memory of different nature.

61. What is the use of C-processor?

The C-preprocessor are the statements used for preprocessing of the certain function written before starting of the program. These are written in the beginning of file be '#' sign.

62. What are the different types of C-processor used?

There are three types of C-preprocessors

1. Simple string replacement
2. Micro-function
3. File inclusion

63. What is the purpose of 'include' statement?
The include statement is used for inclusion of files which contains the usermade or readymade function which can be included in the current file.
include<iostream.h>

64. What do you mean by string and how it is represented in C-language ?
A string consist of bunch of characters and it is written in double inverted colon " ".

65. What is a null character and how it is indicated ?
A null character is a terminating blank space and it is indicated by '\0' sign. A string can be terminated by a null character.

66. Explain how to declare a string and store in a char array ?
The string can be declared by

```
char C[6] = { 'H','e','l','l','o','\0'}
```

It can also be declared as

```
char C[6] = {"Hello";
```

67. What is a string function?
The string functions are the functions which performs certain operation on characters such as
1. finding length of string
2. Copying of string
3. joining of string
4. finding a character
5. finding whether it is equal or not

68. What is the concept of pointer ?
A pointer is a variable which acts like a broker for transaction of value between two variables. The pointer is capable of accessing the address of any other variable and modifying the values of variable and modifying the values of variable.
It is declared by

```
int *ptr;
```

where ptr -- pointer variable
The use of * convert the variable to pointer variable.

69. What is a pointer of array ?
A array when it becomes pointer of its own or is given to a pointer as argument of function program, then it captures the base address of array. This makes it easier to make movements on the other values of array.

70. What is a function pointer ?
A pointer which can access the address of function programs are called function pointer. They are declared as

```
void (*fptr) ();
```

where fptr —— function pointer.

71. What is the concept of structure ?
It is association of number of variables having main variable which is attached with sub-variable having multiple memories.

72. Explain how a structure can be declared.
The structure can be declared by indicating name of structure and sub-variables of structure.

```
struct xx
{
int x,y,z;
```

```
} ;
xx      —    name of structure
x,y,z   —    names of variables
```

73. Explain how a reference of structure is made.

The structure can be refered as

```
struct xx yy ;
```

The structure of xx is referred to yy so that all sub-variables of xx can be received by yy.

74. Explain how a structure variable can be written.

The structured variable can be written as

yy. x = 5

main variable subvariable

The value of x sub-variable of yy main variable is 5 or value of structured variable yy.x is 5.

75. Explain how a main variable of structure is referred.

The main variable of structure can be referred by using

```
Struct xx yy;
```

This refers the structure of xx to yy.

76. Explain how array of structure is declared.

The structure of 'xx' is referred to an array variable 'yy' which has memory of 5.

```
struct xx yy[5];
```

In this case the structure of xx is referred to yy which is array variable.

77. Explain how structure can be referred to pointer variable.

The main variable of structure can be a pointer variable which can be written as

```
struct point *P ;
```

The 'point' is structure of two variable P1 and P2

```
struct point
{
int P1;
int P2;
};
```

78. Describe the process of scanning of structure.

The structure can be scanned by independent scanning of structured variable.

```
scanf\"%d", & yy. a, & yy.b,& yy. c);
```

The structure of 'today' consists of date, month, year. These are scanned by using above statement.

79. Explain the structure of pointer.

This is a structure of pointers in which all the members of structure becomes pointer variable.

```
struct P
{
int * P1 ;
int * P2 ;
} ;
```

80. Explain how a sub-variable of structure as pointer receives a value.

The structure variable with sub-variable as pointer can be indicates as

```
* point p1 = a ;
```

where

a — normal variable

point — main variable of structure

P1 — Pointer sub variable of structure.

81. Explain why file operation are required.

The file operation are required because the repetitive data can be preserved and read from the file and the results obtained from program can be stored in the file. This operation allows for storage of data, editing of the stored data, deletion and addition of new records or result. The data base operation can be easily performed through file operation. The graphic images can be stored by use of files.

82. What is a file pointer ?

A file pointer is a pointer which can access the address of any file. It can open a file and close a file. It is capable of reading a data from file and writing the results on the file. It is declared by

```
FILE * fptr;
```

83. Explain how a file is opened.

A file can be opened by using 'fopen' function in which the file pointer receives the address of file name and the mode of opening file.

```
ftpr = fopen ("name", mode");
```

84. Explain how a file can be closed.

The file can be closed by fclose function.

The file can be closed by

```
fclose(fptr);
```

This closes the file opened by 'fptr' pointer.

85. How many file can be opened in C-program ?

In C-programming as many number of file can be opened and closed according to the requirement. But only one file can be opened by a file pointer. It is possible to use number of file pointers to open number of files. The file pointer can accept the address of file and once the work is over it can closed. Then the pointer can open another file.

86. How to open and close a file ?

It is necessary to open a file by file pointer using 'fopen' function.

```
fptr = fopen ("name", "mode");
```

where fptr — file pointer used for opening file

This function opens a file on the memory device and provides address file to file pointer by given name and mode.

The file can be closed by

```
fclose()
```

function.

87. What are the different types of modes?

There are various modes of opening file

1. reading file —

   The reading file is used for reading of data from the file.

2. writing file —

   This mode is to be used for writing of result on the file.

3. reading writing (append) file —

   This mode is to be used for reading as well as writing of results on the file.

4. reading append mode :

   If file exist then it is reading operation otherwise it is writing operation.

5. write append mode:

   If file exist then it is a writing to be performed at the end of file. If file do not exists then the file is to be opened and writing is done in new file.

6. Binary file :

   If the writing is to be performed in a binary mode, then it is a binary file.

88. What are the functions used for reading and writing operation file ?

There are three types of function which can be used to perform reading and writing operation on file. For reading purposes three function are used:

1. fscanf 2. fputs
3. fread

For writing purposes there are three functions used:

1. fprintf 2. fgets
3. fwrite

89. What is the use of 'exit' function ?

The 'exit' function is to be used for intermediate termination of execution of program. The program can be terminated at any point if it is found that abnormal condition is likely to occur. There are such conditions possible as

1. zero divide error
2. Under root of negative quantity
3. file not opened
4. any other conditions.

90. What is the use of NULL flag ?

In case if the file is not opened successfully then the file pointer receives NULL flag. The opening of file operation fails under the circumstances that

1. Reading file not created or do not exist.
2. The drive or directory specified in the path of not exists.
3. Memory device do not have space or bad sectors are found on disk.

91. What is meant by object oriented programming ?

It is technique in which the classes are utilized for storage of large amount of data which may be private or public . The object are created from the classes and these objects create memories under private and public variable . The object are utilized for performing manipulations on the given data through the function members of the class.

92. What do you mean by a class ?

A class consists of private and public members of data variables and function members. The private variables and member functions could be accessed by public member functions.

93. How class programs are written in C^{++} ?

In C^{++} the programs uses class are arranged in following fashion

include files
class declaration
class functions and definitions
main functions

94. How a class declared ?

A class declared by a word class preceded by name of a class and the body of class is enclosed in braces. The class body contains the private member functions and public member functions. These member functions can be of Two varieties:

1. data members
2. function members

Ex:
```
class item
{
    int number;
    float cost;
public :
    void getdata( int a,int b);
    void putdata();
};
```

95. How the object are declared ?

The object of are declared by reference to a class and supply of name of object.

```
item i;
```

item is a name of a class

i is a name of object

96. Can array become private member of class ?

An array variable can become private member of class and can access the information of a class in the object. The array variable can be declared as member of class.

```
class item
{
    int n[10];
    ______
public :
    ______
}
```

In this class n is declared as an array of private member data type .

97. Can function member be a private member of class ?

A function member can be a private member of class and such a function member can be access by public member function of the class.

```
class item
{
    void read();
public :
    void compute();
    ____
}
```

In this class item the read function is a private function which can be access by a public function compute by giving a call to read function.

98. Is it possible to have array of objects ?

It is possible to create array of objects by reference of a class to the array. If xx is a name of a class then

xx   y[20]

yy can become array of xx class.

99. How a pointer can become object of class ?

If a pointer variable is refered to a class then the pointer variable can become object of a class. For example

If xx is a class which is refered to *x, then *x become an object of a class.

100. What is meant by nested classes?

The placement of a class inside another class is a nested class. A class declared in a outer class and it becomes a member of outer class is called nested class.

101. What is a static data member?

A variable of a class can become a static member by declaring the variable to be a static member using a word static. Such a member of a class can be initialized with any desired value.

102. Can external function becomes a member of class?

A friend function can become a member of class means a function which is not a member of class can become friend member of class and declared as friendly function.

EXERCISE 1

Identify syntax errors in the program and correct the errors, indicate the output of the following :

```
# define PI 3.142
main ()
{
    int R ,C;
    float perimeter ;
    float area  ;
    C = PI
    R = 5 ;
    perimeter = 2.0 * C *R;
    area = C*R*R ;
    printf("%f","%d",&perimeter,&area)
}
```

EXERCISES 2

What will be the output of the following program ?

(i)

```
main()
{
    int i = 1;
    for (; i++;)
    printf("%d" , i);
}
```

(ii)

```
main()
{
    int x=3,y,z ;
    z = y=x;
    z *=y|=x;
    printf("x=%d y=%d z=%d",x,y,z);
}
```

EXERCISE 3

Evaluate the expression given below assuming.

a = 5, b = 2, c = 4

(a) b%c && a*b/c +c+b || a || b

(b) a%c && a*c/b&& b||a

(c) a%b *c && c%b*a

(d) b%c * a && a%c*b

(e) b > 15 && c < 0 || a > 0

(f) a = = c || b > a.

EXERCISE 4

What will be the output of the following programs?

(a)

```
main()
{
    int a = 3, b = 2 ,c = 1, d;
    d = a | b & c;
    printf ("d = %d \n",d);
    d = a | b & ~c;
    printf ("d = %d \n",d);
}
```

(b)

```
main ()
{
    int a = oxff;
    if (a << 4 >> 12 )
            printf("left");
    else
            printf("Right");
}
```

(c)

```
main()
{
    int i = +1;
    while (~i)
```

```
    printf("Happy New Year");
}
```

```
(d)
main()
{
    static int b[]= {1,2,3,4,5};
    int i ;
    for(i = 0; i <=4; i++)
            printf("%d", i[b]);
}
```

```
(e)
main()
{
    static int b[]={10,20,30,40,50};
    int i,*k;
    k = & b[4] – 4;
    for(i = 0; i <= 4; i++)
    {
            printf("%d",*k);
            k++;
    }
}
```

```
(f)
main()
{
    int i = 45;
    float c;
    c = ckhe(i);
    printf("c=%c",c);
}
    ckhe(ch)
    int ch
    {
    (ch >= 45? return 3.14: return (6.28));
    }
```

```
(g)
main()
{
    int i = 400*400/400;
    if(i ==400)
            printf("students");
    else
            printf("staff");
}
```

```
(h)
main()
{
     int i;
     for(i = 0,ch = 'A';i<4;i++,ch+ =2*i)
               putchar(ch);
}
```

```
(i)
main()
{
     printf("%d%d%d%d",4%3,4%-3,-4%3,-4%-3);
}
```

```
(j)
main()
{
     float a = 0.7;
     if(a<0.7)
               printf("true");
     else
               printf("false");
}
```

```
(k)
main()
{
     int a=10,b,c;
     b=!a;c=!!b;
     printf("%d%d%d",a,b,c);
}
```

```
(l)

main()
{
     int x=-1,y=2,z=3,a;
     a=++x && ++y && ++z;
     printf("%d%d%d%d",a,x,y,z);
}
```

```
(m)
main()
{
     int i=3,k,l;
     k = add(++i);
     l = add(i++);
     printf("i = %d,k = %d, l = %d",i,k,k);
}
```

```
add(i)
int i;
{
    ++i;
    return(i);
}
```

(n)

```
main()
{
    char ch='B';
    switch(ch)
    {
    case 66 :
            printf("capital B");
    break;
    case default:
            continue;
    }
}
```

(o)

```
main()
{
    int i,j;
    for(i=1;j=2;;)
    {
            i+t; j+=2;
            if(i+j>20)
                    break;
    }
}
```

(p)

```
main(int argc,char *argv)
{
    printf("%d%s",argc,argv[0]);
}
```

(q)

```
main()
{
    FILE *fp;
    fp = fopen("e.dat","rb");
    if(fp==NULL)
    {
    printf("unable to open file\n");
    exit();
    }
}
```

26

COMMON PROGRAMMING ERRORS

26.1 INTRODUCTION

When a C–Program is written on the screen of monitor, there are possibilities of errors in programming by the programmer. These are to be corrected.

The detection of errors is a very difficult task in programming and such errors depend on the complexity of the program and system of programming.

There are various types of major errors in the program :

1. Compilation error
2. Memory error
3. Logical error
4. Under flow or over flow error
5. Statement errors
6. File operation errors

26.2 COMPILATION ERROR

These errors occur due to grammatical mistakes in the language of the program. The errors are due to the procedure of writing program in the given system of the language which has not been followed. The errors may occur in the conversion of the program into machine language which is not possible due to internal errors in the program.

These errors occur in the stage of compilation because of incorrect use of words or writing procedure in the program . Some of these can be as below :

(i) A variable is used in program, but not declared in the program.

(ii) The statement is not closed by a semicolon " ; "

(iii) The " , " are missing in the `printf' statement. and 'scanf' statement between two variables.

(iv) Brackets '()' not matching in arithmetic statement.
The number of opening brackets are not equal to number of closing brackets.

(v) Errors in name of function program and number of variables used as arguments.

(vi) Ampersand missing before non-pointer variables in a 'scanf ' statement.

26.3 MEMORY ALLOCATION ERROR

This error occurs in the program where the array variables are used. The array variable is declared and maximum number of memories are specified as

intm[10];

In case if the numbers read through program are more than the allotted memory then such errors occur in the program.

26.4 LOGICAL ERRORS

These are the errors created in the program because of incorrect logic in the program. These are created because of improper writing or execution or iteration in the program.

These errors may occur due to:

(a) Endless cycle of iteration in program.

(b) The decision to be taken at certain value is unknown.

(c) Modification 'index' in a 'for' statement.

(d) Unknown function call.

(e) Memory of array is deficient to store values of array.

(f) Incorrect decision making.

(g) Non-inclusion of files for required to execute function used in program.

26.5 UNDERFLOW AND OVERFLOW ERRORS

These errors occur due very low value which can not be accepted by the computer or the value obtained is very high which goes out of the memory of computer.

26.6 STATEMENT ERRORS

These are the errors which are not detected during compilation process, but produce incorrect results due improper execution of program.

The common errors are listed below :

(i) Incorrect format in scanning/printing

The format is incorrect in scanning because of different format for different types of variables. Like

Ex:
```
scanf("%d%d" &a,&b);
printf("a=%d,b=%d", a,b);
```
Where,

a & b are float variables.

(ii) Insufficient format for variables

If number of variables used and their format do not match, then the values will not be available correctly.

Ex:
```
scanf("%d%d", &a, &b, &c);
printf("a=%d,b=%d", a,b,c);
```
Where,

a,b,c are integer variable.

Sometimes formats are given, but no variables are written in 'printf' statement.

(iii) Integer division

The division between two integer variables is an integer value like

```
b = a/2;
```
Where,

'a' is integer variable

This division may be consisting of decimals which are cut off due to the use of integer variable division.

(iv) Unnecessary semicolon

If a semicolon is given unnecessarily to 'if' or 'for' statement, then the 'if' statement cannot take decision or 'for' statement does not execute the cycle.

Ex: (1)
```
if(j==100);
    j=0;
```
(2)
```
for(i=1;i<=10;++i);
{
    a=a+i;
}
```
In these case 'for' and 'if' statements are closed by semicolon, which is incorrect.

(v) Use of incorrect logical operator

The '==' logical operator is confused with '=' operator.

Ex:

```
if(a=2)
        printf("This is C\n");
```

The 'if' statement uses logical operators, which is missing in 'if' statement.

(vi) Using wrong indexes for an array

```
for(i=0;i<100;++i)
        sum += a[i];
```

In this case calculation starts from 0 value and ends at 99 rather than 100. Total 100 cycle are executed from 0 to 99. But if values are present between 1 to 100, then results will be wrong.

(vii) 'break' statement not in 'switch' statement

```
switch(opr)
{
case 1:
c = a+b;
case 2:
c = a–b;
case 3:
c = a*b;
default:
c = a/b;
}
```

In this statement, the break statement is not used which results in checking of all cases and the last value of c will be retained by calculation of 'switch' statement. Which is an error in use of switch statement.

(viii) The use of braces '{', '}' or ';' at wrong places, results in inaccurate execution of program in case of 'Nested for' and 'Nested if' statements.

```
if(a>b);
        c=a+b;
if(a>b);
        c=a+b;
else
        c=a*b;
```

(ix) Use of mismatch operation on indexes in a 'for' statement

```
for(i=0;i<m;++m)
        {
                ----------
                ----------
                ----------
        }
```

This statement increments 'm' rather than 'i' hence results in wrong calculation of the cycle.

(x) Mismatch in call of function program

The function call may be by wrong name in the main program or the arguments of function program may be missing or less than given at the function program. The name function program and number of argument must match in sequence at the place of giving call to function program in the main. The nature of argument variables should also match with nature defined in function program.

26.7 FILE OPERATION ERRORS

The errors occur while using file operations. If input file is not opened and saved in memory device by the given name, then reading file is not available or a reading file does not contain data, which we want to read from file or incorrect data may be written in the file. Then the data reading error occurs in file.

EXERCISE

1. Explain the errors in the following statements :

(a) int a, b,c,float d;

(b) int a,b; float b,c ;

(c) char a,b;c;

(d) int a=12.78;

(e) char c= 24;

(f) scanf("%d%d\n",&a,&b);

(g) scanf("%d%d",a,b);

(h) scanf("%d%d",*ptr,a);

(i) scanf("%d%d",&a&b);

(j) scanf("%d%d%d",&a,&b);

(k) scanf("%d%d",&a,&b,&c);

(l) printf("a=%d,b=%d,c=\n",a,b,c);

(m) printf("a=%d,b=%d,c=%d\n",a,b);

(n) printf("a=%10.3d,b=%–0.4f",a,b);

(o) /* Nice C–programming /

(p)
```
if(a>b);
  {
        c=a+b;
  }
```

(q)
```
if(a>b);
    c=a+b;
else
    c=a–b;
```

(r)
```
if(a=b)
    c=a+b;
else
    c=a–b;
```

(s)
```
if(a)
    c=a+b;
else
    c=a-b;
```

(t)
```
if(a>b)
    c=a+b;
    d=c+x;
else
    y=a*b;
```

(u)
```
for(i=0;i<=m; ++m)
    y=a+b;
```

```
(v)  for(i=0;i<=m;++i)
       i+=2;
(w)  while(i=15)
     {
         i *=2;
         printf("i=%d",i);
     }
(x)  while(x>25);
     {
         x +=4;
         printf("x=%d\n",x);
     }
(y)  do
     {
         i +=5;
         printf("i=%d\n",i);
     }while(i<34)
(z)  int  a[4] = { 12,3,6,7,19,34};
```

2. Find the error in the following program :

Program 1

```
main ( )
     {
          int a, b,c;
          printf ("Enter the values of a,b,c\n");
          scanf("%e%c", &a,&b,&c);
          printf (%g%g%g\n",a,b,c);
     }
```

Program 2

```
main ( )
     {
          int a,b,c;
          a = 2;
          b = a*c;
          printf ("a = % d, b = % d\n", a,b);
     }
```

Program 3

```
main ( )
     {
          int a,b,c
          printf ("Enter the values of a,b,c\n");
          scanf ("%c%c", &a,&b);
          c = a+b;
          printf ("c=%d\n",c);
     }
```

Program 4

```
main ( )
        {
                int a = 12.25 , b = 13.96;
                printf ("a = %f , b= %d\n", a,b);
        }
```

Program 5

```
main ( )
        {
                int a = 12 , b = 15;
                if (a = b)
                        printf("a = %d\n",a);
                else
                        printf ("b=%d\\n",a);
        );
```

Program 6

```
main ( )
        {
                int a = 9, b = 32, c;
                if (a > b);
                        c = a+b;
                else;
                        c = a – b;
                printf ("c = %c\n",C);
}
```

Program 7

```
main ( )
        {
                (int a,b,c,d;
                printf("Enter the values of a,b,c\n");
                scanf ("%d%d%d", &a,&b,&c);
                if ((a>b) & (a>c))
                        d = a+b;
                else;
                        d = a–b;
                        printf("d = %d\n",d);
        }
```

Program 8

```
main ( )
        {
                int x, y, a;
                printf ("Enter the value of x,y,\n");
                scanf ("%d%d", x+y);
                printf ("%d%d,x,y,z);
        }
```

Program 9

```
main ( )
        {
                int i, m;
                print("Enter the value of m\n");
                scanf("%d",&m);
                while(i<=15)
                {
                        i = i*3;
                        print("i=%d\n",i)
                }
        }
```

Program 10

```
main ( )
        {
                int a [5] = {6,7,–12,19,3}
                int sum = 0;
                for(i = 1; i<5; ++i)
                {
                        sum += a[i];
                }
                printf("sum = %d\n,"sum);
        }
```

Program 11

```
main ( )
        {
                int a[20], i,m, sum;
                printf("Enter the value of m\n");
                scanf("%d", &m);
                for(i=0; i<m; ++i)
                        scanf("%d", &a[i];
                        sum = 0;
                        for (i=1; i<=m; ++i)
                                sum = sum + a[i];
                                printf("sum = %d\n,"sum);
        }
```

Program 12

```
#define PI = 3.5
        main ()
        {
                float a;
                printf("Enter value of radius");
                scanf("%f", &a);
                a = PI*a*2.0;
                printf("Area is %f", a);
        }
```

Program 13

```
/* C++*/
        # include "stdio.h"
        void main()
        {
                int i,j;
                void show (int,int);
                show (i,j);
        }
        void show (a,b)
        int a, b;
        {
                printf("Value of a and b = %d  %d", a,b);
        }
```

Program 14

```
/* C++ */
        #include "stdio.h"
        void main ()
        {
                float a;
                a = 5;
                printf("value of a = %d", a);
        }
```

Program 15

```
main ( )
        {
                int a = 5 , b ;
                if (a > b)
                        b = 2 * a ;
                if (a < 5 )
                        b = 3 * a;
                printf ("b = %d\n",b);
        }
```

Program 16

```
main ( )
        {
                int i ;
                printf("Enter the value of i\n");
                scanf ("%d", &i);
                switch (i)
                {
                        case 1:
                                c = a+b;
                        case 2 :
                                c = a – b;
```

```
            case 3:
                    c = a*b;
            default :
                    c = a/b;
        }
        printf(" c = %d\n", c);
}
```

Program 17

```
Compute (a,b,c)
        float a,b,c;
        {
                c = a*b;
        }
        main ( )
        {
                float p,q,r,s,z;
                printf ("Enter the values of p &q\n");
                scanf("%f %f", &p,&q);
                compute (p,q,z);
                printf("c = %g \n",z);
                r = p + 2.0 ; s = q +3.0;
                compute (r,s,a);
                printf ("c = %g\n", z );
        }
```

Program 18

```
main ( )
        {
                int a [5] , i,m;
                m = 10;
                for (i = 1; i < = 10; ++i)
                scanf("%d ",&a [i] ) ;
                for (i = 1 ; i< = 10; ++i)
                printf ("%d, a [i]);
        }
```

Program 19

```
compute (a,b)
        {
                int c;
                c = a*b;
                printf ("c%d\n",c);
        }
        main ( )
        {
                int a = 2, b = 3;
                compute (a);
        }
```

Program 20

```
int compute (a,b)
        {
                int c;
                c = a*b;
                return (c);
        }
        main ( )
        {
                int a = 2, b = 3;
                compute (a,b);
        }
```

Program 21

```
main ( )
        {
                int x = 4, y = 5;
                while (y <= 10)
                {
                        ++x;
                        – –y;
                        printf("%d   ", y++);
                        printf("%d   ",--x);
                }
```

Program 22

```
test  (x,y,z)
        int x,y,z;
        {
                if x > y
                        return x;
                else
                        return  y;
        {
        main ( )
        {
                int x = 10, y = 20;
                test  (x,y,z);
        }
```

Program 23

```
main ( )
        {
                int x = 3;
                if (x > 5)
                        int y = 2*x;
                else
```

```
            int z = 3*x;
        printf("x =%d, y = %d, z=%d\n", x,y,z);
    }
```

Program 24

```
main ( )
    {
        int x = 3,y,z;
        if (x > 5)
            y = 2*x;
        else
            z = 3*x;
        printf("x =%d, y = %d, z=%d\n", x,y,z);
    }
```

Program 25

```
main ( )
    {
        file *fptr;
        int x, y, z;
        fptr = fopen("data.bmp","r");
        fscanf(fptr,"%d%d%d", &x ,&y, &z);
        printf("x=%d, y = %d, z=%d\n", x, y, z);
    }
```

Program 26

```
main ( )
    {
        FILE *fptr;
        int x, y, z;
        fptr = fopen("data.bmp","w");
        fscanf(fptr,"%d%d%d", &x ,&y, &z);
        printf("x=%d, y = %d, z=%d\n", x, y, z);
    }
```

Program 27

```
main ( )
    {
        FILE *fptr;
        int x, y, z;
        fptr = fopen("data.bmp","r");
        if(fptr ==null)
            printf("unable to open a file\n");
        else
            printf("file successfully opened");
        fscanf(fptr,"%d%d%d", &x ,&y, &z);
        printf("x=%d, y = %d, z=%d\n", x, y, z);
        fclose(fptr);
    }
```

Program 28

```
main ( )
        {
                FILE *fptr;
                int x, y, z;
                fptr = fopen("data.bmp","r");
                while (feof(fptr))
                        fscanf(fptr,"%d%d%d", &x ,&y, &z);
                printf("x=%d, y = %d, z=%d\n", x, y, z);
        }
```

Program 29

```
/*overflow error if y > 1.5*/
        main()
        {
                float x,c,y,k,sum,term;
                clrscr();
                printf("enter the value of y maximum upto 1.14 \n");
                scanf("%f",&y);
                x = 0; term = 1;
                for (k=1;k<500;++k)
                {
                        if(k<=250)
                        {
                                c = k *k;
                        }
                        else
                                c = 4*(k*k*k);
                                term = term*y;
                                x = x+c*term;
                        }
                        printf("the value of y =%g and the values of x=%g\n,y,x);
                }
```

Program 30

```
float x, bm;
        main()
        {
                float x = 5;
                printf("Enter the value of bm\n");
                scanf("%f", &bm);
                compute();
        }
        compute()
        {
                float z;
                z = x*bm;
                printf("z = %g\n",z);
        }
```

Program 31

```
main ( )
      {
            float i, n, fact;
            printf("Enter the value of n\n");
            scanf("%f", &n);
            fact = 0;
            for (i = 1; i<=n; ++i)
                  fact *= i;
            printf("fact = %g\n",fact);
      }
```

Program 32

```
main ( )
      {
            float i, n, fact;
            printf("Enter the value of n\n");
            scanf("%f", &n);
            fact = 1;
            for (i = 0; i<=n; ++i)
                  fact *= i;
            printf("fact = %g\n",fact);
}
```

Program 33

```
main ( )
      {
            float x, rem;
            printf("Enter the value of x\n");
            scanf("%f", &x);
            rem = x%3;
            printf ("rem=%g\n", rem);
}
```

Program 34

```
main ( )
      {
            int, x, n;
            printf("Enter the value of n\n");
            scanf("%d", &n);
            if(n>4)
                  x = n*n;
                  printf("The value of n<4&x=%g\n",x);
            else
                  x = 2*n;
                  print("The value of n<4&x=%g\n",x);
```

```
}
```

Program 35

```
main ( )
        {
                int num;
                printf("Enter your number\n");
                scanf("%d", &num);
                if(num<0)
                        num = –num;
                        printf("The absolute value of number is \n",num);
}
```

Program 36

```
main ( )
        {
                float a[10],i,m;
                m = 5;
                printf("Enter 5 elements of array\n");
                for(i=1; i<=m; i=i+0.1)
                {
                scanf("%f", & a[i]);
                }
                sum = 0;
                for(i=1; i<=m; i=i+0.1)
                {
                sum = sum + a[i];
                }
                printf("%g\n", sum);
}
```

Program 37

```
main ( )
        {
                char C[10];
                printf("Enter your string\n");
                scanf("%d", C);
                printf("The string entered was %d", C);
}
```

Program 38

```
main ( )
        {
                char C[10];
                printf("Enter your string\n");
                scanf("%c", C);
                printf("The string entered was %c", C);
}
```

Program 39

```
main ()
        {
                int l,b,h,v;
                printf("Enter value of l,b,h\n");
                scanf("%d%d%d", &l,&b,&h);
                v = l*b*h
                printf("The volume is %d \n",l,b,h);
}
```

Program 40

```
main ()
        {
                int l,b,h;
                printf("Enter value of l,b,h\n");
                scanf("%d%d%d", &l,&b,&h);
                Volume(l,b,h);
}

Volume (l,b,h );
int l,b,h;
        {
                int v;
                v = l*b*h
                printf("The volume is %d \n",v);
}
```

Program 41

```
main ()
        {
                int a, b,c;
                cout<<"Enter the values of a,b,c\n";
                cin<<a<<b<<c;
                cout>>a>>b>>c;
        }
```

Program 42

```
        main ()
        {
                int a,b,c;
                a = 2;
                b = a*c;
                cout<<"a ="<<a<<"b =<<b<<"\n";
        }
```

Program 43

```
main ()
        {
```

```
        int a,b,c
        cout<<"Enter the values of a,b,c\n";
        cin>>a>>b;
        c = a+b;
        cout<<"c="<<c;
    }
```

Program 44

```
main ()
    {
        int a = 12.25 , b = 13.96;
        cout<<"a = "<<a<<" b= "<<b<<"\n";
    }
```

Program 45

```
main ()
    {
        int a = 12 , b = 15;
        if (a = b)
            cout<<"a ="<<a;
        else
            cout<<"b="<<b;
    );
```

Program 46

```
main ()
    {
        int a = 9, b = 32, c;
        if (a > b);
            c = a+b;
        else;
            c = a – b;
        cout<<"c = "<<C;
}
```

Program 47

```
main ()
    {
        (int a,b,c,d;
        cout<<"Enter the values of a,b,c\n";
        cin>>a>>b>>c;
        if ((a>b) & (a>c))
            d = a+b;
        else;
            d = a–b;
            cout<<"d = "<<d;
    }
```

Program 48

```
main ()
    {
        int x, y, a;
        cout<<"Enter the value of x,y,\n";
        cin>>x+y;
        cout<<x<<y<<z;
    }
```

Program 49

```
main ()
    {
        int i, m;
        cout<<"Enter the value of m\n";
        cin>>m;
        while(i<=15)
        {
            i = i*3;
            cout<<"i="<<i;
        }
    }
```

Program 50

```
main ()
    {
        int a [5] = {6,7,-12,19,3}
        int sum = 0;
        for(i = 1; i<5; ++i)
        {
            sum += a[i];
        }
        cout<<"sum = ", sum;
    }
```

Program 51

```
main ()
    {
        int a[20], i,m, sum;
        cout<<"Enter the value of m\n";
        cin>>m;
        for(i=0; i<m; ++i)
            cin>>a[i];
            sum = 0;
            for (i=1; i<=m; ++i)
                sum = sum + a[i];
                cout<<"sum = ", sum);
    }
```

Program 52

```
#define PI = 3.5
        main ()
        {
                float a;
                cout<<"Enter value of radius\n";
                cin>>a;
                a = PI*a*2.0;
                cout<<"Area is"<<a;
        }
```

Program 53

```
/* C++*/
        # include "stdio.h"
        void main()
        {
                int i,j;
                void show (int,int);
                show (i,j);
        }
        void show (a,b)
        int a, b;
        {
                cout<<"Value of a and b ="<< a<<b;
        }
```

Program 54

```
/* C++ */
        #include "stdio.h"
        void main ()
        {
                float a;
                a = 5;
                cout<<"value of a ="<<a;
        }
```

Program 55

```
main ( )
        {
                int a = 5 , b ;
                if (a > b)
                        b = 2 * a ;
                if (a < 5 )
                        b = 3 * a;
                cout<<"b = "<<b;
        }
```

Program 56

```
main ()
        {
                int i ;
                cout<<"Enter the value of i\n";
                cin>>i;
                switch (i)
                {
                        case 1:
                                c = a+b;
                        case 2 :
                                c = a – b;
                        case 3:
                                c = a*b;
                        default :
                                c = a/b;
                }
                cout<<" c ="<<c;
        }
```

Program 57

```
Compute (a,b,c)
        float a,b,c;
        {
                c = a*b;
        }
        main ()
        {
                float p,q,r,s,z;
                cout<<"Enter the values of p &q\n";
                cin>>p>>q;
                compute (p,q,z);
                cout<<"c ="<<z<<"\n";
                r = p + 2.0 ; s  = q +3.0;
                compute (r,s,a);
                cout<<"c = "<< z;
        }
```

Program 58

```
main ()
        {
                int a [5] , i,m;
                m = 10;
                for (i = 1; i < = 10; ++i)
                        cin>>a [i] ;
```

```
        for (i = 1 ; i< = 10; ++i)
            cout<<a [i];
    }
```

Program 59

```
compute (a,b)
    {
        int c;
        c = a*b;
        cout<<"c= "<<c;
    }
    main ()
    {
        int a = 2, b = 3;
        compute (a);
    }
```

Program 60

```
int compute (a,b)
    {
        int c;
        c = a*b;
        return (c);
    }
    main ()
    {
        int a = 2, b = 3;
        compute (a,b);
    }
```

Program 61

```
main ()
    {
        int x = 4, y = 5;
        while (y <= 10)
        {
            ++x;
            --y;
            cout<<y++;
            cout<<--x;
        }
```

Program 62

```
test (x,y,z)
    int x,y,z;
    {
```

```
        if x > y
                return x;
        else
                return y;
    {
    main ( )
    {
        int x = 10, y = 20;
        test (x,y,z);
    }
```

Program 63

```
main ( )
    {
        int x = 3;
        if (x > 5)
                int y = 2*x;
        else
                int z = 3*x;
        cout<<"x ="<<x<<" y = "<<y<<"z="<<z;
    }
```

Program 64

```
main ( )
    {
        int x = 3,y,z;
        if (x > 5)
                y = 2*x;
        else
                z = 3*x;
        cout<<"x ="<<x<<"y ="<<y<<" z="<<z;
    }
```

Program 65

```
main ( )
    {
        FILE *fptr;
        int x, y, z;
        fptr = fopen("data.bmp","w");
        fscanf(fptr,"%d%d%d", &x ,&y, &z);
        printf("x=%d, y = %d, z=%d\n", x, y, z);
    }
```

Program 66

```
    /* C++*/
    # include "stdio.h"
```

```
void main()
{
        int i,j;
        void sh(int,int);
        show (i,j);
}
void show (int a,int b)
{
        cout<<"Value of a and b = <<a,b;
}
```

Program 67

```
/* C++ */
#include "stdio.h"
void main ()
{
        float a;
        a = 5;
        cout<<"value of a ="<< a;
}
```

Program 68

```
#include "stdio.h"
void main ()
if (a < 5 )
        b = 3 * a;
cout<<"b ="<<b;
}
```

Program 69

```
main ( )
{
        int i ;
        cout<<"Enter the value of i\n";
        cin>>i;
switch (i)
{
case 1:
        c = a+b;
case 2 :
        c = a - b;
case 3:
        c = a*b;
default :
        c = a/b;
}
```

```
cout<<" c = "<< c;
}
```

Program 70

5.

```
Compute (a,b,c)
float a,b,c;
{
        c = a*b;
}
main ()
{
        float p,q,r,s,z;
        cout<<"Enter the values of p &q\n";
        cin>>p>>q;
        compute(p,q,z);
        cout<<"c ="<<z;
        r = p + 2.0 ; s = q +3.0;
        compute (r,s,a);
        cout<<"c = "<< z ;
}
```

Program 71

```
main ()
{
        int a [5] , i,m;
        m= 10;
        for (i = 1; i< = m; ++i)
                cin>>a [i] ) ;
        for (i = 1 ; i< = m; ++i)
                cout<<a[i]<<"\t";
}
```

7.

```
compute (a,b)
{
        int c;
        c = a*b;
        cout<<"c="<<c;
}
main ()
{
        int a = 2, b = 3;
        compute (a);
}
```

Program 72

```
int compute (a,b)
{
```

```
        int c;
        c = a*b;
        return (c);
}
main ()
{
        int a = 2, b = 3;
        compute (a,b);
}
```

Program 73

```
main ()
{
        int x = 4, y = 5;
        while (y <= 10)
        {
                ++x;
                --y;
                cout<< y++;
        cout<< --x;
        }
```

Program 74

```
test (x,y,z)
int x,y,z;
{
        if x > y
                return x;
        else
                return y;
        {
main ()
{
        int x = 10, y = 20;
        test (x,y,z);
}
```

Program 75

```
main ()
{
        int x = 3;
        if (x > 5)
                int y = 2*x;
        else
                int z = 3*x;
```

```
        cout<<"x ="<<y<<" y ="<<y<<" z="<<z;
}
```

Program 76

```
main ()
{
        int x = 3,y,z;
        if (x > 5)
                y = 2*x;
        else
                z=3*x;
        cout<<"x ="<<x<<"y = "<<y<<"z="<<z;
}
```

Program 77

```
/*overflow error if y > 1.5*/
main()
{
        float x,c,y,k,sum,term;
        clrscr();
        cout<<"enter the value of y max upto1.14\n";
        cin>>y;
        x = 0; term = 1;
for (k=1;k<500;++k)
{
        if(k<=250)
        {
                c = k *k;
        }
        else
                c = 4*(k*k*k);
                term = term*y;
                x=x+c*term;
}
cout<<"the value of y ="<<y
  <<" and the values of x="<<x;
}
```

Program 78

```
float x, bm;
main()
{
        float x = 5;
        cout<<"Enter the value of bm\n";
        cin>>bm;
        compute();
}
```

```
compute()
{
        float z;
        z=x*bm;
        cout<<"z="<<z;
}
```

Program 79

```
main ()
{
        float i, n, fact;
        cout<<"Enter the value of n\n";
        cin>>n;
        fact=0;
        for (i=1; i<=n; ++i)
                fact *=i;
        cout<<"fact="<<fact;
}
```

Program 80

```
main ()
{
        float i, n, fact;
        cout<<"Enter the value of n\n";
        cin>>n;
        fact=1;
        for (i=0; i<=n; ++i)
                fact *=i;
        cout<<"fact="<<fact;
}
```

Program 81

```
main ()
{
        int i=3, K, l;
        K=add(++i)
        l=add(i++)
        cout<<i<<K<<l;
}
add (int ii)
{
        ++ii;
        return(ii);
}
```

Program 82

```
# define PI 3.14159
main ()
{
```

```
        int R, C;               /*      Radius of Circle–R */
        float perimeter;  /* Circumference */
        float area;             /*      Area of circle */
        C = PI
        R = 5;
        perimeter = 2.0 * C * R;
        Area = C * R * R;
        cout<<perimeter<<Area;
    }
```

Program 83

```
class comp
    {
                int a,b;
        public :
                void getdata();
                void putdata();
    };
    void getdata:comp
    {
        cout<<"enter the values of a & B\n";
        cin>>a>>b;
    }
    void putdata:comp
    {
        cout<<a<<'\t'<<b;
    }
    main()
    {
        comp a,b;
        a.getdata();
        b.putdata();
    }
```

Program 84

```
class comp
    {
                int a,b,c;
        public :
                void getdata();
                void putdata();
    };
    void getdata::comp
    {
        cout<<"enter the values of a & B\n";
        cin>>a>>b;
```

```
}
void cal::comp
{
        c=a*b;
        cout<<a<<'\t'<<b;
}
main()
        {
                comp a;
                a.getdata();
                a.putdata();
                cout<<"c="<<c;
        }
```

Program 85

```
/*overflow error if y > 1.5*/
        main()
        {
                float x,c,y,k,sum,term;
                clrscr();
                cout<<"enter the value of y maximum upto 1.14 \n";
                cin>>y;
                x = 0; term = 1;
                for (k=1;k<500;++k)
                {
                        if(k<=250)
                        {
                                c = k *k;
                        }
                        else
                                c = 4*(k*k*k);
                                term = term*y;
                                x = x+c*term;
                        }
                        cout<<"Value of y ="<<y<<" and the values of x=<<x;
                }
```

Program 86

```
float x, bm;
        main()
        {
                float x = 5;
                cout<<"Enter the value of bm\n";
                cin>>bm;
                compute();
        }
```

```
compute()
{
        float z;
        z = x*bm;
        cout<<"z = "<<z;
}
```

Program 87

```
main ()
{
        float i, n, fact;
        cout<<"Enter the value of n\n";
        cin>>n;
        fact = 0;
        for (i = 1; i<=n; ++i)
                fact *= i;
        cout<<"fact = "<<fact;
}
```

Program 88

```
main ()
    {
        float i, n, fact;
        cout<<"Enter the value of n\n";
        cin>>n;
        fact = 1;
        for (i = 0; i<=n; ++i)
                fact *= i;
        cout<<"fact = "<<fact;
}
```

Program 89

```
main ()
    {
        float x, rem;
        cout<<"Enter the value of x\n";
        cin>>x;
        rem = x%3;
        cout<<"rem="<<rem;
}
```

Program 90

```
main ()
    {
        int, x, n;
        cout<<"Enter the value of n\n";
        cin>>n;
```

```
        if(n>4)
                x = n*n;
                cout<<"The value of n<4&x="<<x;
        else
                x = 2*n;
                cout<<"The value of n<4&x="<<x;
}
```

Program 91

```
main ( )
    {
        int num;
        cout<<"Enter your number\n";
        cin>>num;
        if(num<0)
                num = -num;
                cout<<"The absolute value of number is \n"<<num;
}
```

Program 92

```
main ( )
    {
        float a[10],i,m;
        m = 5;
        cout<<"Enter 5 elements of array\n";
        for(i=1; i<=m; i=i+0.1)
        {
        cin>>a[i];
        }
        sum = 0;
        for(i=1; i<=m; i=i+0.1)
        {
        sum = sum + a[i];
        }
        cout<<sum;
}
```

Program 93

```
main ( )
    {
        char C[10];
        cout<<"Enter your string\n";
        cin>>C;
        cout<<"The string entered was "<<C;
}
```

Program 94

```
main ( )
     {
          int l,b,h,v;
          cout<<"Enter value of l,b,h\n";
          cin>>l>>b>>h;
          v = l*b*h
          cout<<"The volume is "<<l,b,h;
}
```

Program 95

```
main ( )
     {
          int l,b,h;
          cout<<"Enter value of l,b,h\n";
          cin>>l>>b>>h;
          Volume(l,b,h);
}

Volume (l,b,h );
int l,b,h;
     {
          int v;
          v = l*b*h
          cout<<"The volume is "<<v;
}
```

Program 96

```
main()
{
     short int x;
     x = foo();
     Printf(" foo= %d",x );
}
short foo()
{
 short int a,b,c;
 b=10;
 c = a + b;
 return c;
}
```

27

BIOS/DOS FUNCTIONS

27.1 INTRODUCTION

These functions are used for accessing the hardware components by using the commands in C-programming language.

The data bus is the set of wires used for flow of data between the microprocessor and the memory. Each wire in this bus carries a bit of data at a time either zero or one in the form of an electric pulse. The data bus has 8 wires then 8 bits or 1 byte of data can flow in it at a time and this is called a 8-bit data bus. Similarly, we have 16-bit data buses which can carry 16 and 32 bits at a time respectively.

A microprocessor with a 32-bit data bus is faster than the one with a 16-bit data bus. This is because, in the former, four bytes of data are brought to the microprocessor at a time, while in the latter only 2 bytes of data are brought at a time.

The pentium processors are used currently which allows for

Data Bus =64

Maximum memory= 2^{44} MB

The address of the first byte in CGA video memory.The segment address of video memory is OxB0000 (20-bit address), whereas the offset value of the first CGA byte in this segment is OxB0000 address in 16-bit segment register. The first byte in CGA video memory is referred using segment:offset format as OxB000:0x8000. Thus, the offset register works relative to the segment register. Using both these, it is possible to point to a specific location anywhere in the 1 MB address space.

For example to write a character 'A' at location OxB000:0x8000. It is necessary to convert this address into a form which C-language compiler understands. This is done by simply writing the segment and offset addresses side by side to obtain a 32-bit address. In this case , address would be OxB000:0x8000.

If the data model used are small , then a keyword used as 'far'

```
char far *s;
```

where s is a character pointer using small memeory model.

The address could be given to 's' as below

```
s = OxB000:0x8000;
```

A far pointer is always treated as a 32-bit pointer and contains both a segment address and an offset address.A huge pointer is also 32 bits long, again containing a segment address and an offset. However, there are a few differences between a far pointer and a huge pointer.

A near pointer is only 16 bits long. It uses the currents of the Code segment register for the segment part, whereas the offset part is stored in the 16-bit near pointer.

The far pointer (32 bits) contains the segment as well as the offset. By using far pointers it is possible to have multiple code segments, which allows to have programs longer than 64 KB worth of data .

27.2 DOS FUNCTION

The functions are used in DOS operations for accessing the hardware by using the DOS interrupt by C-programming commands. To use these functions "DOS.h" file must be included.

27.3 int 86 FUNCTION

This function is used for accessing the hardware components in the program by use of the programming commands. The various hardware components which can be accessed are mouse,monitor,printer and harddisk which can be accessed by this function.

int86(no,in,out);

Where

no – hardware interrupt number

in – pointer created by using the union of REGS as union REGS *in

out – pointer created by using the union of REGS as union REGS *out

The variety of hardware interrupts which are used as below

interrupt	device
0 × 10	video
0 × 33	mouse
0 × 17	printer
0 × 19	disc access

27.4 int 86x FUNCTION

This function is used by following commands

int 86x(no,in,out,se);

Where no – hardware interrupt number

in – pointer created by using the union of REGS as union REGS *in

out – pointer created by using the union of REGS as union REGS *out

se – pointer created by using the structure of REGS as struct REGS *out

27.5 intdos FUNCTION

This function is used for performing DOS function by following commands intdos (&i,&o);

Where

i – pointer created by using the union of REGS as union REGS *in

o – pointer created by using the union of REGS as union REGS *out

27.6 intdos x FUNCTION

This function is used for performing DOS function by following commands

intdosx (&i,&o,&s);

Where

i – pointer created by using the union of REGS as union REGS *in

o – pointer created by using the union of REGS as union REGS *out

s – pointer created by using the structure of REGS as struct REGS *out

Program 27-1

This is the program to delete a file which exists. The service 0x41 under interrupt number 0x21. Since this is a DOS service under interrupt 0x21.The intdos() function to used to carry out the file deletion. The service number is always placed in the AH register. The segment address of the file to be deleted must be stored in DS register, where as the offset address must be stored in the DX register.

```
#include *dos.h*
main()
{
    Union REGS i,o;
    char fn[100];
    puts("\nEnter name of file to be deleted");
    gets (fn);
    i.h.ah = 0x41 ; /*service number*/
    i.X.dx = fn ;/*offset address of filename*/
    intdos (&i,&o);
    if (o.x.cflag = 0)
            printf ("\n%s file successfully deleted", fn);
    else
            printf("\n%s file could not be deleted", fn);
}
```

Program 27-2

This program uses 'intdosx' function for creating directories and which is normally done in the DOS system by MD command without realising that internally DOS calls interrupt 0x21 function 0x47 to achieve this.

```
#include "dos.h"
main()
{
    union REGS i,o;
    struct SREGS s;
    char far dn[100];
    puts ("\nEnter namedirectory name:");
    gets (dn);
    i.h.ah = 0x39; /*service no.*/
    s.ds = FP_SEG (dirname);
    i.x.dx = FP_OFF (dirname);
    intdosx (&i,&o, &s);
    if (o.x.cflag ==0)
            printf ("Directory has been successfully created");
    else
            print ("Could not create %s directory",dn);
}
```

Program 27-3

Disk input/output is under the control of interrupt number 0x13.

This program uses int86x function for reading sectors from the disc.

```
#include "dos.h"
main()
{
      union REGS i,o;
      struct SREGS s;
      char far b [600];
      int r;
      i.h.ah =2; /*service number*/
      i.h.dl = 0; /*drive no.*/
      i.h.al = 1; /*number fo sectors to read*/
      i.h.ch =  4; /*track number*/
      i.h.cl = 1;/*sector number */
      i.h.dh = 1 ; /*head number*/
      s.es = FP_SEG (b);
      i.x.bx = FP_OFF (b);
      int86x (0x19, &i, &o,&s);
      if (o.x.cflag == 0)
      {
      printf ("\nReading sectors successfuled");
      printf("\nNo.of sectors read is %d",o.h.al);
      }
      else
      printf("/nReading sectors failed");
}
```

28
C – SHARP

INTRODUCTION

The programming in C and C^{++} languages have has been most widely used for commercial and technical software development. The object based programming in C^{++} allows programmer to handle complexcity of data structure and data base programming. The major difficulties in these programming techniques is the development required for every module in the programming. The C–sharp the designated as C # is a modern object oriented language which allows the programmer to quickly build wide range of application for the new microsoft.net plateform. The C-sharp is a object oriented language which is uses the concepts of classes and objects and develops new programs using readymade functions. The C-sharps is a internet based language having connectivity with html, xml and object access protocol. The language allows the storage of complex data in variables and eliminates the manual memory management burden. The variables in C-sharp are automatically initized by the environment. It is possible to protect the data values by use of private and public variables. The concepts of inheritance and polymorphism are very well available in C-sharp. The multiple inheritance internal interfaces rather than external interfaces as been done in java. The garbase collection is an important features C-sharp. The garbase collector governs all manage objects and they are freed when they are no longer needed. The C-sharp object determinastric destruction as in C^{++}. The C # destructors are really finalizers because they perform a final resource freeing on the object before it is released from memeory. The C-sharp works with hirarchical names space model. These are C # program elements design to organise programs. The objects are grouped into names space and perticular names space has to be included in the program to access the classes the objects. The C # has limited data types as boolean integer float and double. The boolean provides true and false which is not used in C and C^{++}. The C # is meant for writing COM + and window base program for enterprise computing. The C # supports four common APIs on the window plateform. The C # omits pointers as data type. However, access to pointer types becomes an assecity. Hence C # provide the ability to write the unsafe code. In the unsafe code it is possible to declare and operate on pointers and perform conversion between pointer and integeral types. The error handling and debuging is a importing part of any program the C # provide integeral support to try, catch, and through methods with improved model. The goto statement is allowing in the C # has been replaced in the java by continue statement which allows for transfer of control vary easily to any other location.

The C # has simplicity in writing of program. It has modern techniques of writing systems and it has a consistancy which allows easy writing for the programer. The C # is object oriented progrmming technique allowing for multiple inheritance for creation of **COM +** virtual object systems. It allows for creation of multi-dimensional array and they arrays can have any number of elements different dimension. The length of an array can be very easily to determine as similar to java interfaces.

29

Appendix-I
Standard Library Functions

1. 'abs' Function

This function provides the absolute value of an integer number

Use the library file to include the function

#include <math.h>

y =abs (x);

Where x — number whose absolute value is to be calculated.

y — integer variable

2. `pow' Function

This function calculates power of any number.

z = pow (x, y);

This calculates x to the power of y.

Use the library file to include the function

#include <math.h>

On success, `pow' the value calculated, x^y.

3. `sin' Function

This function calculates sine of any angle.

Use the library file to include the function

#include <math.h>

y= sin (x);

y — double variable

x— value of angle in radians

This function computes the sine of the input value. Angles are specified in radians.

4. `sqrt' Function

This function calculates the positive square root of value.

Use the library file to include the function

#include<math.h>

y= sqrt(x);

y — double variable

x— value of angle in radians

This calculates square root of the positive square root of the input.

5. `tan' Function

This function calculates the tangent of the given angle.

Use the library file to include the function

#include <math.h.>

y=tan (x);

This calculates the tangent of angle are specified in radians.

6. `atoi' Function

This function converts a string to an integer.

y = atoi (S);

where y — integer variable

S — char array or pointer

This converts the numeric char value of the input string into integer value.

7. `gevt' Function

This function converts floating-point number to a string.

Use the library file to include the function

#include<dos.h>

S = gevt (v, n, b);

where v — double variable

n — integer variable

b — char variable

This function converts value to a null-terminated ASCII string and stores the string in b variable. It produces n significant digits.

6. `atoa' Function

This function converts an integer to a string.

S = itoa (v, s, r);

where v — integer variable

s — char variable

r — char variable

This function converts value to a null-terminated string and stores the result in string.

r — specifies the base to be used in converting

value it must be between2 and 36, inclusive.

7. 'isspace' Function

This function specifies the value by table look up using ASCII coded integer value. Use the library file to include the function

#include <ctype.h>

i= isspace (c);

where c — integer variable

This function is a macro that classifies ASCII-coded integer values by the table look up. It is defined only when isscii(c) is true or c is EOF.

8. `tolower' Function

This function translates all characters to lowercase alphabets.

i= tolower(ch);

where ch — character variable

This function converts an integer ch to its lowercase (a-z) value if it is uppercase (A-Z); all others are left unchanged.

9. `toupper' Function

This function translates all character to uppercase alphabet.

i = toupper(ch);

where ch — char variable

This function converts an integer ch to its uppercase value (A-Z) (if it is lowercase (a-z); all others are left unchanged.

10. `strcat' Function

This function concatenate one string with another.

S = strcat(s1, s2);

where s1 — char array

s2 — char array

This function joins s2 string to s1 string and stores in S string

11. `strlen` Function

This function finds the length of string

i = strlen (s)

where s — char array

i — integer variable

This function finds the length of string s and stores in integer variable i .

12. `strcmp' Function

This function compares one string to another.

i = strcmp (s1, s2);

s1 – char array

s2 – char array

i – integer variable

This function performs comparison of s1 to s2, starting with the first character in each string and continuing with subsequent characters until the corresponding characters differ or until the end of the strings is reached.

This function returns a value as

i<0 if s1 is less than s2

i=0 if s1 is same as s2

i>0 if s1 is greater than s2

13. `strcpy' Function

This function copies one string into another string.

strcpy (s1, s2);

This function copies string s2 to s1, stopping after the terminating null character has been moved.

14 `qsort' Function

This function sorts using the quicksort algorithm.

qsort (b, n, w, f)

qsort is an implementation of the quicksort algorithm.

b -points to the base (0th elements) of the table to be sorted.

n-the number of entries in the table.

w- the size ofeach entry in the table, in bytes.

fcmp -the comparison function which accepts two arguments, **elem1** and **elem2,** each a pointer to an entry in the table. The comparison function compares each of the pointed-to items(*elem1 and*elem2), and returns an integer based on the result of the comparison.

fcmp returns a value that is

<0 if *elem1 <*elem2

==0 if *elem1 == *elein2

> 0 if *elem1 > *elem2

15. `ftell' Function

This function indicates the current position of file pointer.

Use the library file to include the function

```
#include<stdio.h>
i=ftell (s);
```

This function returns the position of current file pointer s in the file. The offset is measured in bytes from the beginning of the file.

16. `inportb' Function

This function reads a byte from a hardware port.

```
inportb (p);
```

where p — integer variable

This reads byte from the input port specified by p port.

17. `inport' Function

This function reads a word from a hardware port.

```
inportb ( p);
```

Where p — integer variable

This function reads a byte from the input port specified by p.

18. `outportb' Function

This function outputs bytes to a hardware port.

Use the library file to include the function

```
#include <dos.h>
        outportb ( p, v);
```

This function writes a byte given by value to the output port specified by p.

19. `getcwd' Function

This function provides current working directory.

Use the library file to include the function

```
#include <dir.h.>
S = getcwd (buf, b);
```

This function gets the full path name of the current working directory up to buflen bytes long, including the drive, and stores it in buf. If the full path name length (including the null- terminator) is longer than buflen bytes, an error occurs.

20. `memmove' Function

This function copies a block of n bytes

Use the library file to include the function

```
# include <mem.h>
    void *memmove (void *dest, const void *src, int n);
```

This function copies a block of n bytes from src to dest. Even when the source and destination blocks overlap and bytes in the overlapping locations are copied correctly.

21. `memcpy' Function

This function copies a specified number of characters from one buffer to another.

Use the library file to include the function

```
#include <mem.h>
void *memcpy (void *dest, const void *src, int n);
```

This function copies a block of n bytes from src to dest. If src and dest overlap, the behaviour of memcpy is undefined.

22. 'memset' Function

This sets n bytes of block of memory to byte c.

Use the library file to include the function

```
#include <mem.h>
```

void *memset (void *s, int c, intn);

This function sets the first n bytes of the arrays to the character c.

23. `setdisk' function

This function sets current disk drive

i=setdisk (drive);

This function sets the current drive to the one associated with drive : 0 for A, 1 for B, 2 for C, and so on.

24. `getdisk' Function

This function gets current drive number.

i= getdisk (void);

This function gets the current drive number. It returns an integer: 0 for A, 1 for B, 2 for C, etc.

25. `calloc' Function

This function allocates main memory.

Use the library file to include the function

```
#include <stdlib.h>
```

void *calloc (int nitems, int size);

This function provides access to the C memory heap. The heap is available for dynamic allocation of variable-sized blocks of memory. Many data structures, such as trees and lists, naturally employ heap memory allocation.

All the space between the end of the data segment and the top of the program stack is available for use in the small data models (tiny, small and medium), except for a 256-byte margin immediately before the top of the stack. This margin is intended to allow the application some room to grow on the stack, plus a small amount needed by DOS.

26. `realloc' Function

This function reallocates main memory.

Use the library file to include the function

```
#include <stdlib.h>
```

void *realloc (void *block, int size);

This function attempts to shrink or expand the previously allocated block to size bytes. The block argument points to a memory block previously obtained by calling malloc, calloc, or realloc. If block is a null pointer, realloc works just like malloc.

realloc adjusts the size of the allocated block to size copying the contents to a new location if necessary. This function returns the address of the reallocated block, which may be different than the address of the original block. If the block cannot be reallocated, or size ==0, realloc returns NULL.

27. `int86x' Function

This function provides general 8086 software interrupt interface.

Use the library file to include the function

```
#include<dos.h>
int int86x (int intno, union REGS *inregs,
union REGS *outregs, struct SREGS *seg)
```

This function executes an 8086 software interrupt specified by the argument intno. Before executing the software interrupt, it copies register values from inregs into the registers.

After the software interrupt returns, int86x copies the current register values to outregs, the status of the carry flag to the **x.cflag** field in outregs, and the vlaue of the 8086 flag register to the x.flags field in outregs.

If the carry flag is set, it indicates that an error occurred.

29. `time' function

This function gets time of day

Use the library file to include the function

```
#include <time.h>
long time (long *timer);
```

This function time gives the current time, in seconds, elapsed since 00:00.00 GMT. January1,1970, and stores that value in the location pointed to by timer, provided that times is not a null pointer.

30
APPENDIX II
C-LANGUAGE KEYWORDS

Types of Formats

d	—	Integer variables
f	—	Floating variables with six decimal precision printing
e	—	Floating values with exponent printing
g	—	Floating values with printing in the minimum space
c	—	Character variable
s	—	String or char array

Modifier

-	—	changes start of writing of values
n	—	field with number to specify minimum number of field for the values
l	—	long variables
.m	—	m is a integer number to specify the number of decimal precision.

White Space Character

\t	—	this gives a tab or blank space of five
\n	—	new line character
\f	—	form feed character

Comment

It is a string consisting of number of characters or words or numbers used for representing a dummy sentence to be printed at the time of printing the values of variables. It is enclosed in

/* -----------------------------*/

Mathematical operators :

- a	- ve give negative value of a
a + b	addition between a & b
a - b	subtraction between a & b
a * b	multiplication between a & b
a / b	division between a and b
a % b	gives remainder after division of a & b.

Arithmetic expression :

It is a joining of variables and constants by arithmetic operators such that it form a mathematical expression whose value can be calculated by computer. The circular brackets can be used in program, but number of opening bracket must be equal to number of closing bracket.

((a + b) / (c + d))

In this case, addition between a & b and c & is performed and then division between two occurs.

Logical operators :

a < b	true if a is less than b
a > b	true if a is greater than b
a < = b	true if a is less than or equal to b
a > = b	true if a is greater than or equal to b

a = = b true if a is equal to b
a ! = b true if a is not equal to b
a ! = b true if a is not equal to b

These logical expression does a comparison and find whether the condition is true or false.

Logical expression

When two variables or one variable and one constant are joined by logical operator then it is a logical expression. Like

a > b

Where

a , b — variables

Compound logical operators

The two logical expression are joined by compound logical operator like and operator

if ((a > b) && (b > c)

This is true when a > b and b > c both logical expression are true or operator

if((a > b) ¦¦ (b > c))

This is true when a > b or b > c is true or both are true negation operator

if(! (a > b))

This is true if a is less than b.

Increment and Decrement Operators

+ + i increments value of i by 1 and uses the value in the expression
i ++ uses the value of expression and increment later value of i by 1
- - i decreases the value of i by 1 and uses the value in the expression
i - - uses the value in the expression and decreases the value of i by 1

'if' statement

1. Simple ' if ' statement

```
if ( x1 )
        y1;
```

where

x1 ------ logical expression
y1 ------ program statement.

If value of x1 is true, then execute y1

2. 'if - else' statement

```
if ( x1 )
        y1;
else
        y2;
```

if x1 is true execute y1, otherwise execute y2
y1, y2 -- program statement.

3. Nested ' if ' statement

```
if ( x1 )
if ( x2 )
        y1 ;
else
        y2 ;
```

x1, x2 --- logical expressions.
y1, y2 --- program statement

if x1 and x2 are true then y1 is executed, otherwise if x1 is false, y2 is executed.

'if - else' construct statement :

```
if (x1 )
        y1 ;
else
if (x2)
                y2;
        else
        if ( x3 )
                        y3;
                else
                                y4;
```

x1, x2, x3, x4 ---- logical expression
y1, y2, y3, y4 ---- program statement
if x1 is true execute y1, otherwise
x2 is true execute y2, otherwise
x3 is true execute y3, otherwise
execute y4 as last alternative

'Switch' statement

If is a special case of 'if-else' construct statement, that if logical expression has '= =' logical operator, then it is used 'switch' is used to check the condition of operator and execute the statement

```
Switch (o)
{
case n1 :
        y1;
break;
case n2:
        y2;
break;
case n3:
        y3;
break;
default :
        y4;
break;
}
```

n1, n2, n3 are values and 'o' is variable to work operator of switch.
y1, y2, y3, y4 are the program statement
if the valve of 'o' is n1, then y1 is executed
if the value of 'o' is n2, then y2 is executed
if the value of 'o' is n3, then y3 is executed
otherwise y4 is executed.

'for' statement

This statement is used to provide cycle of iterations.

for(x1; x2; x3)

```
{
        y1;
        y2;
        y3;
}
```

y1, y2, y3 – program statement
x1 – arithmetic expression to indicate begin values of index of 'for'
x2 – logical expression to indicate maximum value of index
x3 – arithmetic statement to indicate increment or decrement

This statement is executed as index of for start with begin value given in x1, the cycle are continued upto maximum value of index x2 and in every cycle index is modified as given in x3.

'While' statement

This statement is used when index is modified in the cycle by a relation.

```
while (x1)
        {
                y1;
                y2;
                y3;
        }
```

where,

x1 — logical expression
y1, y2, y3 — program statement

The y1, y2, y3 are executed in cycle till condition the x1 is true.

'do-while' statement

This statement is used when the begin value of index is unknown in the first cycle

```
do
{
        y1;
        y2;
        y3;
} while (x1);
```

y1, y2, y3 are executed in cycle till x1 is true. But for first cycle there is no checking carried out.

'continue' Statement

This statement is used in the cycle and because of this statement all feature statement of the cycle are skipped and second cycle is executed.

```
for (i=0; i < = + + i)
{
        if (i ==3)
                continue;
        -----------
        -----------
}
```

In this case if i is equal to 3 first cycle is terminated and second cycle is started.

'break' statement

This statement breaks the cycle of operation and comes outside the cyclic operation

```
while (i<=5)
{
        ----------
        -----------
        if (i < = 0.5)
                    break;
}
```

In this statement, the cycle breaks if 'i' value goes below 0.5.

Array variables

The array variables can be declared as

x y [z] ;

where

x --- type of declaration int,float , char

y --- name of variable

z --- maximum number of memory location as

int a[20] ;

where

int ---- type declaration of variable

This statement declares that 'a' is integer type of array variable with 20 memory spaces.

Equivalent expression statement

The general form is

x = x opr 2

is equivalent to

x opr = 2

where

opr ---- mathematical operator

z ---- constant or variable name

x ---- variable name.

as

y = y * 2 ;

is equivalent to writing

y * = 2 ;

User Specified data :

1. enum statement : This statement enumerates the 'x' variable as given ax, ay, az ....

enum x (ax , ay , az ....) ;

x --- integer variable name

ax, ay, az --- string to replace value as number

Ex.

enum colour [RED, BLUE , GREEN] ;

mean enumerate colour 0 as RED

colour 1 as BLUE

colour 2 as RED

Then using

colour = RED ;

means

colour = 0 ;

2. 'typedef' statement

This statement allows replacement of a any string by a new string .

It is written as

```
typedef  xx yy ;
```

xx is equivalent to yy string.

3. unions

These can be declared as

```
union xx
{
int a;
float b;
char c;
};
```

xx is a union of a, b,c having single memory and maintaining different types of values.

C - Preprocessors

The c - processors are the beginning statements of any file. These are

1. simple string replacement :

This is used to indicate a value of a constant in the program.

It is written as

```
#define  xx  n
```

xx ----- string

y2 ----- value of string

such as

```
#  define  P I   (22.0/7.0)
```

in the program substituted as (22.0/7.0)

2. Micro - expansion :

This is a micro - function defined on one single line.

It is written as

```
#define    xx(z)  (yy)
```

xx ---- name of function

z ----- argument of function

yy ----- expression of the function.

it is written as

```
#define    f(x)   (x * x * x)
```

This means whenever the function f (x) is called with any value of x in the program cube of x is calculated and substitute in the program.

3. File Inclusion :

This is used to include function programs in file in the current file

```
#include   " file name "
or
#  include < header file name >
```

The first is used for any type of file where as the second is used for header file only.

This allows function other file to be accessed by current file.

For example to obtain mathematical function.

```
#include < math.h >
```

library file.

String functions :

1. gets (x)
   This gets a character string from screen in a char array x.
2. puts (x)
   This prints character string on the screen in a char array x.
3. getchar (a)
   This get a character directly from a input device as keyboard.
4. putchar (c)
   This writes a character in ' c ' char variable to user screen.
5. strcat (s1 , s2)
   This joins two string in char array s1 & s2
6. strcpy (s1 , s2)
   This copies string in char array s2 to s1
7. strlen (s)
   This find the length of string in char array 's'
8. i = getch()
   This accept one character directly from keyboard.

Declaration of pointer variable

It is declared as

```
xx * yy;
```

where

xx ----- type of pointer int, float, char

yy ----- name of pointer variable

Like

```
int *ptr ;
```

supply of value to pointer

The pointer can be supplied with a value

```
*ptr = a ;
```

where value of 'a' variable is given to pointer 'ptr' alternately

```
ptr = &a ;
```

In this ptr is supplied address of a as such automatically receives value of a at the address.

declaration of structure

The structure of 'day' can be declared as

```
struct day
{
int date ;
int month ;
int year ;
} ;
```

In this case day has sub-variable date, month, year which forms a structure.

Reference of structured variable

The structure can be referred to a another variable.

```
Struct day today ;
```

This means that day is referred to 'today' for supply of value.

Representation of structured variable

The structure variable is represented as x . y

x --- main variable

y --- sub-variable

Like

today.date

In this case 'today' is a main variable and 'date' is a main variable and 'date' is sub-variable is a structured variable to receive value.

Declaration of file pointer

FILE *fptr;

Where

*fptr ---- file pointer.

Opening of File

A file can be opened by using 'fopen' function.

fptr = fopen ("file name ","mode");

File name — file name with any extension can be written

mode ---- write /read/ append mode like

fptr =fopen ("data.bmp","r");

This opens a file 'data.bmp' in reading mode.

File closing

The file can be closed by

fclose (fptr);

or

fclose ("file name");

File input functions

(i) fgetc function

This is used for reading of a character from a file

c = fgetc (fptr) ;

Where

fptr ---- file pointer

c ---- character variable

This statements reads a character from file referred by file pointer 'fptr' and stores in 'c' char variable.

(ii) fscanf function

This is used for scanning of the data from a file

fscanf (fptr," formats", variable list);

This statement reads the data for variables in the list according to the given sequence of formats from the file referred by 'fptr' file pointer.

Ex. fscanf (fptr,"%d%d %d",&a,&b,&c);

File Output functions

(i) fputc function

This writes a characters to a given file

fputc (c,fptr);

The character in char variable 'c' is written on a file referred by file pointer 'fptr'.

(ii) fprintf function

This prints the results of program in a give file.

fprintf (fptr, " formats " , variables) ;

This statement prints the results in different variables on a file referred by 'fptr ' pointer in given formats.

Ex. fprintf (fptr,"a=%d, b=%d",a,b);

'feof' function

This indicates whether the control is at end of file or not.

It is written as

feof (fptr) ;

fptr ---- file pointer.

'exit' function

This is used to terminate the running of program

exit(x) ;

x ---- condition or non-zero number.

'fwrite' function

This is used to write a string in a char array

fwrite (s , l , y , fptr) ;

s — char array

l — length of char array

y — position in a file

fptr — file pointer to which string is written.

This is used to write a string in char array 's' of length 'l' at position y in a file referred by file pointer fptr.

'fseek' function

This is used to seek a particular position in a file

fseek (fptr , x, y) ;

where

x ---- new position relative to the position given by y

y ---- position in a file indicated as

SEEK_SET

SEEK_CUR

SEEK_END

'ftell' function

This function is used to indicate the size of file

i= ftell (fptr) ;

i – integer variable to store the size of the file .

This indicates the size of file given by 'fptr'.

'rewind' function

This function is used to rewind the file and to obtain start position of file.

rewind (fptr) ;

'fgets' function

This function is used to scan 'n' characters from the given file referred by file pointer 'fptr ' and store in the 's' char array .

fgets(s,n,fptr);

where

s — char array

n — number of characters

fptr — file pointer

'fputs' function

This function is used to prints characters form 's' char array on the given file referred by file pointer 'fptr '.

fputs(s,fptr);

where

s — char array

fptr — file pointer

C++ KEY WORDS

'cin' STATEMENT

cin >> x >> y;

This scans values of x and y from user screen.

'cout' STATEMENT

cout << x << y;

This prints values of x and y from user screen.

'comment' STATEMENT

// This is the computer programming in C++

This is used for giving a title to the program. It is a non-executable statement of the program.

'endl' STATEMENT

cout << " m = " << m << endl;

This is used in output statement to shift the control to new line.

MANIPULATORS

1. **cout.width(10);**

   This sets a width of '10' for printing of variables.

2. **cout.precision(2);**

   This sets the precision of decimal value printing of '2' for printing of values of variable.

3. **cout.fill('*');**

   This sets the filling pattern of blank spaces by '*' character at the time of printing of variables.

4. **setw(10);**

   This sets a width of '10' for printing of variables.

Scope Resolution Operator

:: x

In C++ language a scope resolution operator is used to indicate the scope of variable in the block. The '::' symbol is used for scope resolution operator. This operator can be used for accessing the global variable in the program.

'void' FUNCTION

void compute(int,int);

This is non-returnable function program which can be declared by word 'void' in the main program.

'inline' FUNCTION

inline double cube (double a){return(a * a * a);}

This is a single line function program which returns a cube of a given argument.

Enumerated Data Type

enum{i = 4, z = 200};

This statement declares a constant as 'i' and 'z' whose value is '4' and '200'.

'void' Pointer

void * gp

The 'gp' is a 'void' type of pointer . These are the pointer variables declared as void which makes them capable of accepting a data from any type of pointer.

'new' and 'delete' Operator

The new and delete operator are used in C++ -Language to obtain the required memories and to delete the unrequired memories. The new operator assist in opening of new memories and the delete operator deletes the created memories.

'constant' Pointer

int const * ptr1 = &m;

These are pointer utilised for the constant used in the program. These pointers can accepts a value from constants and can access the address of the constant.

'get ()' Function

cin.get(x);

These statements reads a character from the userscreen and stores in 'x' char array .

'put()' Function

cout.put (x);

This statement writes a character on the userscreen from 'x' char variable.

'getline' Function

cin.getline(x,y);

These statements reads a line from the userscreen consisting of 'y' number of characters and stores in 'x' char array.

'write' Function

cout.write(x,y);

These statements writes a line on the userscreen consisting of 'y' number of characters and stores in 'x' char array.

'fstream' function

fstream infile;

This function is used for declaring a file object 'infile'.

'open' function

infile.open ("data1.dat");

This function is used for opening of a file 'data1.dat' using a file object 'infile'.

'close' function

infile.close ();

This function is used for closing of a file opened by 'infile' object.

'fail' function

infile.fail ()

This is a logical function which checks whether the object is in position to open a file.

'eof' function

infile.eof ()

This is a logical function which checks that whether the object is at the end of file or not.

'seekg' function

infile.seekg (x,y);

This function seeks a position in a file at a distance 'x' from 'y' position flag.

ios::beg

ios::end

ios::cur

class

The class can be declared as

```
class item
{
    int x;
```

```
    int y;
  public :
  void read(int,int);
  void write(int,int);
}
```

The class 'item' consist of two private member variables 'x' and 'y' and two public members function read and write.

Reference of Class to Object

```
item p;
```

This is a reference of a class to an object 'p' which can utilised public member function and stores the data in private member function.

Reference of Class to array of Object

```
X p[20];
```

This is a reference of a class to an object `p' which is array of objects and these objects can utilize public member function and stores the data in private member of the class 'X'.

Protected variable

```
class X
{
        protected:
                int a, b;
        public:
                int c;
                void getdata(void);
                void putdata(void);
};
```

In this case 'a' and 'b' are protected variables and 'getdata' & 'putdata' are the public functions. The 'c' is a public variable.

Inheritance

This is a process of extending existing classes to form new classes by way of inheritance.

```
class X
{
        protected:
                int a, b;
        public:
                int c;
                void getdata(void);
                void putdata(void);
};
class Y : public X
{
        private:
                int d, e;
        public:
                void get_new(void);
                void put_new(void);
};
```

In this case class 'Y' inherits from class 'X' and can be utilized public member functions and protected variables of the class 'X'.

31

EXERCISES & PROJECTS

Exercise 1:

Write algorithm and program to find from given array

(i) total number of even integers

(ii) total number of odd integers

(iii) sum of all even integers

(iv) sum of all odd integers

Exercise 2:

Write a program using function which reverses a list of n integers stored in an array passed to it. The main should read n integers into an array and print the reversed list.

Exercise 3:

Exaplin the difference between "call by value " and "call by reference" with suitable programming example

Exercise 4 :

Wrtie a program using function and pointers to determine the length of string

Exercise 5 :

Write a program to find the sum of upper off diagonal elements and sum of lower off diagonal elements of a given square matrix

Exercise 6:

Wrtie a program to read three sides of a triangle and check whether it is a right angled triangle

Exercise 7:

Write a menu driven program that has the following menu:

(1) Get Number

(2) Determine if Number is Odd or Even

(3) Determine if Number is Positive or Negative

(4) Determine How Many Digits are in the Number

(5) Determine What Digit is at a Specific Position from the Right

(6) Exit

Functions

You must create the following functions.

DisplayMenu:

This function will accept a parameter passed by reference that will represent the user's choice. The function will then Display the menu and ask for the user to enter their menu choice, which is stored in the parameter.

DoChoice:

This function will accept one parameter that is passed by value. This number represents the menu choice. Call the appropriate functions depending upon the selected menu item.

GetInput:

This function will prompt the user to enter a number from -35536 to 35536. If the number entered is out of range, display an error message and allow them to re-enter the number. This function will return the number entered.

IsEven:

This function will take the integer (passed by value) that wasentered at the keyboard and then determines if the number is odd or even. This function will return 0 if odd, -1 if zero, and 1 if even.

IsPos:

This function will take the integer (passed by value) that was entered at the keyboard and then determines if the number is positive or negative. This function will return –1 if the number is negative, zero if the number is 0, and 1 if the number is positive.

NumDigits:

This function determines the number of digits in the number that is passed by value and then returns the number of digits.

DigitPosition:

This function accepts two parameters, the number and another number that represents the position from the right of the number. Find the digit at that position. If the position number is greater than the number of digits in the number, return a –1 else return the digit.

After the function is done executing display the appropriate response depending on the return value. Don't display the response in the function.

Hint

To determine the number of digits in a number, divide it by 10 repeatedly. When the number reaches 0, the number of divisions is the number of digits the original number has.

Exercise 8: Array & Files

The must accept an input from a file, a person's name, Social Security number, wage and the number of hours worked in a week. Also, if a person is a full time employee Rs.50.00 is deducted from their wages for union fees. A person is full time if they have an F in their record. Time and a half is paid for any time worked after the forty hours in a week. The output must display the person's name, Social Security number, wage, number of hours, straight time pay, over time pay, whether they are a part time or full time employee, and their net pay. Make sure the output is formatted into rows and columns and self-documenting with the appropriate titles and column headings.

Use the following information as data for your data file:

Rajesh 123-09-8765 9.00 46 F

Suresh 432-89-7654 9.50 40 F

In this program

(1) You must use arrays where appropriate. Single or Multi-Dimensional.

(2) You must use functions in your program.

(3) The output must go to the screen as well as an output file.

Exercise 9:

Construct a program to accept as input from a file, a person's first name, last name, phone number and birth date. This program will be menu driven with the following options:

(1) Find a person's information

(2) Add a person to the database

(3) Edit a person's information

(4) Print all records to the screen

(5) Quit

Option 1
will allow the user to enter a name after which you will search for and display the person's information.
Option 2
will allow the user to add a person to the database.
Option 3
will allow the user to change any information related to a specific individual.
Option 4
will display to the screen all of the records in the data base.
Option 5
will end the program.

The data will be read from the file only once, and will only update the file after the person has chosen option number 5 from the menu.

(HINT: Use two-dimensional arrays.)

(1) There must have at least 5 initial people in your database.
(2) It must read the data from a file.
(4) It must read the data into two-dimensional arrays.
(5) It must add at least two people to the database.
(6) It must edit the information of two different people.
(7) It must sort the information in ascending order by their last name.

Exercise 10:

Design a software for maintaining accounts in the bank.

A mini- bank holds 20 accounts out of which there are 10 general accounts and the remaining 10 are special accounts. The Bank has a single cash-machine. The cash machine takes the account number and a password from an account holder. It then asks how much money the account holder wants to withdraw. If there is that much of money then it prints a message that the transaction has succeeded and shows the remaining balance on the screen: otherwise it tells that the transaction has failed. An account holder can also query the mini-bank about his balance(without asking for money). The cash- machine asks a single password from the general accountholder whereas it asks two passwords from the special account holder. A special account must always have a minimum balance of $1000 whereas there is no such limitation for a general account.

The important function to be done by the software are

1. A general account holder withdrawing some money
2. A general account holder wants to withdraw but there is not enough balance in the account.
3. A special account holder wants to withdraw some money but the transaction is refused because the transaction would violate the restriction that the account must hold a minimum amount.
4. A special account holder queries about his balance.

Exercise 11:

This project to develop an Airline Reservation System (ARS). The following operations are supported:

1. Make a reservation (Make Reservation)
2. View all reservations for a flight (View Flight Reservations)
3. View flights by date (View Flights by Date)
4. View flights by destination (View Flights by Destination)
5. View flights by source (View Flights by Source)

6. View reservation information from reservation number (View Reservation Information)
7. Print reservation available (Print Reservations)
8. Print flights information (Print Flights)
9. Exit

When the program starts, a menu should be shown on the screen such as the menu shown below:

1. Make Reservation
2. View Flight Reservations
3. View Flights by Date
4. View Flights by Destination
5. View Flights by Source
6. View Reservation Information
7. Print Reservations
8. Print Flights
9. Exit

The details of the operation are as below:

1. Make Reservation:

The program asks the user to enter the source, destination, and date of reservation. Flight numbers for the source and destination for that date along with number of seats available will be listed from which the user is requested to select one. The user is requested to enter the number of people traveling. If the reservation is possible, it is made (also saved to file) and a reservation number is printed; otherwise, the message "NOT ENOUGH SEATS ARE AVAILABLE" is displayed.

2. View Flight Reservations:

The user is requested to enter a flight number and date. If a valid flight number and date were entered, all reservations for that flight are listed along with the reservation number, date and time; otherwise, a message such as "INVALID FLIGHT" is displayed.

3. View Flights by Date:

The user is requested to enter the date. If a valid date is entered, all flights on that date are listed along with the source and destination.

4. View Flights by Destination:

The user is requested to enter a destination. If a valid destination is entered, all flights schedualed for that destination are listed along with the number of seats available, the date, and time information. If an invalid destination is entered, a message such as "NO FLIGHT TO DESTINATION" is displayed.

5. View Flights by Source:

The user is requested to enter a source. If a valid source is entered, all flight schedualed from the source are listed along with the number of seats available, the date, and time information. If an invalid source is entered, a message such as "NO FLIGHTS FROM SOURCE" is displayed.

6. View Reservation Information:

The user is requested to enter a reservation number. If a valid reservation number is entered, all flight information for that reservation is listed; otherwise, a message such as "INVALID RESERVATION NUMBER" is displayed.

7. Print Reservations:

print all reservation in reservations.dat to the screen.

8. Print Flights:

print all flights in flights.dat to the screen.

9. Exit:

quits the program.

Exercise 12 :

The *point-slope equation* of a line having slope *m* and passing through point *P* with coordinates (x_1, y_1) is

$$y - y_1 = m(x - x_1).$$

(a) Write a class for a **CartesianPoint**, described by its *x*- and *y*- coordinates, with all appropriate operations on such objects.

(b) Write a **LineSegment** class, described by two **CartesianPoint** endpoints. In addition to the usual operations, this class should provide operations to compute

(i) The midpoint of the line segment joining two points and

(ii) The equation of the perpendicular bisector of this line segment.

(c) Write a class for a **Line**, described by its slope and a point on the line, with operations that

(i) Find the point-slope equation of the line and

(ii) Find the slope-intercept equation of the line.

(d) Write a program to read the point and slope information for two lines and to determine whether they intersect or are parallel. If they intersect, find the point of intersection and also determine whether they are perpendicular.

Exercise 13

A *rational number* is of the form *a/b*, where *a* and *b* are integers with *b != 0*. Write a program to do rational number arithmetic, representing each rational number as a class that has instance variables for the numerator and the denominator. The program should read and display all rational numbers in the format *a/b*, or simply *a* if the denominator is 1. The following examples illustrate the menu of commands that the user should be allowed to enter:

Input	Output	Comments
3/8 + 1/6	13/24	a/b + c/d = (ad + bc)/bd reduced to lowest terms
3/8 – 1/6	5/24	a/b – c/d = (ad – bc)/bd reduced to lowest terms
3/8 * 1/6	1/16	a/b * c/d = ac/bd reduced to lowest terms
3/8 / 1/6	9/4	a/b / c/d = ad/bc reduced to lowest terms
3/8 I	8/3	Invert a/b
8/3 M	2 + 2/3	Write a/b as a mixed fraction
6/8 R	3/4	Reduce a/b to lowest terms
6/8 G	2	Greatest common divisor of numerator and denominator
1/6 L 3/8	24	Lowest common denominator of a/b and c/d
1/6 < 3/8	true	a/b < c/d?
1/6 <= 3/8	true	a/b = c/d?
1/6 > 3/8	false	a/b > c/d?
1/6 >= 3/8	false	a/b = c/d?
3/8 = 9/24	true	a/b = c/d?

Exercise 14 :

A demographic study of the metropolitan area around particular area is divided into three regions (urban, suburban, and exurban,) and published the following table showing the annual migration from one region to another (the numbers represent percentages):

	Urban	Suburban	Exurban
Urban	1.1	0.3	0.7
Suburban	0.1	1.2	0.3
Exurban	0.2	0.6	1.3

For example, 0.3 percent of the urbanites (0.003 times the current population) move to the suburbs each year. The diagonal entries represent internal growth rates. Using a two-dimensional array with an enumerated type for the indices to store this table, write a program to determine the population of each region after 10, 20, 30, 40 and 50 years. Assume that the current populations of the urban, suburban, and exurban regions are 2.1, 1.4, and 0.9 million, respectively.

Exercise 15 :

A certain professor has a file containing a table of student grades, where the first line of the file contains the number of students and the number of scores in the table; each row of the table represents the exam scores of a given student and each column represents the scores on a given exam. The maximum possible score on each exam was 100 points. Write a program that, given the name of such a file, generates a report summarizing the overall percentage for each student and the average score on each exam.

Exercise 16 :

Suppose that a certain automobile dealership sells ten different models of automobiles and employs eight salespersons. A record of sales for each month can be represented by a table in which each row contains the number of sales of each model by a given salesperson and each column contains the number of sales by each salesperson of a given model. For example, suppose that the sales table for a certain month is as follows:

0	0	2	0	5	6	3	0
5	1	9	0	0	2	3	2
0	0	0	1	0	0	0	0
1	1	1	0	2	2	2	1
5	3	2	0	0	2	5	5
2	2	1	0	1	1	0	0
3	2	5	0	1	2	0	4
3	0	7	1	3	5	2	4
0	2	6	1	0	5	2	1
4	0	2	0	3	2	1	0

Write a program to produce a monthly sales report, displaying the monthly sales table in the form:

				Salesperson					
Model	1	2	3	4	5	6	7	8	Totals
1	0	0	2	0	5	6	3	0	16
2	5	1	9	0	0	2	3	2	22
3	0	0	0	1	0	0	0	0	1
4	1	1	1	0	2	2	2	1	10
5	5	3	2	0	0	2	5	5	22
6	2	2	1	0	1	1	0	0	7
7	3	2	5	0	1	2	0	4	17
8	3	0	7	1	3	5	2	4	25
9	0	2	6	1	0	5	2	1	17
10	4	0	2	0	3	2	1	0	12
Totals	**23**	**11**	**35**	**3**	**15**	**27**	**18**	**17**	

As indicated, the report should also display the total number of automobiles sold by each salesperson and the total number of each model sold by all salespersons.

Exercise 17:

Suppose that the prices for the ten automobile models in Problem 7 are as follows:

Model	Model Price
1	₹1,74,500
2	₹1,99,950
3	₹2,65,000
4	₹2,59,990
5	₹2,00,400
6	₹1,88,850
7	₹1,17,000
8	₹1,44,400
9	₹1,79,000
10	₹1,95,500

Write a program to read this list of prices and the sales table given in the previous exercise and calculate the total amount of sales for each salesperson and the total amount sales for all salespersons.

Exercise 18:

A certain company has a product line that includes five items that sell for ₹ 100, ₹ 75, ₹120, ₹ 150, and ₹35. There are four salespersons working for this company, and the following table gives the sales report for a typical week:

Salesperson Number	**Item Number**				
	1	**2**	**3**	**4**	**5**
1	10	4	5	6	7
2	7	0	12	1	3
3	4	9	5	0	8
4	3	2	1	5	6

Write a program to do the following:

(a) Compute the total amount sales for each salesperson.

(b) Compute the total commission for each salesperson if the commission rate is 10 percent.

(c) Find the total income for each salesperson for the week if each salesperson receives a fixed salary of ₹ 500 per week in addition to commission payments.

Exercise 19 :

Write a program to display a calendar for any month of any year of the twentieth century and on.

```
The program should prompts like
Enter month number: 13
Month must be between 1 and 12, please re-enter: 0
Month must be between 1 and 12, please re-enter: 2
Enter year: 98
Year must be 1900 or later, please re-enter: 2002
February 2002
Su Mo Tu We Th Fr Sa
12345678 9
10 11 12 13 14 15 16
17 18 19 20 21 22 23
24 25 26 27 28
Another? (y or n)
```

To determine the day of the week on which the month starts: know that January 1, 1900 was a Monday, and then find the number of days difference between that day and the first day of the month for which you are making the calendar. This difference plus one mod 7 (i.e. (totaldays+1) % 7) tells you the day of the week (0 meaning Sunday, 1 meaning Monday etc.). Finding the number of days from 1/1/1900 to the first day of any other month can be further broken down into the following subproblems:

1. Number of days in whole years (i.e., (Year - 1900) * 365);
2. One day for each year in the above range which is a leap year;
3. The number of days in each month from January thru the previous month of the year making a month calendar

Remember the rule for leap years:

A year is a leap year if it is divisible by 4, unless it is divisible by 100 (in which case it's not a leap year) UNLESS it's also divisible by 400 (in which case it's a leap year). year%4==0 && year%100!=0 || year%400==0 (1900 was not a leap year, but 2000 is, 2100 will not be).

Exercise 20 :

This is program on production reporting database. Production performance information would be inputted by part number into one database on a shift basis (each 8 hours) and reports generated comparing performance to standards entered into another database. The standards could be added, edited, or deleted, as needed. The production performance information would require approx. 30 data entries per part number. A maximum capacity of 500 part numbers would be required. Reports would be configured to present information per sample reports provided and reports could be generated by shift, day, part number, and customer. The perfromance indicators would be generated by shift, day, week, month, part number, and customer.

Exercise 21:

Write a recursive function, vowels, that returns the numbers of vowels in a string. Also, write a program to test your function.

Exercise 22:

A palindrome is a string that reads the same both forward and backward. For example, the strings "madam" and "madam I'm adam" are palindromes. Write a program that uses a recursive function to check whether a string is a palindrome. Your program must contain a value-returning recursive function that returns true if the string is a palindrome and false otherwise. Do not use any global variables; use appropriate parameters.

Exercise 23 :

Write a program that uses a recursive function to print a string backwards. Your program must contain a recursive function that prints out the string backward. Do not use any global variables; use appropriate parameters.

Exercise 24:

Write a program that computes batting averages. There are 20 players on the team, identified by the numbers 1 through 20. Their batting records are coded in a file as follows. Each line contains four numbers: the player's id number, the number of hits, walks and outs he/she made in a particular game. Here is a sample:

3 2 1 1

The example indicates that during a game, player number 3 was at bat four times and made 2 hits, 1 walk and 2 outs. For each player there are several lines in the file. Each player's batting average is computed by adding the player's total number of hits and dividing by the total number of at-bats.

A walk does not count as a hit or a time at bat. Print a table showing the player id number, batting average (to 3 decimals), and number of walks. (Remember Id numbers are 1-20, but array indexes start at 0. Also, beware division by zero).

Exercise 25 :

Write a program to help a local restaurant automate its breakfast billing system. The program should do the following:

a. Show the customer the differenct breakfast items offered by the restaurant.

b. Allow the customer to select more than one item from the menu

c. Calculate and print the bill.

Assume that the restaurant offers the following breakfast items (the price of each item is shown to the right of the item):

Samosa	₹ 6/-
Kachori	₹ 5/-
Dosa	₹ 18/-
Idli	₹ 12/-
Uttappa	₹ 15/-
Bhelpuri	₹ 10/-
Coffee	₹ 4/-
Tea	₹ 3/-

Define a struct, menuItemType, with two components: menuItem of the type string and menuPrice of the type double. Use an array, menuList, of the struct menuItemType.

The program must contain the following functions:

Function getData:

This function loads the data into the array menuList.

Function showMenu:

This function shows the different items offered by the restaurant and tells the user how to select items.

Function printCheck:

This function calculates and prints the check.

(Note that the billing amount should include a 5% tax.)

A sample output is:

Welcome to Sahayog Restaurant

1 Dosa	₹ 18/-
2 Samosa	₹ 12/-
1 Coffee	₹ 4/-
Tax	₹ 1/70
Amount Due	₹ 35/70

Exercise 26:

The value of pi (3.14….) can be computed according to the following formula:

pi/4 = 1 – 1/3 + 1/5 – 1/7 + 1/9 - …

Write a C++ program to compute pi using above formula . Since the formula is an infinite series and an algorithm must stop after a finite number of steps, you should stop when you have the result determined up to six significant digits.

Exercise 27:

Write a procedural C++ program that calculates and displays the mortgage payment amount given the amount of the mortgage, the term of the mortgage, and the interest rate of the mortgage. In this program, hard code the amount = ₹ 200,000, the term = 30 years, and the interest rate = 5.75%. Insert comments in the program to document the program.

Exercise 28:

Modify the mortgage program to input the amount of the mortgage, the term of the mortgage, and the interest rate of the mortgage. Display the mortgage payment amount. Allow the user to loop back and enter new data or quit. Insert comments in the program to document the program. This program should still be a procedural C++ program.

Exercise 29:

Modify the mortgage program to input the amount of the mortgage, the term of the mortgage, and the interest rate of the mortgage. Display the mortgage payment amount. Then, list the loan balance and interest paid for each payment over the term of the loan. On longer-term loans, the list will scroll off the screen. Do not allow the list to scroll off the screen, but rather display a partial list and then allow the user to continue the list. Allow the user to loop back and enter new data or quit. Insert comments in the program to document the program. This program should still be a procedural C++ program.

Exercise 30:

A company ABC needs a system to track employees and their work projects. All employees have First and Last name and 9-digit ID number. Some employees are trained in one of 50 skills used in the company. Training in the company is absolute; an employee is either trained or not trained in a skill, there is no middle ground.

All projects groups have:

* a 3-digit project number.
* a project name.
* a room assigned to that project
* and a list of employees who are members of that group.

  Membership in most projects is open to any employee except the company classified trained projects. For these projects one or more of the 50 skills is required for membership.

The Program should be able to:

* enter information for an employee,
* enter information for a project,
* assign an employee to a project(the program should check to make sure that it is a valid assignment) Both the project and the employee would be referred to by number,
* remove an employee from a project,
* list all employees,
* list all projects and the employees who work on them,

Use object-oriented design to make the program. You do not have to store the project or employee information in a file, the number of employees and projects is fixed.

Exercise 31:

This is program on computer (PC) management system. For each computer, the system stores the following information:

Brand/Model	(a string)
Inventory ID#	(a unique integer value for each computer)

Date of Service	(day, month, and year put into service)
Location	(a string)
Processor Speed	(a floating point number (Ghz) ranging from .500 – 3.0)
Memory	(.25 (256 MB), .5 (512 MB), 1 (1 GB), 2 (2 GB))
Disk Space	(30 GB, 40 GB, 60 GB, 80 GB, 120 GB)

The program collects and reports data for the company's computer tracking system. The options are:

(1) A list of all computers within the organization sorted by inventory
(2) A list of all computers within the organization sorted by location
(3) A list of all computers matching a user specified brand/model
(4) A list of all computers matching a user specified location
(5) A list of all computers matching or exceeding as user specified date (older)
(6) A list of all computer information for a user specified computer inventory#
(7) Add a new computer to the inventory
(8) Remove an existing computer, based on inventory#
(9) Exit processing

BIBLIOGRAPHY

1. The Art of C : Elegant Programming Solution *—by Herbert Schildt*
2. Computer Aided Design *—by Dr. S.S. Khandare*
3. Computer Aided Design *—by Krishnamurty*
4. Programming in C and C^{++} *—by Jayshree*
5. Programming in C —by Kochan
6. Programming in C^{++} *—by Balaguruswami*
7. Programming with C^{++} *—by D. Ravichandran*
8. Programming with C *—by B. S. Gottfried*
9. Programming ANSI C *—by Ramkumar and Rakesh Agarwal*
10. Programming C *—by Kris A. James*
11. Programming in C^{++} *—by Edgar Huckert*
12. C for Professional Programmers *—by Tizzart, Keith*
13. Programming in C For Unix *—by Schirmer*
14. Thinking in C-including object oriented programming with C^{++} *—by P.B. Mahapatra*
15. The Art of C Programming *—by R. Jones.*
16. Introduction to Data Structures Using C —Sunil B.C.
17. Computer Graphics Including CAD, Autocad & C —A.M. Kuthe
18. Computer Fundamentals —D.P. Nagpal
19. Elements of Computer Science —Sarkar, Gupta
20. Programming in C for BCA —Guru Prasad

INDEX

D

G

H

I

S

T

U

V

W

Z